Connecting Young Adults and Libraries:

A How-To-Do-It Manual®

Fourth Edition

Michele Gorman
and
Tricia Suellentrop

HOW-TO-DO-IT MANUALS®

NUMBER 167

Neal-Schuman Publishers, Inc.

New York   London

Published by Neal-Schuman Publishers, Inc.
100 William St., Suite 2004
New York, NY 10038

Library of Congress Cataloging-in-Publication Data

Gorman, Michele.
    Connecting young adults and libraries : a how-to-do-it manual. — 4th ed. / Michele Gorman and Tricia Suellentrop.
        p. cm. — (How-to-do-it manuals ; no. 167)
    Rev. ed. of: Connecting young adults and libraries / Patrick Jones, Michele Gorman, Tricia Suellentrop. 3rd. ed. c2004.
    Includes bibliographical references and index.
    ISBN 978-1-55570-665-4 (alk. paper)
    1. Young adults' libraries—Administration—Handbooks, manuals, etc. 2. Young adults—Books and reading—Handbooks, manuals, etc. I. Suellentrop, Tricia, 1970– II. Jones, Patrick, 1961- Connecting young adults and libraries. III. Title.

Z718.5.J66 2009
027.62'6—dc22
                                                                        2009017657

Contents

Contents

List of Figures

Foreword

Patrick Jones

This isn't really a foreword; it's a backward. The core of this book discusses services, materials, and resources that didn't exist when I wrote the first edition of *Connecting Young Adults and Libraries* on an Apple IIe in 1991. Here's a quick list of some of the changes between the publication of the first edition of this book and now:

- The Young Adult Library Services Association was still the Young Adult Services Division and one of the smaller American Library Association divisions.

- The Internet was something for academics, not social networking and gaming.

- Very few teens had computers at home, let alone in their laps or palms.

- Gaming in libraries meant a chess board, or maybe *Dungeons & Dragons.*

- Video gaming tournaments did not exist.

- Graphic novels barely existed; the battle was getting teen magazines in libraries.

- So many teen novels were more like an "after-school" special than literature.

- There was no "Excellence in Library Service," Printz, Morris, or Alex Awards.

- There were no Young Adult Library Services Association "best" lists for graphic novels, audio books, nonfiction, or popular paperbacks.

- You shared information with colleagues once a year at conferences, not daily or even hourly through blogs, e-mail, and wikis.

- In your library, you maybe did summer programs, but there was no Teen Read Week or Teen Tech Week.

- Youth participation and book discussion groups existed in some libraries, but they were more about getting numbers for the library, not getting outcomes for the teens.
- I couldn't get enough votes to get a book about professional wrestling on the list now known as Quick Picks; now World Wrestling Entertainment has teamed up with the Young Adult Library Services Association for the Wrestlemania Challenge.

That's not evolution in eighteen years; that's revolution.

Okay, some things are the same: the book is still pink, teens still use libraries, and many library staff are still not tickled pink about *how* teens use libraries. That is why the need for this book remains after all these years.

When I wrote the first edition of *Connecting Young Adults and Libraries*, there was very little in the field about young adult librarianship. *Bare Bones* came out right around the same time, but aside from a few collections of essays, all of the work was about young adult books. I wanted to look at the larger field of library services for teens. Today, electronic discussion lists, blogs, and wikis have made the sharing of information so much easier, quicker, and democratic. But what *Connecting* did in 1992, 1998, and 2004 and does now in 2009 is pull it all together to present a holistic look at how teens use libraries and how librarians serve teens. It is where philosophy and practice come together to present both the big picture and the small details.

For the third edition, I brought Michele and Tricia on board in the summer of 2003. By then, my first young adult novel was in production and I'd started writing my second novel for teens. As much as I loved writing about serving teens, it was time for a change. In addition to focusing on writing fiction for teens, one of my main reasons for letting *Connecting* go in 2003 was because I wasn't doing teen services or interacting with teens anymore. These days I find myself back in high school classrooms, not booktalking, but talking about my books. Often, a teen at one of these schools will say, "I've never read an entire book before in high school, but I read your novel." I'm delighted, and then depressed. Very depressed.

In libraries, we've done all these wonderful high-tech things, like creating MySpace pages for teen spaces, holding gaming tournaments, and developing online summer reading clubs, but still some teens don't know how to use the libraries to find something to read. We have the favorites with cult-like followings such as *Harry Potter* and *Twilight*, but these series that capture both readers and self-proclaimed "nonreaders" are uncommon.

This is one of the reasons that I do school visits: it gives teens a chance to connect with someone, and this brief relationship empowers them. The following is a message left by a teen on my MySpace page:

> You visited my school on Friday, and I got a copy of your book *Things Change*. I just wanted to let you know how good that book was. I haven't been through an abusive relationship with another guy, like you had said other girls have been through.... So, I just

wanted to tell you that I read your book *Things Change* in about five hours. I absolutely loved it. I really like how you make it so teenagers can relate to the story, and not just think it's some other stupid book. I really don't know where I was getting at with this, just thought I'd point it out. Write back if you want to.

I did write back, and that's why I do school visits and that's why reading still matters. Reading provides teens with a mirror to reflect themselves and a window to show the world who they are and what they believe. During school visits I am often asked how much money I make from writing. The teens laugh a lot when I answer the question. So why do I write for teens? Because it is the right thing to do. And just in case no one told you, you don't and won't make a lot of money working with teens in libraries. So why should you do it? In part, because it is the right thing to do.

The world is full of shades of gray, but part of me always likes to break everything down into black and white, or two choices; there are people in the world who take and people in the world who give. By choosing to work with young people in libraries, you've chosen to give. But as you read this book, become a taker. Take ideas, programs, titles, tools, and tips. Take what you need, match it against your circumstances, and make it work for you and the young people you serve. This journey started in 1991, and my hope is that it will continue with this edition and into the next decade as well, because the work of connecting young adults and libraries is too important to ignore.

Preface

The first edition of *Connecting Young Adults and Libraries* was published in 1992, with a core message of recognizing the value of teens and their right to quality library service. In that book and in all subsequent editions, the focus has been on developing an attitude of service to teens, for teens, and with teens to make this core message a reality. This attitude is called a "YAttitude" (YA stands for young adult), and it is all about recognizing the value of young adults, defending their right to quality library services and having the passion needed to serve them. The goal of *Connecting Young Adults and Libraries* has been and will continue to be to educate, enlighten, and inspire librarians serving teens in public and school libraries as well as educators, administrators, and graduate students who will be the next generation of librarians serving teens. This book, like the three preceding editions, will include practical suggestions, personal experiences, best practices, and synthesis of the latest research about adolescents.

Librarians without YAttitudes might find themselves "converted" after reading this book. Those who already have the attitude will find new tools in this edition as they seek new ways to meet the needs of the millennial generation. For either audience this book will increase awareness about what teens want and need and how libraries and librarians can best respond to this challenge. For those of you who are up for it, the challenge awaits, and not just because it is your job but because it is enjoyable, rewarding, and an increasingly indispensable adventure that provides the essential function of supporting healthy youth development.

According to a recent survey conducted by the American Library Association about how youth utilize libraries, 78 percent of preteens and teens reported owning a library card.[1] If you currently work in a library you know that this statistic does not jive with your library's patron base. Many of these self-proclaimed teen-cardholders never set foot in the library. Those who do drop in several times a month are coming in, grabbing a book, and dashing back out the door. Sure, libraries have core teen patrons; however, very few libraries can honestly say that 78 percent of the community's teen population patronize their spaces and utilize their services. When every teen with a library card actually comes into the library to find something to read, or do homework, or play video games, or simply hang out and read comic books, there will no longer be a need for this book. Until then, *Connecting Young Adults and Libraries* will live on, shining a spotlight on best practices and highlighting some of the most successful teen programs, spaces, and collections in school and public libraries today.

In the past 15 years libraries around the country have really stepped up their game, providing record numbers of developmentally appropriate spaces, programs, collections, and staff for teen patrons. Now is a great time to be serving teens in libraries, but we can always do more.

Throughout this book we will cover new trends in young adult library services as well as long-standing programs and ideas that have stood the test of time. We'll focus on librarians who are continually coming up with new ways to engage teens and get them meaningfully involved with their library community, and we will dissect the research that has been collected in the past six years about what teens want, how they think, and how we can best serve their interests. We will address cutting-edge trends, success stories, and new and exciting opportunities for change and growth in our profession and how they affect library services to teens, including the following:

- Social networking and library 2.0
- New awards for young adult nonfiction, graphic novels, and first-time YA authors
- A decade of celebrating literary merit in teen literature: Michael L. Printz Award
- New annual celebration of teens and technology: Teen Tech Week
- New research about teen behavior, library usage, and technological savvy
- Instantaneous sharing of information via professional blogs
- Global collaboration via wikis focusing on teen library services
- YALSA membership growth
- Explosion of gaming in libraries
- Continued growth and mainstream acceptance of the graphic novel format

The first chapter looks at the philosophical basis for serving teens in school and public libraries. Chapter 2 provides an in-depth look at our audience, helping readers understand adolescent development, the developmental needs of teens, and the Search Institute's 40 Developmental Assets®, along with new research about the adolescent brain as it relates to and impacts library services. Chapter 3 examines the past, the present, and the future of connecting young adults and libraries. Customer service, building relationships, teen reference, and readers' advisory services are all addressed in Chapter 4. Chapter 5 is about information literacy, and Chapter 6 is about collection development. Chapter 7 focuses on the best ways to promote those collections, including booktalking. Chapters 8, 9, and 10 look at other ways to meaningfully involve teens with various aspects of the library, including outreach and collaboration, programming, the development of teen-friendly spaces, and the promotion of these teen services. Chapter 11 takes on teens and technology, including ways to incorporate existing and emerging technologies into your daily library services for teens. Meaningful youth involvement, which is really a core idea behind all of these services, is examined in Chapter 12, with an emphasis on teens as programmers, volunteers, and interns, as well as working with library administration to encourage and sustain youth involvement with both daily practices and strategic planning. Chapter 13 appropriately ends this book by asking you, the reader, to ask yourself some of the hard questions about why and how we can all best serve teens.

In the end, it is the very nature of all of these services that presents libraries, librarians serving teens (LSTs), policymakers, and teen patrons with various "issues," which are presented as updated, real-life case studies in the final chapter. The fourth edition also includes works cited and suggested further readings for each chapter, an index, and "The Librarian Serving Teens (LST) Tool Kit on CD-ROM," which includes editable core tools to help you put into practice all of the programs and services discussed throughout the book.

This symbol highlights related core documents located on The LST Tool Kit on CD-ROM.

One final note for those of you who have been fans of *Connecting Young Adults and Libraries* for years: You are likely aware by now that the book's original creator, Patrick Jones, is no longer working on new editions of this book. Patrick is focusing on writing fiction for teens while we are focusing on writing nonfiction about serving teens. As Patrick mentioned in the foreword, he has entrusted us with carrying on the legacy of the "The Big Pink Bible of Teen Services." His are big shoes to fill, but we trust Patrick knew what he was doing when he asked us to join him in writing the third edition to prepare us for flying solo with this fourth edition. Like Patrick did for the first 15 years of his career, we both work directly with young people in the library on a daily basis. We have also spent the past seven years traveling around the world conducting workshops and talking to thousands of librarians, LSTs, and teens about developing and carrying out exceptional library services to teens. We may not have Patrick's hair, but we do have his passion, enthusiasm, commitment to teens, and dedication to our profession and colleagues. We like to consider ourselves PJ 2.0 and we're thrilled to be your continued guides on this journey, a journey that begins and ends with all of us collectively providing outstanding library services for teens.

Sources Cited in This Chapter

1. American Library Association. "American Library Association Youth and Library Use Study." Available: www.ala.org/ala/mgrps/divs/yalsa/Harris YouthPoll.pdf (accessed January 13, 2009).

Acknowledgments

The authors would like to collectively thank their library systems (The Public Library of Charlotte and Mecklenburg County and Johnson County Library) for their support and for allowing them to reproduce original core documents; Charles Harmon and the editorial team at Neal-Schuman for their support; Jim Rosinia for allowing them to reproduce his original "teens and customer service" scenario/training exercise; Michael Giller (school librarian extraordinaire) for his unique perspective and for helping librarians serving teens see the importance and value of information literacy; Mary K. Chelton, Jack Martin, and Pat Feehan, for their insightful and candid feedback of the first draft; graduate student Rebecca L. Buck for creating, implementing, and analyzing the "2008 Teen Reading Habits and Perceptions" Survey; and the following public library systems and schools who participated in the aforementioned survey: Ann Arbor District Library (MI), Austin Public Library (TX), Broward County Library (FL), Carnegie Library of Pittsburgh (PA), The Public Library of Charlotte and Mecklenburg County (NC), Coshocton Public Library (OH), Fairport Public Library (NY), The Girls' Middle School (CA), Houston Public Library (TX), Johnson County Library (KS), Kansas City Public Library (KS), Laramie County Library (WY), Schaumburg Township District Library (IL), Sno-Isle Libraries (WA), St. Louis County Library (MO), and West Ottawa Public Schools (MI).

Michele would like to thank her family and friends for always sticking with her through the endless hours of research, writing, editing, and rewriting. She promises this is the last one for a while. Michele also owes a debt of gratitude to current and former Loft at ImaginOn staff members and ImaginOn and PLCMC staff and administration for their support, feedback, contributions, and often necessary distractions from the writing process: Jimmeka Anderson, Melanie Baron, Beck Buck, Kelly Czarnecki, Seth Ervin, Catherine Haydon, Lois Kilkka, Pamela McCarter, Beth Murray, Jesse Vieau, and Amy Wyckoff. You guys make my day-to-day a lot of fun, and that's worth more than you might know. Paula, Tricia, Marin, and Sarah—you guys really are the best. Marli: thanks for the help with all of the music. And finally, Michele wants B.D. to know that this book wouldn't exist without her patience, motivation, and mad organizational skills.

Tricia would like to offer thanks to the brilliant staff of the Johnson County Library for their creativity, patience, humor, and understanding. Thanks to the Sharpnacks for the use of their computer and for feeding me with television, dinner, and love. Thanks to Sarah D., Kathy M., C. J. S., Kate P., Scott S., Jackie B., Stuart H., Dave H., Erica R., Erin H., and Kasey R. for the distractions and laughter. Thanks to Paula for setting me straight on almost everything, and the biggest thanks goes to iMEG for doing all of the work. Really, truly, thanks.

The Language of the Librarian Serving Teens

Glossary

Throughout the text we will refer, in true librarian fashion, to a plethora of acronyms and jargon. Therefore, we decided to start with the glossary so that we're all on the same page from the beginning. As you read through the glossary, you'll notice definitions for words you know, new words we coined since this book's inception in 1992, and other important terms that are necessary for understanding this text and work with teenagers in a school or public library. The three most critical are listed first, followed by more definitions listed in alphabetical order. Boldfaced terms within definitions indicate a corresponding entry in the glossary.

LST: A term coined in the third edition of *Connecting Young Adults and Libraries* that stands for "librarian serving teens." Although we do not have an exact number of how many young adult librarians are out there serving teens in public libraries, we do know that **YALSA** is the fourth largest division of the **American Library Association**, with more than 5,800 members. While this number does not tell us how many of these dedicated library workers actually hold the title "young adult librarian," it does tell us that interest in serving teens in libraries is growing and will likely continue to grow during the next decade. Whether they hold the title of YA or Teen Librarian or not, it is obvious to us that many librarians across the country actively create original programming, develop outstanding teen collections, and otherwise engage teens on a daily basis. The point we want to make by using this term throughout the book is that any librarian in any library who counts young people between the ages of 12 and 18 among their patrons is an LST. Some do this full time, while others only do it from 3:00 p.m. to 6:00 p.m. across the reference desk. The term *librarian* is also broadly defined to include any library staff member or volunteer. It is also used for school librarians, media specialists, and teacher-librarians who work with students between the ages of 12 and 18 in a school setting. While school librarians play different roles, have different ways of measuring success, and provide different services than public librarians, they are still LSTs.

YALSA: Young Adult Library Services Association. A division of the American Library Association, YALSA is the primary professional association for librarians serving teens in libraries. The mission of YALSA is to advocate, promote, and strengthen service to young adults as part of the continuum of total library service and to support those who provide service to this population. Many of the booklists, awards, and projects we will refer to in the text emerge from the work of this organization and its members.

YAttitude: Someone with YAttitude recognizes the value of young adults, their right to quality library services, and the passion needed to serve them. This term was coined in the first edition of *Connecting Young Adults and Libraries*. A YAttitude doesn't imply that LSTs are "cooler" than other librarians but merely that they understand the unique information needs of teens and advocate for others to share a similar understanding. YALSA continues the tradition of associating outstanding teen services with YAttitude by publishing a quarterly electronic newsletter by the same name.

In alphabetical order, here are other important terms, documents, people, and definitions that we mention in the text of this book and/or we consider essential for LSTs to know in order to best connect young adults and libraries.

AASL: American Association of School Librarians. The mission of this ALA division is to advocate excellence, facilitate change, and develop leaders in the school library media field. About one-half of all YALSA members are school librarians. The primary document spelling out the AASL agenda is *Information Power*.

adolescence: The transitional period of time during which a young person moves from childhood to adulthood. Young people in the midst of adolescence often experience a wide range of events and opportunities that contribute to their growth and development.

adolescent literacy: The concern that teenagers are actively engaged in reading. The most successful adolescent literacy activities are based on research that suggests that time spent reading is related to reading skills, academic success, attitudes about reading, and knowledge of the world.

ALA: American Library Association. The ALA is the oldest and largest library association in the world, with more than 64,000 members. Its mission is to promote the highest-quality library and information services and public access to information.

ALAN: Assembly on Literature for Adolescents. ALAN is one of the **NCTE**'s special-interest groups. Founded in November 1973, ALAN is made up of teachers, authors, librarians, publishers, teacher-educators and their students, and others who are particularly interested in the area of young adult literature.

ALAN Review: Official publication of ALAN, which contains articles on YA literature and its teaching, interviews with authors, reports on publishing trends, current research on YA literature, a section of reviews of new books, and ALAN membership news.

Alex Awards: A YALSA book selection committee charged with awarding, from the previous year's publications, ten books written for adults that have special appeal to young adults ages 12 through 18. The major sponsor of the Alex Awards is the Margaret Alexander Edwards Trust. The awards were named "Alex" after **Edwards**, who was called "Alex" by her friends.

alliterate: A person who has the ability to read but chooses not to pursue reading as a recreational activity.

ALSC: Association for Library Service to Children. ALSC is another division of ALA. In 2009, ALSC had approximately 4,230 members, including children's and youth librarians, children's literature experts, and publishers committed to improving and ensuring the future of the nation through exemplary library service to children, their families, and others who work with children.

anime: The Japanese term for animation. The word *anime* is derived from the French word *animé*, which means animated or lively.

App: An abbreviation for application, this term has become popular with the proliferation of the Apple iPhone, which allows users to download custom applications for use on their phones.

ARC: Advance reading copy. A book printed by a publisher in a limited quantity expressly for members of award selection committees, professional reviewers, and librarians for prepublication review and consideration for awards. Also known as a "galley."

assets: The building blocks of adolescence. Assets represent strengths and opportunities for young people.

at-risk youth: A broad term used to describe teens in trouble. A young person defined as "at risk" is generally under the age of 21 and at a high risk of becoming or has become a substance abuser, victim of abuse, or school dropout; has experienced chronic failure in school or mental health issues, including suicidal tendencies; and/or has committed a violent or criminal act. While some equate "at risk" with urban or minority youth, all teens are at risk in one way or another. Research tells us that teens without assets are more likely to be at risk and to engage in self-destructive behavior.

BBW: Banned Books Week. BBW is a weeklong celebration of the freedom to read, held during the last week of September. In existence since 1982, this project is sponsored by the American Booksellers Association, American Booksellers Foundation for Free Expression, Association of American Publishers, American Society of Journalists and Authors, National Association of College Stores, and ALA.

Bare Bones: Shortened name for *Bare Bones for Young Adult Services: Tips for Public Library Generalists*, a book originally written by **Mary K. Chelton** and Jim Rosinia to provide basic service tips for public library generalists in the early 1990s. A second, expanded edition written by **Renee Vaillancourt** was published in 2000.

BBYA: Best Books for Young Adults. BBYA is a YALSA committee charged with annually creating a list of the year's best young adult and adult fiction and nonfiction of interest to teens.

Big6: A popular information and technology literacy model created by Robert Berkowitz and Michael Eisenberg that provides students with a framework for thinking about research by following a series of six steps.

blog: An online diary or journal.

***Booklist*:** An annual ALA publication that reviews more than 2,500 titles for youth. *Booklist* also publishes a wide variety of feature articles, including author interviews, bibliographies, book-related essays by well-known writers, and a selection of columns, including one dedicated to young adult literature. The youth editors for *Booklist* serve as advisors to some YALSA book selection committees.

booktalk: A prepared introduction to a book, usually in the form of a mini-performance. Like a movie trailer or the well-written flap copy of a book, a booktalk is a presentation with the same intention. The goal for the librarian is to have the teens in the audience at a book-talking presentation check out the books being promoted.

Broderick, Dorothy M.: The author of many publications about library services to teens and the cofounder of *Voice of Youth Advocates (VOYA)* magazine.

Cart, Michael: A past president of YALSA, writer, lecturer, and consultant. Cart, whose column "Carte Blanche" appears monthly in ***Booklist*** magazine, was one of the primary forces behind the establishment of the Michael L. Printz Award for young adult literature.

Chelton, Mary K.: Another past president of YALSA, a highly respected young adult advocate, SLIS professor, and one of the cofounders of ***VOYA***. Dr. Chelton is also the editor of three volumes of *Excellence in Library Services to Young Adults* and the coauthor of the first edition of *Bare Bones*.

CIPA: Children's Internet Protection Act. Signed into law in December 2000, CIPA was designed to safeguard children against objectionable or harmful material on the Internet. CIPA amends the Elementary and Secondary Education Act of 1965 and the Communications Act of 1934. The amendments direct schools and libraries to have in place a policy of Internet safety and a technology-based method of blocking access to visual depictions on the Internet that are obscene, pornographic, or harmful to minors.

collection development: The process of selecting (and deselecting) materials for a library's physical and virtual collections. More than just buying and weeding materials, collection development is a series of choices based on each library's mission, community, and operating procedures. Collection development isn't about buying books; it's about resource allocation.

developmental tasks: The emotional, social, sexual, intellectual, and psychological changes that make up adolescence.

digital divide: Originally this term was used to define the gap between those who have physical access to new information and communication tools, such as the Internet, and those who do not. With the passage of time and the proliferation of technology, this definition has expanded to include the divide between those who have the skills to use these technologies and those who do not.

digital immigrant: A term coined by Marc Prensky to define a person who was born and raised before the proliferation of digital technologies like personal computers, cell phones, and the Internet.

digital native: Also coined by Prensky, this term is generally used to define anyone who was raised with digital technology—a native speaker of the digital language of computers, video games, and the Internet.

DOPA: Deleting Online Predators Act of 2006. DOPA passed once before by the House 410–15 in July 2006 before dying in the Senate. The bill would have withheld federal e-rate funding from libraries and schools that did not restrict the use of social networking Web sites by minors.

Edwards, Margaret: The administrator of young adult programs at Enoch Pratt Free Library in Baltimore for over 30 years and author of the first "manifesto" of YA librarianship. Edwards' trust fund has backed many YALSA projects, and her name is YALSA's award for lifetime achievement in young adult literature.

ephebiphobia: The fear and loathing of teenagers.

ESRB: Entertainment Software Rating Board. ESRB is a self-regulatory organization that independently applies and enforces ratings for computer and video games in North America.

Excellence in Library Services to Young Adults: A YALSA-sponsored project started by ALA past president Hardy Franklin in 1993. All five rounds of the project have been funded by the Margaret Alexander Edwards Trust. Each round's selected programs have been included in a book by the same name, each of which highlights 25 of the best programs across the country that can be adapted and replicated in school and public libraries around the country.

The Fair Garden and the Swarm of Beasts: Book by Margaret Edwards, often considered the "manifesto" of young adult librarianship. It has been updated twice since its original publication in 1969.

fan fiction: Unofficial, unlicensed fiction created by fans using characters from existing books, games, manga, comics, television shows, movies, etc.

focus group: A technique used in marketing to gather a representative sample of a certain market to ask questions in a controlled setting to discover the participants' feelings about a certain product or service.

folksonomy: A means of classifying and categorizing online data, also referred to as "tagging." This process is a collaborative one in which online users generate a list of open-ended and user-controlled labels to help classify online content like images, blogs, videos, podcasts, etc.

40 Developmental Assets®: A framework developed by the **Search Institute** to identify the elements of a strengths-based approach to healthy development. This framework identifies 40 critical factors for young people's growth and development. When drawn together, the assets offer a set of benchmarks for positive adolescent development. The assets help show how all families, schools, congregations, neighborhoods, youth organizations, libraries, and others in communities all play a role in helping shape young people's lives.

Free Access to Libraries for Minors: A core ALA document originally adopted in 1972 (last amended in June 2004) that is an interpretation/extension of the **Library Bill of Rights**, which states that any attempt by libraries to deny minors equal access to resources violates the Library Bill of Rights.

"Freedom to Read" Statement: An important ALA statement originally adopted in 1953 (last amended in June 2004) that spells out the association's belief that the freedom to read is essential to our democracy.

friending: The act of requesting someone be your friend or adding a friend to your account on a social networking site (like MySpace or Facebook).

GNLIB-L: Graphic Novels in Libraries E-mail Distribution List. GNLIB-L is where LSTs can discuss issues and share information about graphic novels.

graphic novel: Term coined by artist/writer Will Eisner in 1978. A graphic novel is a book-length story that is written and illustrated in comic book style. It can be an original, self-contained story or it can be a collection of previously published comic books that together tell one story. It can also be an original publication that features traditional comic book characters.

Grolier Award: Past ALA award, sponsored by Grolier Publishing, that was presented annually to a librarian whose unusual contribution to the stimulation and guidance of reading by children and young people exemplified outstanding achievement in the profession. Grolier sponsored this award from its inception in 1954 through 2005. Scholastic began sponsoring this award in 2006, so it is now known as the **Scholastic Library Publishing Award**.

Guys Read: A Web-based literacy initiative for boys and young men created by children's author Jon Scieszka.

Hinton, S. E.: Author of the *The Outsiders*, the young adult book considered by many to be the first "modern" teen novel, and the mother of all young adult literature

homework center: Normally more than just a physical space, but instead a public library program that provides homework assistance and/or tutoring to teens after school.

Horn Book: Review journal that focuses on the best literature for youth.

IM: Instant Messaging. A form of real-time communication between two or more people based on typed text. Also known as "chat," teens often IM with other teens who are on their "buddy list" or a list of predetermined and vetted online friends and acquaintances.

IMLS: Institute of Museum and Library Services. IMLS is a federal government agency from which much library funding flows.

information literacy: The ability of any person, but in this context a secondary school student, to be competent in the skills of selecting, retrieving, analyzing, evaluating, synthesizing, creating, and communicating information in all formats. Information literacy is focusing on youth learning as a process for solving information problems rather than simply product- or even project-based learning.

Information Power: AASL document created in 1988, revised in 1998, which provides the framework for working in a school library media center. This book provides school library media specialists the tools they need to fulfill their libraries' mission and to ensure that students and staff are effective users of ideas and information.

IRA: International Reading Association. The IRA is a nonprofit, professional organization for those involved in teaching reading to learners of all ages. Specific IRA groups that directly impact library services to teens include the Middle School Reading Special Interest Group, the Network of Adolescent Literacy, and the Commission on Adolescent Literacy.

Jones, Patrick: The original creator of *Connecting Young Adults and Libraries*, world-renowned trainer of young adult librarians, champion of teen services, young adult author, and lover of all things professional wrestling.

Kirkus: A biweekly review journal that publishes more than 5,000 reviews a year, including fiction, mysteries, science fiction, translations, nonfiction, and children's and young adult books.

KLIATT: A bimonthly magazine that publishes reviews of paperback books, hardcover fiction for adolescents, audiobooks, and educational software recommended for libraries and classrooms serving young adults.

Library Bill of Rights: Core ALA document that advocates for free and fair access to library materials.

lifelong learning: A common term used by libraries to help define the act of and importance of the process of continued learning throughout one's life. A library that provides lifelong learning service helps address the desire for self-directed personal growth and development opportunities. Lifelong learning is an outgrowth of effective teen services. If collections, programs, and other elements of the service response reach the teen patron, the outcome will be to create a lifelong library user and, ultimately, a lifelong learner.

literacy: The ability to read, write, communicate, and comprehend meaning locally and globally through print, visual media, and increasingly cross-platform multimedia.

LM_NET: An electronic e-mail distribution list sponsored by the Educator's Reference Desk that is open to school library media specialists interested in general discussion as well as idea sharing, problem solving, and networking.

LSTA: Library Services and Technology Act. The LSTA came into existence due to the Museum and Library Services Act of 1996. This formed the Institute for Museum and Library Services and changed federal funding for LSCA Titles I, II, and III from the Department of Education to LSTA from **IMLS**. The LSTA provides library funding to the states. Some states use a competitive grant process that allows libraries or library systems to get money for specific projects that fit that state's priorities.

manga: Japanese comics in print form that traditionally read back to front, right to left, when they are translated into English.

Margaret Edwards Award: Established in 1988, this award honors an author's lifetime achievement for writing books that have been popular over a period of time. The annual award is administered by YALSA and sponsored by *School Library Journal* magazine. It recognizes an author's work in helping adolescents become aware of themselves and addressing questions about their role and importance in relationships, society, and in the world.

Millennials: Generation of young people born between 1980 and 2000 characterized by self-confidence, acceptance of diversity, optimism, individuality, and an affinity and talent for multitasking. Young people who fall under this umbrella term have grown up surrounded by digital media and have never known a world without personal computers, cell phones, and video games. Millennials are also called Generation Y, the i (Internet) Generation, Echo Boomers, Nexters, the Nintendo Generation, the Digital Generation, and the Net Generation.

NCTE: National Council of Teachers of English. NCTE is devoted to improving the teaching and learning of English and the language arts at all levels of education. Since 1911, NCTE has provided a forum for the profession, an array of opportunities for teachers to continue their professional growth throughout their careers, and a framework for cooperation to deal with issues that affect the teaching of English.

NEA: National Education Association. NEA is the nation's largest professional employee organization committed to advancing the cause of public education.

New Directions for Library Services to Young Adults: Written by Patrick Jones and edited by Linda Waddle, this document represents YALSA's broad philosophical vision. The purpose of the document is to help libraries, with their communities, develop their teens into healthy, competent, and caring adults.

OIF: Office of Intellectual Freedom. Established in 1967, ALA's OIF is charged with implementing ALA policies concerning the concept of intellectual freedom as embodied in the **Library Bill of Rights**. The goal of the office is to educate librarians and the general public about the nature and importance of intellectual freedom in libraries.

Opposing Viewpoints: A series of books and a subscription database that provide teens with the types of resources (short, argumentative essays) they need to complete term papers about various issues.

outcomes: The effect a service, such as library services, has on the life of a person. Outcomes, which are considered essential, are often easy to define but much harder to measure. Outcomes might include youth contributing to their community, doing well in school, developing social skills, learning work or marketable skills, and developing positive and responsible family and social relationships.

outcomes-based education: A curriculum practice used in schools that establishes clearly defined learner-outcomes based on the premise that all students can be successful learners.

out-of-school time: Critical nonschool hours, notably the hours after school and before a parent gets home, generally identified as 3:00 p.m. to 7:00 p.m., when teens need access to high-quality programs, activities, and opportunities to keep them off the streets and out of trouble.

output measures: A measurement tool used in both school and public libraries to capture both quantitative and qualitative data to "prove" the success of services.

outreach: Library services that take place outside the library setting. Outreach refers to either a community relations function (promoting services) or actual service delivery, such as booktalking in a classroom.

The Pew Internet and American Life Project: An initiative of the Pew Research Center, a nonprofit "fact tank" that provides information on the issues, attitudes, and trends shaping America and the world. The Pew Research Center has been instrumental in collecting information about how teens use technology and the Internet in their daily lives.

PLA: Public Library Association. PLA is a division of ALA that enhances the development and effectiveness of public library staff and public library services.

podcast: A digital recording of a radio broadcast or similar program distributed over the Internet using syndication feeds for downloading and playback on a personal audio player or personal computer.

positive youth development: A process of creating environments that support the social, emotional, spiritual, physical, moral, and cognitive development of young people. Positive youth development addresses the broader developmental needs of youth, in contrast to deficit-based models that focus solely on youth problems.

PPYA: Popular Paperbacks for Young Adults. PPYA is a YALSA committee that prepares one to five annotated booklists of different genres of current interest to teens each year.

Printz Award: The Michael L. Printz Award recognizes several young adult books each year that exemplify literary excellence in young adult literature. It is named for a Topeka, Kansas, school librarian who was a longtime active member of YALSA and it is sponsored by *Booklist*, a publication of the American Library Association.

program: Generally defined as a library-sponsored activity that takes place outside the context of reference services designed to inform, entertain, or enrich users as well as promote the use of the library and its collection.

puberty: The physical change that occurs in young people when the secondary sexual characteristics start to appear. Research indicates that puberty is beginning earlier and earlier with each generation. Puberty is usually seen as a physical milestone that marks the beginning of the process of adolescence.

PUBYAC: An Internet discussion list concerned with the practical aspects of children and young adult services in public libraries, focusing on programming ideas, outreach and literacy programs for children and caregivers, censorship and policy issues, collection development, administrative considerations, job openings, professional development, and other pertinent services and issues.

Quick Picks: A YALSA committee charged with developing an annual reading list for young adults (ages 12–18) who, for whatever reasons, do not like to read. The purpose of this list is to identify titles for recreational reading (not for curricular or remedial use) of interest to the **reluctant reader**.

reluctant reader: A term used to describe a teen who is not interested in reading. Reluctant readers generally fall into four categories: teen who is intelligent and interested in reading but doesn't read well, teen who seems to have no interest in reading and is falling behind as a result of not reading regularly, teen who is dealing with specific learning problems that impedes his or her ability and willingness to read, and teen who reads well but has little interest in doing so.

Scholastic Library Publishing Award: Award that recognizes a librarian for outstanding achievement in the profession for his or her contribution to the stimulation and guidance of reading by children and young people. Formerly the **Grolier Award**, Scholastic took over the sponsorship of this award in 2006.

Search Institute®: An independent, nonprofit organization whose mission is to provide leadership, knowledge, and resources to promote healthy youth and communities by conducting research, developing publications and practical tools, and providing training and technical assistance to all sectors of society including K–12 and higher education, faith communities, **youth-serving organizations**, social-service organizations, families, businesses, and the public sector.

social media: Internet and mobile-based tools for sharing and discussing information. These tools might include blogs, podcasts, online forums, instant messaging software, e-mail, voice-over IP, etc.

social networking: The act of connecting online with friends, family, and colleagues as well as meeting people with similar interests or hobbies via various Web sites and services that focus on creating networks of like-minded individuals. Popular social networking sites include Facebook, MySpace, Digg, and LinkedIn.

SLJ: *School Library Journal. SLJ* is a professional publication whose mission is to serve librarians who work with young people in school and public libraries by providing information needed to manage libraries, from creating high-quality collections to understanding how technology can assist (or hinder) learning.

student achievement: The success of students on standardized tests, often used as a measure of school success and therefore an important factor for LSTs in secondary schools to consider.

student learning: A term that encompasses the broad process of learning. Similar to student achievement, student learning is an important measure of success for LSTs in a school setting.

TAC: Teen Advisory Council. TACs are sometimes referred to as Youth or Teen Advisory Groups and are usually formal groups put together by an LST to provide assistance in all aspects of planning, developing, implementing, and evaluating library services.

teen: The term that most persons ages 12–18 prefer to be called based on research inside and outside of the library field.

texting: Shorthand for text messaging, texting via cell phone (sending a written message from one cell phone to another) has become the dominant form of communication for teens in the past few years.

TRW: Teen Read Week. Sponsored by YALSA, TRW is a national literacy initiative aimed at teens, their parents, librarians, educators, booksellers, and other concerned adults. Since its inception in 1998, TRW has been celebrated annually during the third week of October in libraries throughout the country.

TTW: Teen Tech Week. Sponsored by YALSA, TTW is a national celebration that focuses on connecting teens with different technologies, especially those available through the library. Since its inception in 2007, TTW has been celebrated annually during the month of March in libraries throughout the country.

tween: People between the ages of 8 and 12 who are often served by children's departments but who seek to define themselves as teenagers.

Twitter/tweet: Twitter is a free social networking and micro-blogging site that allows users to send and read others' updates. A tweet is a message sent through Twitter, usually via cell phone (an act referred to as "twittering") and up to 140 characters in length.

UGC: User-Generated Content. UGC is an umbrella term for various kinds of media content produced by nonmedia professionals that is often made publicly available via the Internet. UGC might include videos, images, audio files, and written content (posted on Web sites, social networking sites, or blogs). Popular UGC created by teens include machinima, home videos posted to YouTube, fan fiction, and cell phone-to-phone photo messaging.

ULC: Urban Libraries Council. ULC is an association of public libraries in metropolitan areas and the corporations that serve them. Believing that thriving public libraries are a result of collaborative leadership, the trustees, library directors, and corporate officers of member institutions work together to address shared issues, grasp new opportunities, and conduct research that improves professional practice.

vlog: Video blog, or blog that primarily uses video as its primary information-sharing format.

VOYA: *Voice of Youth Advocates* is a bimonthly professional journal for librarians, educators, and other professionals who work with young adults. The only magazine devoted exclusively to the informational needs of teenagers, it was founded in 1978 by librarians and renowned intellectual freedom advocates **Dorothy M. Broderick** and **Mary K. Chelton**.

Web 2.0: A buzzword coined by Tim O'Reilly and Dale Dougherty to define a more dynamic and interactive World Wide Web. The original Web (or Web 1.0) is more about static Web pages, search engines, and surfing from one Web site to another, whereas this new generation of Web (2.0) is about Web-based communities and hosted services (such as social-networking sites, wikis, and blogs) that aim to facilitate creativity, collaboration, and sharing between users.

wiki: A collaborative Web site that represents the ongoing, collective work of many authors. Similar to a blog in structure and logic, a wiki allows anyone to edit, delete, or modify content that has been placed on a site, including the work of previous authors, using only a browser interface.

Williams, Mabel: Generally considered the first official young adult librarian, Ms. Williams was the first librarian to serve older youth at the New York Public Library in the early 1900s and was belatedly awarded the Grolier Award for her services to teens in 1980.

YA: Young adult. In the library field, the term "young adult" generally refers to a person between the ages of 12 and 18. In the business world, this term often refers to twenty-somethings. Generally, "young adult" is used in professional settings when referring to this age group, while "teen" is used when interacting with members of this age group.

YA-Lit Symposium: Held for the first time in 2008, YALSA's YA Lit Symposium is a biannual professional development conference that focuses specifically on library materials and programming for a teen audience. Funded in part by the William Morris Endowment, the YA Lit Symposium is largely focused on young adult literature and connecting teens with books and other reading materials.

YALS: *Young Adult Library Services* is the official journal of YALSA. *YALS* primarily serves as a vehicle for continuing education for librarians serving young adults ages 12 through 18, in addition to serving as the official record of the organization.

YALSA-BK: A YALSA-sponsored e-mail distribution list with the primary purpose of providing librarians a forum to discuss young adult literature and other issues concerning young adult reading and young adult literature. Teens, especially those who belong to book discussion groups, are encouraged to subscribe and participate by sharing their thoughts about what they are reading.

YALSA-LOCKDOWN: A YALSA-sponsored e-mail distribution list with the primary purpose of providing librarians a forum to discuss issues unique to librarians working with incarcerated youth, including teens in juvenile halls, group homes, treatment centers, mental institutions, etc.

YA-MUSIC: A YALSA-sponsored e-mail distribution list started by YALSA's Teen Music Interest Group, whose primary purpose is to develop recommended practices in collections, programming, and related topics in the field of music and media, including CDs, MP3s, and emerging technologies and services in music media for teens. This list is open to anyone interested in teen music and media.

YA-URBAN: A YALSA-sponsored e-mail distribution list with the primary purpose of providing librarians a forum to discuss issues unique to librarians who work in large urban libraries.

YA-YAAC: A YALSA-sponsored e-mail distribution list with the primary purpose of providing teen library advisory councils and the librarians who coordinate them in school and public libraries opportunities to share information and ideas.

youth advocacy: Supporting young people in all areas of service by speaking up, writing in favor of, recommending, or urging library administration, members of your community, or your local, state, or national government to share in this support.

youth advocate: An adult who acts in the best interest of a young person, ensuring his or her rights while at the same time aiding in skill development and supporting his or her emotional, physical, and mental growth.

youth-serving organization: An institution whose activities are deliberately structured to provide a set of operational procedures, values, and mores that teach and encourage responsible behavior. These organizations include extracurricular, school-based organizations as well as broad-based community organizations such as Boys and Girls Clubs, 4-H clubs, church groups, and sports leagues.

YP: Youth participation. YP is defined by YALSA as the involvement of young adults in responsible action and significant decision making that affects the design and delivery of library and information services for their peers and the community.

zine: An abbreviation of fanzine or magazine. Issued independently and usually produced today using desktop publishing and photocopiers, zines are a relatively low-budget, low-circulation means of self-expression.

The Philosophy of Service to Young Adults

In countless workshops, people ask us questions about how to improve services to teens. These are the right questions, but everyone needs to supply his or her own answer to what an improved, quality young adult services program looks like in a particular school or public library. Throughout this text, we will provide you with the tools and techniques and introduce you to the best practices and innovative ideas that will help you to turn this vision into a reality at your library. Is this really the best vision for your library? It depends on the unique wants and needs of your teen users. And you will never learn, unless you ask them and provide them opportunities to work alongside you.

Let's start by laying down one golden rule of young adult library service: always put the customer first. Most librarians spend all day answering questions, but planning for young adult services is about asking questions. Let's start with these six important questions:

- What do the teens want and need from their library?

- What can your library do in the short term to meet these wants and needs?

- What should your library do in the long term to meet these wants and needs?

- Can your library afford it, and is it a priority?

- What obstacles does your library need to overcome?

- How do we know that we have successfully met those wants and needs?

But maybe before we ask those six important questions we should ask some more basic ones:

- Why are we here?

- Why do libraries exist?

- Why do we work in libraries?

- What do we want to achieve?

It is time to step back from the day-to-day, the desk, and the demands of programming, to think about these most basic issues. It is time to form a strong foundation, to reexamine and reaffirm our values, and to refine our role. While libraries have many service responses, they are all aimed at achieving positive outcomes for our patrons. Why do teens matter? Why should we care?

How to provide all children and adolescents with a solid foundation for life is a pressing social issue in the United States. Evidence that the foundation is fragile appears year after year in newspaper articles and scientific studies that call attention to the challenges and problems facing too many youth. Those of us who work with teens realize, in so many ways, that as a society we are failing to offer our young people the solid footing they need to grow safely and successfully into adulthood. In almost every community, a library in a school or public setting can provide that foundation, if the powers that be make serving teens a priority.

What Is a Vision of Service for Connecting Young Adults and Libraries?

In a perfect world, every public and school library would have a librarian dedicated to serving teens. All teens who encounter a library staff person would be treated with respect, and teen volunteers and interns would have opportunities to be meaningfully involved in developing and implementing library services for teens. Teens would have unfettered access to a comprehensive collection of materials and would be free to spend time in the library doing whatever they want, be it reading, doing research, playing games on the Internet, reading comic books, socializing via MySpace, or downloading music online. Teens would still use the library for homework, but in addition they would have access to a broader selection of recreational materials, including magazines, downloadable audio and video, and graphic novels. They would also have an opportunity to help plan, carry out, and participate in a wide selection of teen-driven programs.

Each library would have a dedicated space for teens with comfortable seating and relaxed rules about eating, drinking, and socializing, as well as a range of outreach services, after-hours services, and Web-based services that would expand the library beyond normal open hours. All policies, procedures, and services for teens would be planned, promoted, and implemented with the assistance of teens serving on formal or informal advisory groups as well as with the input of community partners. All rules that govern the library's services to teens would be fair and impartial and created for the good of the library community and not to censor or inhibit teens from using the library, and library administration would acknowledge that teens deserve the same financial support as other departments within the library, including children's services and adult services.

Teens would be knowledgeable about the library's resources and would know how to utilize technology to find information. They would also have the skills necessary to locate, use, and evaluate information from a wide variety of sources. Finally, every teen who had a library experience could honestly say that it was a positive experience, and one they would recommend to their peers. These positive interactions will contribute to the healthy development of young adults.[1]

This vision, of course, is perfectly lined up with the larger institutional vision/mission and will vary by community, but a vision gives us a place to start, a road to follow, and an objective to achieve.

What Are Six Key Goals for Reaching This Vision?

If this vision is to become a reality, a process has to happen. Visions flow into missions that flow into goals and for LSTs (librarians serving teens), youth involvement is the river that runs through it all. In the following sections are six key goals toward which a library, regardless of its size, needs to work. Associated with each of these goals are practical tasks that most libraries could undertake, many with little expense. We will cover more details on how to do each of these tasks within this book, but start planning, advocating, and building by knowing what you need to do and how to achieve it, one step/task at a time.

Goal 1

Libraries are committed to providing services that are suitable to the developmental needs of young adults and the principles of positive youth development.

Tasks

- Remind everyone that nowhere in any library mission statement does it read "except for teenagers." Here is another reminder: Look at your library's annual report. If there are pictures, no doubt the majority of them are of young people using libraries. That is the message we send to our public: Young people matter.

- Organize teens to write e-mails to library/school board members about the importance of library services and the need to keep them a priority. Engage groups of teens already organized (school clubs, faith-based groups, etc.) to lobby for services based upon their needs.

- Plan services and programs based not on the needs of the library but on the developmental needs of teens. Then, remind staff and the public about those needs by posting the Search Institute's list of 40 Developmental Assets[2] around the library, including staff areas. Send information to board members and others about products from the Search Institute, such as the "150 Ways to Show Kids You Care" poster,

If your library system is resistant to change, start small and grow your program teen by teen, step by step. Success breeds success.

the "40 Ways Anyone Can Build Assets" poster, and "Asset-Building Bookmarks" (perfect for libraries). Get serious about adopting the asset framework.

- Be direct with your director, or advocate your principles with your principal. Ask her what she wants the library to do for teens and what resources she is willing to dedicate to make it happen. Good intentions are not good enough. Also, reward your director for any steps taking you closer to realizing the vision.

- Find partners in the community who share a passion for building assets. Just go to the Search Institute Web site and learn about communities involved in asset building (www.search-institute.org/communities/partner.htm). Teach them what libraries can do for teens.

Goal 2

Libraries employ young adults or certified school library media specialists and train staff members, volunteers, youth participants, and others to serve teens.

Tasks

- Provide all library staff with training about adolescent development, the developmental needs of teens, and adolescent brain research. To find someone who can deliver this training, contact your state library's youth consultant or YALSA (Young Adult Library Services Association), who can recommend someone in your area who has been certified to train staff on these topics. It is self-defeating for an energetic teen librarian to be working 50 hours a week to get teens to come into the library if, on their first visit, teens encounter staff who have not been trained to effectively meet the needs of teens (or, worse, who are unwilling to do so).

- Develop a program to recruit and employ teen volunteers through improved communication with school service learning personnel and other entities providing community service volunteers. If you want staff to treat teens well, then get teen volunteers who will present positive images to the staff.

- Develop employment opportunities for teens that allow for flexibility in scheduling—including internships and work-study programs. One way to acquire additional funding for young adult staffing is to seek grants and other funding for short-term projects with definable outcomes.

- Staff must work toward continued improvement to ensure that they meet the competencies established in the "Young Adults Deserve the Best Competencies" document created by YALSA. Hold people accountable for their work with youth. Get managers to write teen customer service objectives into performance reviews. It is hard to fire the wrong people; it is a lot easier to hire the right ones. Educate managers to ask each job candidate, regardless of the level in the

> Research supports a greater quantity and higher quality of service to teens when a young adult librarian is present.

organization, behavioral interview questions that will weed out the "teen haters" at the onset.

- Develop young adult librarian positions. Few libraries are adding new positions, but they can still change existing ones that no longer meet the needs of the library's patron base.

Goal 3

Libraries provide for the unique needs of teens as part of the library's general service responses; for example, readers' advisory, information services, cataloging, circulation, data collection.

Tasks

- Work with technical services staff to ensure that young adult use of the collection is measured. Make sure to count not only use of the YA collection but also use of the entire collection by teens. In all measurement matters, argue for a separate teen report that has the same status as children's and adult services. We can't improve until first we can accurately gauge how well we are doing.

- Get involved within the library system, school, or profession to support teen services at all levels. Always ask the question, "Where do teens fit in this?"

- Train staff to understand the unique information needs of teens, and identify the unique skills that your librarians may need to develop to assist teens with information and readers' advisory services online and in person.

- Increase the library's capacity to serve teens by increasing the awareness of all staff through a presentation on teen services during staff development day, distribution of information about teens and teen services through various library communication vehicles, and presentations to various library teams.

- Involve teens through formal and informal means to have an effect on service responses. Make suggestion and comment forms available not just at the reference desk but in the physical and virtual spaces teens use. Consider forming a focus group periodically. Just talk to teens.

Goal 4

Libraries set aside space(s) for teen use in the library's physical and virtual space.

Tasks

- Make better use of public library meeting rooms to expand services and programs to young adult customers. Study halls, the "teen time" recreation program, as well as tutoring and after-school programming held in the meeting rooms would increase the capacity of the library to serve teens.

- Realize that the best "space" to provide library services to teens might not be in the library but rather in their schools and online. Develop effective outreach services from the public library to schools, particularly in the areas of booktalking, that promote reading and information literacy instruction. Outreach is an effective and efficient method to provide a high level of service in a short amount of time. It does not require increasing the library's hours; however, you will need to redistribute staff during open and closed hours.

- When building new library spaces, engage teens in all phases of the project, including planning, space development, aesthetic design, and implementation.

- Create and utilize virtual spaces for teens that support interactive services, such as instant messaging, commenting, and discussion boards.

Goal 5

Libraries develop unique collections of resources for teens and provide plentiful resources and enriching experiences to build and strengthen adolescent literacy skills. Libraries provide remote information and resources needed by teens for information, education, and recreation needs.

Tasks

- Develop or support a strong selection of adult titles of interest to teens, particularly in the genres of science fiction, fantasy, and horror. Popular bestsellers as well as classics, both established and contemporary or cult favorites, will meet the reading needs of older teens.

- Develop or support a well-rounded collection of print materials, including award winners, pop fiction, genre fiction, series books, and graphic novels in both hardback and paperback.

- Develop or support a nonfiction print collection specifically for teens that includes both popular and informational materials (in particular in the areas of pop culture, health and sexuality, and materials related to college and careers) and titles that support the formal education needs of students, including multiple copies of series books that are in high demand.

- Develop collections that are heavy in nonbook items, such as magazines, music CDs, audiobooks, comic books, DVDs, and video games.

- Develop methods to involve youth in the collection development process, such as reading-interest surveys, participation in magazine and music selection groups, or genre selection committees.

- Develop a comprehensive and cooperative plan for information literacy instruction to ensure that all secondary school students and their teachers understand how to access, use, and evaluate online resources. Educate teachers on the information resources critical to student achievement and then provide teachers with resources to educate their students.

Goal 6

Libraries utilize the experience and expertise of teens.

Tasks

- Develop a program that better uses teen volunteers, through improved training and sharing of knowledge among staff, to ensure meaningful work for young adult volunteers. Work with school counselors to make the library a preferred site for students to do community service projects for school.
- Develop methods to gather teen input, such as formal and informal focus groups, print or online surveys, exit interviews, discussions during class visits, and forming a teen advisory council.
- Invite teens to take part in planning, implementing, and evaluating library programs and services.
- Engage teens as program providers and active participants in programs that allow them to express themselves creatively.

What Are the Core Values That Drive Our Work?

In June 1994, the YALSA board adopted the following vision statement:

> In every library in the nation, quality library services to young adults are provided by a staff that understands and respects the unique informational, educational, and recreational needs of teenagers. Equal access to information, services and materials is recognized as a right not a privilege. Young adults are actively involved in the library decision-making process. The library staff collaborates and cooperates with other youth-serving agencies to provide a holistic community-wide network of activities and services that supports healthy youth development.[3]

A vision statement represents many things to an organization; it is the reservoir from which missions, goals, and objectives flow. It tells everyone what the organization, representing its members who work directly with young adults in school and public libraries across the nation, believes to be important. The vision responds to the needs of teens, not librarians. The vision provides the foundation on which service responses are built. But mostly a vision statement is a statement of values. There are many values expressed here, but perhaps the five most important are these:

- Respecting unique needs
- Equal access
- Youth participation
- Collaboration
- Healthy youth development

Consider developing your own mission statement for teen services that is in alignment with your library system's mission statement. This microvision will help you stay true to your original purpose while at the same time communicating your goals and intentions to your colleagues.

These are also the foundation on which *Connecting Young Adults and Libraries* is based. These values have not changed much over time; they are the values that have always guided librarians working with teenagers. Research, anecdotal evidence, and success stories from the field demonstrate that services planned, implemented, and evaluated based on core values achieve results. They are values that remain because they work.

What Do We Mean When We Speak of These Core Values?

- **Respecting unique needs** means recognizing that teens are not adults, and they are not children; they are their own package, but they are also library customers who deserve to be treated with the same respect as every customer. This means respecting teen reading choices rather than dismissing them with the "At least they are reading something" idiocy. This means that if a teen chooses to use an Internet computer that has no posted restrictions regarding use to chat or to play games, then that use is important to him or her. To say to a teen, "We need this computer for something important" is tantamount to telling an adult patron checking out romance novels that we won't be buying those books anymore because we only spend money on things that are important. This means we accept teen behavior, correct it when necessary, understand and explain it, but don't dismiss it. This means building an atmosphere where teens are respected by the library. Respecting means letting teen tastes and input drive collection development, programming, and space design.

- **Equal access** means being as true to the idea of equal access as allowable by law. It means advocating against censorship from outside community groups and from inside in terms of self-censorship. It also means questioning administrative decisions that will directly impact the library's services to teens. It means working with partners to share our values in order to gain access to students in their care in schools, youth organizations, or correctional institutions. It also means acknowledging that access is not the same as availability. Databases like Opposing Viewpoints might be available to teens, but a failure to promote these in a way that teens understand is denying access through neglect. This is about policies at the administrative level and procedures at the managerial level, but, most important of all, this is about practice at the frontline staff level. Equal access is as much about attitude as it is about the ALA (American Library Association) Bill of Rights.

- **Youth participation** means embracing teens as collaborative partners. This means rather than providing services *to* teens, you are working *with* teens to transform the delivery of services into a collaborative context. This is crucial to the planning process, as it requires adults to recognize that teens can make a positive contribution. It also requires adults to trust teens.

- **Collaboration** means that in addition to collaborating with teens, we join forces with all those around teens who share our values and seek the same positive outcomes for teens. We look at the lives of teens through the connections in their lives: family, school, faith-based organizations, other government entities, businesses, youth organizations, and media. The library is not the only institution in your community with a vested interest in raising healthy teens. We forge connections with others who reach teens in other parts of their lives. We learn to collaborate successfully by engaging people from all aspects of the community. We agree on outcomes, then work backward to achieve them. We take small steps, succeed, and then build on our successes. We speak the same language—that of healthy youth development—and we learn from one another. We seek to strengthen existing programs and resist the temptation to create new projects to solve problems; instead we collaborate to strengthen our own organization's ability to build assets in young people.

- **Healthy youth development** means that we are aware, in everything we do, that we are contributing to the healthy development of young people by taking into consideration the developmental needs of teens, the stages and milestones of adolescence, and the Search Institute's 40 Developmental Assets (which we'll talk about more in Chapter 2) as we plan and carry out library services for teens in our community.

Libraries don't serve young people because it is good for the library, but because it is good for young people. What is good for young people, it follows, is good for the community. The library is an asset for teens. The more assets they have, the less likely they are to engage in destructive behavior and the more likely they are to thrive, to engage in positive behavior, and to become competent, caring adults. Relationships are the key to asset building. As adults encounter kids, we need to learn their names, support them, encourage them, and empower them. We are not talking about social work; we are talking about people work; we are talking about library work. These relationships are not about the payoff for us, but for the teen. For years we have justified youth services to administrators, saying, "Be nice to them now and these kids will remember us later, when it comes time to vote or pay taxes." That is true, and let's keep this in mind, but be careful not to view youths as merely a means to an end. Teens are the end.

How Do You Know If Your Teen Program Is Successful?

If your comprehensive teen program (including your young adult collection, programming, customer service, space, and staff attitude) is successful, it will do these things:

- Provide a transition entry and a buffer into adult reading and collections

- Respond to the school-related demands of teens
- Involve cooperation between schools and libraries
- Encourage reading for personal enrichment and independent learning
- Model for other staff an example of service
- Allow for young adult participation
- Reach out to at-risk or special groups of teens
- React to social and cultural trends
- Advocate for free and equal access for teens
- Contribute to the healthy development of teens

Conclusion

Connecting Young Adults and Libraries is not about treating teens as "special," but it is about serving them uniquely, as we do other market segments of the public library, including toddlers, genealogists, seniors, college students, and small business people. Each group of users places different demands on libraries, reflecting their different needs, based on what each is trying to accomplish. Above all else, teens are trying to accomplish one thing—to form an identity. If we believe that libraries are good things for a community, then does it not follow that we want teens, as they are forming this identity, to recognize this value? If we believe libraries have value, then we will want teens to learn through our deeds and actions. If we believe that our work has value, then we need to know that it matters. If we believe that libraries should be supported by the community, then we need to show and prove this belief to the community. When LSTs work with teens, they are building community. This is not just theory—the results of case studies of successful services to teens are too clear, too obvious to miss or deny. So what is the essential argument for serving teens in libraries? Because it works.

Sources Cited in This Chapter

1. Jones, Patrick, and Linda Waddle. 2002. *New Directions for Library Service to Young Adults*. Chicago: American Library Association.
2. Jones, Patrick, and Linda Waddle. 2002. *New Directions for Library Service to Young Adults*. Chicago: American Library Association.
3. Young Adult Library Services Association. 1994. "About YALSA: YALSA Vision Statement." Available: www.ala.org/ala/yalsa/aboutyalsab/yalsavisionstatement.cfm (accessed June 13, 2008).

Recommended Sources for Further Reading

Anderson, Sheila B. 2006. *Serving Young Teens and 'Tweens*. Westport, CT: Libraries Unlimited.

"Blending Youth and Organizational Cultures." 2005. *Contemporary Youth Culture: An International Encyclopedia.* Westport, CT: Greenwood.

Brautigam, Patsy. 2008. "Developmental Assets and Libraries: Helping to Construct the Successful Teen." *Voice of Youth Advocates* 31, no. 2 (June): 124–125.

DeMarco, Pat. 2003. "Teens Are a Work in Progress: Finding Our Way in a Construction Zone." *Voice of Youth Advocates* 25, no. 6 (February): 440–442.

Halsey, Richard Sweeney. 2003. *Lobbying for Public and School Libraries: A History and Political Playbook.* Lanham, MD: Scarecrow Press.

Hilly, Nancy Milon. 2008. "Teens—Perpetual Problem or Golden Opportunity?" *Public Libraries* 47, no. 1 (January/February): 24–32.

International Federation of Library Associations and Institutions. 2009. "Guidelines for Library Services for Young Adults." Available: www.ifla.org/VII/s10/index .htm#GuidelinesYA (accessed April 3, 2009).

Jones, Patrick. 2001. "Why We Are Kids' Best Assets." *School Library Journal* 47, no. 11 (November): 44–47. Available: www.schoollibraryjournal.com/article/CA179493.html (accessed April 3, 2009).

MacRae, Cathi Dunn. 2002. "A Quarter Century of VOYA: Visible Acts of Youth Advocacy." *Voice of Youth Advocates* 25, no. 1 (April): 5.

Miller, Donna P. 2008. *Crash Course in Teen Services.* Westport, CT: Libraries Unlimited.

National Clearinghouse on Families and Youth. 2007. *Putting Positive Youth Development into Practice: A Resource Guide.* Washington, DC: U.S. Department of Health and Human Services. Available: www.ncfy.com/publications/pdf/PosYthDevel.pdf (accessed April 3, 2009).

Shek, Daniel T.L., and C.L.Y. Wai. 2008. "Training Workers Implementing Adolescent Prevention and Positive Youth Development Programs: What Have We Learned from the Literature?" *Adolescence* 43, no. 172 (Winter): 823.

Tuccillo, Diane. 2001. "Positive Youth Development: A Positive Move for Libraries." *The Unabashed Librarian* 119: 21–23.

Whelan, Debra Lau. 2007. "Adolescents Aren't That Stupid After All." *School Library Journal* 53, no. 1 (January): 17.

Understanding the Audience

It is a normal day at Normal Public Library. It is 10:30 a.m. and story time lets out. Young children run from the story room into the library, filling it with noise, no doubt stemming from the excitement of the program. The library staff smile. At 11:30 a.m., a library customer, who just happens to be on the Board of the Library Friends, comes to the desk to place a long list of books on hold. Even though you've shown her many times how to do the holds herself, she insists you do them for her, and all the while her booming voice supplies commentary on each book. You place the reserves and you smile. At 12:30 p.m. the noise level increases dramatically as the staff talk about where they are going to lunch. Everybody smiles. At 1:30 p.m. an adult walks into the library, sits down at a computer, and then begins loudly talking into a cell phone. The library staff sigh, thinking that coming up with a policy on cell phones would solve the problem. At 2:30 p.m., two seniors are leaving a program on living wills you've just held. They are standing by the front door when one turns to the other and says very loudly, "How did you like that, Chester?" to which Chester replies, "Huh?" and the library staff smile, knowing we've met the information needs of our seniors. At 3:30 p.m., two teenagers walk in, one giggles and the entire staff starts frowning, shushing, and wondering why teens can't behave in libraries.

Let's examine the unusual treatment given to the teenagers in this story. Why did the librarians feel it was fine to tell the teens how to behave and not the others? As adults we are often uncomfortable and find it embarrassing to approach other adults and tell them how to behave. Perhaps there's a bit of power politics thrown into the equation. We go out of our way not to offend certain groups of people: story time moms, the Friends members, the always supportive senior population, or our colleagues. Any action with these special groups might risk negative consequences. Why is telling a teen an easier power trip to take? Are we confident that we can tell them what to do because there are no adults to defend them? Is it easy to shrug and think, *Oh well, even if I reprimand them, what are they going to do about it?*

Are there unspoken assumptions underpinning this behavior? One implicit idea revolves around the notion that many teens don't choose to be in libraries in the first place. They are there because they have to be. They have to come to the library to find information they aren't interested in, to write a paper they don't want to write, for a teacher they don't even like, to get a grade in a class they can't stand, so they can graduate from the school that they loathe, so they can get away from their parents whom they also might just detest. On top of that, they come unprepared, bringing only a notebook or a pen and even sometimes forgetting those basic tools. By far the worst crime committed is that teens come to the library with an attitude. It's the surly attitude of someone being someplace she doesn't want to be. Perhaps it's the bored attitude of someone who doesn't have any other place to go.

Many teens come to us after school out of burden and boredom, not exactly the best motivations for a successful relationship. When they get there, what do they find? Normally, they find an overworked staff without enough resources to do their jobs well. They find staff members who are feeling underappreciated and underpaid, feeling overwhelmed in an environment of rapid technological improvement and budget cutting. They don't find people working in libraries who look like them, act like them, or even seem to care about them. And in walks the 14-year-old who would rather be anywhere in the world. Unfortunately, he needs to finish a paper by tomorrow on symbolism in the plays of Arthur Miller and the library is his only hope for finding the "reputable" resources required by his teacher. But he can't figure out how the online catalog works, he has no idea how to access any of the library's databases, and the only thing he can find online is in Wikipedia—which his teacher specifically said he couldn't use as a resource. Fifteen minutes before closing, he comes up to the desk and mumbles something that resembles a reference question. This doesn't sound like a success story in the making.

The uniqueness of serving young adults, of course, stems directly from the uniqueness of teenagers as people. Understanding how this uniqueness impacts teens as library patrons/customers is crucial because the problems libraries have in serving—and reasons for not serving—teens often stem from misunderstandings and misinformation. Too often libraries allow the few "problem patron" teens to become the image of how all teens use or misuse libraries. Many of the behaviors that librarians have always found annoying among teens—mainly loudness and rudeness—are directly related to the physical and psychological changes taking place in a teen's life. Most things a teen does or doesn't do in a library can be explained, understood, and then responded to by first understanding the various developmental stages that make up adolescence.

What Are the Stages of Adolescence?

Teens develop at different paces, so not every behavior can be plugged into one slot. Physical development is not always in synch with emotional or psychological development. Teens also differ on when they hit these

> "Adolescence is the time when young childhood is left behind and your young teen begins to cross the long bridge that separates childhood and the adult world."
>
> — David B. Pruitt, MD, *Your Adolescent: Emotional, Behavioral, and Cognitive Development from Early Adolescence through the Teen Years*

stages for a variety of factors, including, but not limited to, environment, demographics, family history, and national origin. All of those disclaimers aside, some universals do exist. There are three primary stages of adolescent development, each one characterized by different tasks or "milestones": early adolescence (generally ages 11–13), middle adolescence (generally ages 14–16), and late adolescence (generally ages 17–18). Most of the behaviors that drive us crazy about teens stem from these developmental tasks/milestones. Developmental tasks are those emotional, social, sexual, intellectual, and psychological changes that make up a young person's normal developmental cycle. While certainly one size doesn't fit all, and it is important to respond to teens as individuals and not representations of a type, these tasks should guide our work. Older teens might be attracted to youth involvement where they are given adult roles, while younger teens often just want to have fun. Middle teens are curious about the world around them and are gaining interest in ideas, forming skills, asking questions, and setting their values. What all teens have in common is that they are in a process of growth and change.

If you commute to work in a city of any size, then you know all about sitting in traffic on roads under construction. It is one of the most stressful of all activities. The area is messy and disorganized, and it makes everyone short tempered because there is only so much patience a person can have. You want to get going, but you are surrounded by the symbol of commuter frustration: the orange cone. You somehow just have to remember that this road construction is a work in progress; when completed, things will look and work much better. That is also what a teen is: a work in progress. A teen is an orange cone.

Is the Teen Brain a Work in Progress?

Neuroscientists conducting research on the adolescent brain during the past 25 years have discovered that teens' developing brains are as much a part of their erratic behavior as the newly present hormones coursing through their bodies. Surprisingly, this process of growth and change in the brain will continue throughout adolescence and into a young person's early twenties. In contrast to the idea that a person's brain is fully formed in the first three years of life, ongoing research proves that critical brain development goes through several phases, the first in the womb, the second during early childhood, and the third in adolescence. According to Dr. Jay Giedd from the National Institute of Mental Health, what is happening in this period of proliferation during adolescence is that the brain is not developing new brain cells but "pruning" those already in existence. This is where Dr. Giedd's "use it or lose it principle" comes into play; brain cells and neuron connections that are used will "survive and flourish. Those cells and connections that are not used will wither and die."[2]

The adolescent brain is also going through structural changes during this time. The frontal lobe/prefrontal cortex, which is the part of the brain that allows a teen to process information and make decisions, continues changing and growing throughout adolescence. This is one of the main

---

THE THREE STAGES OF ADOLESCENT DEVELOPMENT

Tasks/milestones of early adolescence:
- Feels increased concern about appearance
- Seeks independence from family
- Displays rebellious/defiant behaviors
- Importance of friends increases
- Peer group dominates
- Ego dominates viewing of all issues

Tasks/milestones of middle adolescence:
- Becomes less self-absorbed
- Makes decisions on own
- Experiments with self-image
- Takes risks/seeks new experiences
- Develops sense of values/morality
- Begins to make lasting relationships
- Becomes sexually aware
- Intellectual awareness increases
- Interests/skills mature
- Seeks out "adventures"

Tasks/milestones of late adolescence:
- Views world idealistically
- Becomes involved with world outside of home/school
- Sets goals
- Relationships stabilize
- Sees adults as "equals"
- Seeks to firmly establish independence[1]

You may think the phrase "teen brain" is an oxymoron, but we promise it's not. We recommend Barbara Strauch's *The Primal Teen: What New Discoveries About the Teenage Brain Tell Us About Our Kids* for an easy-to-digest guide to what's going on inside the teen brain.

reasons teens are notorious for problems with planning, organization, complex thinking, and impulse control. While the prefrontal cortex is developing, teens often use their temporal lobe/amygdala to process information and make decisions. The amygdala is the home of emotional, impulsive, and instinctual behavior. To give you a better idea of how this impacts a teen's behavior, here's a breakdown of how these areas of the brain work and how the growth/maturation of these areas of the brain directly impact how a teen responds to any given situation:

Frontal Lobe/Prefrontal Cortex

- Responsible for reasoning, motivation, judgment, problem solving, and rational decision making
- Governs impulsivity, aggression, ability to organize thoughts, and plan for the future
- Controls ability to think abstractly, perform higher-level thinking, see consequences of actions
- Undergoes significant changes during adolescence
- Is one of the last areas of the brain to fully develop; not fully developed until a person reaches his or her early to mid-twenties

As this area of the frontal lobe matures through experience and practice, teens can reason better, develop more impulse control, and make better judgment. Sometimes an adult must function like a "surrogate" set of frontal lobes (auxiliary problem solver) for a teen; we can't just tell a teen what to do, but we can set boundaries and help them figure things out for themselves.

Temporal Lobe/Amygdala

- Responsible for instinctual reaction; used by teens to process situations, often causing them to overreact, get emotional, and erupt for no reason
- Regulates emotions and motivation, particularly those related to survival, such as fear, anger, and pleasure
- Matures around ages 18–19

Simply put, the frontal lobe can be categorized as reason and the temporal lobe as emotion. Due to the later maturation of the frontal lobe, the temporal lobe tends to dominate in teens, which often results in a decrease in reasoned thinking and an increase in impulsivity.[3]

How Does Adolescent Brain Development Impact Your Job as an LST?

Knowledge is power, and nowhere is this more applicable than when it comes to reacting appropriately to typical teenage behavior. Understanding adolescent brain development is the first step in acknowledging that while teenagers are no longer children, they are also not quite adults. A major part of adolescence is learning how to assess risks and consequences because adolescents are not yet skilled at these tasks. As teens begin to look like us, we often expect them to act like us, but it doesn't work that way. We need to use this information to build on our professional awareness so that we are more thoughtful in how we act and react when dealing with teens.

Adolescence is a time when physical and mental growth collide, wreaking havoc on a young person's psyche. Keeping the following things in mind will help you remember that, as frustrating as teens can be, there is a very real reason, backed up by the research discussed here, for teens' emotional responses, unreasonable behavior, and general "flakiness" when it comes to doing things like checking out a book for a report due tomorrow or missing a program they helped plan.

- Normal adolescent development includes conflict, facing insecurities, testing out different identities, mood swings, self-absorption, etc.
- Because of immature brains, adolescents do not handle social pressure, instinctual urges, and other stresses the way adults do.
- As a teen gets older, his or her ability to reason gets better. This is why trying to have a rational conversation with a 12-year-old about choices and consequences can be frustrating, but having the same conversation with a 16-year-old can be productive.
- You cannot change what is physically happening within a teen's brain. You can change how you work with teens by trying to accommodate them when they exhibit some of the characteristics adults find so annoying, like requiring instant gratification, making terrible judgment calls, or reacting immediately and irrationally to an external stimulus.

How Do the Developmental Needs of Teens Relate to Libraries?

While each stage of adolescence is unique, some overlap and we would argue that four common themes exist in the lives of all teenagers, regardless of race, religion, age, sexuality, or other factors. The core needs of all teens relate to issues of independence, excitement, identity, and acceptance. For each of these core needs, let's look at how libraries can or have responded.

Independence

From birth, children learn to depend on their parents or other adults. During the teen years, this basic child/adult relationship morphs into a more equal relationship in which teens begin making decisions for

You don't always need to understand why a teen acts the way he or she does; you just have to accept it as a natural part of life and attempt to find a way to work together for the good of a common goal.

themselves and learning to do things on their own. As teens become more independent, they also begin to learn to accept responsibility and participate in the decision-making process.

How can your library promote teen independence?

Library Cards

All teens should have their own library cards, not only to check out materials independent of their parents, but also to help them learn responsibility. Schools and libraries together should wage campaigns to get every teen registered for a card at the beginning of each school year. There are caveats to consider here. Many libraries are struggling with library card issues, such as minors' access to DVDs, and debating confidentiality of records balanced against a parent's "right to know." An increase in teen library cards will create more lost cards, more problems at the circulation desk, and more headaches. But the gain is great. If libraries want teens to feel welcome, they cannot deny teens the ability to access materials. With more noncirculation functions in libraries requiring a card, like access to a computer with Internet or checking out a laptop for in-library use, it is vital that teens have access. Also, if a teen does not have his own card and wants a book that he is not comfortable asking his mom or dad to check out for him, he is going to either steal it (we lose) or not borrow it (we both lose).

Information Literacy Instruction

By teaching teens how to effectively use our resources, we allow them to work independently. Instruction can help teens learn about the information gathering and evaluating process, develop critical-thinking and decision-making skills, and teach them time management. For libraries, instruction is time management because it is certainly more efficient to provide teens with instruction in a controlled setting than to give the same instruction in the more frantic over-the-desk routine. In school libraries this is one of the most important, if not the most important, roles. Similarly, part of the message to teens is that information literacy is time saving for them as well. It's a win-win. For more information about information literacy instruction, see Chapter 5.

Volunteer Programs

A teen volunteer program gives a young person a chance to experience independence and responsibility and be a meaningful part of the library community. Training, supervising, and encouraging teen volunteers will take time and effort up front, but in the end there will be a huge payoff for both the library and the teen engaged, either in burning off community service hours or in learning, growing, and changing into a healthier person because of the experience.

Teen Advisory Councils (TACs)

Teen advisory councils or groups provide teens with a forum to learn decision-making skills, to take on new responsibilities, and to participate in different programs and projects. One important caveat about TACs:

If you form a group of teens and call it an advisory council, this group needs to play an advisory role. If you form a group and the teens have no responsibility, opportunities for meaningful involvement, or oversight, then you do not have an advisory council—you have a club. This is fine, but you need to be upfront about the responsibilities of the group, and this begins with the name and description. If you form an advisory council and then do not allow teens to make decisions or contribute in a meaningful way, then the message you are sending to council members is that they are not worthy of actual advisory responsibilities. Also, if you ask your advisory council for help or feedback, be sure to carry out the group's suggestions and recommendations. If this is not possible, provide them with an explanation about why something isn't possible or didn't happen. For example, if your TAC is charged with helping you order new manga, and then you do not order the manga they requested, let them know why this didn't happen. Teens may not mention that the books never showed up on the shelf, but we guarantee they'll notice. It's also important to allow your TAC members to provide feedback about their participation as active members of the council. This opportunity to provide feedback will let them know their opinions matter and it will help you plan and carry out future tasks for your council.

(CD) Tool 31. TAC (Teen Advisory Council) Participation Survey

Excitement

Because everything changes, everything is possible. Teens experience physical changes wrought with emotional changes. The world becomes a more exciting and scary place with more possibilities, opportunities, and dangers. Excitement manifests itself in the abundance of energy, wild enthusiasm, good humor, bad pranks, vandalism, and the lack of desire to slow the body or quiet the mind.

How can your library capitalize on this excitement?

Programming

When done right, programs offer teens the chance to actively participate rather than passively react. They can generate enthusiasm and channel energy into productive pursuits. Programming may be educational or informational in nature, but it almost always needs to be interactive and entertaining. Teens want to act, not just be told. The model for teen programming isn't that which always creates the best statistics, but rather that which provides the teen participating with the best experience. For more information about programming, see Chapter 9.

Teen Space

A separate teen space in the library both answers teens' need for independence and provides the possibility of a place where exciting things can happen. Secondarily, a separate teen space will provide staff with a set destination to send teens who are looking for a place to hang out in the evening or after school. This teen area needs a collection of young adult materials, comfortable furniture, spaces for teens to hang out and congregate, spaces for teens to spend time alone reading or listening to music, computers with Internet access, wireless access, and a comfortable atmosphere where teens feel like they are welcome. For more about teen spaces, see Chapter 10.

Magazines

Because the teen attention span can be short, magazines are often desired reading materials. In addition, magazines are current, so they talk about what is "hot," and they are full of photos. Magazines present libraries with a simple, low-cost, bang-for-the-buck opportunity to do something that teens will view favorably, given the interest in periodicals and the importance many teens place in them. Serialized comic books also help meet this same need.

Games

Teen areas should have board games, access to popular computer games (like Runescape), and a video game console like a Nintendo Wii, Sony PlayStation or Microsoft Xbox 360. The library should also sponsor gaming tournaments and host groups for tabletop role-playing games (RPGs) like Dungeons & Dragons. Games are social in nature, require mind energy, and are a medium for laughs. The drawback, however, is noise. Be proactive: offer headphones for computer games; buy board games that don't require beepers, buzzers, and shouting out answers; and limit the availability of the gaming console to Friday afternoons, weekends, and some evenings. It is possible to find a happy medium between meeting the needs of teens and keeping the library a safe and sane place where everyone in the community will want to spend time.

Reasonable Expectations

You cannot expect a group of teens full of stored-up energy from a day of school to walk into the library and be perfectly still and quiet. Expectations have limits and must be based on circumstances. If these expectations resist flexibility, then an impossible situation is created for both you and the teens.

Identity

"Who am I?" is the basic teen question. Teens define themselves in many ways, and it is a constant balancing act of trying to be similar to their peers so they fit in while also trying to be as unique as possible so they stand apart. It is a full-time job, and teens may be seeking a mixture of the two at any point during the day. The search for identity produces even more changes as teens attempt to say, scream, or whisper, "Who am I?" in what they wear, do, watch, listen to, and read.

So how does the library assist a teen in his or her quest for identity?

Readers' Advisory

Reading choice is personal, and it varies greatly from teen to teen. Helping teens select materials they want to read is one of the best ways for an LST to contribute to a teen's development of identity. Promote popular materials, but remember that not every teen is a fan of the *Naruto* manga series, *J-14* pop magazine, the *Gossip Girls* series, or the latest Stephenie Meyer vampire novel. The teens who are not into "what's hot" need and want materials that reflect their wide variety of interests, from Kerouac to *Thrasher* magazine. Teens' wide diversity of interests can be a training challenge; LSTs might field one request from a 12-year-old for a copy of the next title in the *Cirque de Freak* series followed by a request from a 17-year-old for Vonnegut's *Cat's Cradle*. This same LST might spend an hour later in the day helping a teen find books and Web sites about the Wiccan religion. It's important for all staff who work with young people to understand that teens often explore alternative lifestyles and personas through their reading materials. Therefore, as difficult as it might be for some staff members to mind their own business, it's important to recognize that young people have the right to read whatever they want, no matter if staff find the topic personally offensive or question the age appropriateness of the material.

Shared Interest

Despite what mainstream movies and television tell us, all teens are not the same. Although this may come as a surprise to some of you, teens often share interests with library staff members, from a passion for classical music to an obsession with zombie movies. You'll never know unless you ask. Engaging a teen in a conversation about his or her passions and pleasures is not only a great way to provide personalized customer service but also an excellent jumping-off point for developing a meaningful relationship. While you will not have something in common with every teen who enters your library, chances are good that you will find you have more in common with more teens than you think. So how does this correlate to the development of a teen's identity? Sometimes you will find that the teens who are library regulars are having trouble forming an identity; they do not fit in with the other kids and seek refuge at the library. When you have something in common with these teens, the chances of them opening up to you are greater. The more they open up, the more opportunities they have for self-definition.

Writers' Programs

By definition, writing is an exercise in self-exploration. When we offer teens the opportunity to express themselves through writing, we help meet the core need of developing identity. You will be amazed, even shocked, at the things teens produce when you ask them to share their thoughts and stories. Do keep in mind that adolescence is a time of extremes, so chances are very good that some of the writing will be painfully real and often times edgy, moody, and dark in tone. To take a library writing program a step further, consider producing a literary magazine or zine in print or online.

Artists' Programs

Like a writers' program, a library-sponsored program for teen artists is about providing young people with a platform for self-expression. From one-shot art shows to ongoing displays and exhibits, library programs for teen artists should provide teens with opportunities to showcase their work in whatever form they find most appealing, including fashion, graffiti, painting, video production, photography, collage, computer-generated art, Web page design, comic-style art, and even skateboard decoration. Consider expanding the aforementioned literary magazine to one that includes teen art in addition to writing.

Individual Relationships

Because teens often travel in packs, it can be hard to get to know teens as individuals. Some teens will respond to you immediately, while others might be harder to reach. The key to helping any teen develop identity is to begin treating him or her as an individual.

Diversity

Libraries are great melting pots, or microcosms, of their communities, where people from different backgrounds, creeds, and colors (race, gender, socioeconomic status, sexual orientation, and religious affiliation) come together for a shared purpose. Over the years we have seen teens from a local, private school (in uniform) playing cards with teens from the housing shelter next door and Goth/emo drama teens sharing space (and MySpace layout tips) with the loud hip-hop crowd who congregate in the teen area after school. We've seen gay teens talking with bangers and nerdy gamers engaged in conversations with cheerleaders. By sheer necessity (someone needs information or a place to go), libraries bring people together who might not otherwise spend time together. Your goal as an LST should always be to create a welcoming space for all members of the community, not just a place that mirrors your community's dominant culture. The simple truth is that LSTs are often not reflective of the race/gender makeup of the teens they serve. Keep this in mind as you plan and implement services because awareness goes a long way in bridging divides.

So how else can the library honor diversity and model genuine acceptance of all people?

Modeling Behavior

We are all responsible for modeling behavior. How we treat those who are different from us will directly impact how teens in our libraries treat one another. This is basically the golden rule in action. It also means walking the walk: using multicultural photos in marketing teen programs, seeking diverse teen representation for your library's teen advisory council, selecting books and other materials that feature a diverse cast of characters, making sure your library is compliant with the Americans with Disabilities Act and inviting to physically disabled teens, and helping your staff or colleagues understand the importance of creating a safe space for all in the library. This is certainly not an exhaustive list, but it's a beginning.

Communication

That old adage about "sticks and stones" isn't true—words can hurt and they can also divide. Slurs like "fag," "retard," or "white trash" are often thrown around casually, but the truth is that this is hate speech and it should not be tolerated (much less accepted) in any library. The same holds true for allowing a teen to repurpose a word into a slur—for example, the word "gay" to mean stupid or "ghetto" to mean poor or low class. Although the allowance of some words over others will be local or regional (what's offensive in your community might not be offensive in ours), the ultimate decision about what is and what is not appropriate should hinge on this simple premise: If it has the potential to hurt someone's feelings, then it's not appropriate for the library. Finally, we hope it goes without saying that we should never allow one teen to make fun of another for his or her physical appearance, IQ, age, clothing, haircut, or physical disability.

Youth Involvement

Diversity is everyone's responsibility, and this means getting teens involved in how we develop and implement library services for all teens. See Chapter 12 for more ideas about getting teens involved in a meaningful way.

Programming

Another responsibility we have is to plan and carry out programs and special events that are as diverse as the teens we serve. Examples include, but are certainly not limited to, hosting book discussions about books that address nondominant cultures, showing movies that espouse beliefs that are different from our own, planning programs about topics that might be seen by some as outside the mainstream (e.g., world religions, GLBTQ teen health and safety, Mehndi tattoos and tribal art, etc.), and celebrating various cultures and segments of the population with special events (e.g., Dia de los Niños, Dia de los Libros, National Coming Out Day, Women's History Month, etc.).

Acceptance

Because teens seek independence from everything they know and hold dear, because they look for risk and excitement but often find trouble, and because they are developing an identity, the last core need is, not surprisingly, acceptance. As they are doing all of these things, and at the same time redefining themselves and their relationships, they are going to make mistakes. They will need reassurance on various levels that they are on the right track, and this acceptance is what will give them the courage to go out and try again, confident that they can return and be welcomed.

So how does the library model acceptance for teens?

Youth Involvement

When we actively invite teens to participate in volunteer programs, community service activities, and youth councils, we are showing them that we accept them. When we focus on their works and their words and not on their hair color or clothing choice, we are showing them that it is their actions that matter, not their appearance. When we create opportunities for teens to be meaningfully involved, we are not just talking about being accepting but are actually accepting them as meaningful contributors to our world. Additionally, since many of the teens drawn to these activities are often those shunned by their peers, these programs provide a vehicle for acceptance from another set of peers. This acceptance from outside of their "regular" world can give them the perspective to weather the tough encounters.

Positive Experiences

A teen who comes to the library and finds unfriendly service, no information for schoolwork, and frustrating technology will have a negative library experience. We need to set a tone for all patrons, especially teens, that the library is a place where they can "win." It is an inviting place, and teens will find people there who are both helpful and patient. Teens remember those who are rude and take such offenses personally because they are very self-conscious. A teen's ego is fragile and ranges from bravado to shyness, and these extremes make a reference interview by a "kid hater" tricky to endure.

Discipline with Dignity

The most well-behaved teens in the world have been known to tear pictures out of magazines or search for porn on library computers. Teens make bad choices, and for those who break the rules there must be consequences. Our job is to make sure we are fair, firm, and consistent in how we dole out those consequences. The message to teens who break the library's rules needs to be that some *behaviors* are unacceptable, not that the teens themselves are unacceptable. We should all strive to correct the behavior and not the person. Anything less will set up the teen and the library for future problems. Also remember that disciplining teens with dignity is everyone's responsibility, not just the LST's. This means that everyone who works in your library, from the circulation clerk to the security guard, needs to be on the same page when it comes to addressing inappropriate behavior, doling out punishment, and beginning every day as a new day for any teen who finds himself or herself on the wrong side of library law.

Outreach

Many teens may never come into the library. Other teens will come into the library, find (or not find) what they need, and head back out the door, never coming into contact with a library staff person or finding out what the library offers outside of what is immediately available on the shelves. The only way to meet the needs of these teens is to go out into the community. One way to do this is to conduct outreach at schools. Another way is to set up a booth at community festivals where teens will be present. We need to tell these teens about what we do, what we offer, and how we can help. We also need to let them know that they are welcome in our space and we are interested in both their thoughts and their contributions. We need to demonstrate to them that their interests are important, their opinions valid, and their requests and

CD **For more information about developing a youth-friendly discipline plan, see Tool 26. Progressive Discipline Policy.**

needs worth our time and support. See Chapter 8 for more information about outreach to teens.

Meeting Special Needs

We need to be conscious of the fact that there is no "average" teen; there are teens who score off the IQ charts but have no social skills, teens who cannot read, teens who do not speak English, teens who work two jobs to support their families, teens who drop out of high school to raise babies, teens who are blind, deaf, or both. Our job is to ensure that all teens are not only accepted but welcomed into the library. If the library cannot cater to everyone, then it needs to be aware of the resources in the community that can assist these teens.

What Is Wrong with These Damn Kids?

Teens congregate in the library for a variety of reasons: because they have an information need that the library can meet, they need Internet access, they have nothing else to do, or their friends are there. Some teens use the library for homework. Some teens use the library as a social center after school, in the evenings, or on the weekends. In many communities, the only place for teens to gather is their local public library. The library is free, easily accessible, and known. It is also an acceptable place for parents to send their teen, as libraries are often considered "safe" spaces. Libraries are, normally, easy to get to, close to schools or other institutions, and have comfortable furniture and air-conditioning. Although many teens do have computers at home, some don't have Internet access and some need to share the computer with many family members. All of these reasons can create havoc when it comes to limited library space and overworked and often impatient staff members.

One of the first steps in minimizing this craziness is to develop realistic expectations of behavior. Three of the most common challenges for LSTs include overcoming stereotypes, managing large crowds, and enforcing boundaries.

Overcoming Stereotypes

Most of the time the conflict in libraries with teens isn't their actions, but our reactions. If we had a better understanding of teens as a whole, we would be more respectful of them. If we were more respectful, we would get that respect returned to us. The environment would be less stressful for staff, more conducive to building assets, and geared toward ensuring that teens have a positive library experience. When teens find what they need, do not feel frustrated, and feel that they have been helped and not hindered, they have had a successful library experience. When a teen returns again and again, each successful library experience contributes to his or her development as a lifelong library user.

Achieving a positive experience is not always easy. When teens need to use the library, they cannot find the materials they need or the services they deserve. Often, one negative interaction between a teen and a library staff person becomes the model, causing teens to view library staff members as uninviting or unfriendly and library staff members to view teens as disrespectful troublemakers. No one is without blame here. At the heart of these negative interactions are stereotypes.

What stereotypes of teens do library staff members hold? What stereotypes of library staff members do teens hold? Are these stereotypes accurate? Yes and no. They are based on some knowledge, often limited and often a result of a negative incident. Many of the stereotypes of teens match up perfectly with the stages and milestones of adolescence; many of the librarian's stereotypes match up just as well with the personality indicators of the Myers-Briggs in which most librarians fall (INTJ). Let's face it: we are a profession of people who don't like other people, but we do know what is wrong with them. This is a joke and an exaggeration, but it also works because it is based on some truth; often we do act out these stereotypes and become our worst enemies in interacting with teens. Stereotypes are warped perceptions, based on selected truth, that need to be replaced by facts derived not from anecdotal evidence but from actual experiences. In other words, building relationships that build assets probably does more to knock down stereotypes than any other function. Like all relationships, it takes time, involves effort, and requires patience. Knowing the stages of adolescent development and moving behind stereotypes doesn't mean excusing or allowing obviously inappropriate behavior; it means instead understanding it and redirecting it in a way that is not disrespectful.

Figure 2.1. Librarian and Teen Stereotypes

Librarians	Teens	Librarians	Teens
Boring	Not interested in libraries	Not interested in teenagers	Appearance conscious
Stuffy	Loud	Out of touch with the times	Travel in packs
Mean	Destructive	Rigid	Physical/sexual
Read all day	Uncaring	Serious	Smart alecks
Old-fashioned	Wild	Suspicious	Unpredictable
Cold and uncaring	Obsessed with being online	Solemn	Techno-savvy
Overprotective	Flippant and disrespectful	Technophobes	Obnoxious
Judgmental	Full of energy	Anal retentive	Energetic
Only care about books	Disorganized and chaotic	Female	Pressured
Asexual	Drug-dealing gangsters	Detail freaks	Unpredictable
Bad hair, ugly shoes	Dangerous	Out of touch with the times	Obsessed with the latest and greatest
Obsessed with quiet	Driven by their hormones		

Managing Large Crowds

For those libraries located near schools, the crowd that gathers after school can be intimidating for no other reason than sheer numbers. When this happens, as it does in libraries around the country every day, a single LST cannot be the answer to serving or policing 75 teens at once. The person in charge of the library must set the tone and, with the LST, develop the strategy for all staff. If library staff are acting as security guards, we recommend assessing the situation to determine what's really happening to cause staff to need to police the crowd. If the library is physically too small to accommodate the after-school crowd and library staff or other patrons are at risk, we recommend discussing this situation with your administration to secure funding for an actual security guard whose job will be to manage the masses during your library's busiest hours. If this is a situation where staff are not comfortable dealing with the after-school crowd, we recommend training for the entire staff so that everyone feels better equipped to meet the needs of the teens. As a whole the staff need to plan and agree on appropriate behavior for the library as well as programs and events to keep the after-school crowd engaged. This is not going to happen overnight, and often it will be a lengthy process to get consensus and policies and procedures in place to handle the after-school crowd. The good news is that once the problem is being addressed, staff will feel more confident that they have support and a plan for consistently meeting the needs of the teens. We also recommend working with schools to develop after-school programs, working within the community to find recreational alternatives, and working with other youth-serving organizations to share solutions about working with large groups of teens.

Enforcing Boundaries

Every day, teens are learning about accepting responsibility. They are told what to do as children, and as they grow older they face choices despite not having clear ideas about personal limits. Thus, they test the limits. Confrontations between library staff members and teens often revolve around this very issue—how much is allowed and who decides. This task is tedious for everyone involved, as adults in positions of authority are rarely consistent, and teens are unable to predict the unwritten limits imposed against them. This helps explain why some teens are constantly challenging authority in an ongoing dialogue about the library's rules and expectations. Although this can be annoying, it is developmentally appropriate for teens to test limits and boundaries. This is even more reason for staff to be fair but consistent in their enforcement of the rules and handling of inappropriate behaviors. This is where the old adage of "correct the behavior and not the person" comes into play. We know this is easier said than done. When you are confronted with a group of boys cursing loudly or a group of girls shouting in front of the library's front door, it is easier to kick the teens out than it is to have a conversation about why their behavior is inappropriate in the library.

So What Are Some Strategies for Dealing with Disruptive Behavior?

Our strategies for dealing with teens' disruptive behavior revolve around the four Rs: relationships, rules, reactions, and respect. Of these four, we believe the most important when it comes to managing teens is respect. Some library staff members don't like teens. It is likely this is never going to change. Some staff don't like crying children, some don't like soccer moms, and some don't like the elderly. Thankfully this job is not about liking people but serving them. With each of these groups, teens included, the key is respecting everyone as a library patron. It is the responsibility of all staff to treat all patrons with respect, no matter their personal feelings. Characterizing teens as "those loud kids" or the LST's problem is not the solution. We need to treat teens as patrons who demand, require, and deserve our respect. If we don't see them that way, then library staff are the real disruptive element, not the teens.

Relationships

With Teens

Once you actually get to know teens as people, it is harder to stereotype them or judge them. The first step in redirecting inappropriate behavior is to develop a relationship with the disruptive teen. As you nurture the relationship, put the onus on the teen who is behaving inappropriately. Make it his or her choice and say, "Look, your behavior is inappropriate because it is disrupting others. If you choose to behave this way, then you are choosing to leave. If you wish to stay, then you must be less disruptive; you decide." As you begin developing relationships with the teens who hang out in your library, it will be easier for teens to see you as the person who helps them with research for school, who recommends great new books, and who carries out cool programming instead of the quiet cop who spends all day "shushing" them.

With Staff

It is also important that your colleagues make it a priority to build relationships with the teens who frequent your library. Since dealing with disruptive teens needs to be everyone's responsibility, all staff (not just whoever bears the brunt of serving teens) need information and education about redirecting behavior. It serves no one to have an LST working hard to improve relationships if the circulation clerk at the checkout desk is being rude and insulting. Not everyone on staff can or will be a teen advocate, but, then again, everyone must understand that teens are patrons just like anyone else who walks through the door.

With the Community

Network with schools, youth groups, churches, and other youth-serving agencies. What about working with businesses that also cater to teens and maybe face some of the same problems? Also, a relationship with the police department is essential. Sometimes teens, like other patrons, do get out of hand and you might need some help. But, what are your expectations? Do you want the police just to show the badge, or is the library willing to follow through on prosecuting patrons who engage in criminal behavior? If disruptive patrons refuse to correct their behavior after reasonable attempts on the part of staff, then it is no longer a library problem, but a criminal one.

With Yourself

It is important to be confident within yourself when dealing with teens. It takes toughness to deal with teens, even if you understand their actions. If they belittle you, it is just to make them feel bigger because feeling bigger or better is what they are trying to do all the time; self-esteem is a teen's daily concern. Sometimes it seems that many of us working in libraries have the most trouble dealing with teens who remind us of teens we didn't like when we were growing up. Let's accept this and then move beyond it. Remember, we're the adults.

Rules

Written rules, especially to teens, are often interpreted as a series of challenges. A simple posted rule like "No gum allowed" seems clear, but teens could argue for heated minutes with retorts of, "It says no gum, not no chewing gum." Although we might feel safer with written rules of conduct, unless you allow the teens to develop the rules, this is just trouble waiting to happen. There are, admittedly, many valid reasons, some of them legal, for having such rules, so this may not be negotiable. Any written rules of conduct should not, however, be directed only toward teens. There is much literature regarding problem patrons/ situations in libraries; in order to be fair, teens deserve the same treatment as adults.

Noise versus Disruptive Behavior

Even without posted rules for using the library, there is one overriding rule and it applies to everyone—if your behavior disrupts others, then that behavior is inappropriate and you must stop it or leave the building. This is a fine line, especially with teens who tend to become carried away. Sometimes the best way to deal with noisy teens is simply to remind them that they are in a library. If teens are consistently disruptive with their noise, then it's probably a good idea to ask them to go outside. If possible, find other options for teens, like a study room for after school or specific hours of the day being designated as "for youth," when visitors can expect a certain amount of noise throughout the building.

Fair, Firm, and Consistent

You cannot treat the honors students differently from the ones who take shop—there is no playing favorites in the teen world. You must also be firm when you redirect a group of teens for inappropriate behavior. Meek or mild will not work, and quietly suggesting, "Gee whiz, can you please not be so loud" will get you nowhere. Your best bet is to be polite, but direct, with a firm statement about how inappropriate behavior cannot continue, followed by a choice for the offending teens to modify their behavior or leave. This must be as consistent as possible among all staff members. The rules cannot change from day to day; it confuses the teens and creates problems for everyone. Furthermore, teens have a sharp sense of injustice. If reprimanded for being loud only to witness a group of the staff talking at a high volume, they will react. Rightly so, as we are not practicing what we preach.

Hidden Agendas

Librarianship is a female-dominated profession, and the role of teen hell-raiser is usually a male-dominated one. This, too, presents itself as a contradiction. In many libraries it is also a race issue as well; in many public libraries the staff is certainly not a "mirror" of the community it serves. Some additional training from outside your library might help staff handle situations in which the problem for staff isn't so much teen issues but issues related to race. Sometimes the real issue is not teens, but dealing with the diversity of our users.

Enforcing the Rules

You cannot threaten to throw teens out eight or nine times, or just ignore them and hope they go away. If you are going to intervene, then you need to be prepared to follow through with that action. If you follow through and the behavior continues, then seek assistance in enforcing your decision. If they realize you are all bark and no bite, then teens might just sit around the table figuring out what to try next.

Crossing the Line

CD See Tool 26. Progressive Discipline Policy and Tool 2. Banned Patron Appeal Form

Unfortunately, in spite of good intentions, thoughtful planning, and the creation and implementation of developmentally appropriate programs and services, there will be times when you do have to involve security or ban a teen from the library. When this happens, deal with the situation and the teen with patience, respect (even if it is not given in return), and understanding. That same teen who broke a major rule today will be back in a year, more grown up, more prepared to deal with the library's rules and regulations, and hopefully more aware of what he or she missed out on in the year away from the library. This is the time to offer up the proverbial "olive branch" and start anew; this is the time to forgive and, more important, forget past transgressions in order to move forward with developing a new relationship with the teen.

Don't Escalate

When you are enforcing the library's rules, teens will often challenge them. They will want to ask you questions or say things like, "It is a public library, so I'm allowed here." Without being obnoxious, you merely need to restate your position—correct the behavior or leave. While it is impossible to avoid all confrontations, it is possible to derail heated conflict. This is not a time for discussion, as discussion often leads to debate, and debate often leads to an angry argument with you flustered and the teen defiant. If a teen knows he or she can fluster you, the teen will likely try harder to do it again. This cyclical behavior should be avoided at all cost, as it will only lead to a no-win situation in which everyone ends up angry and there is no resolution.

Make the First Impression a Positive One

A teen's first encounter with a library staff member is often negative, with the teen playing the role of the rule-breaker and the LST playing the role of enforcer. Instead, LSTs need to be proactive about greeting, meeting, and developing relationships with the "regulars" who use libraries. Tell them clearly what the expectations are, but also tell them what they can expect of you—assistance, fairness, and respect.

Reactions

Don't Power Trip

One of the reasons teens have a bad image of people who work in libraries is because they see us as mean and controlling. Unfortunately, this image has roots; sometimes we think it is "our" library, when really the library belongs to the community, including teens. Sometimes there are library staff members who abuse their power, act unfairly, or are prejudicial in their behavior toward teens. These staff members need to be reminded that if they humiliate, embarrass, or humble a teen and consider it a "win," then the library and the community are the ones who have really lost.

Keep Your Cool

If you lose your cool or become rattled, then teens get the reaction they wanted and a payoff for their inappropriate behavior. It is difficult, but you need to remain relaxed and just let the situation bounce off you. They will test you like they do a new teacher or a substitute.

It's Not Personal

If a teen calls you a name, it is usually because he or she feels a need to test you or to strike out at you as an authority figure. Rarely are incidents like this personal in nature. Although it might be upsetting, try not to take it personally. Of course, there are certainly limits here—racist, homophobic, sexist, or sexually harassing tirades should not be tolerated from teens any more than they would be from any other patron. To help you set and enforce limits, have predefined guidelines for what is and what is not appropriate behavior for your library. These guidelines will help you be fair, firm, and consistent in your delivery of library services to all teens.

CD See Tool 55. Youth Behavior Guidelines

Lighten Up

Teens make mistakes because they are in the process of growing up and into themselves. Most of these mistakes are not the end of the world, and we need to remember that most of us made our fair share of mistakes growing up as well.

The best thing you can do when you are standing on one side of a situation with a teen who made a mistake on the other is to ask yourself, "Is anyone going to die?" If the answer is no, then everything is going to be okay.

Remember

No one really wants to remember their teen years—there's a reason why most of us have blocked out our own adolescence. However, it would serve us all well if we could take a moment to remember our own insecurities, confusion, and bad decisions before we react to any given situation involving a teen.

Respect

None of these strategies is foolproof. Like any situation dealing with a problem patron, dealing with a problem teen requires a large dose of good judgment, timing, and people skills. Despite the contradiction of librarians and teens, we have some things in common. Our emotional makeup is often the same: librarians, like teens, often feel underappreciated and disrespected. It might be hard for some to think teens deserve respect, but the minute teens walk through the door, they become library patrons who deserve respect. Librarians and teens might be opposites in many ways, but we share the same ground and should learn to live with one another. More than that, we need to engage in those services that will do more than handle teens, but instead see that they thrive.

What Do Young Adults Want and Need from Libraries?

Despite differences in geography, demographics, and experiences, what teens want and need from libraries is similar:

It Pays to Read! The Public Library of Charlotte and Mecklenburg County (PLCMC) has an ongoing program where teens can read down their fines, called "Project Payoff." Consider creating a similar program in your library to help teens start fresh. This type of program is win-win: Teens have an opportunity to start over and you have an opportunity to start again. Use PLCMC's program as a template and modify it so that it works for your library.

CD See Tool 9. Fine Reduction/Waiver Program (Project Payoff)

- Opportunities to be involved
- The library to be a bright and cheerful place
- A space of their own/relaxed atmosphere with comfortable furniture
- Computers with Internet access and access to various social networking applications
- Up-to-date collections with multiple copies of materials (especially those used for school projects)
- New fiction and nonfiction specifically for teens
- Alternative formats like graphic novels, manga, teen magazines, and comic books
- Downloadable music and other content and new DVDs available free of charge
- Longer weekend and evening hours/24-hour access
- No fines or a way to work/read down fines (negotiable system regarding fines)
- Staff to recognize their right to be there and to be treated with respect

- Good customer service and helpful staff that look like them
- Homework help and access to resources for school
- Potential for job opportunities
- Easier ways to find information in the library (in person and online)
- Programs and promotional events featuring giveaways, food, and fun, teen-relevant activities
- Freedom to eat and drink

In many ways, teens have a very traditional view of library services. The unanswered question, however, is if the library offered more programming, opportunities for youth involvement, and a separate space for them, would teens' view and use of the library change?

What Do Young Adults Need in Their Lives?

The word "thrive" emerges from the literature on youth development, in particular from the Search Institute. The Search Institute is an independent nonprofit organization whose mission is to provide leadership, knowledge, and resources to promote healthy children, youth, and communities. The Search Institute has reviewed the research in the field of youth development and has conducted its own studies on thousands of adolescents. The institute concluded that teens require certain positive conditions and experiences in their lives, or what Search has called "Developmental Assets." The research led the Search Institute to identify 40 such assets, 20 external and 20 internal. The external assets are about the relationships available to young people. Internal assets are the values and skills that teens develop to guide themselves. These 40 assets are the positive experiences, opportunities, and personal qualities that youth need to become responsible, successful, and caring adults. They are the foundation teens need in order to thrive.

Figure 2.2 is a simple chart listing the asset type and name, followed by a definition. The last column shows a library connection: a program, idea, or service that libraries could undertake in order to build each asset.

The key conclusion is this: The more assets young people accumulate, the less likely they are to engage in a wide range of risky behaviors and the more likely they are to engage in positive behaviors, including succeeding in school, helping others, and valuing diversity. Other positive behaviors could include maintaining good health, resisting danger, exhibiting leadership, delaying gratification, and overcoming adversity.

Public and school libraries are unique in that they have an opportunity to meet a majority of these 40 Developmental Assets. Libraries are not really in the information business or the book business, but the people business—connecting people and information and providing opportunities for teens to be meaningfully involved in their community. Churches, homes, and youth-serving organizations are often more

Simply put, teens want three basic things from a library:
- A positive experience
- To be treated fairly
- To make a difference in their lives

Figure 2.2. Developmental Assets® and Library Connections

Assets Type	Asset Name	Asset Definition	Library Connection
EXTERNAL ASSETS			
Support	Family support	Family life provides high levels of love and support.	Intergenerational programming supports this asset, such as mother/daughter book discussion groups.
	Positive family communication	Young person and her or his parent(s) communicate positively, and young person is willing to seek advice and counsel from parents.	Libraries support this asset through workshops for parents of teenagers and by promoting books on parenting teens in the collections.
	Other adult relationships	Young person receives support from three or more nonparent adults.	Library staff can develop strong bonding relationship with teens, either through organized groups or through daily interaction.
	Caring neighborhood	Young person experiences caring neighbors.	Library outreach in the community contributes to a caring neighborhood.
	Caring school climate	School provides a caring, encouraging environment.	Programming at the school media center teaches information literacy skills and demonstrates a caring school climate.
	Parent involvement in schooling	Parent(s) are actively involved in helping young person succeed in school.	Parent technology nights at school or public library provide skills parents need to help their teens succeed in school.
Empowerment	Community values youth	Young person perceives that adults in the community value youth.	Teens are actively involved in library decisions and are asked for their opinions either formally or informally.
	Youth as resources	Young people are given useful roles in the community.	Teens are used as volunteers, workers, and mentors supporting the library's mission.
	Service to others	Young person serves in the community one hour or more per week.	Year-long volunteer programs provide an opportunity for service, from helping the children's librarian with story times to helping the library build its physical and virtual collections.
	Safety	Young person feels safe at home, school, and in the neighborhood.	Library often acts as a safe haven for teens and provides them with a place to be alone.
Boundaries and Expectations	Family boundaries	Family has clear rules and consequences and monitors the young person's whereabouts.	Libraries support this asset though workshops for parents of teenagers and by promoting books on parents of teens in the collection.

(Cont'd.)

Figure 2.2. Developmental Assets® and Library Connections (Continued)

Assets Type	Asset Name	Asset Definition	Library Connection
EXTERNAL ASSETS (Cont'd.)			
Boundaries and Expectations (Cont'd.)	School boundaries	School provides clear rules and consequences.	Positive discipline practiced in the library media center supports this asset.
	Neighborhood boundaries	Neighbors take responsibility for monitoring young people's behavior.	Libraries are neighborhood institutions. Through positive discipline and redirecting inappropriate behaviors, librarians can play a role in setting boundaries.
	Adult role models	Parent(s) and other adults model positive, responsible behavior.	Librarians can serve as role models for youth if they allow teens "in."
	Positive peer influence	Young person's best friends model responsible behavior.	Peer programming such as book discussion groups support this asset.
	High expectations	Both parent(s) and teachers encourage the young person to do well.	The school librarian takes an active role in encouraging student achievement and supports it through a proactive plan of service.
Constructive Use of Time	Creative activities	Young person spends three or more hours per week in lessons or practice in music, theater, or other arts.	Programs that promote creativity such as creative writing programs, talent shows, literacy magazines, book reviews, newsletters, poetry slams, and other library-sponsored creative expression activities.
	Youth programs	Young person spends three or more hours per week in sports, clubs, or organizations at school and/or in the community.	After-school homework help program at school and the public library functions as a "club" as would a youth participation group.
	Religious community	Young person spends one or more hours per week in activities in a religious institution.	NA
	Time at home	Young person is out with friends "with nothing special to do" two or fewer nights per week.	NA
INTERNAL ASSETS			
Commitment to Learning	Achievement motivation	Young person is motivated to do well in school.	Homework assistance program involving tutors at the school or public library motivate students to achieve.
	School engagement	Young person is actively engaged in learning.	School media specialist involved in designing assignments that provide students with active learning in regard to information literacy.

(Cont'd.)

Figure 2.2. Developmental Assets® and Library Connections (Continued)

Assets Type	Asset Name	Asset Definition	Library Connection
INTERNAL ASSETS (Cont'd.)			
Commitment to Learning (Cont'd.)	Homework	Young person reports doing at least one hour of homework every school day.	Initiate homework assistance programs as well as collections to support homework; reference services in person, over the phone, via chat and e-mail, and assist teens in completing homework.
	Bonding to school	Young person cares about her or his school.	By involving youth in the school media center, as workers or volunteers, this bonding is encouraged.
	Reading for pleasure	Young person reads for pleasure three or more hours per week.	Everything we do: our collections, our programs, our displays, and our readers' advisory work.
Positive Values	Caring	Young person places high value on helping other people.	Youth advisory groups/volunteer programs can involve teens in projects, such as reading to seniors or working with preschoolers, which gives them the opportunity to help others.
	Equality and social justice	Young person places high value on promoting equality and reducing hunger and poverty.	Collections and programming illustrate this asset.
	Integrity	Young person acts on convictions and stands up for her or his beliefs.	Youth participation groups encourage the development of this asset.
	Honesty	Young person "tells the truth even when it is not easy."	This value is learned while serving as a teen volunteer or worker.
	Responsibility	Young person accepts and takes personal responsibility.	Participation in after-school programs and daily behavior, libraries help young people learn about responsibility.
	Restraint	Young person believes it is important not to be sexually active or to use alcohol/drugs.	Collections and programs can speak to this asset.
Social Competencies	Planning and decision making	Young person knows how to plan ahead and make choices.	Youth advisory groups can involve youth in planning programs and services.
	Interpersonal competence	Young person has empathy, sensitivity, and friendship skills.	Youth advisory group, book discussion group, or other such groups support this asset.
	Cultural competence	Young person has knowledge of and comfort with people of different cultural/racial/ethnic backgrounds.	Both groups as well as our collections support this asset. Multicultural programming plays a role here as well.

(Cont'd.)

Figure 2.2. Developmental Assets® and Library Connections *(Continued)*

Assets Type	Asset Name	Asset Definition	Library Connection
INTERNAL ASSETS *(Cont'd.)*			
Social Competencies *(Cont'd.)*	Resistance skills	Young person can resist negative peer pressure and dangerous situations.	Collections and programs illustrate this asset.
	Peaceful conflict resolution	Young person seeks to resolve conflict nonviolently.	Collections and programs can speak to this asset.
Positive Identity	Personal power	Young person feels he or she has control over "things that happen to me."	Collections and programs illustrate this asset.
	Self-esteem	Young person reports having a high self-esteem.	Collections and programs illustrate this asset.
	Sense of purpose	Young person reports that "my life has a purpose."	Collections and programs illustrate this asset, while youth participation provides teens with something of value in their life.
	Positive view of personal future	Young person is optimistic about her or his personal future.	Collections and programs illustrate this asset.

narrowly focused in their offerings, but libraries have collections, spaces, programs, personalized service, and hopefully a dedicated teen-serving staff member to help meet the needs of young people. With these offerings, libraries have a great chance of reaching or providing for the needs of many teens in the community.

Think for a second about libraries. What, at the basic level, do we do? We solve problems and, in doing so, provide our customers with good feelings. This is what teens want on their trip to a library. It is what they want out of their lives—solutions to problems and good feelings. We do this through relationships, from simple interactions that take place during a reference interview in person or online to longer commitments like programming, readers' advisory, outreach, or taking the initiative when it comes to treating teens with respect.

Relationships are the key to asset building. As we encounter teens, we need to learn their names, support them, encourage them, and empower them. We are not talking about social work; we are talking about people work; we are talking about library work. Relationships are the key to demolishing stereotypes, improving services, and building assets. When all library staff start serving teens as customers and not problems, then relationships will flourish. When we form relationships, we help teens succeed, but also help libraries thrive.

Conclusion

Throughout this chapter, we've identified the stages of the teen experience and how we respond, respect, and understand it in the library. The information in this chapter is about building a foundation for providing outstanding library services for teens. Everything else in this book builds on this foundation. So often when we do workshops about the information included in this chapter we know that we are preaching to the choir. Chances are good that you, as an LST, know the importance of this information. Your mission now is to share this information with your colleagues and your library administration. Meeting the needs of teens in the library is everyone's responsibility, and this responsibility begins by *truly* understanding the audience.

Sources Cited in This Chapter

1. Fenwick, Elizabeth, and Tony Smith. 1994. *Adolescence: The Survival Guide for Parents and Teenagers.* New York: Dorling Kindersley.
2. Frontline. 2008. "Inside the Teenage Brain: Interview with Dr. Jay Giedd." Available: www.pbs.org/wgbh/pages/frontline/shows/teenbrain/interviews/giedd.html (accessed August 8, 2008).
3. Strauch, Barbara. 2003. *The Primal Teen: What New Discoveries About the Teenage Brain Tell Us About Our Kids.* New York: Anchor Books.

Recommended Sources for Further Reading

Brautigam, Patsy. 2008. "Developmental Assets and Libraries: Helping to Construct the Successful Teen." *Voice of Youth Advocates* 31, no. 2 (June): 124–125.

Gorman, Michele. 2006. "Teenage Riot: The Terrible Teens." *School Library Journal* 52, no. 6 (June): 34.

Jones, Jamie. 2005. "Teens Will Be Teens." *School Library Journal* 51, no. 1 (January): 37.

Perlstein, Linda. 2003. *Not Much Just Chillin': The Hidden Lives of Middle Schoolers.* New York: Farrar, Straus, and Giroux.

Pierce, Jennifer Burek. 2007. *Sex, Brains, and Video Games.* Chicago: ALA Editions.

Strauch, Barbara. 2003. *The Primal Teen: What New Discoveries About the Teenage Brain Tell Us About Our Kids.* New York: Anchor Books.

Wallis, Claudia. 2004. "What Makes Teens Tick? Secrets of the Teen Brain." *Time,* May 10.

Walsh, David. 2004. *Why Do They Act That Way: A Survival Guide to the Adolescent Brain for You and Your Teens.* New York: Free Press.

Wolf, Anthony. 1997. *Get Out of My Life, but First Can You Take Me and Cheryl to the Mall: A Parent's Guide to the New Teenager.* New York: Farrar, Straus, and Giroux.

History and Trends

The field of library services for teens is, on the surface, stronger than ever as libraries enter the second decade of the twenty-first century. A scan of the history of teen services shows how today's library services for teens have emerged from an evolution of ideas and activities on both the national and local levels—sometimes progressing in leaps, and other times in lulls. The history of teen services in libraries is an interesting one, with a similar waxing and waning cycle that produces two common themes. First, there is a huge gap between what libraries know they should do and what they actually do. This gap comes from the normal factors that separate library dreams from library reality, but with teens there seems to be a deeper question underneath: Should young adults be treated as a special group? To classify teens as a special population is to admit that they need a special service, and this means special staff and collections. Young adults are not a group with extra needs, but they do have unique needs and they do require staff with specialized training and materials. The second theme is approaching teen services holistically. YA literature, programs, and information literacy are not enough in themselves, but libraries must be able to provide teens the opportunities to take full advantage and benefit from a full range of library services. If the aim for twentieth-century young adult librarianship was to gain recognition as a real and vital part of the library world, then the profession, in the twenty-first century, aims to show that serving teens in school and public libraries is a real and vital part of creating a strong community. Equally as important, for many library directors, is that young adult services are seen as "cutting edge" and part of a library's success. While directors and principals take their cues from their community and their staff, they also look around the field at what other libraries are doing that is producing an effect. The drivers of public library work in the twenty-first century—technology, diversity, and supporting lifelong learning—are the essence of services to teens.

IN THIS CHAPTER:

✔ What Is the History of Library Services for Young Adults?

✔ Where Are Young Adult Services Now?

✔ Conclusion: What Is the Future of Young Adult Services?

What Is the History of Library Services for Young Adults?

The history of services to young adults in the public library is a little less than 100 years old. Like so much library work, it is difficult to capture a true snapshot of work being done in the field; instead, we'll look at the "top" of the field, in terms of professional associations and publications, as an indicator of the status and state of the art of services. We focus on history to give some context to the trends of the present and our predictions for the future.

1913: Two library students from New York Public Library's (NYPL) Library School present a study at ALA Midwinter asking whether libraries need a separate department for young people.

1921: Kansas City Public Library (KCPL) in Missouri sets up a separate area of library services for young people.

1925: Four years later, public libraries in Cleveland, Ohio, New York City, and Trenton, New Jersey, join KCPL in establishing library services for young people.

1927–1928: Many libraries follow suit by creating separate divisions for library services to young people, including Dayton, Ohio, Los Angeles, Duluth, Atlanta, Nashville, and Pittsburgh, Pennsylvania.

1929: Formation of Young Peoples Reading Round Table (YPRRT) as part of ALA's Children's Library Association. New York Public Library publishes its first edition of *Books for Young People* (which would later become NYPL's much-acclaimed *Books for the Teenage*).

1930–1932: First youth services textbook, *Library Work with Children*, by Effie L. Powers was published in 1930. It is the first of its kind to include a chapter about library services to adolescents. In 1932 Margaret Alexander Edwards joins the staff of Enoch Pratt Free Library in Baltimore, Maryland.

1937: *The Public Library and the Adolescent*, by E. Leyland, the first professional book solely about library services for young adults, is published.

1941–1943: YPRRT becomes a part of ALA's Division of Libraries for Children and Young People. Margaret A. Edwards takes horse-drawn book wagon service to youth in poor neighborhoods in Baltimore.

1944: The term "young adult" is first used in the title of bibliographies published in *Library Journal.*

1948–1950: ALA publishes *Public Library Plans for the Teen Age.* YPRRT becomes a separate section under the title of Association of Young People's Librarians. *Booklist* carries annotated list of "Adult Books for Young Adults" for the first time in 1948. Amelia Munson's *An Ample Field* is published in 1950.

1954: *School Library Journal* becomes its own entity, separate from *Library Journal.* The Grolier Award is established to honor a librarian for his or her unusual contribution to the stimulation and guidance of reading by children and young people.

1957: Young Adult Services Division (YASD) splits from the Children's Library Association to establish itself as a separate division within ALA. Margaret A. Edwards is the first provider of young adult library services to win the Grolier Award.

1960: ALA's Committee of Standards for Work with Young Adults publishes *Young Adult Services in the Public Library*.

1966–1967: In 1966 YASD publishes *Guidelines for Young Adult Services in Public Libraries* and holds first preconference at an ALA Convention. In 1967, G. Robert Carlsen publishes *Books and the Teen-age Reader* and "age" is added to the ALA Library Bill of Rights, guaranteeing young people the right to use the library as they wish.

1969: Margaret A. Edwards publishes *The Fair Garden and the Swarm of Beasts*.

1976: YASD establishes its own office and part-time staff as well as its own intellectual freedom committee.

1978–1981: *Voice of Youth Advocates (VOYA)*, founded by Dorothy M. Broderick and Mary K. Chelton, makes its debut in 1978. This was the first professional journal devoted to the informational needs of teenagers. YASD publishes *Directions for Library Services to Young Adults* to provide the profession with a document to help them plan services. One year later, Libraries Unlimited publishes *Libraries and Young Adults*, which provides an excellent overview of services entering the 1980s. In 1981, *Young Adults Deserve the Best: Competencies for Librarians Serving Young Adults* is published.

1982–1984: In 1982, YASD establishes annual grants for librarians with vendors' support, including the YASD/*VOYA* Research Grant and the Baker & Taylor Conference Grant. In 1984 the first Frances Henne/YASD/*VOYA* Research Grant is awarded for research that specifically addresses young adult library services.

1988: *Library Trends* publishes "Library Services to Youth: Preparing for the Future," a document that looks at various issues regarding serving teens in libraries in the 1980s. The same year, the National Center for Education Statistics (NCES) releases a report called "Services and Resources for Young Adults in Public Libraries," the first comprehensive survey of our profession. This same year the YA Author Achievement Award to honor an outstanding teen author was created by YASD, funded by *School Library Journal*, and awarded biannually to a YA Author for his or her contribution to the field.

1988–1989: In 1988 teens from Enoch Pratt Central Library in Baltimore become the first YASD-sanctioned teen group to speak at a Best Books for Young Adults (BBYA) meeting. A year later the first ever YASD Econo-Clad Award was given to a practicing teen librarian for the development and implementation of a unique teen program that involved reading and the use of literature. In 1991 the YA Author

Today *VOYA* is the leading professional publication for LSTs. For less than $50 for an annual subscription, it's the most bang for your buck when it comes to professional development. Each issue contains a wealth of information about providing direct service, programming for teens, and building spaces and collections, and the reviews are from both an adult and a teen perspective.

Achievement Award was renamed the Margaret A. Edwards Award and bestowed annually to a YA author for his or her significant contribution to young adult literature.

1992: YASD changes its name to the Young Adult Library Services Association (YALSA) and Patrick Jones publishes the first edition of *Connecting Young Adults and Libraries* with Neal-Schuman. During this year YALSA also begins a project called "Serving the Underserved: Customer Services for Young Adults in Public Libraries Project," which won a World Book Award. Since the inception of the project more than 10,000 library staff members from public libraries have been trained to provide exemplary service to young adults.

1994: Under ALA President Hardy Franklin, a triple play of publications coincides with the ALA President's Program and a customer service award through the Margaret Edwards foundation. Three publications, *Excellence in Library Services to Young Adults*, a reprint edition of *The Fair Garden and the Swarm of Beasts*, and YALSA's *Beyond Ephebiphobia*, join ALA's *Best Books for Young Adults* and Scarecrow's *Hangin' Out at Rocky Creek* for the most prolific year of YA professional publishing and YA visibility in the history of our profession. This same year Los Angeles Public Library opens "TeenS'cape," the first public library space designed with the help of teens.

1995: Two documents are published that help LSTs prove and measure their worth: YALSA's *Youth Participation in Schools and Public Libraries: It Works* and Virginia Walter's *Output Measures and More: Planning and Evaluating Public Library Services for Young Adults*, which provided teen librarians with a tool to plan, document, and evaluate their work.

1996: By this time, most libraries are connected to the Internet, moving the LST from thinking about "How do we get teens in the library?" to "What do we *do* with all of these teens?" The Internet also opens up new avenues for LSTs to communicate with colleagues.

1997: In addition to the second edition of *Excellence in Library Services for Young Adults*, another key document is published by YALSA titled *Youth Participation: It Works*. This tool provided philosophical and practical information to get librarians involved in youth involvement. Another YALSA product that made life easier, in particular for smaller libraries, was the listing of Top Ten titles for BBYA and Quick Picks. Finally, YALSA's Web site "Teen Hoopla" debuted to huge acclaim from librarians and plenty of scorn from failed television talk show host Dr. Laura Schlessinger.

1998: A banner year, in 1998 both the Alex Awards (adult books for young adults) and Teen Read Week were introduced by YALSA. In the same year, YALSA also rolled out revised competencies for librarians serving youth, while the American Association of School Librarians (AASL) launched **Information Power,** the blueprint for successful school library media programs. As the twentieth century winds down, most of the tools are in place for LSTs to create dynamic services and teen spaces.

1999: Two major milestones occur in cooperation with ALA/YALSA. The DeWitt Wallace–Reader's Digest Fund conducts then reports on a study about programs for school-age youth in public libraries. Following up on the survey results, DeWitt Wallace teams with the Urban Library Council to launch the "Public Libraries as Partners in Youth Development" Project, which provided a handful of large urban libraries with the funding and the philosophy to move away from thinking about services *to* young adults and reconceptualize services *with* young adults.

2000: The Michael L. Printz Award is established to honor one book each year that exemplifies excellence in YA literature. The establishment of this award serves as a recognition of the importance of YA literature, but the naming of the award after the late, great school librarian Michael Printz serves to remind us that librarians must do the work of connecting teens with books. To help non-LSTs do this, YALSA publishes a revised edition of *Bare Bones* that provides generalists with information on how to serve teens.

2001: YALSA kicks off the new century with internal and external success. Its Strategic Plan provides the organization with the framework, while the "Power Up with Print" Training Session held at the AASL Conference provides the organization with a product to deliver the message about the importance of young adult library services to the library community as a whole.

2002: YALSA Deputy Director Linda Waddle, who retired in 2002, left a huge legacy. In addition to the Printz Award, Teen Read Week, "Serving the Underserved" Train the Trainer Program, and a host of other projects, under Waddle's leadership YALSA membership exploded—going from 1,787 personal members to 3,183. One of Waddle's final acts was to edit the latest revision of *New Directions for Library Services to Young Adults*, originally published in 1977. This third edition represents the broad philosophical framework for the association and thus the profession.

2003: For the first time, teens select YALSA's "Teens' Top Ten" Books online. YALSA also publishes a revised edition of *Young Adults Deserve the Best: Competencies for Librarians Serving Teens in Libraries* to help librarians and educators stay in the loop regarding services for teens.

2004: YALSA membership continues to grow exponentially, with a large increase in membership and the addition of a much-needed full-time executive director, Beth Yoke. Our professional association also finally outgrows the small division subsidy from ALA as it begins the climb to financial independence in the fiscal year of 2004–2005. Patrick Jones, with the help of co-authors Michele Gorman and Tricia Suellentrop, publishes the third edition of *Connecting Young Adults and Libraries*.

2005: The Pew Internet and American Life Project publishes a study about how more than half of teens online are creating original content online. This same year the *New York Times* publishes an article about the popular *Gossip Girl* series. This national exposure raises the general public's awareness about contemporary young adult fiction.

If you're a YA lone ranger (LST who works alone), we recommend you join YALSA for the sense of community it provides. YALSA also offers its members excellent opportunities for networking and professional development and growth.

CD See Tool 51. YALSA Committee Volunteer Form

2006: Teen librarians begin mobilizing, and YALSA membership hits more than 5,000. YALSA capitalizes on its continued growth by offering online classes. Adding to the growing acceptance of the graphic novel format in the library world, YALSA develops a new annual selection list: Great Graphic Novels for Teens. This same year, teen librarians around the country begin using social networking tools, like blogs and wikis, to share information about teen services and to collaborate globally with their colleagues. YALSA also jumps on the social networking wagon and creates both a MySpace profile and a blog to communicate with members virtually. As social networking becomes more popular, so does controversy surrounding its use by young people. YALSA Executive Director Beth Yoke testifies at the Deleting Online Predators Act (DOPA) hearing in Washington, DC, about the positive uses of social networking tools and how this legislation would negatively impact teens.

2007: YALSA celebrates 50 years of world leadership in selecting and recommending reading, listening and viewing materials for teens, and it becomes public knowledge that YALSA is the fastest-growing division of the American Library Association. For the first time, YALSA and young adult librarians around the country celebrate "Teen Literature Day" during National Library Week in April and "Teen Tech Week" in March. It is also a big year for awards, with the announcement of the Odyssey Award (a new annual award for the best young adult audiobook) and the selection of a graphic novel for the Printz Award. Many studies are conducted in 2007 about teens' use of libraries and technology, including a study about children and teens using digital technology sponsored by MTV, Nickelodeon, and Microsoft; two Pew Internet studies about teens and social networking and the rising use of social, interactive media; and a poll about youth and library use sponsored by Harris. YALSA also adds a communications specialist to its growing staff to keep up with the growing needs of its members.

2008: For the second time, YALSA undergoes strategic planning to continue to meet the needs of both librarians serving teens and the teens themselves. This is also the inaugural year for YALSA's Young Adult Literature Symposium held in Nashville, Tennessee. In partnership with the Association for Library Service to Children (ALSC), YALSA also hands out the Odyssey for the first time, an award for the best audiobook produced for children and/or young adults during the previous year.

2009: YALSA introduces the Morris Award, an annual award recognizing a first-time, previously unpublished author who has written an outstanding book for the young adult audience.

2010: YALSA names an annual winner of the YALSA Award for Excellence in Nonfiction for Young Adults, which honors the best nonfiction book published for young adults (ages 12–18) during the previous year.

A majority of the information in the timeline was taken from *VOYA*'s "200 Years of Young Adult Library Services History: A Chronology" compiled by Anthony Bernier, Mary K. Chelton, Christine A. Jenkins, and Jennifer Burek Pierce. We highly recommend you take a look at the document as a whole for an even more detailed account of where we've been as a profession.

Where Are Young Adult Services Now?

In spite of ever-present budget cuts, libraries have continued to recognize the importance of developing services for teens since the last edition of this book was published. While some large systems still do not have staff dedicated to serving teens, many others have come onboard in the past five years by hiring librarians specifically trained to work with teens. In both rural and urban libraries, a large number of staff hired for a variety of positions have taken an interest in providing programs for teens because they have seen a rise in the need for serving this demographic. Another trend in our profession has been an increase in professional development activities about successfully serving teens for all staff as well as the development of new classes for library students focusing on more programming for young adults. The much talked about "graying of the profession" has also had a direct impact on library services to teens in that as baby boomers are retiring, younger librarians who began their careers serving teens are now moving into top-level administrative positions. Staying true to their roots, these former teen librarians are continuing to support teen services by advocating for budget, space, and staff for young adults and libraries.

Now that we understand from the previous two chapters whom we serve and why, let's examine five trends exploding in the field of YA services in school and public libraries that should provide you with the context for developing your own services. Throughout the text, we'll discuss in detail about how to turn these trends into services at your school or public library. These trends represent the overarching ideas driving services to teenagers as we charge further into the twenty-first century. What is just as important, however, is realizing that these trends do not stand alone. Most are intertwined with larger societal trends that drive the actions of all institutions involved in the business of positive youth development.

The New Digital Divide

In the last edition of this book, one of the top ten trends identified for its impact on young adult library services was the digital divide, or the gap between young people who had access to computers and the Internet and those who did not. The digital divide makes the list again in this edition, but with a different definition. While the original digital divide continues to exist, the gap between those who have access and those who do not has grown marginally smaller in the past decade due to a decline in the price of desktop computers and laptops, which has contributed to more teens having personal computers at home and schools being able to afford more computers for school labs and classrooms. However, the lingering impact of the old-school digital divide continues to rear its ugly head with the persistently widening gap between teens who have access to technology and teens who have access to technology but who do *not* have the time or opportunity to use computers recreationally and without constraints. Unfortunately, in the United States, this gap is still largely tied to poverty because teens who do not own a personal computer do not have the same opportunities to play with new technologies, immerse themselves in virtual worlds, or become engaged with social networking and other participatory cultures—all opportunities and experiences that indirectly lead to the development of skills that allow teens to effectively participate in today's fast-paced, digital world.

This new digital divide is also about the invisible line separating the digital natives and the digital immigrants, or those who have grown up with technology at their fingertips and those who have not. It impacts today's library services to teens because we are asking library staff (some with a low comfort level with new technology) to work with and even mentor teens who often have a higher level of comfort with new and emerging technologies and applications. For many teens, this increase in comfort level isn't about being comfortable with "technology." It's more organic than that, with teens being more interested in the functionality of the technology because it allows them to stay in constant communication with one another, expand the concept of their immediate neighborhoods for making friends, and share and receive information instantaneously. We are also asking library staff with little or no experience with new technologies and library 2.0 applications to accept these new tools in the workplace and even to use them to reach teens where they are, which is online and on their cell phones. Nowhere has this divide been more apparent than in the battle between teens and library administrations over access to social networking sites. While some libraries have embraced social networking like MySpace and Facebook as a relevant means of communication for teens and an excellent tool for marketing to the teen demographic, others have rallied against it, even banning it from use on public computers in the library. Digital communication in all its forms (instant messaging, texting, tweeting, and social networking) has revolutionized how teens communicate with their peers, and this revolution has the ability to dramatically impact how we serve teens.

Content Delivery

Teens have always looked to libraries for their homework needs, but every day another batch of teens is finding out that libraries have the good stuff they want for their recreational reading. Or are they? Teens and their parents now function in a world in which any content they desire—educational, informational, or recreational—can and will be delivered to them in a variety of ways. Have we rested on our laurels by thinking that purchasing the newest John Green book and ordering *Nintendo Power* magazine equals delivering content? The term that comes to mind is explosion, as in *explosion* of format and of delivery. Many of the teens we serve can and will get their information and recreational needs filled through other sources for the simple reason that it is, well, simple. Amazon, iTunes, YouTube, and Hulu are all simple, easy, fun, and even addictive to use, and they deliver content directly to you 24 hours a day. Where are libraries in that equation? That is up to us.

Libraries are stuck in the middle: we serve everyone, and often this means our services and accompanying technology are geared toward the last of the technologically savvy. Teens as a whole don't fall into this group. They are risk takers, early adopters, and often have the money, desire, and time to demand their content be delivered when and how they like it. Our budgets are limited, so again we play it safe by not expanding our offerings with teens in mind. We would rather have a drive-through window for soccer moms than invest in a service for downloadable music and videos, a service that would clearly appeal to teens on many levels. They get the content they want, when they want it, and they see the library as the benevolent access giver. Every time we turn around there is a new and often better format that can deliver our traditional services better and faster. Twice as many people are designing and marketing new content compared to those of us attempting to deliver it in an equitable manner, so we have to be even more vigilant as to what on the long list of options will help teens in their lives. Content such as television, music, freeware, and even CliffsNotes all have their place in the lives of teens, and it is estimated that 35 percent of teens share their own creations online. It is our responsibility to design and plan for all of it—textual, video, audio, and photo content—all of the resources that will prepare teens for the workforce and higher education. By involving teens in the discussion about and planning for the next wave of service, we get a front row seat at the buffet that is technology and content delivery. Because the buffet of information and delivery options can overwhelm and delight all of us, it is crucial that libraries do not turn a blind eye to this opportunity but rather embrace this trend that will set your library and ultimately the teens you serve on the right track.

Teen Involvement and Radical Trust

The Youth Participation (YP) Movement has been around since the 1970s, so it's certainly nothing new. What is new is that it is now easier than ever to mobilize teens and engage them in meaningful ways by using the Internet and social networking tools to give them both opportunities to contribute to the library community and to build their own set of skills. From designing a library's MySpace page to developing a collaborative wiki for teen advisory council (TAC) members, teens now have more opportunities than ever to get involved and to help contribute to the development and success of a library's teen program. Another new idea in teen involvement is the concept of "radical trust," or the idea that we will trust teens to do the right thing. If we want teens to get involved, we have to allow them the freedom to get involved, and this means doing away with the parental permission forms to post a poem or original drawing in our teen Web site gallery, being more open to the idea of allowing teens to write and post original commentary on a library-sponsored teen blog, or even going so far as to allow teens to tag the library's catalog in order to make it more useful for other patrons looking for recommended reading materials or similar items to some of their favorite books, magazines, or graphic novels. Radical trust also means that we are open to teens planning and carrying out programs, helping develop library policies and procedures that directly impact teens, and even being in on the ground floor of the hiring process when library administration sets out to hire a new youth services director or a new teen librarian. These may seem like revolutionary ideas, but they are happening around the country.

- At the Ft. Worth Public Library in Texas teens plan and carry out an annual "Hip-Hop Symposium" to help shine a light on the importance of hip-hop culture to young people in their area.

- In Mesa, Arizona, a teen serves four years on a citizen committee formally known as the Library Advisory Board as a full-fledged voting member.

- In Charlotte, North Carolina, teens at the Public Library of Charlotte of Mecklenburg County's teen-only library, the Loft at ImaginOn, serve on a panel to help hire teen-serving staff members; they develop the questions, conduct the interview, and give the teen services manager relevant feedback and impressions about all candidates.

- At the Ephrata Public Library in Pennsylvania, teen advocates planned and held a living art exhibition/demonstration titled "Stuck on the Library" to garner voter support of a ballot referendum for a tax to fund local libraries.

Obviously teens want to get involved. Our job is to make these opportunities possible and then to put the concept of radical trust into action by giving over some of the control and giving up some of the control issues that often plague our profession.

> With radical trust we are taking the power out of our hands and putting it in the teens' hands—where it rightfully belongs if we want to tout ourselves as developmentally appropriate youth-serving organizations looking to contribute to the overall development and well-being of teens in both our local and global community.

Adolescent Development and Brain Research

The concept of youth development has been emphasized in every edition of this book. It is no less important now than it was five or ten years ago, but in the past decade two new components of healthy youth development have risen to the forefront: meeting the developmental needs of teens and acknowledging that scientific data about the development of the teenage brain backs up what many of us in this profession have known for years—teens are a work in progress.

Youth development is a perspective that emphasizes providing services and opportunities to support all young people in developing a sense of competence, usefulness, belonging, and power. Positive youth development is a process that prepares young people to meet the challenges of adolescence and adulthood through a coordinated, progressive series of activities and experiences that help them to become socially, morally, emotionally, physically, and cognitively competent. Positive youth development addresses the broader developmental needs of youth, in contrast to deficit-based models that focus solely on youth problems. Youth development is about prevention as opposed to intervention. To keep youth development at the forefront when serving teens, many LSTs are now learning about the stages and milestones of adolescence as well as the seven developmental needs of teens and the Search Institute's 40 Developmental Assets, described by the institute as "concrete, common sense positive experiences and qualities essential to raising successful young people. These assets have the power during critical adolescent years to influence choices young people make and help them become caring, responsible adults."[1] LSTs are using this information to help plan and carry out developmentally appropriate programs, design teen-friendly spaces, and even reassess how they provide traditional library services for teens, like reference and readers' advisory.

Adolescent brain research is a relatively new field of scientific study that has gotten a lot of attention in the past ten years. From a cover article in *TIME* magazine[2] to a feature documentary on PBS,[3] the subject is galvanizing youth workers around the country who are seeking answers about how teens process information and why they do some of the puzzling (and often frustrating) things they do. Barbara Strauch sums it up best in her book *The Primal Teen: What the New Discoveries About the Teenage Brain Tell Us About Kids*, when she ends her introduction with this thought: "As it turns out, teenagers may, indeed, be a bit crazy. But they are crazy according to a primal blueprint; they are crazy by design."[4]

Virtual Library Services

As we move further into the age of information, the role of libraries and the services provided for users of all ages will continue to evolve. LSTs know that young people are often on the forefront of cutting-edge technology, not only aware of the newest stuff but often proficient at first touch. These kids have been raised with technology at home, in the classroom, and in the library, and soon we will have the first generation of teens whose parents were raised with a high level of technology at home. Although not all young people everywhere have the same level of experience with computers and electronic information, as we move further into the digital age, it will be safe to assume that a majority of teens will have at least a rudimentary knowledge of computers, electronic information, and digital media.

As technology advances and information becomes more widely available in electronic formats, librarians who want to move forward with the teens they serve will need to go beyond being familiar with digital information. LSTs will need to accept the nature of the virtual world and embrace the fact that content is everywhere and teens are used to it being delivered directly to them, instantly. As LSTs begin to understand the various uses and benefits the virtual world offers teens, they also grasp the value of being a passive observer and active participant within that world. This level of understanding demands a change in attitude, moving from awareness to use, and within that change a level of celebration about technology and the virtual services it will afford teens. Librarians who work with teens know that your street credit with teens—your value as a source of information—is only as strong as your knowledge of the things that interest them. Just like we must be aware of the music teens listen to and the books they read, librarians who successfully serve this population will have to use technology, offer virtual services, and be comfortable having an online presence and living in an online world.

However, no amount of technological advancement or interest from the library will eliminate the need for an LST who can serve as intermediary between teens and technology. There is a genuine need to extend, modify, and reconfigure dynamically the behavior of our existing library services as we move further into a virtual world. This human interface is what sets the library experience apart from a kid doing research on the Internet at home. In the future, as computers become more accessible and the Internet a more congested labyrinth of information, the human interaction between a teen patron and an LST will be what helps a library remain more than a repository of information. The working relationships that make each library experience an individualized encounter must move seamlessly between the virtual and physical world, an experience that is a teen's daily life. A relationship founded in the quest for information often breeds trust between the finder and the findee, and with this trust often comes a sense of comfort. Once a teen is comfortable with you as a source of information, chances are good that he or she will risk asking you for help with other things, including that elusive request for readers' advisory—an LST's dream.

While it is safe to say that the future of young adult librarianship is no place for technophobes, a library of the future remains one that provides a space for teens along with quality programming and opportunities for young people to share their voices and their unique experiences. Whether these spaces and opportunities exist physically or virtually, they contribute to the development of lifelong library users. The future of teen services is about LSTs, not just knowing computer networks, but becoming equally adept at mastering human networks, both within and outside of their own organization.

Conclusion: What Is the Future of Young Adult Services?

We have glimpsed the amazing benefit that a holistic approach to serving teens in school and public libraries will yield. Libraries across the world are working toward this goal. We have teens who are part of the decision-making process on a micro level, running their TAC and more on a macro level, being voting members of the library board, and getting involved in collection development and true advocacy for libraries. We also see that the more virtual our world becomes, the greater the need for libraries to function as a connector for teens, giving them the space and experience to become a vital part of their community. The challenges will remain, as always.

Previously those challenges were experience, technology, and the ability to connect (both in person and geographically), but we see the new challenges on the horizon as being attitudes, values, and legislation. Libraries are facing more intellectual freedom challenges on a local level and more proposed legislation that will limit what an individual can access, and of course this directly impacts teens; limiting their access to printed and electronic materials will affect their ability to negotiate higher education and the workplace. This type of legislation is often couched in "protecting children" terms, but is limiting teens really protecting them? LSTs are constantly championing this group by making sure teens are not forgotten in this battle.

For the teens in your community to succeed, they need advocates inside and outside of the library. Youth advocacy means believing in treating youth as first-class citizens in the library world, not as a marginalized group.

Youth advocacy means being a voice with and for youth at all levels of a library organization, ensuring that circulation systems can measure teen use, selecting appropriate furniture, providing information literacy instruction, and employing programs that increase student learning and achievement. We want to be successful advocates, not marginalized martyrs. Advocacy is a core value, but it is about expanding beyond our core supporters and finding others in the library and community who share our vision and core values. True youth advocates engage allies, share resources and successes, and create a stronger community for teens.

Let's think about teens we are working with for a minute. In the next five years we will be providing services to the first generation of teens whose parents grew up in an Internet world. What does that mean for libraries? According to a Pew Internet Study,[5] it means teens will be more self-directed and less dependent on top-down instructions, more reliant on feedback and response, more tied to group knowledge, and more open to cross-discipline insights. It seems like the traditional methods of library service delivery are contrary to all of these characteristics—our catalog, our rules, and our virtual interaction all seem to be opposite of how teens function best. As teens are transitioning to adulthood we must look at the big picture: How will their parents treat technology in and outside of the home? How will teens deal with the limits government wants to impose? What role do the library and LSTs play in that equation? That is the future of young adult services.

Sources Cited in This Chapter

1. Search Institute. 2007. "What Kids Need: Developmental Assets." Minneapolis, MN: Search Institute. Available: www.search-institute.org/assets/forty.htm (accessed January 10, 2009).
2. Wallis, Claudia. 2008. "What Makes Teens Tick." *Time*, September 26. Available: www.time.com/time/magazine/article/0,9171,994126,00.html (accessed January 10, 2009).
3. Spinks, Sarah. 2002. "Frontline: Inside the Teenage Brain." Arlington, VA: Public Broadcasting System. Program #2011 (January 31). Available:

www.pbs.org/wgbh/pages/frontline/shows/teenbrain/etc/script.html (accessed January 10, 2009).

4. Strauch, Barbara. 2003. *The Primal Teen: What New Discoveries About the Teenage Brain Tell Us About Our Kids.* New York: Doubleday.

5. Rainie, Lee. 2006. "Life Online: Teens and Technology and the World to Come." Pew Internet & American Life (March 23). Available: www.pew internet.org/ppt/Teens%20and%20technology.pdf (accessed January 10, 2009).

Recommended Sources for Further Reading

Bernier, Anthony, Mary K. Chelton, Christine Jenkins, and Jennifer Burek Pierce. 2005. "Two Hundred Years of Young Adult Library Services History: A Chronology." *Voice of Youth Advocates.* Available: www.voya.com/whats invoya/web_only_articles/Chronology_200506.shtml.

Bernier, Anthony, and Cathi Dunn MacRae. 2007. "Two Hundred Years of Young Adult Library Services History: A Chronology: Update 2007." *Voice of Youth Advocates.* Available: http://pdfs.voya.com/VO/YA2/VOYA 200708chronology_update.pdf.

The Young Adult Library Services Association. n.d. "About YALSA: History." Available: www.ala.org/ala/mgrps/divs/yalsa/aboutyalsab/yalsahistory.cfm.

Customer Service

How do teens see themselves when it comes to customer service in libraries? The following are actual teen responses from a series of teen focus groups conducted by the California State Library:

- "If we went into a library, the librarian would look at us, like, why are they here? Like we're going to cause trouble or something, like we're being watched."

- "Some of the librarians don't even care about you. Librarians at school, they are nice. But outside, they are kind of rude and they don't really care."

- "If I ever go when I need a book, I'm scared to ask them where it is, because I don't want them to think I'm stupid."

- "When you ask them how to find something, they'll just tell you to go over there."

- "I don't think it's so much the age [of the librarian]; it's the way they speak to you. The point is that a person needs to know how to communicate with people no matter what age they are. They're supposed to help you and that's what they are there for, but they don't take it like that."

- "Some librarians just don't like you. They pick on you, especially us teens."

- "The library is so very serious. Everyone has a very solemn look. It's depressing. It's very, very depressing to walk into a library."[1]

Not an attractive picture of how teens view libraries, but just because they said it, does it mean it is true? It doesn't matter what is true. What matters is the perception that these things are true. What matters is that teens shop with their feet, and many teens prefer researching at home or finding books at Barnes and Noble to visiting a library. Libraries, pre-Internet and pre–mega bookstore, could give lip service to the idea of customer service. It is easy to do when you have a monopoly on the information business. But now teens have a wide variety of choices for where to go to

IN THIS CHAPTER:

- ✔ So Are We Getting Anything Right in Customer Service to Teens?
- ✔ What Is the Ideal Customer-focused Library Service for Teenagers?
- ✔ What Does an Ideal Staff Member Who Works with Teens (Which Means Anyone Who Works in the Library) Look Like?
- ✔ What Skills Does an LST Need to Work with Teens?
- ✔ How Do You Construct Information Services to Provide Teens with a Positive Library Experience?
- ✔ What Does an Ideal Reference Transaction with a Teen Look Like?
- ✔ Is Customer Service with Teens Really That Bad?
- ✔ How Do You Train Other Staff to Provide Quality Customer Service to Teens?

get information, and the responses tell us very clearly that we have not given them a compelling reason to visit a library. While many teens do use libraries, it is clear from these teen focus groups and stories we hear every day from LSTs around the country that teens often do not have positive experiences in the library and/or with library staff. Even more disturbing is that teens often do not believe that library staff want to connect with them or will be interested or able to provide the service they need and deserve.

The summary of the focus groups conducted in California included the following conclusions about teens' general attitudes and perceptions of the library:

- Teens don't see either value or convenience in using a public library.
- Libraries make teens feel uncomfortable, unlike a bookstore.
- Libraries need to be more physically attractive and relaxed.
- Teens believe that library staff view them with suspicion.
- Teens use libraries primarily for homework.
- Libraries need to be more user friendly.
- Library staff need to become more user friendly.

From this we can surmise that teens feel disconnected from and unwelcome in the library. So taking this information into consideration, our challenge is to develop a customer service model that will help us bridge the divide and reconnect young adults and libraries.

So Are We Getting Anything Right in Customer Service to Teens?

Yes. Based on the focus groups conducted by the California State Library, the following are six aspects of libraries teens generally like:

- **Displays.** This certainly confirms what teens often tell us when asked: Make the materials attractive. This also reflects a common theme that teens want libraries to be more like bookstores where they feel comfortable and they can find what they want without a lot of hassle. In many surveys, teens answered that displays were the number one way that libraries could do more to promote reading.

- **Computers and Internet Access.** Teens also consistently report that one of the greatest things about libraries is access to Internet-enabled computers. In addition to access, teens want computers to be fast, have a lot of bandwidth, and have up-to-date software. Teens also want the library to provide free printing. The Internet is clearly a draw for teens, so we need to capitalize on this and stop making it so hard for teens to get online.

- **Homework.** Teens recognize that libraries are a great place to do homework or study, particularly if the library offers both quiet places and areas for group work. Even better, some libraries offer homework centers and writing labs staffed by tutors and teachers and/or virtual homework help from subscription services like tutor.com or brainfuse.com.

- **Free.** For teens who understand that the library lets you "rent" books, movies, CDs, and audiobooks and use a computer *free of charge*, the library is one of the best places on earth. Unfortunately, many teens out there still don't know that a library card is free and that the library, by nature of being a community service, is a place where they can freely borrow materials, get help with problems, seek information, and find fun and interesting things to do during the summer, after school, or on the weekend.

- **Quiet.** In spite of stereotypes or horror stories you might have heard about loud and boisterous groups of teens hanging out in the library after school (don't get us wrong; these stories are often true), many teens are looking for a quiet place to study because they lack this kind of environment at home. Providing nooks and crannies for reading and doing homework, quiet study rooms, headphones for use on the computers, and opportunities for "study halls" where teens can work together on projects in unused meeting room spaces are all ways in which we can meet the needs of these teens.

- **Helpful staff.** We guarantee you that one teen having a positive experience in your library will lead to an increase in your general teen population because teens talk, and word of mouth is the fastest way for teens to know and understand that your library staff is not only welcoming but helpful, courteous, and respectful. You can have the best teen collection and programs in the world, but if you're not friendly and helpful to every teen who walks through your doors then you might as well be flushing your money and energy down the toilet. The things that really matter to teens are the things that don't cost a dime: library staff who smile, make eye contact, and offer assistance without attitude or prejudice.

So, yes, we do plenty of things right in libraries for and with teens, but none of this means we can't continue to improve or that everyone on your library's staff knows how to "do it right." We can always take it to the next level, and that means creating raving fans by improving our customer service and helping create a paradigm shift in how we serve teens in libraries, from what works for us to what is best for our teen patrons.

> Teens remember when they have been treated kindly and fairly. One of the goals of this book is to educate library staff about why it's important to work with, and not against, teens who frequent the library.

What Is the Ideal Customer-focused Library Service for Teenagers?

In 2008, staff at the Johnson County Library (JCL) in Kansas posed a series of questions to teens, with the goal of having them describe their "ideal library."[2] Many of the answers provided by the teens during these focus groups offer insight into what young people want from a library. Teens want and expect libraries to emulate the retail experience; they want a high-tech experience, but mostly they want a positive customer service experience where they enter with a problem (I need a book; I need to do research; I need to access my e-mail) and leave with a solution delivered by a staff member who is above all else "friendly." They also wouldn't mind these features:

- A quick, self-service checkout system
- A space in which they can relax, laugh, and talk with other teens (hammocks, beds, seats in windows with pillows, a loft, a water feature)
- Music piped into the teen area
- Up-to-date collections
- Home delivery of materials (like Netflix)
- Food and beverages sold/permitted within the library
- Helpful and friendly staff
- Newest software loaded on computers
- A handheld device that locates books on the shelf
- A supply area that includes paper, pencils, glue sticks, etc.
- Areas for private computer use and/or group study
- Laptop computers/checkout
- Better way to communicate online with staff
- Better computer programs to search for books (or, better yet, one place to search for everything in the library)
- Book synopses or book recommendations by staff available online
- Popular series separated into their own section
- Drive-through where they can pick up and drop off books
- A "free day" (or amnesty day) where they can return past due books without a charge
- Longer periods on the computer
- No late fees (this was probably the number one complaint)
- Open longer hours
- The fastest computers and Internet connections

Are all of these things possible? Yes, with time, money, a change in attitude about the role of the library, and a commitment to develop a space where the customer's wants and needs come first. If we don't choose to make these improvements in libraries, it is because we have not made it a priority.

CD See Tool 21. Laptop Circulation Policy and Agreement Form

Ask the teens who frequent your library what they'd like to see change. You'll likely be surprised by their responses and teens will see you as a potential change agent. A focus group is an excellent way to get feedback and provide teens with an opportunity to be meaningfully involved. If you want more casual feedback, consider handing out a survey.

CD See Tool 11. Guidelines for Running a Teen Focus Group

CD See Tool 35. Teen Focus Group Questions

CD See Tool 36. Teen Library User Survey

What Does an Ideal Staff Member Who Works with Teens (Which Means Anyone Who Works in the Library) Look Like?

Over the past several years we have both hired a number of teen librarians, and we always include teens in the interview and selection process. The following list presents attributes our teen interviewers think are ideal when hiring an employee who works with teens (which means anybody who works in the library):

- Friendly, knowledgeable, and helpful
- Has a sense of humor
- Treats everyone with respect
- Knows what is going on (translation: keeps up with pop culture)
- Is younger, but old enough to help them
- Knows how to use technology
- Has customer service skills

Correspondingly, teen marketing guru Peter Zollo, who works with business professionals and company executives looking to attract a teen audience, cites the following rules for engaging teens:

- Use humor/be funny
- Be honest
- Be clear with message
- Be original
- Don't try so hard to be cool[3]

If you are a library staff member who works with teens, use the previous lists as a primer. If you are a library administrator looking to hire a new staff member, use them as a checklist.

What Skills Does an LST Need to Work with Teens?

Working with teens in a library setting is an interesting job filled with challenges and unexpected experiences, but it's not for everyone. If you want to become a teen librarian solely because you love young literature, this is not the job for you. If you want to become a teen librarian because you love YA lit *and* you believe in advocating for teens and being passionate and creative in your work life, then this might be the perfect job for you. From experience we know that there are two sets of skills that LSTs need to survive the job. The first set of skills is very difficult to teach. These are innate qualities one is born with, and while they are not absolute necessities, they do make this job easier on a day-to-day basis.

Being an LST is not a job for the meek, but for the bold, outgoing, creative, and enthusiastic. If you are planning to be an LST, take note of these skills and set out to master those that can be learned. If you are a manager or administrator planning to hire an LST, review the following two lists for 20 skills to look for when interviewing candidates.

Innate Skills or Character Traits That Will Serve You Well as an LST

- **Initiative.** This trait didn't make the top spot on a whim. Initiative is the backbone of being an LST. In a typical day an LST must take the initiative with colleagues, teens, parents, teachers, publishers, and community organizations. If you can't or won't take the initiative on behalf of teens, then there is no need to keep reading.

- **Ability to build and maintain relationships with adults and teens.** This is important in any job, but there is a level of finesse involved with building relationships as an LST. Developing and maintaining relationships with teens is the cornerstone of youth involvement, but the ability to establish working relationships with adults, including parents, teachers, and administrators is just as important to working successfully with teens.

- **Enthusiasm/passion.** We hope a passion for serving teens is what brought you here. We can promise you it will be tested time and time again. We can also promise you that enthusiasm and a passion for working for and with teens is what will win you the hearts of the teens you are serving.

- **Organization.** Serving teens when and where they are can be the opposite of a typical business day. To be an effective LST, you need to be organized and ready to roll when a large group of unexpected teens comes into your library at 3:45 p.m., when your manager asks for your monthly program report, or when a local youth-serving organization calls you up at the last minute and asks you to speak at a fund-raiser...that night!

- **Creativity.** Working with teens requires you to be creative on a daily (sometimes hourly) basis, with triage reference for the masses, readers' advisory, unique and innovative programming, emerging technologies, and simple communication with teens from all walks of life. Being creative is not as much a skill as a necessity for working with teens.

- **Flexibility.** This skill is key when working with teens because you have to be willing to adapt to new ideas quickly.

- **Sense of humor.** This might be the most valuable skill in the group because humor can get you into and out of many crucial situations when working with teens on a daily basis. Working with teens will often require you not to take things personally, and having a sense of humor makes this process a lot easier for everyone.

- **Open-mindedness.** You will work with teens who are prickly and difficult. Being open-minded and empathic will help you go the distance with and for these teens.

Don't let things sneak up on you! Organization is key when it comes to planning your year as an LST, and these two core documents can help you plan ahead so that you never miss an important teen event or opportunity.

CD See Tool 1. Annual Planning Calendar

CD See Tool 50. YALSA Annual Calendar of Events and Important Dates

- **Easygoing/unflappable.** Working with teens can be anxiety-inducing. If you are not easily flustered, then this job will be easier when the security guard comes to tell you he caught teens having sex in the bathroom or a teen gets upset and storms out of the library calling you all kinds of names on the way out the door.

- **Problem solver.** When you are serving teens this process often takes place on the fly, in the thick of things. You need to be ready to problem solve on the run, in the midst of a million things, and surrounded by packs of teens waiting for help, or an answer, or both.

Skills or Character Traits That Can Be Learned on the Job That Will Serve You Well as an LST

- **Knowledge of adolescent development and the developmental needs of teens.** The more you know about where teens are and what they need to develop into competent, caring adults, the more prepared you'll be to serve them on a daily basis. As you learned in Chapter 2, knowledge of the developmental needs of teens will impact every aspect of your job.

- **Knowledge of young adult literature.** Get reading! Make a plan for staying up to date with your teen reading and stick to it. There is no other way, and you can't fake it because teens can spot a fake a mile away.

- **Communication skills.** Similar to initiative, this is a skill that will help you build relationships with teens and adults. The great thing about communication skills is that they can be improved with practice, and over time you will learn how to adapt your communication style to fit the needs of your audience.

- **Library experience** (circulation, readers' advisory, reference transaction). This isn't so much a skill as it is a need. To be successful as a library employee, you need experiences with all things that happen in a library, including circulation, readers' advisory, the ability to hold a reference interview, etc. The best advice we have for those looking to improve their abilities in library services is to seek out the best people in your library, watch their every move, emulate their styles, and then ask lots of questions.

- **Confidence with emerging technologies.** This isn't about bleeding edge territory; this is awareness—pay attention and experiment. Strike a reading and technology balance because both are important to teens.

- **Planning skills.** The reality is that planning comforts managers. High comfort level equals freedom for young adult services in most libraries.

- **Booktalking.** The ability to mesmerize teens (and teachers) with your book-selling skills is just one of the many secret weapons of an LST.

- **Public speaking skills.** You need to be able to articulate your message to teens, to library staff, to your manager, to the director, and to the library's board of directors. Part of your job is advocating for teens,

The best way to determine the breadth and depth of your library's services to teens is to conduct an in-depth evaluation of the organization's commitment to teens, staff, facilities, collections, programs, and technology.

(CD) **See Tool 22. Library/Teen Services Evaluation**

and sometimes this will require you to pull out the soapbox and confidently and succinctly inspire those who have doubts about why teen services in libraries matters.

- **Understanding the importance of the "big picture."** You need to be able to see how serving teens fits within the bigger picture of library services as a whole. If you don't, who will?
- **Understanding organizational culture.** The sooner you understand your library's organizational culture, the quicker you'll be able to move the teen agenda into the mix.

Here are another dozen traits that will serve an LST well:

- Adaptive
- Articulate
- Collaborative
- Competitive
- Understanding
- Empathetic
- Energetic
- Forgiving
- Patient
- Persistent
- Pleasant and friendly
- Both a rule breaker and risk taker

Of course, none of these skills exists in a vacuum. You cannot be a teen advocate if you are not empathetic and friendly. You cannot be a great booktalker if you have no knowledge of YA literature and are not comfortable speaking in public.

How Do You Construct Information Services to Provide Teens with a Positive Library Experience?

Here's a possible model for excellent customer service based on what we believe teen customers value:

- **Quality.** Teens don't just want answers; they want correct answers. Just as you would for any adult who came to the reference desk asking for help, you need to make sure you are going out of our way to help a teen find the correct answer to any question he or she might have. Part of providing quality service is knowing where to look, but it is just as important that staff know what questions to ask and how to ask them to get to the heart of a teen's question. It is equally important that staff are energetic enough to actually do the work. If you get the answer

The best LST is one who has a majority of these traits and the willingness to work on developing the rest. Never underestimate the power of what you can learn and earn on the job.

right but don't bother to get out of our chair when a teen asks where he or she might find the poetry section, then you have not delivered quality customer service. There is a lot of literature about promoting the quality of reference, but sadly there is little research about measuring the success of reference transactions. To test the quality of customer service at your library, enlist the help of some teens as "secret shoppers" to determine how well your library staff deliver quality service to teen patrons.

- **User-focused.** You need to rethink everything you do in terms of what is best for the user, not what is easiest for the staff, what causes the least amount of headaches, or what makes the clerical staff happy. The implications of this focus are enormous and run through everything you do, from how you design your buildings, to signage, to how you staff your desk, to how you approach your work. Of course, the best way to be user focused is to know what the user wants—youth involvement strikes again, but so does understanding the user.

- **Inviting.** A vision of reference service for teens must include the idea that staff need to be inviting to teens. Inviting is more than approachable; it is an attitude that expresses eagerness to invite teens to use the library, have a positive experience, and return. Successful providers of information services find users where they are—in the stacks or on the computers or any place in between—and then offers assistance. Many teens feel stupid asking for help. Your job, as an information professional, is to approach them in an inviting fashion to determine if they do, indeed, need help. If they don't need you, they'll let you know. If they do, then your openness and approachability will simply make the process of asking for help easier.

- **Convenient.** This is a logical extension of a user-focused approach to customer service. We naturally offer reference in person, but shouldn't we also find ways to meet teens where they are, including online, to make our services as convenient as possible? Virtual reference is not difficult, and it is one more way you can utilize the tools at your disposal (in this case, computer, Internet, and instant messaging software) to offer convenient customer service to our patrons.

- **Knowledge sharing.** We go into more detail in Chapter 5 about organized, formal information literacy instruction, but a vision of reference service for teens must also include the idea that you are open to every opportunity to empower teens to work on their own. To put it simply, customer-focused reference service to teens means turning the computer around; rather than you being the information gatekeeper, be the guide. Once you share your knowledge about how to find the library's resources, then teens will know how to use them when you are not available or when they are at home, online, navigating the catalog or database alone.

CD See Tool 42. Teen Secret Shopper Behavior Checklist

The best way to determine if you're getting it right is to ask teens who spend time in your library.

CD See Tool 33. Teen Comment Card

Finally, services need to be, as the list's mnemonic spells out, QUICK. Teens have always had little patience, and if possible, they will have even less in the future. You must adapt or be left behind.

What Does an Ideal Reference Transaction with a Teen Look Like?

Every reference transaction is about solving a problem: "I need three books about..." or "I need to find who did..." or "Can you help me find this article about..." This is library services 101. What staff who are not familiar with teens may not know is that every teen reference transaction is just as much about finding the answer as it is about validating a teen emotionally. Teens are stars in their own movies, and a reference transaction is just another scene. They can come out of it feeling good about themselves because they solved their problem and someone treated them with courtesy and respect *or* they can exit the scene with their problem intact and feeling bad about themselves and the quality of service they received.

We have bricks (what teens want) and we have mortar (what LSTs need to do), so let's build a house of reference. Drawing on YALSA's vision for exemplary reference to teens,[4] the measurement of a quality teen service relates to how well it accomplishes the following:

- Responds to teens
- Respects teens as individuals
- Readies teens as they move from being children to adults
- Reaches out to the community
- Reaches in to involve everyone on the staff
- Reacts to changes
- Involves youth in the library
- Resists efforts to restrict access
- Advocates for equality for youth
- Creates raving fans

What Are the Elements of Success When It Comes to Teen Reference?

If reference for teens embraces the QUICK model, then what does it look like at the desk? Let's translate these values into actions, or elements of success:

- Always let teen customers know what good service they are getting. This is more than knowledge sharing; this is making sure that teens understand the nature of your work but also how that work revolves around them. This is not just about information service; this is more about marketing—not flyers or posters, but real one-on-one customer building. And it's not just about the new or "special stuff"—the majority of teens have *no idea* about the library's core services. Surveys and focus groups of teens in several large library systems found that teens don't know they can renew books online, ask e-mail reference questions, access databases and interlibrary loan, or even reserve books. Think in your own life about being at a dinner party or family gathering and then sharing a story about some strange telephone reference question, only to have someone be amazed that libraries offer such services. Circulating a flyer about a new chat reference service doesn't do much when you have not done a good job helping teens who visit and don't visit libraries understand what good in-person services you offer. Every transaction with a teen should end with an offer to do one more thing, provide one more service now or in the future.

- Always offer short-term (come back if this doesn't help) and long-term (see me again when you have another paper due) follow-up. If building assets is about relationship building, then we need to rethink the reference transaction as a relationship. Sometimes it lasts 30 seconds, sometimes three minutes, and sometimes longer. Regardless, the onus is on library staff to invite the teen customer to continue the relationship—a business card, a bookmark with the library's phone number, or whatever other collateral can serve to underscore the most basic points: "Thanks for coming; please come back." And we do this not only for teen customers (and their friends) but also for ourselves. Most of us don't get raises or administrative praise for the good service we give kids, so let's start asking for something better: real success stories from teens about the impact of our services. When kids tell you they are working on a paper, invite them to tell you the results. When they check out a book, invite them to tell you if they liked it. It is not research, but getting teens to tell these stories that will help you build anecdotal evidence documenting your effect on creating positive outcomes.

- Always find a way to say yes, always find a way to agree, and, whenever possible, demonstrate your competence. Teens are most disgusted with the number of rules libraries impose, all of them about limits and saying no. While every institution needs policies to function, you should be bound to results for teen customers more than anything else. Look for ways to say yes in everything you do: from signs that tell teens what they *can* do at a library rather than the laundry list of prohibitions, to making sure reference questions are, within limits of common sense, answered with the affirmative. There might be a "but" or "however," but answering a question with a negative to teens shuts down the conversation.

- Always show teens you know stuff—most act impressed rather than intimidated by your knowledge. And by the same token,

> You don't need to know the answer to every question; you just need to know how to find the answer. More important, you need to know how to teach a teen to find the answer.

don't be afraid; ask teens to show you the stuff that they know. Whether it is how to do something on a computer, to a shared pop culture obsession, to, more than likely, a common reading interest, teens are interested in what the adults in their lives know.

- Always be sensitive to a teen's sense of space, in terms of eye contact, body language, and other nonverbal cues. Two sub-rules: Never take the mouse or keyboard away from a teenager working on the computer; you always have to let them drive. When you drive, it sends the nonverbal message that they are not competent, and, besides, they are less likely to learn whatever it is you want to show or teach them. Never ever say, "Well, if you would have come in earlier" to any customer, let alone a teen. They know that; you don't need to remind them. Help them first, and then tell them you will help them even more when they visit again if they provide you with more time to do so.

- Always listen, learn, and then ask open-ended questions. All librarians complain about not getting information from teachers about assignments, but simply by listening to teens ask us information requests we can learn a great deal. While you should be careful never to ask "why" a teen is requesting information (because it is none of your business and this knowledge doesn't really help you do your job), when a teen volunteers that it is assignment related, use that opening. Gather information: What school? Who is the teacher? When is it due? etc. Create digital content, create pathfinders, and send them to the teachers. Most of all, consider the collection development applications (teachers rarely change their assignments; more kids will be in next year looking for the same stuff at the same time).

- Always be prepared to do triage reference when working with several teens at one time. Just as teens are great multitaskers, those of us doing reference with them must have this ability as well. Get teens started, invite them to work with one another, and be visible offering follow-up assistance—all are keys to successful triage. But just as important is prevention. If you are greeting teens when they show up or engaging them soon after they sit down at a computer, you are allowing them to use your services before they get frustrated with the open-ended Google search. Information literacy instruction is the best prevention of all.

- Always be empathetic, stay relaxed, and maintain a sense of humor. You were a teenager once. Remember that experience, accept that teens behave a certain way, and then project that it's a 15-year-old version of you standing on the other side of that desk. This is simply the golden rule in work clothes.

- Always "reward" the teen customer through encouragement, positive reinforcement, politeness, kindness, and by saying yes. The research on positive reinforcement of teenagers is pretty amazing; just saying thank you to teens so unaccustomed to getting that from adults outside of their family is big stuff. Just imagine what services to teens would look like and what "problems" would be avoided if every library staff member simply took the time to sincerely thank teenagers for visiting libraries.

- Always think of every reference transaction as a moment of truth; the success or failure of it will perhaps determine if your teen customer is coming back again. This is now truer than ever as teens do have other options for gathering information and getting help. If you want to create users for life, then you need to make an impact. You need to prove your value every day in every way that libraries matter. You do this by simply reflecting to teens the knowledge that they matter to you.

You must be proactive in doing reference to combat the problem of teens who will not take one step toward a reference desk at all. Some don't ask for help because they want to do it for themselves. Others think they should do it themselves and won't seek assistance. Then there is plain old fear; they are unsure of what/whom to ask, so it's easier not to bother. Whatever the reason, it is safe to say that a large percentage of teens who use libraries do so without seeking assistance.

Reference service to teens requires all the same skills and techniques used with other patrons. In particular with teens, the developmental tasks play a huge role. The self-consciousness of teens is a major barrier—after all, a reference question is admitting that you don't know the answer, and no one likes that, least of all teens.

By utilizing the techniques of customer service, by adopting a proactive posture, and by integrating a customer-centered/problem-solving focus, reference services to teens will create raving fans. But more than that, YA reference can create winning staff. Good customer service solves problems and creates good feelings for patrons, and it is also rewarding for the providers of the service.

What Are the Best Methods for Doing Readers' Advisory Work with Teens?

We would argue that there is only one method for doing successful readers' advisory work with teens, and we're sure this will not be shocking to any of you: You must read the books that teens read. In every area of the library, success is based on your command of the content, from genealogy in the history center to picture books in the children's library. It is incredible for anyone to think that they can connect teens with books when they haven't read these books themselves. The simple fact is that the LSTs who are the most successful at conducting readers' advisory for teens are the ones who read the books teens read.

Plenty of available data (including the 2008 Teen Reading Habits and Perceptions Survey mentioned in the next chapter) let us know that we are not the first place teens turn to for advice about what to read, but maybe this would begin to change if more LSTs and other library staff

> Providing excellent customer service to teens is not just your job; it's the job of everyone who works in a library. Share the information in this chapter with your colleagues and your manager because how your library treats teens must be modeled from the top down.

members made it a point to read more YA lit and engage teens in conversations about books. Unfortunately, most libraries operate in a useless cycle when it comes to readers' advisory for teens: Because teens don't ask us, we don't do it enough. Because we don't do it enough, we can't or don't keep up on the literature. Because we don't read it, we don't feel comfortable recommending titles, or, worse, we end up giving bad advice. Finally, one of the biggest reasons library staff are unable to deliver effective readers' advisory to teens is lack of training. This usually manifests itself in the form of staff making asinine reading suggestions due in large part to their prejudices about what teens should read as opposed to what they want to read. Back to the QUICK model of service—delivering readers' advisory to teens is a perfect opportunity for you to learn to be more customer centered, doing your homework in order to turn teens' needs into your needs.

How Do You Go About Delivering Customer-centered Readers' Advisory to Teens?

The thing to do in every readers' advisory relationship is to determine what the teen will respond to in a book. You do this by learning what they have responded to in the past. A common question, "Why did you like a book?," doesn't always work with teens. This may be because they didn't analyze their reaction to the book or because they don't understand what elements of the book they did like. A better method for drawing out the same information is simply to ask the teen to tell you about books they've read in the past. The answer to this question will likely give you a feel for the teen's taste, and then the teen can tell you what he or she liked, didn't like, what invoked a response, what was exciting, and what he or she remembers most about the book. Now you have a jumping-off point for connecting the reader with other books that may be of interest or cause a similar positive experience. This is the foundation of teen readers' advisory. The following suggestions build on this foundation:

- Don't wait for teens to come to you. Get out from behind the desk. Many teens do want help, but they just won't ask for it due to previous bad experiences or maybe just plain shyness. Your job is to go find them when they are browsing in the stacks.

- For nonreaders, or teens whose only reading are the books assigned and despised in school, asking about reading response isn't going to work. Get creative and ask about magazines, movies, or television shows—anything that will give you an idea about what interests this teen.

- Develop your own core collection. Take some time to develop a core list of authors and/or titles you know are popular. Learn the names of at least three mystery authors you can always recommend; three of the most popular urban lit series, three hot manga series, three "short" books that can pull in a reluctant reader, etc.

- Ask questions to help you narrow the field. Do they care if the main character is a boy or girl? Do they want it to feature older characters or younger? Does the race of the characters matter? Do they want a scary or a funny book? Do they want first person or third person? Hardback or paperback? Rural or urban? Even if you can't suggest specific books that meet all of these criteria, you can help teens develop an idea of what they are looking for and then maybe together you can find something that is a close match.

- Eliminate. A lot of teens are inarticulate, so ask them what they don't want. Use what they say as a checklist to help pick a book they *do* want.

- Use the books. If you have discovered something they have read before, find it and examine it. Many paperback publishers include an "If you liked this book, then try…" ad on the back of the book. Some popular series books list the next couple of books in the series. Many books published under the same imprint (like Kimani Tru) will recommend other titles similar in nature on the back of the books.

- Be smart. If teens haven't expressed a real interest in reading and have told you they have a book report due tomorrow, then set Moby Dick aside. There is nothing wrong with asking if they want a "thin one," but make sure you and the teens understand that thin doesn't always mean easy.

- Be aware. You need to be very sensitive to how teens are reacting to you. If they are kind of quiet, then you should stay low key. This may be their first interaction with a librarian, and we don't want to scare them off. Remember to let their opinions drive your suggestions.

- Things not to say include "I loved [gush gush gush] this book" *or* "I loved this book in school" *or* "My son/daughter loved this book" *or* "Many schools have this book on their summer reading list" *or* "Teachers often recommend this book" *or* "Everyone should read this book."

- Find a fit. If possible you always want to avoid stereotyping. While it is true that teens' clothing, hair, and manner do say something about their identity and possibly their reading tastes, this is not always the case. Just because a Goth teen is dressed all in black doesn't mean he or she wants to read *Sweetblood* by Pete Hautman. Also be careful not to stereotype and hand a person of color any book by an African-American author or a rather effeminate young man a copy of *Rainbow High*. These teens may want these books, but let them lead you by offering information rather than your making assumptions based on their appearances.

- Aim high rather than lower. You will immediately lose whatever minimal credibility you have by suggesting a book that is below the teens' reading levels or tastes. As a rule, figure most teens want to read about kids one to two years older ("anticipatory reading" if you are looking for a smarty-pants term). Thus, your high school juniors/seniors want recommendations out of the adult collection, not "YA kid stuff."

- No advice can be the best advice. If you cannot really peg the teens or nothing comes to mind when they are describing what they are looking for, just admit it. Remember a lot of teens get turned off because they get bad advice rather than no advice at all. The worst thing you can do is suggest the wrong book. If you just can't get a good read, suggest several titles rather than just one, and leave the teens alone to decide. Always make sure you remind teens that you're just picking out books they might be interested in and they are free to take one, several, all, or none at all—it won't hurt your feelings if they leave whatever they are not interested in behind.

- Suggest without request. Sometimes people are just browsing, and they don't want or need help. Not every teen in the library needs your help. What matters is simply that teens know you're around if they do find themselves in need of help.

- Suggest based on a relationship. Once you begin developing relationships with teens who frequent your library, you can begin honing that "book relationship"—you know, the one where you read things they like and they read things you suggest; you make suggestions and ask for feedback the next time they drop by to chat. Once you know your readers, you can always keep an eye out for new things that may be of interest to them.

- Suggest by parent's request. Many times it is Mom who has come in to pick up something for her nonreading son, hoping (again) to find that one book that will hook him. Every teen area should have a print bookmark about YALSA's annual "Quick Picks for Reluctant Readers" reading list for an occasion just like this. If the teen is there with the parent, as with the reference interview, you want to try to get the teen away from the parent long enough to gather information without parental commentary. You want to find out what the teen wants to read, not what the parent thinks the teen should read.

- Use the tools you have at your disposal. These might include readers' advisory databases (like NoveList), recommended reading Web sites created and maintained by librarians (like readingrants.com), suggested reading lists for specific genres (like YALSA's "Great Graphic Novels for Teens" list), thematic reading lists (like YALSA's "Popular Paperbacks" list), Web sites where teens review books (like Flamingnet.com), retail sites where teens can create suggested reading lists (like Amazon.com), collection development books published each year that focus on popular genres for teens (like *Hooked on Horror III*), or professional books that recommend a wide variety of books (like *Best Books for High School Readers, Grades 9–12*).

- Talk to teens. Approach teens you know are avid readers and get input from them about what is good and why they liked it. Listen in on conversation in the stacks, ask opinions, and gather information from readers. Always ask teens what they are reading and get them to tell you the story.

- Use statistics. Do periodic checks about what YA titles have holds and/or are circulating the most, then buy more copies.

Is Customer Service with Teens Really That Bad?

All of these elements of success about reference and readers' advisory are necessary because the perception, among many youth advocates, is that frontline staff still don't "get it." Consider this scenario, originally created by Jim Rosinia and Mary K. Chelton for *Bare Bones*,[5] which we've added to and updated to reflect teens today:

It is 5:45 p.m., 15 minutes before closing after a busy Saturday. At the reference desk is seated the librarian who has been on the desk all day answering one demanding reference question after another. She feels as if she has been slowly nibbled to death by ducks. She is taking the lull to read a professional journal. Meanwhile at a nearby computer terminal, a teen has been using the computer, unsuccessfully, for the past 30 minutes, thus the librarian has been listening to an incessant beeping sound for some time when finally she says:

LIBRARIAN: That's not a toy.

TEEN: I'm using it.

LIBRARIAN: Well, it sounds to me like you are just playing with it. Why don't you take a seat and get to work.

TEEN: (*Walks toward her.*) Um, so like, where are the scary books?

LIBRARIAN: (*Sighs.*) The library does not house a collection of scary books. Do you mean horror novels?

TEEN: Yes, like Stephen King, like that.

LIBRARIAN: Well (*sighs*), as you should know by now, works of fiction are shelved alphabetically by the last name of the author. These materials are located in the last few ranges of shelving which follows the end of the nonfiction area.

TEEN: Whatever. (*Leaves, then comes back.*) I couldn't find anything.

LIBRARIAN: Stephen King writes fiction, right?

TEEN: I think so.

LIBRARIAN: Do you know what letter his last name begins with?

TEEN: K.

LIBRARIAN: Well (*sighs*), then they should be in fiction under K, which is where I just sent you to look. (*Turns to keyboard.*) Are you looking for a particular book by King?

TEEN: No, I have read all of his.

LIBRARIAN: (*Sighs.*) Well, then what is it you need? I have people waiting on the phone.

TEEN: I want a book like his. Aren't all the horror books together?

LIBRARIAN: No, as I've told you, fiction is shelved alphabetically by author unless it is a story collection, then it may be shelved by the editor or the title or in the 800s.

TEEN: I just need a scary book.

LIBRARIAN: Then look under the names of other authors. Don't you know the names of any other authors?

TEEN: No.

LIBRARIAN: Well, there are some bibliographies of horror literature housed in the reference area at the call number 809.092. You should check there.

TEEN: Bibliography? I don't need a book about his life; I just gotta have a book he wrote for tomorrow.

LIBRARIAN: No, not a biography, a bibliography, a collection of citations grouped by subject. (*Sighs.*) Wait a minute. Is this for school or for yourself?

TEEN: No, it's for this stupid assignment in junior English.

LIBRARIAN: In that case, you should read Bram Stoker, Henry James, Edgar Allan Poe, or one of the classic writers in the genre rather than trash like Stephen King.

TEEN: We had to read a story by that Poe guy in class. I didn't get into it at all; it was so boring and there were no monsters or vampires. We can read anything, so do you have a book written by somebody who is alive now?

LIBRARIAN: Well (*sighs*), does it have to be horror?

TEEN: It doesn't have to be; that is just what I signed up for. Don't you have any ideas?

LIBRARIAN: Just a moment. (*Stands, walks out to a table.*) Listen up. There are too many of you at this table and there is far too much talking going on here. You should get to work. This is a library and you must be quiet. If I have to warn you again, I will call the police. (*Returns and sits back down.*) Still don't know the name of a book you want? I can't look it up in the computer unless you know the name.

TEEN: But I don't know any other authors!

LIBRARIAN: Well (*sighs*), then you will just have to go looking through that paperback fiction collection in the children's area. It is just past the charge desk.

TEEN: Where?

LIBRARIAN: (*Points.*) Past the circulation desk.

TEEN: Where?

LIBRARIAN: (*Points again, puts head back in magazine, raises voice.*) Over there.

TEEN: Oh, you mean the front desk. (*Leaves, returns with a copy of* Rosemary's Baby.) Hey, I found this one; it sounds neat. The lady lives with all these Satan worshipers.

LIBRARIAN: (*Interrupts.*) Good. We are closing so you need to check that out now.

TEEN: But I need to a find a book about devil worship.

LIBRARIAN: Didn't you just find one?

TEEN: I need two books for tomorrow: one story and another one about my subject.

LIBRARIAN: So you need a nonfiction work on demonology in addition to contemporary imaginative work from the horror genre?

TEEN: I have no idea what you just said.

LIBRARIAN: Well go look at 974 and be quick about it!

TEEN: (*Leaves; returns.*) There is nothing there.

LIBRARIAN: Well, we just don't have enough books for all you students. Don't you have a school library? All the books must be in circulation or on a hold list.

TEEN: What?

LIBRARIAN: They're all out.

TEEN: Don't you have anything else?

LIBRARIAN: Well (*sighs*), I have these reference books behind the desk; you can use them here and I need ID. And we turn off the copy machine five minutes before closing. You must have exact change.

TEEN: (*Starts behind desk.*) So I take these home? (*Picks up a book.*)

LIBRARIAN: (*Rips out of his hands.*) No! These are reference books. They are noncirculating for use in the library only!

TEEN: What am I gonna do?

LIBRARIAN: Those are the rules. Next time, you should come in earlier.

TEEN: Forget it.

This scenario is a case study in how not to do reference. It takes every positive trait and turns it on its head. Rather than solving the teen's information problem, the librarian is compounding it. The teen isn't leaving with good feelings, nor could one imagine the librarian in this scenario feeling positive about his or her work. If this book is loaded with "to do" lists, consider this scenario the jumping-off point for the "not to do" list. Do not be:

- Immobile
- Intrusive
- Jargon filled
- Judgmental
- Preaching
- Rude
- Unapproachable
- Uninformed
- Uninterested

It does no good whatsoever for a library to employ a high-energy and highly effective teen librarian only to have other staff commit these cardinal sins. Other than trying to do everything themselves (and burning out, thus helping no one), LSTs have three separate paths to pursue to improve customer service in libraries. Two involve training: training our users to become information literate and thus not dependent on libraries, and training staff about teens and customer services so they "get it." The third involves acting as role model, mentor, and coach for other staff. While classroom training and online tutorials are fine, the literature on tutoring is robust, demonstrating that best practices are handed down more through informal one-on-one relationships than through training manuals . . . even how-to-do-it manuals. Don't just mentor youth—mentor adults to better work with youth.

How Do We Train Other Staff to Provide Quality Customer Service to Teens?

Some of the skills and traits described in the beginning of this chapter that define an ideal LST are the same skills and traits your colleagues need to work better and more efficiently with teens: initiative, ability to build and maintain relationships with adults and teens, and understanding organizational culture.

To begin training, spend a few days or weeks observing areas where your library's staff struggle the most in serving teens. Talk with staff about frustrating interactions with teens, make a list of common complaints staff have about working with teens, and devise a simple training with your library's human resources department, using this book as a guide to address these issues. You can also develop information sheets about adolescent development to help staff who have little or no experience working with teens understand better what teens need and why serving them in developmentally appropriate ways matters. You can also work with your human resources department to weave sections about working with teens into existing trainings already being offered to library staff, especially those that focus on general customer service, reference, and readers' advisory. Finally, recruit colleagues who already have a YAttitude to help you model teen-friendly behavior day in and day out in your library so that all staff can see teen-oriented library services in action. Following is more information about some of these ideas as well as other ideas to help you develop an entire library staff of teen fans:

- **Model behavior for your colleagues.** This takes guts, patience, and tenacity because not everyone will be interested in your suggestions. However, it is important—especially for those staff members who are on the fence or who are interested in providing great services to teens but just don't have the skills, experience, or instinct. It is up to you to fill in the blanks for them. Talk with your manager about strategies. Perhaps he or she can schedule you to work with staff who need help but do not regularly come into contact with you during the workday. Or maybe he or she can set up a system of shadowing you for a day.

- **Find your allies.** There are people in your library who like teens, enjoy working with them, and are good at serving them. They may never speak up until you approach them, and then you may discover some undercover LSTs.

- **Get others reading YA lit.** Start a teen book club for staff or display a recommended teen book in the library's break room each week. The more staff read titles they can recommend, the more competent they will feel providing readers' advisory to teens, thereby increasing opportunities for them to develop meaningful relationships with teens. When you witness your colleagues reading a teen book or interacting successfully with a patron, take a minute to thank them for being a part of the solution.

- **Incorporate discussion about teen services into regular staff meetings and daily library life.** This can be as simple as posting an article from *VOYA* or as time intensive as creating a newsletter about teen services for staff. What matters is that library services for teens becomes a topic of discussion around the water cooler, in the break room, and behind the desk when staff are chatting as they get ready to shut down. Too often the only things staff hear about teens are negative. Be the one to change this by interjecting positive anecdotes about teens in the library into everyday conversations with your colleagues.

- **Connect with other LSTs in your area.** Anyone from a library more than 20 miles from your own is an expert. Talk with them to get ideas, but also have them come in to help with training; the cost is less, they are more flexible, and they know the area and perhaps the teens better than a trainer from hundreds of miles away.

- **Hire an expert.** There are YALSA trainers all over the United States who travel and train library staff on all facets of serving teens. These trainers are LSTs who are working with teens every day in their own libraries, face similar issues, and can address the challenges your staff encounter with practical solutions gained from experience. They are also skilled at dealing with resistant staff and are able to address issues head on since they will be leaving the state hours after their presentation. Public shaming might be too harsh a word, but an outside presenter can shine the light on poor service, poor behavior, and bad habits better than anyone. To obtain a list of trainers contact the YALSA office at 1-800-545-2433, x4390, or via e-mail at yalsa@ala.org.

Conclusion

We run into adults every day who are amazed at the services and programs we make available to teens today that were not available to them when they were growing up. They are always appreciative and, we think, secretly resentful. We call this the "Kids today have it so much better than I had it" syndrome. The conversation we rarely have with these adults is whether how we treat teens in libraries today is any better than it was 15, 20, or 30 years ago. Yes, we do more for teens in libraries today in terms of programming and materials, but sadly the way teens are often treated in libraries has not changed much in the past few decades.

Of course, we talk in generalizations. Library staff in buildings all across the country today go out of their way to consistently offer the highest quality of customer service to young people. Unfortunately this is not consistent; it isn't everyone and it isn't everywhere, and this is the problem. We all know teens who have benefited from great customer service in their local library. Sadly, this is not the majority of teens who patronize libraries daily throughout the country. The greatest tragedy is that we will never know how many teens enter our libraries looking for help and walk away with a distaste in their mouth that often lingers permanently, or at least until they return to libraries in adulthood to bring back their own toddlers for story time.

We have daily opportunities to add value to the lives' of teens. We add value through customer service, and we do this by speaking to the core needs of our teen customers. Customer service for teens will succeed when it provides teens with opportunities for independence, excitement, identity, and acceptance.

Sources Cited in This Chapter

1. Marston, Judy. 2001. "Narrative Summary Report of Teen Focus Groups for the Young Adult Services Program." California State Library. Available: www .library.ca.gov/lds/docs/Metareport_12-021.pdf (accessed January 12, 2009).
2. Focus groups held at Johnson County Library, Overland Park Kansas, February 26, 2008.
3. Zollo, Peter. 1999. *Wise Up to Teens: Insights into Marketing and Advertising to Teenagers.* Ithaca, NY: New Strategist Publications.
4. Jones, Patrick. 2000. "Sample Reference Services Program." Young Adult Library Services Association. Available: www.ala.org/ala/mgrps/divs/ yalsa/yalsamemonly/yalsamounder/yalsamotopics/reference.pdf (accessed January 13, 2009).
5. Chelton, Mary K., and Jim Rosinia. 1993. *Bare Bones: Young Adult Services, Tips for Public Library Generalists.* Chicago: American Library Association.

Recommended Sources for Further Reading

Bernstein, Mark P. 2008. "Am I Obsolete? How Customer Service Principles Ensure the Library's Relevance." *AALL Spectrum* 13, no. 2 (November): 20–22.

Brehm-Heeger, Paula. 2007. "Better Late Than Never." *School Library Journal* 53, no. 2 (February): 30.

Brehm-Heeger, Paula. 2008. "Blurring the Lines." *School Library Journal* 54, no. 10 (October): 29.

Casey, Michael, and Michael Stephens. 2008. "The Transparent Library Embracing Service to Teens." *Library Journal* (May 15): 28.

Dresang, Eliza T., Melissa Gross, and Leslie Edmonds Holt. 2006. *Dynamic Youth Services Through Outcome-Based Planning and Evaluation.* Chicago: ALA Editions.

Flower, Sarah. 2008. "Guidelines for Library Services to Teens." *Young Adult Library Services* 6, no. 3 (Spring): 4–7.

Gilton, Donna L. 2008. "Information Literacy as a Department Store: Applications for Public Teen Librarians." *Young Adult Library Services* 6, no. 2 (Winter): 39–44.

Todaro, Julie Beth, and Mark L. Smith. 2006. *Training Library Staff and Volunteers to Provide Extraordinary Customer Service.* New York: Neal-Schuman.

Vilelle, Luke, and Christopher C. Peters. 2008. "Don't Shelve the Questions: Defining Good Customer Service for Shelvers." *Reference & User Services Quarterly* 48, no. 1 (Fall): 60–67.

Information Literacy

Michael Giller

We've all been there—a teenager needs to finish a research paper *today*. It's Sunday afternoon in the library and her father's eyes are glazing over as he watches his daughter struggle to find information and meet the requirements of her physics assignment. You know exactly where to go for the journal articles and books she needs (you have been helping students all week with this assignment). One side of you wants to pull all of the resources together neatly and exhibit your awesomeness, emerging as a hero in the eyes of a parent and teen. The other side of you knows you will always be doing this for people if they do not have basic information literacy skills to function fluently in their lives. The bottom line is this: There is a time for handholding service in the library and there is a time to step up and teach teens how to use the library's resources. Most interactions with teens are moments when LSTs should step up to teach and model the appropriate skills that information-literate adults possess. Whether it is locating materials in the library catalog, using an index, navigating the Web, or finding specialized data on subscription databases, LSTs must embrace this role.

For LSTs—and all librarians for that matter—promoting and developing information literacy skills should be the foundation of everything that we do. Whether in a school or public library, interacting with teens provides limitless opportunities to develop information literacy skills and these opportunities must be seized at every chance. If not promoting these skills, LSTs are not fully serving the needs of teens.

What Is Information Literacy?

Though numerous people and organizations define information literacy, the simple "ability to find and use information"[1] is no longer sufficient. Since the 1998 publication of *Information Power*, AASL has recognized the difficulty of defining information literacy and has incorporated multiple literacies as crucial skills for the new century. The *Standards for the*

It is every LST's responsibility to provide teens with opportunities to develop their information literacy skills, whether you work in a school library or a public library.

Information literacy is not library instruction. Instead, information literacy focuses on youth learning as a process for solving information problems. It is youth development in action; we are working with teens to accomplish these goals.

21st-Century Learner[2] include digital, visual, textual, and technological literacy skills as necessary tools for successful lifelong learning.

Even before teens were raised with Internet access, the *Presidential Committee on Information Literacy: Final Report* defined information literacy as the ability to "recognize when information is needed and have the ability to locate, evaluate, and use effectively the needed information."[3] This means that information-literate teens should know the following:

- When and to what extent information is needed
- How to locate the information they need
- How to evaluate information
- How to evaluate sources of information
- How to synthesize and incorporate information
- Legal and ethical practices in the use of this information.

Why Is It Important for Teens to Be Information Literate?

Teenagers must develop information literacy skills to be successful lifelong learners. While they struggle to become independent and look ahead at life beyond high school, they are making decisions that affect their futures. Some will go to a university, while others will attend junior colleges or vocational schools, join the military, or begin working. However, they all have the same need to find information throughout their lives, and it's your job to guide them.

As LSTs, it is not enough to provide access to online databases, selected Internet sites, and an array of print and audiovisual items. We must provide the skills and resources teens need to become independent successful researchers. The teens that you serve must know how to use and apply these resources to their lives. Your goal is to take every opportunity to guide them in this process; these skills are similar to a student's ability to write a paragraph or solve a mathematical equation in that they are skills that must be learned.

Just as information literacy skills are learned, they are also measured. Are LSTs successfully teaching information literacy skills to teens who will carry them through adulthood? If you look to where many teens end up—college—you will see a void that many universities, junior colleges, and vocational schools are trying to fill. Required classes and programs to educate incoming students about the library and its resources (in an attempt to teach students to effectively find information and use it ethically) are popping up all over the nation. Some programs may be as informal as the library Web site offering online tutorials on how to use the catalog, databases, and various citation styles. While these programs are offered in part because available information changes rapidly in our society, most were initiated because increasing numbers of incoming students do not possess the basic information literacy skills required to be successful learners. This is where LSTs in school and public libraries must pick up the slack and prepare these teens for meaningful and productive futures.

What Are the Information Literacy Standards?

To work effectively within the information literacy movement, LSTs should understand certain standards to have a clear idea of what constitutes an information-literate teen:

- *Information Literacy Standards for Student Learning* (AASL/ AECT)
- *Standards for the 21st-Century Learner* (AASL)
- *Information Literacy Competency Standards for Higher Education* (ACRL)
- *National Education Technology Standards* (NETS)

The standards will continue to evolve as technology and educational theory changes. A thorough understanding helps guide LSTs to develop specific skills, resources, tools, and measurements that will support teens in becoming information literate.

The *Information Literacy Standards for Student Learning*, developed by the American Association of School Librarians (AASL) and the Association for Educational Communications and Technology (AECT), created the foundation for information literacy and learning standards for library media specialists that all LSTs can adopt. Nine standards in three categories are described with 29 indicators. Although only the first three standards are categorized as information literacy, the other two categories of "independent learning" and "social responsibility" are aspects of student learning that directly correlate to information literacy.

The *Standards for the 21st-Century Learner*, also developed by AASL, emphasize reading as the foundational skill for learning, personal growth, and enjoyment because the ability to read is the cornerstone of lifelong learning skills. These learning standards incorporate multiple literacies and are consolidated into four categories that require learners to use skills, resources, and tools to

1. inquire, think critically, and gain knowledge;
2. draw conclusions, make informed decisions, apply knowledge to new situations, and create new knowledge;
3. share knowledge and participate ethically and productively as members of our democratic society; and
4. pursue personal and aesthetic growth.

These standards augment, update, and expand those published in *Information Power: Building Partnerships for Learning*. Beyond defining the skills, these standards include dispositions in action, responsibilities, and self-assessment strategies required of teens to be information literate with specific criteria for each area.

Information Literacy Competency Standards for Higher Education, developed by the Association of College and Research Libraries (ACRL), provide the framework for higher-level skills. At the college level, students are expected to manipulate an array of resources and media to further their understanding of academic subjects. The mission of higher education institutions is the same as AASL's, which is to develop lifelong learners. These standards are not in competition with the AASL standards but rather extend the levels of competencies expected beyond secondary school. The *Information Literacy Competency Standards for Higher Education* provides five standards of competencies and 22 performance indicators. Information literacy skills at the university level should be developed by LSTs so that there is a clear understanding of what is expected of college-bound teens.

Teens cannot be considered information literate in the modern world without exhibiting core competencies in technology. This is acknowledged in both AASL's and ACRL's information literacy standards. LSTs should become familiar with the *National Education Technology Standards* (NETS), developed by the International Society for Technology in Education (ISTE).[4] These six standards address the following:

1. Creativity and innovation
2. Communication and collaboration
3. Research and information fluency
4. Critical thinking, problem solving, and decision making
5. Digital citizenship
6. Technology operations and concepts

The ISTE standards complement the AASL and ACRL standards and give LSTs a framework to use in incorporating technology skills within information literacy instruction.

How Do You Incorporate the Information Literacy Standards into Practice with Teens?

The standards exist to provide the philosophical framework that guides your information literacy instruction and can be used in your formal and informal instruction. All of the standards and competencies include indicators to support them, and by identifying desired outcomes you can develop each competency. Using these indicators, LSTs can increase information literacy by focusing on specific areas of weakness they identify in teens in their community. But the standards and indicators aren't just for LSTs and teachers. Teens need to be aware of the competencies required so that they can understand how to approach and solve information-seeking problems. Ideally, they should develop a conscious approach to their research. Having an awareness of competencies and indicators is a critical component to deepening their understanding.

Quality library instruction to teens naturally incorporates the standards. The best way is to slide your instruction in "under the radar." You'll be surprised how even the most informal interactions build information literacy skills and address competency standards. For example, a teen comes into the library and wants to know whether the library has any Old 97's CDs in the music collection. She is also eager to find more alternative country bands that the library owns. In this teachable moment you walk her over to the catalog and teach her to (1) search the title and subject headings of catalog records and (2) limit searching by material type for compact discs. By doing so, you address Standard 4 (pursue personal and aesthetic growth) of the *Standards for the 21st-Century Learner*:

- Listen for pleasure (4.1.1)
- Connect ideas to own interests (4.1.5)
- Organize personal knowledge (4.1.6)
- Demonstrate motivation (4.2.2)
- Seek opportunities for personal growth (4.3.3)
- Identify areas of interest (4.4.1)
- Recognize limits of personal knowledge (4.4.2)

Labeling information literacy instruction with specific standards allows you to evaluate your instruction. You may discover that you are teaching skills that address some standards too often, while other skills and standards are neglected, and can therefore focus your interactions with teens to improve their weaker skills.

The information literacy standards are not just for school librarians to understand, and LSTs in the public library should use them to teach the teens they serve. Educators have been forced to deal with standards to improve student performance. When you can "talk the talk" of school library media specialists and teachers and intelligently discuss how a collaborative program may help student achievement by addressing specific standards, you will have a much more likely chance of receiving a positive reception and partner in your programs. It is also a sign of respect to school library media specialists and teachers because you are taking the time to understand their curriculum and develop areas of learning for the students whom they teach daily. Perhaps the information literacy program idea you bring to them is not what their students need and you have to adjust the goals and lessons—that's okay. By not focusing solely on your program, your numbers, and your ideas but rather on what the students need to succeed in school, you can build better relationships with school library media specialists and teachers.

Partnerships between school and public libraries reinforce the common goal of creating lifelong learners.

Why Is Teacher/Librarian Collaboration So Important in Developing Information Literacy Programs?

It is important for teachers and LSTs to work collaboratively to build teens' information literacy skills because these skills are applied in their coursework. But what assignments require critical thinking and more sophisticated research skills? Only the teachers know the answer to that question, which is why collaboration is a critical component in developing information literacy. School library media specialists may have access to teens all day in the library media center, but without a context to teach information literacy skills the lessons will have no meaning. Collaborating with teachers is the only way you're going to build information literacy skills in teens because it can directly relate to an assignment, project, or real need.

The information literacy movement is a collective effort, and collaboration allows LSTs to gain a better understanding of teens' lives outside the library. For many LSTs, it is a real eye-opener when they see first-hand what teens go through daily, walking the same public school hallways that students must navigate daily and working with the very teachers that instruct teens. When teens have the opportunity to see public library LSTs, school library media specialists, and teachers integrating lessons that collaboratively develop their information literacy skills, the value of these skills will be emphasized, reinforced, and relevant to their success.

How Do You Help Teens Solve an Information Problem?

Research is a *process*, and models have been developed to aid librarians and educators to teach this process. The models break down the key components of the information problem-solving process into stages that are labeled so that learners can identify where they are in the research process and in what direction they are headed. Using research models can help teens focus on learning new information literacy skills, much as the scientific process helps research scientists focus their research. Some models are linear while others are circular, but the models are designed so that students can start the process over and over again until their research is complete. LSTs should become familiar with research process models because they can help guide your instruction and align lessons with information literacy standards. One of the most popular research models used in high schools is Eisenberg and Berkowitz's *The Big6 in Secondary Schools*. This book aligns information problem solving with AASL's information literacy standards so that LSTs can identify the standards they are addressing with each step of the information problem-solving process. The process of the Big6 includes the following:

1. Task definition
2. Information-seeking strategies
3. Location and access
4. Information use
5. Synthesis
6. Evaluation

In addition to the Big6, Eisenberg and Berkowitz chart other excellent models, for example, the Nine Step Information Skills (Anne Irving) and the Research Process (Barbara Stripling and Judy Pitts).[5] Models that break away from a linear approach include the Circular Model (David Loertscher)[6] and the Research Cycle (Jamie McKenzie).[7]

Take time to review different research process models before trying one out. You will immediately notice that they all feature similar components and can align with the information literacy standards. Teens seeking information in the research process need to be able to identify an information need, determine where to get the information, find the information, and use the information. In addition they must synthesize, analyze, and interpret the information gathered, present the information (written, oral, audiovisual), and be able to evaluate and reflect on the experience. Because these models are so similar, they feature the same general components. LSTs can pick the one suited to their teaching style or their student needs. Better yet, use the different models and tweak them to create your own.

How Does the LST Integrate Information Problem-solving Processes in Everyday Interactions?

Look around any school library media center or public library and where do you find the teens? At computers on the Internet. Still one of the primary reasons that teens use the library, the Internet provides ample opportunities to build information literacy skills. As a starting point, LSTs can use the Internet to develop techniques that challenge teens to use critical-thinking skills in their daily life while pursuing their personal interests. The pursuit of "personal and aesthetic growth" is one of AASL's information literacy standards and incorporates social networks, reading for pleasure, organizing knowledge, and using creative formats for personal expression—all reasons why teenagers are using the library.

By interacting with teens as they operate independently in the library you will begin to create meaningful relationships with them. Use these relationships to increase their information literacy skills. This instruction does not need to be detailed and cumbersome. Ideally, teens will not even be aware that deliberate instruction is taking place. But every moment, your interaction can become a "teachable moment" in building information literacy skills.

One of the advantages of informal library instruction is that it is "one on one" and can occur at any time. Working with individual teens allows you the opportunity to pace yourself, change directions, and focus on fulfilling one need at a time. The best way for teens to acquire information literacy skills is to "learn and practice them in conjunction with course content."[8] In other words, they acquire them while applying information literacy skills to their academic or real-life needs. Tackling information literacy one teen at a time may seem daunting, but LSTs are exposed to countless opportunities to continually build skills should we choose to take them. Some examples of informal instruction in real-life scenarios follow:

- You notice a teen checking her MySpace page obsessively, personalizing it, and updating it regularly. She asks you for information about Mark Twain for a presentation coming due in her literature class. Show her how to access and search your library's subscription to the Biography Resource Center database. Explain what a subscription database is and how the editorial control makes it a reputable source, and teach her to cite the articles she accesses. Suggest that she create a MySpace page for her Mark Twain presentation to her literature class.

- A student is slumped over the computer, head in hands. He is searching for an article his geography teacher suggested he read but he cannot find it on the Internet. He has the journal name, article title, and author's name, but Google cannot produce the article. This is a great opportunity to show him your full-text periodical databases. Take the time to show him how to search for articles in the advanced searching module, using journal name, article title, and author. Explain to him the difference between a subscription database and generic Internet searches.

- Black History Month is approaching and you want to highlight your library's African-American resources. Have your Teen Advisory Board create a bibliography in the Modern Language Association format that includes books, music, films, databases, and Internet sites related to black history that you can publish on the library's Web site. Require them to use all media formats in order to collaboratively examine the collection.

- A teen asks if you have the book *Twilight*. Rather than checking the catalog at the desk and telling her if it's available, walk her over to the library catalog and conduct a title search. Explain to her what you are doing, why you are doing it, and how to tell whether an item is on the shelf or checked out. Be sure to walk her over to the book, casually explaining the general layout of the collection.

- A group of skateboarders—library regulars—are gathered around a computer loudly watching YouTube videos. Skateboarders have a reputation of being nonconformists because they are kicked out of the public places they try to skate and because of their clothing style and music preferences. Tap into their nonconformist attitudes and explain to them what Banned Books Week is about, what their First Amendment rights are, and how libraries try to protect their rights. Show them ALA's Banned Books Week Web site along with other sites about censorship. This is a good opportunity to ask them to help you create a school video for Banned Books Week that can go on YouTube. Give them a video camera, creative control, and ask them to create a video about how teens feel about censorship.

- You notice a student taking notes from Wikipedia and ask if he needs help with any research. He is trying to find literary criticism for the play *Angels in America* for his advanced placement English class and has conducted only a Google search. You tell him about e-books and show him your library's subscription to Drama for Students online. After finding a thorough entry he is happy but then panics because he doesn't have any money to pay for printing charges. You then show him how to e-mail the article and download it to a flash drive so that he can print it later.

Lengthier, casual informal instruction is a great time to work on building relationships with students. There will be gaps in time as you model search strategies and move from the catalog to print resources to online databases and the Internet. These gaps may only be a few seconds but they are great times to make connections to teens. Maybe you notice a Matador T-shirt they are wearing and begin discussing your favorite indie bands, or perhaps you see knitting needles in their backpack and talk about knitting sweaters with cool designs or stitches they haven't learned yet. A casual greeting to simply ask them how their day is going may lead to a short talk about their course work or college and will let them know you care. The point is that through these small moments you can begin to establish a relationship and let them know that there is more to the library—and you—than they might have considered.

Why Is Modeling So Important?

Modeling is exactly what it sounds like: emulating the process, behaviors, ethics, and attitudes of an information-literate adult. Every LST, whether in a school library or public library, should model as a teaching tactic. It is the easiest way to teach information literacy skills to anyone; good modeling effectively teaches new skills to teens while exhibiting best practices. After all, you're spending a lot of time building relationships with these teens; it only makes sense that you should emulate what you want them to become: productive, positive members of society who are information literate and lifelong learners.

Modeling means setting the example in all of your interactions with teens. You may observe teens in the library bootlegging music to download onto their iPods, but participating in such activities with them will nullify every lesson you ever have or ever will teach to them regarding plagiarism, the ethical use of information, copyright, or intellectual property—all things you should be teaching them in accordance with the information literacy standards. Modeling means being the adult and using your guidance in a way that will build their assets, not confuse them with mixed messages. Teens can quickly identify hypocrisy in adults, so don't take the easy way out and shrug off this responsibility.

How Is Technology a Component of Information Literacy?

Just reading any of the information literacy standards reveals that for students to meet the performance indicators they must be fluent in computer applications and technology. Technology is an essential part of using libraries, and computer skills are required to use the library catalog, online databases, digital archives, e-books, or Internet resources. So much information is only available using computers, either via the Internet or local networks, that information literacy in the twenty-first century is interwoven with computer literacy.

The National Education Technology Standards were developed because it became evident that technology impacts the way students think, interact, and develop. Beyond libraries, technology is an important component of information literacy because it can be used for many purposes:

- **Create original works.** Creativity can be exhibited in text, music, film/video, scores, images, or other works of art.

- **Communicate with others.** Communication includes e-mail, chat, social networking, wikis, blogs, image sharing, RSS (really simple syndication) feeds, and allows for easier collaboration.

- **Expand available information.** Technology removes the boundaries of the physical library and enables teens to search library catalogs throughout the world, more easily use inter-library loan, search subscription databases, listen and view streaming audio and video files, discover digital archives, access e-books, and use e-mail/chat with reference librarians and any other Internet resource.

- **Develop critical-thinking skills.** Technology can be used to collect data, visually organize information, discover problems, and explore solutions.

- **Learn ethical behavior.** Becoming a good digital citizen means respecting copyright-protected material, understanding intellectual property ownership, practicing safe online behavior, and being personally responsible with technology and its applications.

- **Further existing technology skills.** Once teens learn how to use one application, they can transfer those skills to other technologies and build on existing skills.

What Are the Core Information Literacy Skills That You Should Teach Teens?

Taking the information literacy movement from the theoretical to asset building in action is a bold step for many LSTs. The task feels daunting at times because we sometimes struggle to keep up ourselves. Nevertheless, LSTs must take action to ensure that teens are prepared to solve their information problems independently. Remember that information literacy skills are learned skills, so teens need opportunities to practice in order to further develop their competencies. Valuable, relevant instruction no longer takes place in traditional "library skills" classes but rather when collaboratively working with teachers and assignments or one on one with teens.

You may know all of the fantastic information resources available in school and public libraries, but teens don't. Core information literacy skills should include the following:

- Organization of information
- Understanding print materials
- Primary and secondary sources
- Boolean operators
- Library catalog
- Keyword and subject searching
- Subscription online databases
- E-books
- Citing sources and information ethics

Organization of Information

If we want teens to use the world of resources available to them in the library, then we must include the key to the map. Using library catalogs to locate materials and online resources to gather documents electronically is useless if they do not understand how the information is arranged.

Information-literate teens should have a clear understanding of the following:

- **Physical arrangement.** They should know the location of fiction, nonfiction, music CDs, DVDs, reference materials, graphic novel collections, local histories, children's collection/ section, computer access, photocopier, and any other specialized collection or spaces available.

- **Library classification system.** Teens should know whether your library uses the Dewey Decimal System, the Library of Congress classification system, or any other system of arrangement.

- **Electronic resources available.** This includes online periodical indexes, streaming audio and video databases, e-books, digital

> LSTs must take the time to incorporate information organization within their daily lessons and interaction with teens to show young people the "big picture."

archives, testing resources, and any other subscription service the library purchases. Online databases should be clearly described as to their scope of coverage. Show teens how to find the title, author, journal/magazine name, volume number, issue number, and date. Teens should be able to fluently identify the components of a bibliographic record.

- **Internet resources.** The various domain names should be examined so that teens can differentiate between commercial sites (.com), organizational sites (.org), governmental sites (.gov), educational sites (.edu), and other domain suffixes.

Understanding Print Materials

Print material is not dead. Although many of the print resources mentioned in this section are available online, effectively using the print collection is a vital skill. Some libraries have fantastic online resources and plenty of computers to accommodate teens, while others have small budgets and a very limited number of computer and Internet resources. It all depends on your library. If you're an LST who still relies heavily on print materials to serve teens, make sure they can use them. When teaching the reference and nonfiction collection, be sure to show them how these materials organize and arrange information.

Important aspects of the print collection teens should know include these:

- What type of information can be found in the public library or school library media center
- How to use dictionaries to determine spelling, pronunciation, and definitions of words
- How to use statistical abstracts
- How to use encyclopedias to gather facts
- How to use glossaries, almanacs, and specialized directories
- How to use maps, atlases, and globes to identify places
- How to use newspapers to locate information
- How to use magazines and journals to locate information
- How to use an index
- How to use bibliographies from books, magazines, and other literature to locate additional sources

Primary and Secondary Sources

We want teens to evaluate information effectively, and to do this they need to understand where information comes from. This gets increasingly difficult as the television media is constantly churning out sound bites, print media is controlled by fewer and fewer individuals, and the Internet is still the publishing house for anybody. Nevertheless, these analytical skills need to be taught to prepare these teens to question everything. Having teens differentiate between primary and secondary sources will help them evaluate information throughout their lives.

- **Primary sources.** Teens need to understand what a primary source is and grasp the value of primary research to their understanding and lives. Primary sources are firsthand accounts of events or ideas and include newspaper articles, news footage, books, films, music, artwork, letters, diaries, statistics and data, online resources, and more. By conducting primary research, teens are able to formulate their own ideas about topics as they make personal inferences through their reading, viewing, and listening.

- **Secondary sources.** The wealth of secondary sources available to teen library users increases every day. Secondary sources are secondhand accounts or descriptions of events and ideas. They include newspaper articles, journal articles, books, music, films, artwork, online resources, and more. Secondary research allows teens to study the ideas of experts and deepens their understanding. In addition, it can help reinforce or reject previous notions.

Be sure to point out the different ways to discover primary and secondary sources. For example, music CDs often provide primary and secondary sources of information. The music on the CD may be the primary source, and the liner notes included may be a secondary source (or another primary source depending on the author) of information on the musician. Liner notes often provide a wealth of information by a music critic or expert. DVDs offer another example where a medium may provide primary and secondary information, such as the director's notes, interviews, and "extras" provided on the disc. These "extras" often offer specific information about a work that is provided directly by the artists who created it.

Boolean Operators

Understanding how to use Boolean operators makes searching everything easier. LSTs should master the use of Boolean logic and model their application in every resource they use. Teens should understand how Boolean operators limit and expand their searches and how applying Boolean operators to their search queries increases efficiency and creates more specific results.

- AND: all terms must be present.
- OR: any one term, some, or all terms must be present.
- NOT: excludes particular terms.

If a teen asks, "Do you have any CDs by The Roots?" the search you model should use Boolean operators to answer that question. Narrating the process will reinforce using this application, and your search query in a library catalog could be AUTHOR = roots AND MATERIAL TYPE = compact disc. This is an important step in teaching teens to effectively use the library catalog, online databases, and the Internet.

CD **See Tool 17. Information Literacy: Using Boolean Operators with Venn Diagrams**

Use a simple exercise to drive home how Boolean operators work:

- Have all students with *brown hair* stand up
- Have all students with *brown* AND *curly hair* stand up
- Have all students with *brown* OR *blond hair* stand up
- Have all students with *brown hair* and NOT *brown eyes* stand up

Point out how each Boolean term expands or limits the results after each time.

CD See Tool 18. Information Literacy: Using the Library Catalog to Locate Materials

The Library Catalog

Whether you're old school or new, teaching teens to effectively search the library catalog is imperative. For library users it is often the first step in answering their information need. Information-literate teens should be able to use the library catalog to search by these fields:

- Author/artist
- Title
- Subject headings
- Keywords
- Material type (books, CDs, DVDs, periodicals, VHS, spoken word recordings)
- Classification scheme

Teens who quickly learn to manipulate the library catalog become confident library users. Their understanding of the library increases as it enables them to explore ideas and materials independently, giving them a sense of empowerment. Teens can learn to ask specific questions with correct terminology, enabling LSTs to serve them in precise and meaningful ways.

Keyword and Subject Searching

A keyword search results in more hits; a subject search results in fewer, more relevant hits.

LSTs must pass on the art of keyword and subject searching. When teens are researching a topic but don't have a specific author or title, they need to use subject or keyword searching. Through time and experience, LSTs instinctively know which search can provide the best results for a particular information need, but teens need to understand the reasoning and decision making involved in deciding what type of search to perform. Show students these aspects of subject searching:

- Searches only the subject field within the record (where "subjects" are listed near the bottom of the record)
- Must match Library of Congress designated term. Explain "controlled vocabulary" and how producers of a library resource (like an online catalog or subscription database) establish terms to represent concepts within that resource. This means that the resource/database can categorize all related materials under the same term regardless of the term used by the author.

Demonstrate these aspects of keyword searching:

- Searches subject fields as well as titles, subtitles, contents notes, series titles, etc.
- Allows Boolean searching to combine concepts.

As you model searching, show teens item records and point out where the search query is looking in a catalog record or database article. For example, as you view the MARC record for an item and point out the subject fields, tell teens, "This is where the computer is looking for your term when you choose a subject search." It needs to be that specific.

Subscription Online Databases

Simply put, they're awesome. Online databases make life wonderful for librarians, as we are able to quickly search for a variety of sources on topics from reputable publications. Information is available in a variety of formats through subscription databases in a quicker, more efficient manner. There is no better way to show the distinction in information quality than by demonstrating the value and relevance of subscription online database searching versus Internet searches. Nowadays, subscription databases go beyond full-text periodical access and include streaming audio, streaming video, artwork, newspaper archives, statistical data, and more.

Although different libraries will offer access to different databases, teens should be prepared to confidently enter any library setting and identify the scope of their information need using any available online databases to aid them.

For Periodical Databases

- **Access.** Show teens where to go to access the library's databases. Proper names of databases should be used because you are showing teens a valid, structured resource. If your library has more than one database from a vendor and it is clustered with others in a group (such as EBSCOhost, InfoTrac, ProQuest, SIRS), be sure to point out how to select individual databases from this group.

- **Scope.** Knowing the scope of each database is the key to selecting the right one. If a teen is looking for current physics articles, they need to be able to distinguish the science database from the visual arts database. They also need to know the limitations of the database and how to determine if it meets their needs. If they are looking for articles in a particular database published before 1992 and full-text access is offered only from 1995 on, they need to understand that the articles will need to be retrieved in another way. Most databases have clear descriptions of the resources covered.

- **Searching.** Accurately searching online databases is a learned skill, and in formal settings it should be taught as such. Whether formally or informally taught, it is equally important to model and narrate search strategies and differentiate between the results. The following search strategies should be understood:
  - Subject searching: students should be able to identify subject headings and when subjects with subdivisions will produce specialized results.
  - Keyword searching: students should understand when and how to use keyword searching to broaden and narrow their searches.

Controlled vocabulary matters when it comes to searching for information. Teach teens that information concepts are categorized into subjects so that a single word or phrase may represent many terms.

- ○ Phrase searching: students should understand the concept of phrase searching and be able to apply it to Boolean operators and keyword searches.
- ○ Truncating terms: students should understand how truncating terms affects search results for fine-tuning their searches.
- ○ Boolean logic: students should understand and apply the Boolean operators AND, OR, and NOT to broaden and narrow search queries.
- ○ Periodical searching: students should be able to search for specific journal titles within a database.
- ○ Title searching: students should understand how to effectively search for the title of a magazine, newspaper, or journal indexed by the online database. This should include any AV (audiovisual) resources.
- ○ Date parameters: students should be able to browse and search by dates within specific journal/magazine titles.

For Audiovisual Databases

Teens should also understand:

- **Source.** This is where the image/clip/file came from. Is it from an audiobook? A film? An image gallery?

- **Browsing features.** Teens need to know how to browse these databases, such as by genre, period, instrument, etc.

- **Retrieving results.** One of the wonderful things about online databases is the variety of ways to retrieve your search results, such as printing, e-mailing, downloading, and creating PDF versions. E-mailing articles is a great way to encourage teens to save printing costs and reduce paper usage. They can read the articles through their e-mail accounts and print needed materials at a later date. If this is an audiovisual database, make sure teens know which software is needed to play the files and if they are able to save them should they want to use them later.

- **Citing sources.** For the many teacher-librarians who work tirelessly each year explaining the importance of documenting research, the database companies have handed them a sweet gift. Most databases now have a citation feature built in that allows teens to select in which format (MLA, APA, etc.) they would like to have the article cited. Usually it is simply a matter of copying and pasting the correct citation into their bibliography. LSTs should promote academic excellence by teaching teens to avoid plagiarism and to correctly cite the sources they consult.

E-Books

E-books offer many advantages to libraries, particularly school libraries with little shelf space and more limited budgets than many public libraries. E-books provide increased access to texts because they are not limited to one user and can be used simultaneously by others. Gone are the days when the one relevant history text or reference book has been checked out to a student for overnight use. The amount of reference books available electronically nowadays is extensive, and it is only going to grow more. It addition to the access, e-books can be searched, and this eliminates the need to remember page or chapter numbers and the constant checking of indexes. Printing and e-mailing options are often available too, and many can be exported to portable devices as well.

Searching with e-books is not a daunting task, but teens should be aware of some key elements when accessing information via an e-book. First of all, make sure teens know that they are accessing an e-book and must comply with copyright laws. Second, they should be aware of the retrieval options available to them via the e-book (print, e-mail, export). Finally, they must know how to correctly cite an e-book. Pointing out to the teen that this electronic resource is also an actual printed book may help them understand that what they are seeing is different from an Internet site or a database article.

Citing Sources and Information Ethics

Teens needs to learn how to correctly cite sources used in academic work and the ethics and laws regarding information. Plagiarism is unacceptable, and this should be regularly reinforced to teens. Just because technologies make it easy to steal does not mean it is right to do so. The issues and laws involved in intellectual property theft are real, complicated, and designed to protect all of our rights. We must teach the value of respecting the intellectual property of others to teens.

By the time students are in middle school/junior high school, they have already begun developing bibliographies for their schoolwork. Because of this, teens are at a very ripe age to learn the importance of citing sources in their schoolwork and research. Build on the skills they are already learning by teaching them how to correctly format citations for their schoolwork. LSTs in the public library can collaborate with teachers and library media specialists in the local schools by finding out what formats are being used. Regardless of the citation manual (MLA, APA, Chicago, Turabian), teens should know the following:

- How the citation manual is arranged
- How to use the index
- How to cite various formats commonly available in their library (books, periodicals, films, music CDs, online database articles, Web sites, statistics, interviews, and works of art)
- How to create a works cited list/bibliography according to the style rules
- How to create quotes, parenthetical citations, footnotes, and endnotes

Many free online citations tools are now available; most online database companies provide correct citations with the retrieval of their documents.

CD See Tool 15. Information Literacy: Creating a Works Cited List

Teens still need to learn how to use the various citation manuals, as there will be times when the manuals will be the only tools that can help them.

How Do You Teach Teens to Evaluate Web Sites?

CD See Tool 20. Information Literacy: Web Site Evaluation Handout

CD See Tool 16. Information Literacy: Lesson Plan for Web Site Evaluation

The need for critical-thinking skills when using the Internet for research cannot be overstated. Teens have grown up using the Internet at home, school, and public libraries, so turning to the Internet for their information needs is natural and second nature to them. Nevertheless, the need to analyze and evaluate Internet information is imperative. Many of the sites that teens use for information have no editorial control or review process, unlike books and other periodical publications. Since the emergence of Web 2.0 technologies, many teachers have embraced the use of wikis, blogs, and social networking sites and have integrated these resources into their curriculum. However, integrating these technologies brings with it the responsibility of teaching students the skills to successfully navigate the Web and distinguish for themselves what is "quality" information and what is not.

Teaching teens to evaluate information on the Web is one of the most important information literacy skills an LST can teach. The Internet is here to stay and will be a resource for them throughout their lives. When you consider how many times you, an LST, refer to the Internet for information throughout the day, just imagine how teen usage is much greater if for no other reason than the fact that for many a computer *is* their library access. For information professionals, most of the criteria are considered subconsciously, with skills developed through experience—this is what LSTs should strive to instill in teens.

Teens should be able to locate valid Internet sources such as the following:

- Sites that support various academic subjects taught in high schools
- Sites with information related to colleges, universities, conservatories, the military, or career preparation
- Sites with statistical information at the local, state, and national levels
- Sites with consumer information
- Sites with primary source documents
- Sites that broadcast audio and video

Teens should also know the criteria for evaluating Web sites:

- **Purpose.** What is the purpose of the Web site? Are there stated goals? Who is the audience? Is this a popular site or scholarly site? Is it a commercial site? Is there advertising? What type of advertising? Is the site trying to sell you something? Is this site to inform you? Persuade you? Entertain you?

- **Authority.** Can the author of the site be identified? Are articles on the site signed by the author(s)? What are the author's credentials or qualifications? Is the author an expert on this subject? Is the author's occupation listed with years of experience, position, and education? Is the author affiliated with any institution? If so, what is its purpose? What is the URL domain (.com, .edu, .gov, .org)?

- **Accuracy.** Is the information presented well researched? Is there a bibliography provided? Are statistics and supporting documents clearly labeled so that they may be verified? Does the site include spelling and grammatical errors? When was the site published? Does the page list when it was last updated? Are there links on the site? If so, where do they point? Are there dead links on the site?

- **Bias.** What are the goals and objectives of this site? Are they clearly stated? What opinions does the author express? Is there bias? Are there opposing points of view? Does this site contain mostly facts or opinion? Does another group, organization, or institution sponsor the site? If so, does it reflect that group's agenda? Why was it written and for whom?

- **Navigation.** Is the site easy to navigate? Is the site well organized? Is there an index or table of contents? Is there a search feature within the site?

- **Conclusion.** Overall, does this site appear to be a complete and well-documented source of information? Does the author or organization appear reputable? Is the information cited correctly?

How Do Web 2.0 Tools Impact Information Literacy?

If you want to know the "bling-bling" of the Internet, it is Web 2.0 technologies. Sometimes it's the real deal, and other times it is all hype. Nevertheless, Web 2.0 technologies are very popular with teens, and many of these tools are an integral part of their lives. Teachers and school library media specialists have observed this trend and already incorporate these technologies into the curriculum. Why? Because Web 2.0 tools such as social networks, blogs, wikis, photo galleries/image sharing, and RSS feeds require students to produce information. This is a key point of Jamie McKenzie's "The Research Cycle,"[9] which strives for students to no longer be consumers of information but rather information producers. As the wildly successful social networking sites reveal, teens love to create information and post it online. If Web 2.0 technologies make teens feel comfortable and confident, teach them to use these tools by applying them to a content area within their studies. For example, teaching students to use VoiceThread (a Web storytelling application using images) to present information about the Holocaust might be a

CD **See Tool 19. Information Literacy: Using Wikipedia in Research**

way to engage them to use technology, inspire creativity, and develop their presentation skills. Another example is discussing the pros and cons of using wikis and having students trace the works cited in a Wikipedia article to evaluate information validity. The key challenges for LSTs will be determining what technologies can enhance student learning and understanding and which ones are just flashy with little educational value.

The bottom line for LSTs who are using Web 2.0 technologies is this: How are you going to make information literacy the most dynamic, the most interactive, and the most cutting edge for teens? The technology changes quickly and that's just fine. What you use this year may be passé next year. Accept this and move on. The idea is not to get married to one specific tool but to instead focus on the big picture—what is happening today with the Web? Teen users no longer want to passively click links and read. They want to create information and use new tools that are fast and flashy. How can you create meaningful activities that fulfill this desire?

Figuring a way to challenge teens to use Internet tools to create and evaluate information is the forever-changing task of the LST. The teens you serve are already using Web 2.0 technologies and may be using them in their research. The following are some tools that can enhance information literacy and critical-thinking skills:

- **Blogs.** Blogs are "Web logs," or Web sites that allow users to post information by date. Blogs can develop writing and communication skills as well as provide opportunities to expand critical thinking as teens read, analyze, create, explain, compare, and contrast information posted throughout the world.

- **RSS feeds.** Really simple syndication (RSS) is a great way to quickly share information among Web users. This is a great collaborative tool, as teens can share information quickly on specific topics of study.

- **Social networks.** Social networks are online networks of individuals or groups connected through common interests, ideas, goals, values, or organizations. Social networking goes beyond MySpace and Facebook, and having teens participate in them to inform, produce, display, or share information is valuable to developing critical-thinking skills.

- **Streaming audio.** Sharing audio files is an easy and quick way for students to create and disseminate information to others. With a variety of formats available and free recorders available online, these resources can help students develop listening, writing, and speaking skills.

- **Video storytelling.** Telling stories with video means understanding the visual language to effectively communicate ideas. Having students practice this form of communication enhances their critical-thinking skills since students must use images to convey information and it also promotes creativity. How does this medium change the concept of "point of view"?

- **Wikis.** Wikis are Web pages on which anyone can add content and/or edit information. Wikis used properly can be used to help teens inquire, research, contribute, and collaborate—all part of the information literacy standards.

How Should You Evaluate Information Literacy Skills?

How can you tell if teens are finding the information they need? Use the performance indicators provided in the information literacy standards to evaluate their progress. Informal assessment is an easy, nonthreatening method of evaluation. You can informally assess competencies in many ways—during a reference interview, circulating among classes of students during formal instruction, beginning an open discussion, or simply observing the actions before you. Informal observation allows you to note weaknesses and plan for future instruction. Pay attention to the questions teens ask you, their responses to the answers you give to them, and the skills they exhibit in the library. These observations and conversations may offer you more information about the type of skills they need to develop more than anything else.

You may also more formally assess students' skills in a variety of ways. You may observe specified tasks, such as a project, an exam, or any other structured tool to implement evaluation. Since tests taken in the library (school or public) may be taken less seriously, work to create worksheets with specific information tasks that are seamlessly integrated with their lessons so that you can formally evaluate students' information literacy skills at the same time. Teens voluntarily attending information literacy programs should not feel pressured about meeting high performance goals or undergoing difficult exams.

How Can Information Literacy Change the Way Teens See the Library?

Tell any teen that a great place to spend the afternoon is the library, and most will roll their eyes, shake their head, or openly mock you. When you prove to teens the advantages of fluently manipulating and using information, you will open up their world to lifelong learning. In turn, this can positively change the way teens perceive and participate in the library. Maybe their afternoons in the library will be spent reading, listening to music CDs, watching streaming videos on the Internet, or playing video games online—things they may be doing in their spare time whether they are in the library or not. It's all a matter of perception. Building information literacy skills in teens builds their confidence. It helps change their perception of the library. It becomes "their space" and they know just how to use it. This sense of ownership shows them the library is a place "where they can come to find answers."[10]

When teens are information literate, they may do the following:

- View the library's resources as relevant to their lives
- Value the knowledge of LSTs
- Ask specific, thoughtful questions related to their information needs
- Maneuver the library and its resources with confidence
- Feel a sense of "ownership" of the library

Is every teen going to be best friends with the LST? Of course not—LSTs won't want to be best friends with all of their patrons either. It is far more important to strengthen your relationships with teens by building collections that meet their needs and by showing them how to use their library in ways that can improve the quality of their lives.

What Are Some Outstanding Libraries Actively Engaging Teens in Information Literacy?

The following libraries are examples of institutions that deliberately integrate information literacy within their services to contribute to the positive development of teens. These are not your typical libraries. Each library has a different mission and serves a unique population. However, these libraries share the common goal of creating independent lifelong learners who are equipped with the flexibility that will help them adapt to the forever-changing landscape of information. Using a variety of techniques, technologies, and services, these libraries strive to make teens adaptable for the futures that await them. They raise the bar in what teens expect from libraries, and their commitment to youth development is evident through the quality materials and services they provide.

Public Libraries

School Corps, Multnomah County Library

Multnomah County Library
801 SW 10th Avenue
Portland, OR 97212
www.multcolib.org/schoolcorps/

The School Corps program is a model public library–school community partnership. The goal of the Multnomah County Library School Corps is to increase the information literacy of Multnomah County students by working with local schools. To meet this goal, School Corps offers services and programs to Multnomah County K–12 public and private schools and connects students and educators with the information resources of the public library. School Corps serves students, teachers, student teachers, and school library staff of Multnomah County.

Ongoing programs and services integrate information literacy skills within the K–12 curriculum of the county and are customizable. Presentations to Multnomah County Schools for online research include Library Catalog (grades 3–12, adult), Using the Multnomah County Library of Web Sites (kids, homework center, or teens), Library Databases A–Z (grades 4–12, adult), Introduction to Search Engines and Web Site Evaluation, Live Homework Help (grades 4–12, adult), and Think Before You Click (grades 4–12). They also offer a presentation on censorship, Feasting on Forbidden Fruit (grades 4–7 and 8–12), that discusses how censorship affects children and teens, an overview of challenged and censored books, and a chance for students to review challenged and censored books. School Corps will also customize booktalks for all grade levels and keeps up to date with what's hot, award winners, and award nominees. Presentations for parents are also offered on social networking and homework resources.

One of the strengths of School Corps curriculum support is its ability to customize services to the needs of the teachers and students. School Corps provides Bucket of Books, which are tubs containing 24–30 books on a topic plus a teacher's guide with an annotated list of age-appropriate Web sites, a pathfinder for doing research on the topic at Multnomah County Library, and instructions on how to obtain additional copies of the books. If there is no Bucket of Books on a topic, you can check out the booklist Web site that has copies of the most popular booklists as well as instructions on how to create your own booklist, or they can create a booklist for you. Customized "Webliographies" with annotated Web sites can be created for audiences if one is not already available at the homework center on your topic. If students are going to be using the public library for their research, they will create customized pathfinders for starting public library research on specific topics. Other unique services include library card campaigns for students in grades K–5 and 6–12 and an "educator" card for teachers, which has an extended loan period of six weeks and allows 40 unfilled holds at any time.

School Libraries

John I. Smith Charities Library, South Carolina Governor's School for the Arts and Humanities

South Carolina Governor's School for the Arts and Humanities
15 University Street
Greenville, SC 29601
www.scgsah.state.sc.us
Michael Giller, Assistant Director of Library Services

The South Carolina Governor's School for the Arts and Humanities is a public residential high school for talented artists living in South Carolina. Students audition for acceptance in one of five art areas: creative writing, dance, drama, music, and visual arts. This school of 245 students consists of primarily upperclassman, although underclassman are accepted in the dance and music departments. The library collection supports both the arts and academic curricula of the school through a specialized print collection and an extensive collection of music compact discs, DVDs, and electronic resources. The library's Web site provides access to the catalog and online materials, while the computer lab and student production center offer students access to computers and software that encourages creative expression of understanding.

Information literacy is integrated on all levels and subjects through teacher-librarian collaboration. Streaming audio databases such as the Classical Music Library, American Song, African-American Song, Smithsonian Global Sound, and the Naxos Music Library allow music faculty to create customized playlists they put on electronic reserve for student listening, and students can also create customized playlists. Streaming video databases such as Opera in Video, Dance in Video, and ETV Streamline allow students to use video footage in their research and presentations. The ARTstor database provides image galleries for the visual arts faculty and students to view high-quality digital reproductions of artwork from around the world, and librarians instruct usage of this for primary research and student projects. The library encourages integrating technology into the curriculum by providing faculty workshops and teaching students bibliographic instruction formally and informally in the classroom and library as requested by teachers.

Librarians use diverse resources across all curricular areas to maximize student exposure to the library's collection. Librarians work with the required 11th grade American history and literature classes to teach them primary and secondary research skills, searching online databases, and citing sources in the schoolwide adopted *MLA Handbook for Writers* for their projects and assignments throughout the year. The use of databases is emphasized in the curriculum, as students discover primary sources such as the nineteenth-century U.S. newspapers, the *London Times* Digital Archive 1785–1985, and the *Times Literary Supplement.* Utilizing other databases such as the Biography Resource Center, Literature Resource Center, Expanded Academic Onefile, Project MUSE, the History Resource Center, and the African-American Studies Center, librarians work to build the confidence of students in determining the scope and relevancy of electronic resources.

All students are required to take a two-year humanities course in which students research an approved topic in-depth throughout the course. Collaborating with humanities teachers begins with topic selection and preliminary research and then continues with research papers and advanced research practices, which eventually culminates into a final presentation. Student projects developed in the library's production center allow students to produce video projects using Adobe Premiere Pro and iMovie, Web sites with Macromedia Dreamweaver and Flash, images with Photoshop, and original scores using Sibelius and Finale. Equipment such as digital video cameras, scanners, LCD projectors, DVD players, drawing tablets, and laptops are available for student use. The library has established several interlibrary loan agreements that include the University of South Carolina libraries, Wofford College, and the Public Library of Charlotte and Mecklenburg County so that access to information is extended beyond the campus.

Maggie L. Walker Governor's School for Government and International Studies

Maggie L. Walker Governor's School for Government and International
  Studies
1000 N. Lombardy St.
Richmond, VA 23220
http://mwlibrary.wordpress.com
Wendy Sellors, Library Media Specialist

The Maggie L. Walker Governor's School for Government and International Studies (MLWGSGIS) is a public high school serving 700 gifted and talented students from 11 surrounding school districts. Students apply for acceptance and are evaluated based on both qualitative and quantitative measures. In relation to its curricular focus on government and international studies, MLWGSGIS offers 11 languages; extensive advanced placement (AP) options in history, politics, and government; competitive academic extracurricular activities such as Model Congress, Model UN, and We the People (constitutional law); and senior mentorships and seminars. Several AP courses in math and science are also offered, as are numerous dual enrollment courses with Virginia Commonwealth University (VCU), primarily in math, science, and the fine arts.

The library's print reference and circulating nonfiction collections reflect a range of topics and reading levels commensurate with the blend of high school and college content in the school curriculum. A selective menu of online resources supports academic rigor and research, including numerous e-books, Gale's Opposing Viewpoints, Making of Modern Law, and Declassified Documents databases, JSTOR, Project MUSE, CIAO, EBSCO's Literary Reference Center, and Elsevier's Science Direct. A small fiction collection focused on cultural/historical fiction and literature and CD collection focused on international and classical music round out the library's offerings. For additional resources, students have community borrower privileges at VCU Libraries.

In collaboration with teachers, information literacy is integrated throughout the curriculum, beginning with a required course for freshmen: Foundations of Independent Research and Communication (FIRC) and culminating with a senior seminar or mentorship. Freshmen rotate through four sections of FIRC: English (speaking and writing for an audience), Math (gathering and using statistics), Science (scientific method), and Social Studies (public policy research). The librarian collaborates with FIRC instructors to teach students how to develop guiding questions for their research based on preliminary reading, distinguish primary from secondary sources, and evaluate sources for bias (including bias in the manner that survey/poll questions are written). In other 9th grade courses and in succeeding years, information literacy skills taught through librarian-teacher collaboration include note-taking strategies, paraphrasing, documenting and citing sources, finding foreign language news, mining the deep Web, and conducting a literature review.

Information literacy skills are taught by the librarian at the point of need for students with examples tailored to the assignment at hand. Emphasis is on research as an iterative process with use of related resources integrated as appropriate (e.g., Noodle Tools when teaching how to document sources, news search engines and databases when teaching how to find news, etc.). Most lessons include time for students to apply the skills taught in an activity that the librarian assesses to determine whether a follow-up lesson is necessary to clarify or reinforce a particular concept. In addition to direct instruction for whole classes, the librarian also meets with individuals and small groups for research coaching sessions as her schedule permits.

As a complement to information literacy instruction, several online library resources help students learn or renew their information literacy skills. Project guides (on Delicious) created by the librarian in consultation with teachers often serve as a starting point for assignments. Even though a full list of databases appears on the library's blog, links to the databases most relevant to an assignment are included on its project guide. Many teachers also add links to project guides and/or the library's databases page to their Web sites. For research topics requiring more extensive tips or tutorials about an information literacy skill (e.g., conducting a literature review) or online tool (e.g., Google Scholar), pages are added to the Library Research Wiki.

Unlike the library's Delicious account, which only the librarian can update directly, the wiki can be edited by any member of the school community. This encourages student-librarian as well as teacher-librarian collaboration, with drafts sometimes developed on Google Docs until a page is ready for its public debut. Although the library's main online space is its blog, a wiki, bookmark account, Google Calendar, photo gallery, and private online social network for discussing books and reading (Dragons Reading Room hosted on Ning) combine to provide a multifaceted, multifunctional online library presence.

University Laboratory High School at the University of Illinois

University Laboratory High School at the University of Illinois
1212 W. Springfield Avenue
Urbana, IL 61801
(217) 333-1589
www.uni.uiuc.edu/library/
Frances Jacobson Harris, Librarian

University Laboratory High School is a public laboratory school for gifted students on the campus of the University of Illinois at Urbana–Champaign. The school has 300 students in five grade levels, "subfreshman" through senior. Being part of a large research university is both a blessing and a challenge for information literacy. Students have access to a collection of ten million volumes and literally hundreds of electronic databases. The library Web site is designed to scaffold student learning by presenting a customized selection of these resources and linking to a variety of support materials. Students can access all online materials from home as well as from school. The library has an active blog (www.uni .uiuc.edu/library/blog) and hosts an online book discussion forum (www.uni.uiuc.edu/bbs/viewforum.php?f=5). The "Recommended Reads" page (http://unihighlib.pbwiki.com) is a wiki to which students and teachers can contribute.

Information literacy is integrated throughout the curriculum through collaborations with teachers that typically include multiple class sessions in the library. Information literacy is also taught in the computer literacy course sequence. Research guides for current class assignments are posted online at www.uni.uiuc.edu/library/classprojects. A number of these guides are now built as wikis, enabling students and teachers to add resources to them. Some feature RSS news feeds. Students in the younger grades learn to use the online catalog and general interest databases such as Academic OneFile, WilsonSelectPlus, Teen Health and Wellness, and LexisNexis. Older students use more specialized sources such as America: History and Life, JStor, Science Direct, Biography Resource Center, and ProQuest Historical Newspapers. All students routinely use the citation software Noodlebib, creating bibliographies in both MLA and APA styles depending on individual teachers' requirements.

The librarian team teaches a two-semester computer literacy course (one semester in the subfreshman year, and one semester in the freshman year) with three other teachers. Her area of responsibility is teaching information literacy skills, with an emphasis on information evaluation and the ethical use of information and communication technology. The focus on evaluation and ethical use is particularly critical in a school where no Internet filtering software is installed. The librarian also shares in supervising the ten-week small group projects conducted in the freshman course, many of which involve Web 2.0 technologies. For example, one group of students entered the library's graphic novel holdings into LibraryThing. Teaching materials for both computer literacy courses are posted online at www.uni.uiuc.edu/library/computerlit.

Conclusion

Trying to cover all aspects of information literacy in one chapter is impossible. LSTs in schools and public libraries must take the initiative to develop their own information literacy and technology skills in order to teach others effectively. The standards and indicators offer the framework, with core skill areas provided to make sure that teens are ready for life beyond high school. Don't try to teach it all at once—find your voice and the methods that work best for you. Develop your methods skill by skill, step by step, until you have a bank filled with techniques and lessons that will withstand the test of time. As technology changes, many of the retrieval and organizational methods will change too. This is okay because the essential skills remain the same and you can look to the standards to guide you.

Sources Cited in This Chapter

1. American Association of School Librarians and Association for Educational Communications and Technology. 1998. *Information Power: Building Partnerships for Learning.* Chicago: American Library Association.
2. American Library Association. 2007. *Standards for the 21st-Century Learner.* Available: www.ala.org/ala/aasl/aaslproftools/learningstandards/standards.cfm (accessed February 25, 2008).
3. American Library Association. 1989. *Presidential Committee on Information Literacy: Final Report.* Chicago: American Library Association.
4. International Society for Technology in Education. 2007. *National Education Technology Standards.* Available: www.iste.org/AM/Template.cfm?Section=NETS (accessed February 25, 2008).
5. Eisenberg, Michael B., and Robert E. Berkowitz, with Robert Darrow and Kathleen L. Spitzer. 2007. *Teaching Information & Technology Skills: The Big6 in Secondary Schools.* Columbus, OH: Linworth.
6. Indiana Department of Education. 2008. "An Organized Investigator." Office of Learning Resources. Available: www.indianalearns.org/infolitinvest.asp (accessed March 3, 2008).
7. McKenzie, J. 1999. "The Research Cycle." *From Now On* 9, no. 4 (December). Available: http://questioning.org/rcycle.html (accessed February 25, 2008).
8. Smith, Jane Brandy. 2005. *Teaching and Testing Information Literacy Skills.* Columbus, OH: Linworth.
9. McKenzie, J. 1999. "The Research Cycle." *From Now On* 9, no. 4 (December). Available: http://questioning.org/rcycle.html (accessed February 25, 2008).
10. Carmichael, Maribeth. 2007. "If You Build It, They Will Come: Creating a School Library That Embraces Students and Teachers." *Teacher Librarian* 34, no. 3 (February): 40–3.

Recommended Sources for Further Reading

American Association of School Librarians. 2007. *Standards for the 21st-Century Learner.* Available: www.ala.org/ala/aasl/aaslproftools/learningstandards/standards.cfm.

American Association of School Librarians and Association for Educational Communications and Technology. 1998. *Information Power: Building Partnerships for Learning.* Chicago: American Library Association.

American Library Association and the Association for Educational Communications and Technology. 1998. *Information Literacy Standards for Student Learning: Standards and Indicators.* Chicago: American Library Association.

Association of College and Research Libraries. 2000. *Information Literacy Standards for Higher Education.* Available: www.ala.org/ala/acrl/acrlstandards/informationliteracycompetency.htm.

Behen, Linda D. 2006. *Using Pop Culture to Teach Information Literacy.* Westport, CT: Libraries Unlimited.

Birks, Jane, and Fiona Hunt. 2003. *Hands-on Information Literacy Activities.* New York: Neal-Schuman.

Burkhardt, Joanna M., Mary C. MacDonald, and Andrée J. Rathemacher. 2003. *Teaching Information Literacy: 35 Practical Standards-based Exercises for College Students.* Chicago: American Library Association.

Eisenberg, Michael B., and Robert E. Berkowitz, with Robert Darrow and Kathleen L. Spitzer. 2000. *Teaching Information & Technology Skills: The Big6 in Secondary Schools.* Columbus, OH: Linworth.

Geck, Caroline. 2006. "The Generation Z Connection: Teaching Information Literacy to the Newest Net Generation." *Teacher Librarian* 33, no. 3 (February): 19–24.

Gibson, Craig, Ed. 2006. *Student Engagement and Information Literacy.* Chicago: Association of College and Research Libraries/ALA.

Gilton, Donna L. 2008. "Information Literacy as a Department Store." *Young Adult Library Services* (Winter): 39–44.

Graboyes, Alanna S. 2007. "No Gifted Student Left Behind: Building a High School Library Media Center for the Gifted Student." *Gifted Child Today* 30, no. 2 (Spring): 42–52.

Hunt, Fiona, and Jane Birks. 2008. *More Hands-On Information Literacy Activities.* New York: Neal-Schuman.

International Society for Technology in Education. 2007. "National Education Technology Standards." Available: www.iste.org/AM/Template.cfm?Section= NETS.

Jacobson, Trudi E., and Thomas P. Mackey, Eds. 2007. *Information Literacy Collaborations That Work.* New York: Neal-Schuman.

Johns, Sarah Kelly. 2008. "AASL Standards for the 21st Century Learner: A Map for Student Learning." *Knowledge Quest* 36, no. 4 (March–April): 4–8.

Lane, Nance, Margaret Chisholm, and Carolyn Mateer. 2003. *Techniques for Student Research: A Comprehensive Guide to Using the Library.* New York: Neal-Schuman.

Loertscher, David. 2008. "Information Literacy: 20 Years Later." *Teacher Librarian* 35, no. 5 (June): 42–43.

Loertscher, David V., and Blanche Woolls. 1997. "The Information Literacy Movement of the School Library Media Field: A Preliminary Summary of the Research." School of Library and Information Science, San Jose State University. Available: http://slisweb.sjsu.edu/courses/250.loertscher/modelloer.html.

Loertscher, David V., and Blanche Woolls. 2002. *Information Literacy: A Review of the Research; a Guide for Practitioners and Researchers,* 2nd ed. Salt Lake City, UT: Hi Willow Research.

Long, Deborah. 2007. "Increasing Literacy in the High School Library: Collaboration Makes It Happen." *Teacher Librarian* 35, no. 1 (October): 13–16.

Marzano, Robert J., Debra J. Pickering, and Jane E. Pollock. 2001. *Classroom Instruction That Works.* Alexandria, VA: Association for Supervision and Curriculum Development.

McKenzie, Jamie. 1999. "The Research Cycle 2000." *From Now On: The Educational Technology Journal* 9, no. 4 (December). Available: http://questioning .org/rcycle.html.

McPherson, Keith. "Mashing Literacy." *Teacher Librarian* 35, no. 5 (June): 73–75.

National Commission on Libraries and Information Science. *Why Care About School Libraries?* Available: http://www.fundourfuturewashington.org/ resources/WHYCAREABOUTSCHOOLLIBRARIES-1.pdf.

Rich, Motoko. 2009. "In Web Age, Library Job Gets Update." *International Herald Tribune: New York Times,* February 16. Available: http://www.iht .com/articles/2009/02/16/arts/16libr.php.

Riedling, Ann Marlow. 2006. *Learning to Learn: A Guide to Becoming Information Literate in the 21st Century*. New York: Neal-Schuman.

Salpeter, Judy. 2008. "Make Students Info Literate: There Remains a Larger Challenge for Schools: How to Develop a New Generation of Knowledgeable Digital Citizens Who Can Operate in the Unregulated Online World." *Technology and Learning* 28, no. 10 (May): 24–28.

Shalaway, Linda. 2005. *Learning to Teach...Not Just for Beginners*, 3rd ed. New York: Scholastic.

"SLMAM Skills Correlations—New (2007) to Old (1998)." 2008. *School Library Media Activities Monthly* 24, no. 6 (February). Available: www.schoollibrarymedia.com/articles/correlations2008v24n6.html.

Smith, Jane Brandy. 2005. *Teaching and Testing Information Literacy Skills*. Columbus, OH: Linworth.

Stripling, Barbara K., Ed. 1999. *Learning and Libraries in an Information Age: Principles and Practice*. Englewood, NJ: Libraries Unlimited.

Thompson, Helen P., and Susan A. Henley. 2000. *Fostering Information Literacy: Connecting National Standards, Goals 2000, and the SCANS report*. Englewood, NJ: Libraries Unlimited.

Wiggins, Grant, and Jay McTighe. 2005. *Understanding by Design*, 2nd ed. Alexandria, VA: Association for Supervision and Curriculum Development.

Collections

Collection development isn't about buying books—it's about resource allocation. The decision to create a vital graphic novel collection isn't a random choice—it results from a series of choices that an LST makes on both a macro and micro level about collections. These decisions are based on the library's priorities, space considerations, and the reading interests of teens. Although not as prevalent as it was in the past, many still correlate teen services with teen collections, and teen collections with YA (young adult) literature. While we recognize the importance of teen literature, this chapter provides information about books published for teens as well as other materials used by teens.

We like teen literature too, but we believe that the majority of library use by teens has very little to do with teen literature. One reason for pushing teen literature aside is that so many other professional sources address it, such as the standard text in most teen literature courses.

So what is a teen collection in a library? Is it both fiction and nonfiction? Does it meet just recreational needs, or do materials also speak to the educational and informational needs of teens? And what about formats? Teen areas and collections in both public libraries and school library media centers are all different based on allocated resources, interests of teens in each community, freedom (or lack thereof) to order materials of interest to teens, and each library's LST or other staff member responsible for collection development. One thing we do know is that there is no *best* teen collection; instead, LSTs have a series of choices to make, with support from their administrators, about what materials should make up their teen collection. In this chapter, we'll lay out the many choices available to LSTs as they work to create (or help create) an exciting collection for teens.

What Are the Best Books for Teenagers?

Deciding the best books for teenagers is a topic that interests many LSTs and library school students. It is the basic collection development decision, yet the statement itself is a loaded question. Why books? Couldn't the

During any given day, the percentage of an LST's time spent dealing with YA literature is minimal; a lot more time will be spent fielding questions for research papers, answering inquiries for homework, and enforcing discipline than it will be noting the literary merits of the latest novel with a starred review in *Booklist*. That is the literature that library school students study and librarians put on BBYA (Best Books for Young Adults), but it is not primarily what teens read. Materials that are popular with teens are the glut of mass-market paperbacks, manga, and magazines found in bookstores, libraries, and passed around among teens.

best reading collection or experience be a magazine? What does "best" mean? Does it mean highest literary quality, most popular, or something with a little of each? What does "teenager" mean? Does it mean books written for teens or books read by teens? Does it mean 12-year-olds or 18-year-olds? So what are the best books for teenagers? These are all good questions, but we have no definitive answers. The most accurate answer we can provide is another question: "Who is asking the questions and what kinds of answers are they looking for?" Helpful, right?

To be honest, the answers to most collection-development questions begin at your library, not in the editorial offices of *Booklist* or at a YALSA (Young Adult Library Services Association) "Best Book for Young Adults" (BBYA) meeting. These end-of-year lists produced by YALSA committees and review magazines represent the best books in one year for the teen audience as chosen by a group of informed adult observers. Pay attention here: Did you catch if any living, breathing teens were a part of that process? For the most part teens aren't involved in any of those groups, so this may or may not indicate that they are the best books for the teens in your library or for the customers you serve or want to serve. While YALSA's Quick Picks list gets the closest to listing books by perceived popularity, the function of these lists is to name the best books, and this is almost always defined by quality. Moreover, none of these lists name best books for their audience; they name the best "new" books for an audience. Definitely use the lists, but consider them just one tool in your collection development tool kit.

Also remember that collection development is not just about buying new books but an ongoing process that includes developing a collection that mixes new titles with older ones. It is also about weeding and maintaining, not just ordering everything on BBYA or ordering just the "hot" series. Since many youth collections, in particular those aimed at teens, weigh more heavily on the side of collecting items based on real customer popularity than pure literary quality, the most important lists that LSTs need to consult each year do not come from journals or committees but from your own IT (information technology) departments or your circulation system. The BBYA and other lists tell us what others think are the books we need to buy, but the homegrown lists (garnered from circulation reports) allow teens to tell us the books they read, need, and even steal.

At the end of every year, but probably more often than that, LSTs need to obtain reports on collection use, including the following:

- The items with the most circulation (raw numbers)
- The items with the highest turnover rate (ratio of circulation to number of copies)
- The items with the most reserves
- The items with the highest ratio of reserves to copies owned
- The items that are reported lost or damaged or long overdue
- The items that are reported missing (which often means "stolen")
- The overall circulation of the teen collection for the current year

- The increase/decrease in the circulation of the teen collection over the past three to five years

If possible, these lists should be by collection (teen items) and by customers (checked out by teens). Not every circulation system can generate reports by user type or birthday, but since so much of teen circulation does not come from the teen area, it is vital that LSTs work with their library's IT department to gather this data. If these lists can't be produced by your circulation system, then perhaps LSTs need to get themselves involved in work teams that look at migration or automation issues. We need information to manage our collection and must push for systems that produce the data we need to do our jobs.

Yet, even with that report, we get only half of the story since we might learn about only those items cataloged as "teen" or "YA" that are missing. But this doesn't represent the collection used by teens. We serve teen customers, not teen collections. A real teen collection needs to be a collection for teens, not a collection of teen books or a collection in the teen area. It is not only a matter of semantics but a shift in thinking about who drives collection development and the role, especially in a public library, of the LST. Developing a collection is customer focused; it does not matter to the teen where the book is located, just that the library owns it. In most libraries, this is much easier said than done. Collection budgets are broken down by materials, not customers. Some library systems won't buy duplicate copies of titles that have teen and adult appeal; some libraries won't shelve a book like *The Hobbit* or a biography of Tupac Shakur in more than one part of the collection. If you are an LST, your goal can't be only to develop a teen collection but to make sure that adult and children's collections contain those items that teens want and need. In addition to working with your IT department, working with the children's and adult selectors is important as well. Teens use the library in a holistic way, borrowing materials from a variety of collections as they move from childhood to adulthood over their time in middle school and high school. Homework may take them to both the juvenile biographies and the adult fiction collections. A new movie may take them to the folk/fairy tales collection for the source material, a friend's recommendation may take them to the teen collection, and changes in their bodies may take them to the adult nonfiction collection.

What Are the Reading Interests of Teens?

Perhaps nothing demonstrates the wide scope of teen reading interests better than a series of recent surveys asking teens about their favorite books. The first survey was conducted by SmartGirl, an online community for young women predominantly ages 11–17. Overall, 1,144 youth took this survey during Teen Read Week in the fall of 2007.[1] The second survey, which we'll call the Teen Reading Habits and Perceptions

One of the best ways to develop a teen collection is to ask the teens in your library what they like to read.

(CD) **See Tool 41. Teen Reading Interest Survey**

Survey, was created by us and distributed among more than 20 public and school libraries. This survey was also made available to the general public online for one month during the fall of 2008, garnering 1,092 responses from teens ages 12–18.[2]

The following are some general conclusions about teens and reading that can be surmised by reading the results of both of these surveys:

- Teens that consistently see family members read at home read more often.

- Teens do find time to read for pleasure.

- Online content and periodicals are very popular.

- Young adults' interest in "pure" YA literature decreases with age.

- The most popular genres for teen readers include fantasy, mystery, and true stories. Historical fiction is almost always rated among the least popular.

- Science fiction and fantasy both have a strong and consistent following among teen readers of all ages.

- Audiobooks and books available in other electronic formats are not as popular as print books.

- The majority of readers prefer fiction, followed by nonfiction and then books created in a graphic format (comic books, graphic novels, and manga).

Earlier studies and surveys about the reading interests of teens were also included in the first, second, and third editions of *Connecting Young Adults and Libraries*, and, not surprisingly, these reports documented similar findings. What this tells us is that in spite of the doom-and-gloom reports about teens not reading, they do read. They may not read what adults want them to read, but they *do* read.

The following teen responses from the 2008 Teen Reading Habits and Perceptions Survey clearly articulate the varying attitudes teens have about the act of reading:

- "I read to expand my mind and open my eyes to the world."

- "I only read books for school, or if I am grounded."

- "Reading is the best thing invented since . . . EVER!"

- "I like to read sometimes, but it's kinda hard to find the right book."

- "I read because my girlfriend wants me to."

- "I heard you get smarter by reading."

- "I read to escape reality."

- "Most books are not very appealing, also they are very wordy."

- "Books are boring and I'd rather skate and hang with friends."

- "Nothing keeps me from reading."

Like adults, some teens enjoy reading to escape, some read to find information, and some don't read unless they absolutely have to. Some teens cannot read and others can read but choose not to. One of the biggest mistakes we can make when serving teens in a library setting is to stereotype or make generalizations about how, why, when, or where teens read.

Teens and Reading: Influences, Perceptions, Attitudes, and Expectations

The responses shown in this section's figures provide a snapshot of how teens throughout the country perceive themselves as readers, including why they read, what they read, and what influences their reading choices.

There is a common discussion that adults like to have, and it goes something like this: "These kids today, they don't read books, they don't read the newspaper, they don't read anything... not like when I was a kid." Well, my cranky adult friends, the survey results in Figures 6.1 and 6.2 disagree. Teens ages 12–18, those people we consider to be among the busiest, most scheduled, and least interested in reading *are* reading. And why are they reading? **For the fun of it.** The same reason you read when you were a kid and quite possibly the same reason you read now as an adult. So what does this mean for us? It means you better get your game on and be ready to serve them the books they want, the books they like, and the books that they are interested in reading.

None of the responses in Figure 6.3 should be a surprise to anyone who works with teens, but we can do something about the 22 percent of teens who would read more if they could find a good book to read.

Figure 6.1. Why Do You Read? 2007 SmartGirl Survey

Just for the fun of it	63%
To learn new things	62%
I get bored and want something to do	35%
Because my parents encourage me to read	24%

Figure 6.2. Why Do You Read? 2008 Teen Reading Habits and Perceptions Survey

Just for the fun of it	57%
I have to read for school	46%
I get bored and want something to do	38%
To learn new things	33%
My parents encourage me to read	18%
I don't read much	12%
So I know what's going on with my friends	9%

Figure 6.3. What Keeps You from Reading More? 2008 Teen Reading Habits and Perceptions Survey

I don't have time. I'm too busy.	39%	It puts me to sleep or gives me a headache.	3%
I can't find a good book.	22%	Books are too long.	3%
It's not social—I'd rather hang out with my friends.	8%	It's too much like schoolwork.	2%
I prefer to watch television/movies.	7%	I'm not very good at it.	2%
I'd rather go out and do something.	7%	My friends would make fun of me.	2%
Reading is boring. I can't get into it.	6%		

We can't build an extra hour into the day for voluntary reading, but we can help teens find books they might like to read. We begin this process by making sure our libraries are welcoming to teens and that our collections are up to date. Our next step is to make sure teens know where to go and whom to ask for help when they enter the library, and our final step is to go out of our way to make sure we know what's new, what's hot, what's popular, and what's interesting so that we can make recommendations the next time a teen asks us for a "good book."

Fiction was selected as the format teens read most often, but one-third to one-half of the teens who responded to this survey selected magazines, online content, comics, and graphic novels as their preferred format (see Figures 6.4 and 6.5). This kind of information often makes

Figure 6.4. Which of the Following Do You Read Most Often? 2007 SmartGirl Survey

Books for pleasure	76%	Newspapers	19%
Online reading (Web sites and blogs)	59%	Comics	19%
Magazines	54%	Textbooks	19%
Assigned reading for school	33%	Listening to audiobooks	5%

Figure 6.5. Which of the Following Do You Read Most Often? 2008 Teen Reading Habits and Perceptions Survey

Books (fiction)	72%	Comic books, graphic novels, manga, Web comics	29%
Magazines	44%	Newspapers and news Web sites	18%
Social networking sites	32%	Fan fiction	13%
Books (nonfiction)	29%	None of the above	3%

adults nervous, because unfortunately many parents, teachers, and librarians still don't count this kind of reading as "real" reading. However, what this survey shows us is that if we don't stop and pay attention to what teens are reading and want to read, then we are going to lose opportunities to help develop readers by utilizing these formats and promoting these formats as legitimate options for reading in the classroom and for pleasure.

Secondarily, these results shine a spotlight on teens' increased interest in reading content online, from postings on their MySpace page to online news. It is likely that this percentage will continue to grow as more content becomes available online and social networking becomes even more pervasive as the leading medium teens use to share information with one another.

These results also mean that we all need to pay more attention to creating a teen library collection that is reflective of the needs and wants of our teen community. For years we have asked teens what they like to read, but our questions have usually been limited to books. Sure, inquiries about magazines have snuck in there recently, but is anyone asking teens what online content they are regularly reading? Asking and getting specific answers will also give you valuable information about the stories and topics of interest to teens. Do they follow an author blog or fan fiction? If so, you can use this information to purchase accompanying or support materials. The goal is not to eliminate teens' online reading but to give them options and support their reading interests. If an adult patron followed a local chef's blog and then that chef published a book, the library would buy that book without a second thought. We would also make finding that chef's blog easy on our Web site—we would give our adult patrons those options and support their reading interest. Why then do we hesitate to give the same respect to teens and their reading interests?

Magazines continue to rank high among teen preferences for reading for a lot of reasons, including the fact that they are portable, attractive, high interest, timely, inexpensive, easy to dip in to and out of, and unintimidating for those who struggle with reading. One statistic to watch is how teens regard electronic books and audiobooks. Is the low percentage of teens listening to audiobooks low because they don't like the format or because they can't afford the players to listen to them? After all, most adults listen to audiobooks in their cars, during their commute to work. Very few teens have that option, and those who do have commutes to school in their own car or on a bus usually have an iPod—a notoriously unfriendly piece of hardware when it comes to playing audiobooks that a patron has checked out from the library. This may change as MP3 players become more compatible with audiobooks and as Playaways (all-in-one players that do not require any outside hardware or software) become more widely available, but until then it bears taking notice that audiobooks do not generally rank very high as a preferred format for teen readers. This doesn't mean you shouldn't purchase them for your collection, but it does mean you should keep an eye on the percentage of dollars you spend on them in comparison to how much money you put toward growing your collection of popular series books, graphic novels and comics, and magazines, all preferred materials with teen readers.

Teens today have been raised in a world where fantasy rules and books like *Harry Potter* and *Twilight* inspire a frightening (in a good way) sort of mania. Therefore it's no surprise that teens in both 2007 and in 2008 selected fantasy as their favorite genre (see Figures 6.6 and 6.7). We do think some LSTs might be surprised by the popularity of mystery books among teens responding to these surveys. After all, most LSTs can name a number of fantasy series off their top of their heads but might be hard-pressed to come up with a similar list of titles that fall under the mystery genre category. In the write-in option for this question on the 2008 survey, some of the feedback we found insightful with regard to collection development is that teens also want to read books that are funny, urban fiction, and, believe it or not, classics.

From the responses in Figure 6.8, we can deduce that four areas of nonfiction are the most popular: Biographies/Memoirs, Art/Music/Movies, Poetry, and History. This may help those of you who are inclined to buy historical fiction—resist and buy the true stuff instead. Teens are telling us they want to read about history but they want to read the truth, not some fictionalized version.

If you were expecting "The librarian suggests it" to score high on the question about how teens choose what to read (see Figure 6.9), we're sorry to disappoint you. The reality is that as much as we may want our

Figure 6.6. What Kind of Books Do You Read for Fun? 2007 SmartGirl Survey

Fantasy	48%	Romance	40%
Humor	46%	Horror	34%
Mystery	46%	Short in length	27%
Adventure	41%	Chick Lit	25%

Figure 6.7. What Kind of Fiction Do You Read for Fun? 2008 Teen Reading Habits and Perceptions Survey

Fantasy	50%	Science fiction	28%
Mystery	43%	Historical fiction	19%
Romance	39%	Fan fiction	12%
Realistic fiction	38%	I don't read fiction for fun	8%
Thriller/Suspense	35%	Whatever is short in length	6%
Horror	31%	Westerns	3%

Figure 6.8. If You Read Nonfiction, What Subjects Do You Read about for Fun? 2008 Teen Reading Habits and Perceptions Survey

Poetry	27%	Science and technology	16%
History	26%	Spirituality, religion, or magic	15%
Art, architecture, music, and movies	26%	Other countries and cultures	15%
I don't read nonfiction for fun	25%	Philosophy, logic, ethics, or psychology	12%
Biographies and memoirs	24%	Politics, law, or the economy	7%
Food, exercise, or cooking	19%	Whatever's short in length	7%
How to do something (sewing, car repair, foreign languages, drawing, etc.)	19%		

Figure 6.9. Which of the Following Help You Pick a Book to Read? 2008 Teen Reading Habits and Perceptions Survey

My friends say it's really good.	53%	Parent/teacher makes me.	19%
The cover looks interesting.	48%	The librarian suggests it.	15%
I like other stuff by this author.	41%	It's short.	10%
It's on display with other books I like.	31%	It's available in the format I like (paperback, hardcover, audiobook, etc.).	8%
It's on a bestseller list.	26%		

recommendations to be worth their weight in gold, this is not the case. In actuality, teens care what their friends are reading and they listen to their recommendations when it comes to picking books for themselves. Use this information to your advantage and solicit teen input to build your collection and create displays to market your collection. Use "Teen Picks"—let other teens know that these books in the display have been chosen for teens, by teens.

Not surprisingly, the second greatest influence on teen selection was the cover of a book. The old adage is certainly true that teens do judge a book by its cover, so use this information to your advantage and involve teens in selecting, shelving, weeding, and creating displays. Encourage teen volunteers (and staff) to shelve books face out when possible, and remember that covers matter when you begin ordering replacement copies of classics. After all, there is a reason mainstream publishers often update the covers of older books when they decide to reprint a title. Of course, one option we didn't think to include in the survey was the plot summary, or flap copy, included inside the dust jacket of a book or available on the back cover of a book. Many teens wrote in to let us know that they often use this information to decide if a particular story seems interesting. Finally, a handful of teens also wrote

CD See Tool 37. Teen Picks Card Template

Figure 6.10. Do You Consider Reading...? 2008 Teen Reading Habits and Perceptions Survey

Something fun to do	36%
A good way to escape	26%
A way to learn stuff	16%
Boring	13%
Nerdy	6%
A waste of time	4%

Figure 6.11. What Do You Think Teachers and Librarians Count as Reading? 2008 Teen Reading Habits and Perceptions Survey

Books (fiction)	81%
Books (nonfiction)	79%
Newspapers and news Web sites	42%
Magazines	29%
Comic books, graphic novels, manga, Web comics	24%
Fan fiction	21%
Social networking sites	13%

in to let us know they often read the first few sentences of a book before deciding if they want to read more. This is just one more reason to keep book displays in your library's teen area current and ever-changing.

Both of the questions for Figures 6.10 and 6.11 address perceptions: How do teens perceive the act of reading and how do they perceive what "qualifies" as reading by some of the adults in their lives? The 2008 survey reports positive results for both questions. Not too long ago many teachers had a narrow definition of what teens were allowed to read for book reports and silent reading. Thankfully, this seems to be changing for the better, and teens feel more empowered to select materials and formats that they find interesting and their teachers find suitable.

So how should either of these questions (and subsequent teen answers) affect your collection development choices? You need to be prepared for teens to require a variety of materials to complete their homework, and you are likely going to have to reeducate yourself and your colleagues about what are "suitable" materials for a teen who is looking for help finding resources for a school project.

What Are the Reading Interests of Boys?

Almost any LST who has visited a secondary school classroom or done a booktalk in a middle school or high school could tell the tale about the student, often a male, who will defiantly and proudly announce to the librarian that he doesn't read. Chances are that this response is mainly for show, to mark turf, and to challenge authority; chances are that these boys do read, but not the stack of novels the booktalking librarian no doubt has in front of her. ("Her" is the correct pronoun to use as the overwhelming majority of LSTs are female.) Instead, that male is probably reading newspapers (comics, sports, and entertainment), magazines (same list as newspapers, but add video gaming magazines), graphic novels or collected comics, and maybe even heavily illustrated nonfiction. Thus, the boy at the booktalk session saying he doesn't read might simply be saying that he doesn't read what libraries offer.

Most teen sections in public libraries are filled with fiction; the recreational nonfiction is scarce and is often in the adult area. If there is recreational nonfiction, it is more than likely self-help, health related, about teen issues, or pop star biographies. There might be magazines, but the chances are that they are aimed more at girls than boys. Comic books are more than likely not there and collections of graphic novels are generally pretty slim pickings. There also probably isn't a newspaper lying around. Additionally, boys who venture into the teen area will find shelves so jammed that there won't be an opportunity for them to be captivated by an interesting cover. They also won't find any interesting books on display because most displays are created by female librarians or library staff members, who generally select new fiction for the purposes of merchandising materials.

Given these choices, the teen boy, especially a younger one, will opt for something safe like a series book, only to get the message from a teacher, parent, or maybe even a librarian that the book is only okay because "at least he is reading something." What the boy is getting, given the choices available, is maybe the best by his own standards, not by those of a librarian or committee. His best book is one that will provide him with information or entertainment. It is one he will read.

Michael Smith's book *Reading Don't Fix No Chevys, and Going with the Flow: How to Engage Boys (and Girls) in Their Literacy Learning* reviews a dozen major findings of research done regarding boys—not just teens—and reading:

- Boys don't comprehend narrative (fiction) as well as girls do.
- Boys have much less interest in leisure reading than do girls.
- Boys are more inclined to read informational texts.
- Boys are more inclined to read magazine and newspaper articles.
- Boys are more inclined to read comic books and graphic novels than girls.
- Boys like to read about hobbies, sports, and things they do or want to do.

Boys often prefer nonfiction because they are reading for a purpose (to find information, answers, directions, etc.). Nonfiction often answers the question "Why?," thereby satisfying many boys' natural curiosity about why things work the way they do.

Creating a "Guys Read" Bookclub is a good way to get young guys interested in reading. It's also an excellent way to begin developing relationships and modeling behavior between reluctant readers and reading mentors.

(CD) See Tool 12. Guys Read: Mission, Objectives, and Goals

(CD) See Tool 13. Guys Read: Sample Program Setup

(CD) See Tool 14. Guys Read: Why Does This Program Matter?

- Boys tend to enjoy escapism and humor.
- Some groups of boys are passionate about science fiction or fantasy.
- The appearance of a book and cover is important to boys.
- Few boys entering school call themselves "nonreaders," but by high school, over one-half do.
- Boys tend to think they are bad readers.
- If reading is perceived as feminized, then boys will go to great lengths to avoid it.[3]

How Do You Select the Best Books for Teenagers?

These reading surveys show that while there is some continuity in the reading interests of teens across gender, grades, and even over time, teen readers are difficult to stereotype. They read all genres and they read both teen books and adult books they find of interest. The unpredictability of the teen reader presents those developing collections with their greatest challenges, opportunities, and rewards.

So the best way for an LST or a selector to develop the most teen-friendly collection is to get the teens involved in the process. There are numerous ways to get teens involved, from something as simple as having a suggestion box to something as formal as having a collection development advisory council who meets monthly to pour through publisher catalogs, search Baker & Taylor or Ingram's recommended carts, or read reviews in professional journals collected by the LST. When you give up control, you end up with a collection that has its roots in the genuine interests and desires of real teens who will not only check out your materials but send their friends to do the same.

In our travels around the country doing workshops for public librarians and school library media specialists, we often hear about exciting ways LSTs are engaging teens and getting them involved in the collection development process. Some of our favorites include these:

- An LST in California involved teens in the selection process for paperback books. Using a vendor catalog of new paperbacks, the LST made copies, handed them out to her teen advisors, and then placed an order based on their suggestions.
- An LST in Arizona knew she needed to develop a collection of manga, but she was at a loss for how to get started. So she found a group of teens who knew the genre and allowed them, with guidance, to select materials for the library.
- A school librarian in Michigan had her school's science fiction club do the selection. She copied pages from *VOYA*'s spectacular speculative fiction review section and handed them out at a meeting. She then said, "We can only afford five," which both

allowed teens to make suggestions (all of which were taken) and to learn a little bit about the collection development process.

Some libraries make collection development easier by having teens help with weeding—actually pulling the books, not just developing weeding reports. Many libraries involve teens in monthly sessions of choosing music or doing surveys (sometimes with prizes) when it comes time to order new magazines. Brooke Faulkner of the McArthur Public Library in Biddeford, Maine, takes her teen advisory council (TAC) to Border's for an annual shopping spree. She usually asks them to concentrate on DVDs and CDs during this trip because it is often where she has leftover money in the collection budget, but many books are selected on these trips as well. What she has found is it that teens choose things that would never have occurred to her. Two years ago, the teens built up the collection of musicals. She had forgotten how popular musicals are among teens involved in drama and choir at school. This year, teens selected anime series and classic television shows on DVD, vegetarian/vegan cookbooks, coffee-table-style books of British cars—all of these are materials that flew beneath her radar or didn't fit her adult-constructed view of teen interests.[4]

Involving teens in collection development may take more time at first, but it will be worth it in the end. And, yes, it might be faster to do it yourself rather than set up a process for teen input, but can you really argue that you know better than a teen what teens like to read? No, you can't, and you are fooling yourself if you think you can. Don't worry—this isn't giving up your professionalism; instead, it is proving it. By empowering teens, you are creating more powerful services, building better collections, and, more important, building relationships.

What Kind of Teen Collection Do You Want to Build?

A teen section is usually small enough that over a short period of time one can transform it to meet a particular vision. What is your vision? The answer to that question should be influenced by several factors, including these:

- The library's collection development policy and overall total collection development philosophy
- The quality and quantity of school library collections in your area
- Your library's budget, space, and staff available
- The reading interests of teens in your community
- Your own professional values
- What needs the collection should meet

Whatever your "vision" for the collection, you need to set priorities because doing it all will likely not be possible. Most think a "balanced

If your library does not have a collection development policy or your library's collection development policy does not specifically address your teen collection, we recommend setting up a meeting with your library director and the head of your collection development department to talk about creating one or including teen materials in your existing policy. For your convenience, the Librarian Serving Teens (LST) Tool Kit on CD-ROM includes three sample collection development policies from Haverhill Public Library (Massachusetts), Johnson County Public Library (Kansas), and San Francisco Public Library (California) that do include teen materials.

CD **See Tool 52. Young Adult Collection Development Policy: Haverhill Public Library (MA)**

CD **See Tool 53. Young Adult Collection Development Policy: Johnson County Library (KS)**

CD **See Tool 54. Young Adult Collection Development Policy: San Francisco Public Library (CA)**

collection" is desirable, but if you really want to set priorities and concentrate efforts, funds, and space on certain areas, the collection will be out of balance. The whole battle about collection balance (popularity versus quality, breadth versus depth) involves the basic philosophy of your library. To begin, consider the following questions about collection development. As you consider these questions, remember that this is not about want you want, but about what will best meet the needs of the teens in your community.

- **Demand versus quality.** These are always the first questions you need to ask: Do you buy series paperbacks? Do you buy multiple copies? If you have money to buy only one book, and the choice is between a popular book and a quality one, which one would you choose? To answer these questions, think about what the teens who use your library would be more likely to check out and what your local school libraries have available in their collections that could help balance your selections.

- **Circulation versus standards.** Does the library have a "responsibility" to provide teens with materials of *only* high literary quality? This question, which is closely related to the previous one, should always be followed by the following question: Which is easier to quantify on an annual report: an increase in circulation or literary standards being upheld?

- **Permanency versus immediacy.** What should the turnover rate be in a teen collection? Should you choose to stock it with long-lasting hardbacks that will last decades and create a permanent teen collection, or should you choose to fill it with books that meet immediate reading interests but, due to paperback format, will not survive two years? Obviously there needs to be a mix, but given the fact that most teen areas are small and so are most teen budgets, our guess is even if teens did not prefer the paperback format, librarians would.

- **Recreational versus educational versus informational versus cultural.** Again, the answer to this question hinges on the needs of your community and how teens in your area use your library: Is it mostly used for after-school homework? For finding something fun to read in the summer? For providing programming after school for teens who drop by after school, which is located within walking distance of the library? This decision also hinges on the strength of the school library collections in your community as well as the adult/reference department in your library. Does your area have a teen reference section, or does the adult/reference section in your library handle ordering these kinds of materials? And if they do, do they regularly select materials that will be of interest to teens? And do you incorporate nonfiction for teens into your young adult collection, or is this another area handled by the adult department? All of these questions will also help you determine where to spend your dollars.

- **Professional versus careful.** Another debate concerns professional values, personal opinions, and community standards. The bottom line: Do you buy materials that you and most adults would object to but teens would love? Do you respond to your customers—teens—or to supporters in the community? Do you buy rap music? Manga series rated "Older Teen"? A professional wrestling magazine, skateboarding magazine, or a tattoo magazine? Do you buy Zane or Stephen King for the teen collection? Do you collect books for gay and lesbian teens? Do you collect urban street lit? Again, the answers to these questions depend on the values of your community, your flexibility and freedom to create a user-friendly collection, and what kind of administrative support you have to make these decisions.

- **Librarian versus book buyer.** If your focus is popular reading, then have you forsaken your "professionalism" to become a glorified Border's book buyer? A group of teens could probably select a more responsive collection than many librarians charged with developing teen collections. Is the best selector the person who selects the most titles that end up on a "best books" list or the one who selects all of the teen bestsellers?

- **Customers versus collections.** Actually, this is the big question. Believe it or not, even the most traditional librarians and administrators want quality in teen collections; it is just that these two groups measure quality differently. A customer service–centered process puts the customer first. One way to measure customer satisfaction with the collection is to run a circulation report. If your books are being checked out, then you must be doing something right. Another way is to conduct informal surveys of teens who use your library (or the ones who hang outside of your library but never set foot in the doors) and more formal surveys out in the community where teens hang out (booth at a neighborhood festival, table set up in the cafeteria at the local high school, teen librarian in the mall with a clipboard during the back to school weekend, etc.) to find out if the library is meeting the needs of teens in your community. For many teens, paperbacks and popular fiction meet their recreational and emotional reading needs. However, we would be remiss to say this applies to all teen readers across the board. Part of creating a quality collection for teens is creating a diverse collection. Although an all graphic novel collection would be popular, it would be a major disservice to teens in your community who have no interest in that format. Popularity matters, but not to the exclusion of special interest items (acid jazz CDs, books about gothic culture), more narrow genres (satire, short story), and alternate formats (play scripts, zines) that may not be as popular but will be of great interest to subsets of teens in your community. We heard about one LST who totally stopped buying hardbacks for the branch libraries and put the money into magazines. The circulation soared and everyone was happy, except of course those teens who didn't read magazines and who liked new teen literature that came out in hardback. You will not always be able to please everyone all of the time, but if you pay attention to your community and listen to the needs of the teens who do spend time in your library you will likely hit the target a majority of the time.

- **Hardcover versus paperback (which sometimes also means quality versus popularity).** Here's the scenario: It is near the end of your fiscal year and you have a small amount of money (literally, just a few dollars) available to spend on books for young adults. In front of you is Ingram's newest book cart of suggested titles for teens on iPage and the latest issue of *Booklist*. You have $25.00 to spend; you can buy one of the new hardback books being heavily marketed, or you can buy several paperbacks. Some of these paperbacks are not just reprints of hardbacks, but originals, and most of them are parts of a series. How do you spend the money? This choice is as often about choosing quality versus popularity as it is about hardcover versus paperback. Your decision will usually be a reflection of a series of choices that you have already made about how to develop your collection.

- **Series books versus stand-alone titles.** Often, when you choose paperbacks, as in the previous question, you are making a conscious decision to add series books to your library's collection. Your stance on series books and the role they do (or don't) play in your library's teen collection will greatly determine the popularity of your collection with younger teens who often read series (or formula) fiction at a certain point in early adolescence. Series fiction often provides teenagers with the type of reading experience they want at a particular time in their lives, and once that time in their lives has passed, they will move on to something else. It's not because they want to move on to reading "quality" literature but because reading series fiction no longer meets their emotional or recreational needs. And for some teens, series fiction is simply what they want to read because it's predictable, comfortable, and doesn't require much work. That's okay, and it's not just limited to teens. When the newest James Patterson or Danielle Steele book comes out, adult librarians don't ask whether they should buy it (it is, after all, formula fiction for adults) but how many copies they should buy.

- **Reading versus reading something.** This doesn't mean there aren't teen and adult librarians out there wringing their hands about "soiling" the library's shelves with such "trash." Sadly, there's a whole school of librarians in our profession who feel like it's their duty to save people from their own "bad" reading habits. Occasionally, that school of judgmental librarians is overshadowed by another misinformed group who use the "Well, at least they are reading something" argument to "defend" series books. The problem with this argument (or one might call it an attitude) is that the message it really sends to readers of series fiction is that the "something" in question lacks value, and, thus, the subtle message transmitted is that they lack value. This attitude sets up a caste system of reading; it is insulting, absurd, and counterproductive. The only bad reading choice is the one many teens make not to read at all. The best thing librarians can do to influence that choice is provide materials that a teen would want to read. The best types of material for teens to read are materials that meet their needs, have proven popularity, have peer approval, and lead them to reading something else, if only another book that's exactly like the one they just finished.

All of these questions can often lead to big decisions, and LSTs will need to have many discussions before finding answers that fit their library and community. But understand that if you don't ask these questions and analyze your collection, it will flounder. By trying to be everything to everyone, it will end up being nothing to no one. These are just some of the questions an LST might face when making collection decisions. We write "might" because the sad fact is that many large public library systems do not allow LSTs to make any of these choices. Instead, the choices are made for them. Centralized selection is often counterproductive to building a teen-responsive collection. It doesn't allow for differences in communities, in readers, and in the vast skills most LSTs possess. If your library does centralized collection, offer to spend some time with the selectors, sharing feedback from teens and your knowledge of YA literature. Opening the lines of communication between you and your system's selectors of YA fiction, nonfiction, music, and graphic novels can only make your library's YA collection stronger.

In this book, we don't want to load you down with titles that we think you "must buy" because we don't know what is right for the teens using your library. Along the way, we will suggest some titles as examples or best bets, but these are merely suggestions. We don't work with your teens; you do.

How Do You Start Building a Collection for Teens?

We often build or assess a collection by the titles and authors we recognize; they have a reputation, whether good or bad. Teens also assess and judge books, but they generally use a different set of criteria: the story and the cover. The cover may get them to pick it up but the story will keep them reading it. There is a core collection or a core set of authors that one would expect to find in any teen collection, such as Scott Westerfeld, Walter Dean Myers, and Sarah Dessen. There are different ways to go about building your collection—the author/title route or the genre/list route. The author/title route may include comfortable authors that write many different titles and titles that may cross over genres. If you have a grasp of several teen authors, a variety of books are at your fingertips to recommend to teens. The genre/list route may seem like a narrow focus at first, but in the end you may end up with a better collection because you are looking at each genre individually so it gets the attention it deserves.

You may also want to take a hard look at your juvenile and adult collections; if your library has been without a teen collection, there may be titles purchased over the years that are currently housed in these sections that would be a good fit in your teen collection. Topics and formats such as biographies, magazines, music, videos, science fiction, and recreational and informational nonfiction could all be culled from the juvenile and adult collection. By pulling out certain titles that have teen appeal, you give older titles a new audience. You may have to negotiate liberating those titles from the juvenile and adult collections, but it can be a great start. Which route you decide to take in building your teen collection might depend on your budget and purchasing cycle, as well as your library's philosophy, service response, and partnership with other departments to make sure your library is meeting the informational and educational needs of teens. But it is your job as the LST to communicate with your colleagues about these needs and the larger collection need. If you do work in a library that has centralized collections then there is no better relationship to establish than one with the adult selectors; generally you will find youth selectors who have some teen experience and understand teen development and what titles will fill that crossover use of teens. But you are more likely to encounter adult selectors who do not have any teen experience, and it is up to you to help them understand the need to work with you to fill out the collection. Regularly involve them in discussions about the teen collections, bring them lists of titles teens have recommended, invite them to talk with a group of teens about the titles they read, help them identify authors, book awards, and journals that have teen appeal. . . . Okay, train them to be LSTs. There, we said it.

Fiction

Teens are using your fiction collection for recreational reading but also for required reading for school, so be sure that you have done your research and include titles that show up on reading lists for middle schools and high schools in your area. Be proactive about those required reading titles, seek those lists, and work with your selectors. Figure out which schools read which titles and work to buy multiple copies, and then catalog them together in the teen area so teens, parents, and staff have them at their fingertips. Not every title with teen appeal can be located in the teen collection. There are physical limitations, and some titles that have teen appeal are rightly located in the adult collection. As an LST, a comprehensive knowledge of other collections within your library can be very beneficial. You can serve the teens in your community better and spend money wisely. Because of how libraries often determine their collection budgets, you may have to partner with the adult fiction selector to make sure that certain titles appear in your library no matter who is purchasing them. Be aware of teen programming that goes on and of any special library initiatives, such as "United We Read" or "One City, One Book."

The "one book idea" assumes that there is one book that everyone will enjoy reading. That's an unrealistic idea, as teens vary in their reading tastes. Some will read only certain authors, certain genres, while other teens will read numerous subjects, often choosing books by the cover or the title. While teens may choose books for different reasons, what they get out of fiction may not vary much.

If you look at the books that stand the test of time with teens (*The Outsiders* and *Ender's Game*) or those that suddenly become wildly popular (*Twilight*, books in the "Bluford High" series), most will meet many of the emotional needs teens are looking for in fiction. With many teens, fiction isn't just about escaping; instead it's about making a connection with characters who share similar feelings. These characters may be aliens, or wizards, or everyday normal teens—the best teen fiction is not always that which paints, through language, the most beautiful pictures but rather that which presents teens with a mirror in which they see their own lives reflected in the novel. The following list presents many emotional needs that are met when teens read fiction:

- Reassure them they are normal—physically, mentally, emotionally, and socially
- Present opportunities for emotional independence from adults
- Show how to resolve problems
- Allow to experience success
- Picture satisfying relationships
- Provide help establishing roles
- Support development of socially responsible behaviors
- Help determine personal philosophy
- Furnish opportunities for emotional engagement, pleasure, and relaxation

Genres

If you take a survey of what teens enjoy reading, there are a few genres that zoom right to the top of the list; these are what you should be buying. There are some that fall to the bottom of the list; don't ignore those completely. They are probably required reading, so some poor soul is going to need one on Sunday night. Lend that teen a hand and buy the short and really good ones.

- **Adventure.** This is a great example of a genre where the subject matter itself might not be the most important thing in the book. *White Darkness* by Geraldine McCaughrean takes you on Symone's exciting vacation to Antarctica that turns into a desperate struggle for survival when her uncle's obsessive quest leads them across the frozen wilderness into danger. However, the two best parts of the story are the relationship between Symone and Titus and the harsh environment that forces you to ask the big questions about ethics and morality. A few other titles that will get a reader's blood pumping are *Heroes of the Valley* by Jonathan Stroud, *The True Adventures of Charley Darwin* by Carolyn Meyer, and *Fortune's Fool* by Kathleen Karr.

- **Fantasy.** These readers, like science fiction readers, can be vocal in asking for what they want—the next one in the series. So we tend to hear from them more than the 15-year-old girl who likes romances by Sarah Dessen. They are just as interested in the information about where the next book is, but somehow fantasy readers have learned to speak up. These fictitious worlds, like Abarat, Xanth, and Discworld, are places teens triumph over evil and learn about courage, bravery, honesty, and all that other stuff they are supposed to learn to be better adults. It is almost the equivalent of traveling to a different country as a foreign-exchange student. While you learn about the country you are visiting you also learn plenty about yourself. Divide your fantasy and science fiction collections. It will help teens find what they want quicker, and it will also help your adult staff who may not read science fiction or fantasy help your teen customers with more accuracy. A few fantasy titles to rev up the imagination include *The Fledging of Az Gabrielson* by Jay Amory, *Eon: Dragoneye Reborn* by Alison Goodman, and *Dead Is a State of Mind* by Marlene Perez.

- **Historical fiction.** Historical fiction is almost always ranked as the least popular genre, although it is the genre most mentioned on lists of "good books" for teens written by adults. This is one of those genres that adults enjoy, but most teens are not clamoring for it, probably because it gets so much attention from the teacher types. Teens do not see historical fiction as exciting or interesting. Money must be spent on it because of its value in researching assignments, but use your money wisely. Cover the milestones in history but keep the rest current—that which would probably not be considered historical fiction by you and your friends. The 1970s now count as historical fiction to some teens and soon the 1980s will as well. Go for the short and exciting if you can swing it. A few titles that bring history to life are *M+O 4evr* by Tonya Hegamin, *The Red Thread* by Roderick Townley, and *The Winter War: A Novel* by William Durbin.

- **Horror.** This is the genre parents love to hate, but if you think of popular adult television shows, at the top of the list are true-crime mysteries that have their share of blood and decaying bodies. Teens love to be scared and freaked out, and if it is *Goosebumps* or Dean Koontz that does it for them, we need to buy it. The lack of true teen horror books is one challenge that we face; they often deal with the supernatural, paranormal, and are bloody, but not true horror. For most 10th graders searching for true horror, *Cirque de Freak* is going to fall very short. This is where an LST must cooperate with the adult selectors and make sure a teen can get a hold of some true horror books somewhere in the library if not in the teen collection. A few other titles that will horrify you are *Mason* by Thomas Pendleton, *Vintage: A Ghost Story* by Steve Berman, and *Persistence of Memory* by Amelia Atwater-Rhodes.

- **Humor.** Funny is tricky. Funny movies for teens don't translate well into books because most of the time there is a visual need for the laugh. Many titles don't overflow with funny scenes in every chapter, but plenty of teen books have good humor in them. *I Am the Messenger* by Marcus Zusak has some very funny moments that only someone in high school can truly appreciate. Chris Lynch's *Extreme Elvin* combines some painful experiences with a few classic conversations. *The Dark Lord of Derkholm* by Diana Wynee Jones is a funny send-up of the sword-and-sorcery genre. Humor seems silly and a little painful at times, like when you got dumped or your best friend moved away, but, as with adults, the reading tastes of teens change, and after reading a few titles from one genre they will move on to the next. A few titles that will put a smile on your face are *Playing with Matches* by Brian Katcher, *Ten Things I Hate About Me* by Randa Abdel-Fattah, and *Girl, Barely 15, Flirting for England* by Sue Limb.

- **Inspirational fiction.** There is a huge interest among teens in all things spiritual, and this is often reflected in their reading interests. A few years ago numerous mainstream teen publishers were doing series with a Christian fiction theme, and this has expanded to include a variety of religions and experiences. Those titles have led the way to self-help, prayer books, journals, and growing-up and dating-advice titles—all with a religious tone, many written by the 20–28 age crowd, authors fresh from the fire of teen years. This personal touch also has great appeal and credibility with teen readers. A few titles in this genre are *Ask Me No Questions* by Marina Tamar Budhos, *Shift* by Charlotte Agell, *The Patron Saint of Butterflies* by Cecilia Galante, and *Everything Beautiful* by Simmone Howell.

- **Movie and television.** A benefit of the entertainment industry conglomerates is that every big movie comes as part of a package deal. The package includes soundtracks, posters, T-shirts, countless other merchandise, and a rerelease of the book associated with the movie. These books are gobbled up by teens who either want to relive the experience of the movie or the movie was rated "R" and they couldn't go see it.

- **Multicultural literature.** As more children of recent immigrants hit their adult years we have seen an explosion in multicultural literature. This reflects their experiences but also the incredible diversity in teens today. Recent examples are *Tasting the Sky* by Ibtisam Barakat, *Keeping Corner* by Kashirma Sheth, and *Revolution Is Not a Dinner Party* by Ying Change Compestine, which depicts the common experience of growing up outside of and/or immigrating to the United States with high hopes, no matter your background. In these books, teens also learn the cultures of the main characters, the good and the bad. A few other titles in this genre are *Mexican WhiteBoy* by Matt de la Pena, *Dark Dude* by Oscar Hijuelos, and *The House of Djinn* by Suzanne Fisher Staples.

- **Mystery.** Stock your shelves with the scariest titles you can find because scary is always in demand. Hair-raising is one thing, but don't overlook the good whodunit story with a twist. Just as mystery programs in the adult sections of libraries are popular, teens crave both a familiar plot line and a good challenge. Once they graduate from mysteries by Joan Lowery Nixon, we need to have more challenging titles waiting, like *Right Behind You* by Gail Giles or *King Dork* by Frank Portman. Most adults feel comfortable redirecting a high school student to Patricia Cornwell or John Sanford, but these adults are missing some great stories mostly because they aren't familiar with the teen titles. A few titles that will keep you guessing are *Sparrow* by Sherri L. Smith, *Fade to Black* by Alex Flinn, *Frozen Fire* by Tim Bowler, and *Paper Towns* by John Green.

- **Realistic fiction.** You will hear this referred to as the "problem novel," but this is selling it short. These are the stories in which teens find characters in the everyday situations they too are experiencing. These situations may seem like a challenge, obstacle, or issue to the teen, but if an adult begins to call every teenage situation a "problem," teens will begin to look at their lives as problems. Reading about issues like friendship, sexual experience, betrayal, religion, violence, and school encourages teens to consider how they would react in similar situations. It does not mean that every teen who reads *Burned* by Ellen Hopkins is interested in an alcoholic parent or abusive family. It could mean that a teen living in that situation may see a different way or an explanation offered in the story. You can be assured that in most realistic fiction the problem is resolved, the teen protagonist learns from the situation, and things, in general, get better, although "better" may not be what the teen protagonist expected. Realistic fiction offers teen readers options and consolations, instilling feelings that they are not the only person experiencing a particular moment of embarrassment or confusion. Reading about such problems may help teens see the situation from another perspective. These reasons aren't too far from the reasons why adults read novels that deal with tough situations such as *The Glass Castle* by Jeanette Walls or a variety of Oprah's Book Club selections. A few titles in this genre are *The Truth About Truman School* by Dori Hillestad Butler, *Gravity* by Leanne Lieberman, and *Off-Color* by Janet McDonald.

- **Romance.** This is the emotional category that is probably the easiest to match with teens. Just as they are experiencing highs and lows, they are interested in the trials and tribulations of other teens who may not have the bad skin condition or the overprotective parents with whom they find themselves saddled. You could pick up ten YA novels and find a romance in the story in at least four of them. Romance, while maybe not a major theme, is a topic that runs through many YA books. Romance titles for teens vary from the mild first crush to the full-blown bad relationship that is going too far, too fast. Teen romance novels with more than a hint of sex and no negative repercussions are becoming more common. The *Gossip Girl* series, the *Gemma Doyle* series by Libba Bray, and the comedic romantic musings in *The Au Pairs* by Melissa de la Cruz are some of the works that illustrate this trend. A few titles that you might love are *Split Screen* by Brent Hartinger, *Down to the Bone* by Mayra L. Doyle, and *The Possibilities of Sainthood* by Donna Freitas.

- **Science fiction.** Science fiction and fantasy both have a consistent following of nearly 10 percent of all teen readers. Again do yourself a favor and separate science fiction from fantasy. These genres are not the same, and while devoted readers know the difference, library staff may not at first. Your teen customers will be much better served from a divided collection. Even a sticker on the spine, at the very least, will go a long way in their minds. It will be clear that your library knows the difference and puts equal importance on both, which translates into placing importance on the reader. A few titles in this genre are *Things That Are* by Andrew Clements, *Nation* by Terry Pratchett, and *Andromeda Klein* by Frank Portman.

- **Short story collections.** Thankfully, this subgenre has blossomed in the past years. Short story collections now touch every possible genre and topic that a teen might experience. They fulfill assignments for teens who need to read a short story. These collections give teens experience with the literary devices used in short stories, adding the bonus of a teen protagonist and covering teen issues. Teens can connect with both the characters and issues and then move on to higher-level short stories. They give teachers, counselors, and parents a tool with which to introduce discussion on a variety of topics with teen appeal and parental avoidance. They can also act as the catalyst for various creative writing exercises. A few short story collections are

Lunch with Lenin and Other Stories by Deborah Ellis, *Blood Roses* by Francesca Lia Block, and *Owning It: Stories About Teens with Disabilities* edited by Don Gallo.

- **Sports.** These stories are not only about who wins the game; they also do a good job of incorporating the struggles that every athlete faces—balancing studies with responsibilities at home and sports. Expectations of parents, coaches, and other teens from the teen athlete often come to the forefront in these stories, as well as using sports as a vehicle to explore prejudice, honesty, and pressure. Chris Crutcher, Mike Lupica, Will Weaver, John Ritter, James Bennett, and Carl Deuker are all known authors in this genre. A few titles for the sports fan are *Beanball* by Gene Fehler, *Sophomore Undercover* by Benjamin Esch, and *Box Out* by John Coy.

- **Trauma.** This genre seems like a cross between realistic fiction and romance, and the works of these authors, like Lurlene McDaniel, have as much trauma as drama. The disease-of-the-week might strike a family member, or a friend, or the narrators themselves. With teens so full of life, the preoccupation with death is easy to explain and hard to ignore when choosing books. These titles elicit the high emotion that often matches what teens are experiencing in their own lives. A few titles in this genre are *My Tiki Girl* by Jennifer McMahon, *Such a Pretty Girl* by Laura Wiess, and *Jars of Glass: A Novel* by Brad Barkley and Heather Hepler.

- **Urban fiction.** As the influence of hip-hop on teen popular culture and fashion cannot be overstated, YA literature has yet to produce a great hip-hop novel. The works of Walter Dean Myers and Allison van Diepen's *Street Pharm* come close, but they really lack true street credibility for older teens. Many of the books published under the Kimani Tru imprint will be of interest to teens searching for urban fiction, but they are also not exactly a perfect fit. Books written for teens by Coe Booth, like *Tyrell* and *Kendra*, are a good fit, albeit slightly tamer versions of their adult counterparts, like Tracy Brown's *Criminal Minded*, Sister Souljah's *The Coldest Winter Ever*, and anything by Zane. Other titles in this genre include *Dope Sick* by Walter Dean Myers, *This Full House* by Virginia Euwer Wolff, *Hot Girl* by Dream Jordan, and *Amiri and Odette: A Love Story* by Walter Dean Myers.

Series Fiction

For every adult who hopes they never see another *Gossip Girl*, *Star Wars*, *Cirque de Freak*, or *Sweet Valley University*, there is one word for them: "Relax." Seriously, you must relax. Almost everyone goes through a time when they read series fiction; bad things will not happen to teens who read series fiction. In fact good things will happen; all of the research supports the value of reading series fiction. The appeal of series fiction for teens is varied, but, generally, they appreciate the following:

- They enjoy reading, and this enjoyment will lead to more reading, and more times than not reading a variety of genres while they find the subjects that interest them.

- They develop relationships with familiar characters and thus develop and practice empathy.

- They take comfort in predictable endings because their lives are not predictable. Might we mention Danielle Steele, Mary Higgins Clark, Nora Roberts, or Stuart Woods? We may not associate those authors with series fiction but their books do have many similarities to series fiction, and no one is discouraging adults from reading those authors.

- They work out a variety of situations through the characters they already know.

- They pick up on various points of interest in the stories, such as setting, character development, and vocabulary because of the familiarity with the plot and its predictability.

- They achieve something. Series fiction allows readers who are struggling with their reading to progress, keep reading, and become more confident with each success.

- They get more of what they want (horror/romance) without the hassle of asking adults and getting redirected to something they didn't want (mystery/historical fiction) in the first place.

- They move on to other genres and books cranky adults think are "appropriate."

Classics

The term "classic" means different things to different people. One definition is a book that is "never hot, but never cold." Any book for which there is and always will be a demand qualifies as a classic. For titles that fit this definition, you will have to check your catalog periodically because they have a way of disappearing. One definition of a classic might be any book a teen would reasonably expect to find in any library. Again, that covers a lot of ground.

The popular idea of classics are those with a capital C: Dickens, the Brontës, and others. These books are taught in school, often read by teens out of necessity rather than choice, and were primarily written before any teen's great-great-grandparents were even born. You might want to consider getting these in Permabound editions so you don't constantly have to repurchase them. The primary audience for classics is often a person who knows exactly what book he or she wants to read so format doesn't matter. Because of this, don't waste valuable display space; put them on a bottom shelf near the back of the teen area. But another kind of classic is just as important, and it's not handed down from teacher to student, from one generation of teens to the next. They don't always make our lists, but they do make several trips around a group of teens who end up marking the pages. Some of these make the BBYA list, while others escape attention. These titles represent books that teens will be looking for, but rarely asking for, in a library collection. All will be popular, and almost all present selection versus censorship questions. Most of these types of titles obtained that cult status by being controversial (e.g., *Go Ask Alice*, *A Child Called It*, *Fight Club*, *Push*, and *The Coldest Winter Ever*).[3]

Perhaps, though, the most popular classics among teens are all by the same author—the late, great Mr. Cliff. For every copy of *Moby Dick* you should have a CliffsNotes book as well. Some libraries have refused to stock CliffsNotes, but then there are always Barron's and Monarch and SparkNotes, both in print and online.

Nonfiction

Recreational and Informational

Some libraries ignore YA nonfiction altogether or they shelve it with their adult collection. Their rationale is if teens need nonfiction for homework then they will find more sources if YA nonfiction is housed with the adult collection. This may be true; a teen doing a report on the Holocaust may find more sources in the adult collection. But you are assuming that teens are using nonfiction only for educational purposes. This is not true. Teens use nonfiction for recreational, informational, educational, and reference pursuits.

Don't assume that fiction is the only type of book that teens read for pleasure. It just isn't so. Teens are developing special interests and will read whatever comes their way if it pertains to their passions. Often, the best nonfiction to include in your collection is not found in review journals, but by browsing bookstores online or in person. It also helps to pay attention to what teens in your community like and in what special areas they take an interest.

Not all learning that teens do is related to school. They do homework, but they also do lifework. Teen bodies and lives are constantly changing, so naturally they need information on what is, or is not, happening to them and what will be happening in the future. Combine a desire for independence, lack of confidence, and embarrassment, and you get teens who need information but probably won't ask for it. These books may not have high circulation but they will get the highest marks for creative shelving, and the information they provide might just save the life of a teen. While titles change, the subjects in Figure 6.12 seem, year after year, to be of interest to teens who explore topics outside of a school assignment as they develop their personal cultures and become lifelong learners.

Just as many teens' emotional needs are being met through fiction, many teens also enjoy nonfiction for the following reasons:

- They are fascinated with facts.
- They are developing special interests.
- They are developing intellectual curiosity.
- They have short attention spans.

Figure 6.12. Popular Teen Reading in Each Dewey Subject Group

000	Symbols and signs UFOs Unexplained Computer languages World records	600	Inventions Sex Teen health Suicide Eating disorders Mental health
100	Philosophy Witchcraft/Wicca Parapsychology Astrology Handwriting analysis Palm reading Dreams Self-help Eastern philosophy		Depression Substance abuse Yoga/tai chi Vegetarianism Teen pregnancy Bicycles Cars Motorcycles Pet care Cooking

000 | Symbols and signs
UFOs
Unexplained
Computer languages
World records

100 | Philosophy
Witchcraft/Wicca
Parapsychology
Astrology
Handwriting analysis
Palm reading
Dreams
Self-help
Eastern philosophy

200 | Mythology
Angels
Eastern religions
Islam

300 | Teen studies
Relationships
Gay/lesbian/bisexual/transgender issues
Spies
Careers
Civil rights
Legal rights
Armed forces study guides
Child abuse, homelessness, drug addiction, etc.
   (first-person narratives)
Dating violence
Adoption
True crime
Gangs
School success
Cheerleading
Study guides for GED, SAT, ACT, etc.
College admissions, scholarships, and directories
Death customs
Fashion
Urban legend

400 | Sign language
Slang dictionaries
Rhyming dictionaries

500 | Math puzzles
Codes
Animals

600 | Inventions
Sex
Teen health
Suicide
Eating disorders
Mental health
Depression
Substance abuse
Yoga/tai chi
Vegetarianism
Teen pregnancy
Bicycles
Cars
Motorcycles
Pet care
Cooking
Babysitting
Makeup/grooming/beauty
Strength training

700 | Graphic novels
Calligraphy
Origami
Drawing
Comic book illustration
Drawing manga/anime
History of comics
Photography
Music and musicians
Movies and movie stars
Television shows
Professional sports
Professional wrestling
Martial arts
Skateboarding/snowboarding
Sports card collecting
NASCAR

800 | Poetry
Collected writings of teens
Humor
Jokes
Book about fantasy, science fiction, and horror
Haiku

900 | Survival tales
Names
Biographies
Ancient Egypt
Medieval studies/King Arthur
Holocaust survival tales
Vietnam War
Sixties culture
9/11 terrorist attack against the United States

- They want to look at pictures/visuals.
- They find "fiction" difficult.
- They like real-life stories, such as personal narratives.
- They are reluctant readers.
- Nonfiction is relevant to their lives.
- Nonfiction inspires lifelong learning.

Additionally, boys often prefer reading nonfiction, which is a reason unto itself for including this genre in your teen collection.

Be prepared to weed and update your nonfiction section regularly. This section, unlike fiction, loses its popularity quickly. This is also a great place to involve teens because they may have a better sense of what is "in" or "out" than you do, so have them help with the weeding and selection of your nonfiction section.

Educational and Reference

You don't need another study from the Pew Foundation to tell you what you have been observing since 1996: A majority of students who have Internet access will use that first and foremost to do research on any topic, even if it is not the "best" place to gather information. The problem, of course, is that a student who looks for information on abortion using Google is not going to find the same quality or organized quantity of information as a book would provide. Furthermore, the time spent looking for such information would probably be greater than if the student had read a series book on the topic. Also, some teachers will resist technology and still require only printed "book" sources, so there is still a demand for printed academic information. Despite the tremendous amount of information available electronically, providing books for students will continue to remain a central role of libraries for some time to come.

Students do not do research primarily by reading books, but by gathering information from a variety of sources. The genius of most of the YA nonfiction book series is how they organize that information, how they gather material from other sources, and how they present that information in an easy-to-read text, complemented by graphics. Often, when students are looking for material for argumentative papers or a speech, we'll show them *Opposing Viewpoints* in print—or the wonderful online version—and say, jokingly, "Here's the report." But it is not a joke because, like teen nonfiction series, *Opposing Viewpoints* and other YA nonfiction series succeed because they give students not just what they want but also what they need. Currency is the watchword here. New topics become "hot" (who was writing about alternative fuel sources or genetically modified foods five years ago? who is writing papers on legalizing marijuana or affirmative action now?), while other topics (such as abortion and the environment) become almost classic in their constant popularity.

Collecting materials for term papers involves a choice about collection scope and balance. Given funds to purchase ten books on the topic of abortion, how best is the money spent? On ten different titles on the subject or ten copies of the same? Each approach has problems because of how many teens do research; if there are ten titles on a subject available, one teen can take out everything. If you buy ten copies of the same title, then ten teens get a book, but only one title.

What would be the best book to buy ten copies? In libraries without teen librarians determining what might be the best one to buy, the problem is compounded. Coupled with shrinking materials budgets and staffing shortages, librarians are finding it difficult to do collection development to buy books kids need. More now than ever publishers are turning to series nonfiction, flooding the market with series after series. Series nonfiction presents librarians with brand names they can trust to provide good information in easy-to-use formats that meet teen homework assignment needs. While older students often need more in-depth material, younger teens are the perfect market for nonfiction educational series.

Reference books are a separate area. Much of the professional literature concerns books that never leave the library and, with the increased use of technology, are used less and less. While we still need some reference books in print, others like Gale's *American Decades* series are moving to online subscription services. In deciding where reference dollars are spent, print versus electronic is a discussion that goes far beyond just the LST. But from the LST viewpoint, one of the primary ways in which we can serve more teens would be to offer services on their schedules (24/7 using technology) and not ours (reference books available only when the library is open and normally only by obtaining help from library staff). If information is empowering, then let's make sure to empower our teen users by providing them direct and easy access to reference materials online.

Series Nonfiction

Series nonfiction books are often popular with younger teens (especially boys) because they are short, formulaic, and developmentally appropriate. Other reasons to offer series nonfiction include these:

- Teens like them. They are easy to use, well organized, and timely, about "exactly" the topic they are researching, and thin—under 200 pages.

- They fill a collection need. Every collection needs books on "hot topics." Just as paperback series support the need for recreational reading, these support the need for educational materials.

- They save time. If you find a series you like, put it on standing order. If you find a really good series, buy multiple copies to save time and money.

We propose the following criteria when looking at series nonfiction:

- **Readability.** Are the books easy to read? Is the author's style clear, concise, and understandable?

- **Facts/opinions.** Are the books unbiased? Does the author present both sides, including labeling facts and opinions? Are the facts accurate?
- **Organization.** Are the books easy to use? Do they contain detailed table of contents, indexes, and glossaries? If there's no index, how will a reader access the information?
- **Format.** Are the books approachable? Is the format appropriate for teens? Are charts, graphs, and/or photos used? What about margins?
- **Photographs.** Do the books have photos? Do they add to the text? Are they captioned? Are they of good quality? Are they color or black and white?
- **Documentation.** Are the books well documented? Are all statements, statistics, etc., tied to sources?
- **Timely.** Are the books current? Do books in the series get updated? How often and to what extent?
- **Short.** Are the books under 200 pages? Are the chapters short/easy to photocopy?
- **Reluctant readers.** Could a nonreader use them? Is the vocabulary simple?
- **The back pages.** Do the books have addresses for more information? Up-to-date bibliographies? Lists of 800 numbers or Web sites?

Periodicals

Magazines are a great draw to your teen section; they can provide the visual flash and currency that your books, no matter how new, cannot provide. Teens read magazines, and libraries should provide them. There are as many reasons why teens are drawn to magazines as there are teen magazines. Here are some favorite reasons for including magazines in the teen section of any library:

- **Currency.** The only quicker information source is the Internet; magazines spot and drop trends before most book publishers.
- **Visual appeal.** Use good pictures and lots of them.
- **Focus on special interests.** Who could resist a whole magazine devoted to your favorite thing? The library may never buy a book on your skateboarding idol, but he or she will be featured in an article in several skateboarding magazines.
- **Speed.** Teens can get a lot of information in a short amount of time; works with their busy schedules; perfect for those who can't or don't sit still—unlike books.
- **Cool factor.** No one gets laughed at for reading a magazine.
- **Availability.** Magazines are sold everywhere and are generally inexpensive.

- **Decoration potential.** They give useful tips on decorating lockers, bedrooms, and anywhere else a teen could be creative.
- **Reading level.** The variety of ways information is packaged appeals to teens on all reading levels and those who don't consider themselves readers.

If you have given a reading survey recently, the results likely confirmed that teens want, and are reading, magazines. Several reasons become immediately evident when we think about why magazines are so valuable to the library.

- **High circulation.** If you allow your magazines to circulate, they will often circulate much more heavily than books. They will go until they drop, rip, or are mangled or stolen.
- **Word of mouth.** This benefit has two parts. First, teens who read the magazines will tell other teens who aren't reading and therefore increase the number of readers. Second, you will get instant feedback on titles that are popular when teens come to the library and ask if the latest copy of any given title has come in yet.
- **Free posters.** These add decoration and color to the YA area, and they also make nice giveaways.
- **Marketing.** Magazines also are a great way to market your library. Teens will come to read them if they know you have them. Magazine displays are visual magnets; they draw teens to a central area and, while there, teens see what other materials are there for them to use.
- **Reach "nonreaders."** Most reluctant readers give "nothing interests them" as the reason they don't read. With special interest magazines you can reach these teens as well as teens who read on a lower reading level.

There are, however, some drawbacks to magazines. The time and effort required to circulate and claim lost titles can be a hassle. They are popular, so they often walk out the door. Although things that get stolen can be a testament to "on target" selections, it is also an unwise way to spend your budget. Introducing a system in which someone must exchange a library card or some other form of identification for the magazine they desire to read would decrease the number of items stolen. Magazines fall apart. YA magazines fall apart, just like any given children's or adult's magazine. With almost everything else in the library that we select or collect, we try to keep it around and in good condition long enough to serve its purpose. With five circulations, a magazine has served its purpose. Five circulations are often more than some YA fiction titles get in a year. If a teen magazine is around and in one piece after a year, then it is not the right magazine—teen magazines and comic books should be weeding themselves with use. Think of the content of magazines we warehouse. It may be humorous to look at old pictures of celebrities, but most teens want current photos and information.

Magazines should be used and circulated. Policies restricting magazine circulation need to be readdressed. Like card catalogs, those policies seem a relic of a different time. We didn't circulate magazines because we needed to hold them for reference, and most teen magazines have no reference value. Those that do can now generally be found online via a subscription database. Allowing magazine circulation is another step away from professional values and toward customer values.

The best way to select which magazines your library should collect is to involve teens. See what magazines they have access to at their schools and try not to duplicate them. Browse the grocery store and local bookstore and observe the magazines teens are buying and reading. Chances are you might find these are the most popular titles that are used for pure recreation and information. Also remember that many magazines intended for the adult market have huge teen appeal.

The list in Figure 6.13 is by no means all-inclusive. There are plenty of adult magazines, local zines, freebies, and even daily newspapers that teens are interested in reading. For a library that really wants to reach teens, in particular to have something to show nonusers, the quickest and cheapest way isn't through programming or promotion but rather by developing a circulating magazine collection based heavily on teen opinion. While there can certainly be a debate whether a magazine like *Spin*, which has ads for cigarettes and alcohol in it, belongs in a teen area, it certainly does belong in a public library. With the curriculum focus of school libraries, the only way to justify subscriptions to most of these magazines is that they provide "reading motivation" since there is little reference value to *Seventeen*, *WWE*, or *Mad*.

Graphic Novels

To the surprise of many library patrons, teachers, administrators, and even a few disappointed young people, a "graphic" novel is not one that contains explicit content but a book-length story published in a comic book style. But wait. If you rolled your eyes at the thought of comics filled with "Zap!" and "Kapow!" taking up space in your school, then you are in for a pleasant surprise. In the past two decades, the comic-publishing industry has been redefined, producing award-winning, creative works that have as much literary merit as they do artistic credence. These graphic novels are filled with complex characters, well-developed story lines, and literary devices like foreshadowing, imagery, and allusion, and artwork that can leave you breathless. Today's graphic novels are like a third cousin, once removed, from their distant dime-store comics kin that were widely popular in the 1950s. Today, graphic novels are being embraced by librarians around the country for their ability to pull in new audiences of readers, both those who have been reluctant to enter the library and those who are simply reluctant to read. As a format for a new generation of visually literate young people, graphic novels often appeal to teens' predilection to a more visual medium, transcending apathy and the lack of "coolness" sometimes associated with reading.

Title	Topic	Age	Title	Topic	Age
American Cheerleader	Sports	12+	*M*	Entertainment	14+
Anime Insider	Japanese animation	14+	*Mad*	Humor	12+
Black Beat	Music (rap)	12+	*Nickelodeon*	Humor	8-12
Bop	Fanzine	12–14	*Rolling Stone*	Music (general)	14+
Breakaway	Boys' Christian	12+	*Seventeen*	Girls' magazine	12+
Brio	Girls' magazine (Christian)	12–16	*Sci-Fi*	Science fiction entertainment	12+
Brio & Beyond	Girls' magazine (Christian)	16+	*Sister to Sister*	Girls' magazines (African American)	12+
Cosmo Girl	Girls' magazine	12+	*Skateboarding*	Sports	12+
Electronic Gaming Monthly	Computer games	12+	*Skateboarder*	Sports	12+
Entertainment Weekly	Entertainment (general)	14+	*Slam*	Sports (basketball)	12+
ESPN	Sports (general)	14+	*Spin*	Music (general)	14+
Fangoria	Horror movies	12+	*Sports Illustrated*	Sports	12+
Game Informer	Video gamer	12+	*Starlog 12*	Science fiction	12+
Girl's Life	Girl's magazine	8–12	*Teen Graffitti*	Teens' writing	12+
Glamour	Women's magazine	14+	*Teen Ink*	Teens' writings	12+
Hmoob Teen	Hmong teens	12+	*Teen Voices*	Teens' writing/issues	12+
Hot Rod	Automobiles	14+	*Teen Vogue*	Girls' magazine	12+
Ignite	Christian	14+	*Twist*	Entertainment	14+
J-14	Fanzine	12+	*Urban Latino*	Latino	14+
Justine	Girls' magazine	12+	*Vibe*	Music (rap)	14+
Jet	African American	12+	*Word Up*	Music (rap)	12+
Latina	Latino women	14+	*WWE*	Sports (pro wrestling)	12+
Low Rider 14+	Automobiles	14+	*XXL 14+*	Music (rap)	14+
Lucky	Fashion	14+	*YM*	Girls' magazine	12+

Figure 6.13. Magazines with Teen Appeal

So Why Should You Include Graphic Novels in Your Library's Young Adult Collection?

Obviously, they are popular and they will circulate. Additionally, it is important for LSTs to realize the appeal of this format. Here are several possible reasons for collecting graphic novels in your library:

- Graphic novels offer fast-paced action, conflict, and heroic endeavors. This can appeal to boys who like all of these facets in entertainment but can't seem to find them in the pages of a straight narrative.
- Visual learners are able to connect with graphic novels in a way that they cannot with text-only books.
- Graphic novels help young readers develop strong language skills, including reading comprehension and vocabulary development.
- Graphic novels often address current, relevant, and often complex social issues such as nonconformity and prejudice. They also address themes that are important to teens, including coming-of-age, social injustice, personal triumph over adversity, and personal growth.
- Graphic novels often stimulate readers to explore other genres of literature, including fantasy, science fiction, historical fiction, and realistic fiction as well as nonfiction and mythology.
- Many fans of graphic novels become avid book readers.
- Graphic novels are good for the young person who reads English as a second language or who reads on a lower reading level than his or her peers because the simple sentences and visual clues allow the reader to comprehend some, if not all, of the story.

So, in addition to the most important reason, which is that a lot of teens enjoy reading comics and graphic novels, there are plenty of youth development reasons as well.

Is the Graphic Novel a Genre?

No. A graphic novel is a format, not a genre. Like audiobooks, DVDs, and paperbacks, the graphic novel format is an umbrella under which all genres could fall, including the traditional genres like realistic fiction, mystery, romance, western, historical fiction, science fiction, horror, and fantasy. In addition, graphic novels can also fall under a few other categories, or genres.

- **Superhero.** Typified by costumed characters with extraordinary abilities, the superhero genre is often the first genre associated with the term "comic book."
- **Nonfiction.** Like any format, the nonfiction genre of graphic novels is diverse, running the gamut from an autobiography, historical timeline, presentations of scientific theory, and poetry.
- **Graphic (or comic) journalism.** Although titles in this genre could fall under the nonfiction category, what sets them apart is that they often combine a first-person account, told in a narrative style, with images to help tell a tale. Stories that fall under this genre often have a historical significance, documenting civil unrest, war, genocide, and human nature at its best and worst.

What Is Manga, and Is It a Genre That Falls Under the Graphic Novel Umbrella?

The term "manga" is Japanese for "comics," although this is a very simplified definition of a very complex format. And, yes, manga is its own format. Like the term "graphic novel," "manga" is an umbrella term under which all genres such as romance, science fiction, mecha (robot stories), "magic girl" (featuring a seemingly normal girl with powers), historical fiction, and the like reside. Unlike Western comics, manga is created and made available for all ages in Japan, from the youngest, emerging readers to senior citizens. Also, unlike the majority of comics produced in the United States, manga is often created for specific audiences, including teen girls (shojo), teen boys (shonen), grown women (josei), and grown men (seinen)—each with its own defining characteristics. Reading manga is so prevalent throughout Japan that there are also specialty subgenres for targeted audiences, including, but not limited to, pregnant women (tips on pregnancy and child care), fans of the pinball game Pachinko and the Chinese tile game Mah-Jong, video gamers, and more. According to Paul Gravett, author of *Manga: 60 Years of Japanese Comics*, "Comics are so massive in Japan that they make up nearly 40 percent of the sales of all publications."[5]

How Is Manga Different from Western (North American) Comics?

From artistic style to content to layout, manga is very different from traditional Western comics. The art in manga has a definite look to it that is often referred to as "manga style." This artistic style is typified by simple drawings, characters with large eyes (eye shapes and sizes are often symbolically used to represent the character—for instance, bigger eyes will usually symbolize beauty, innocence, or purity, while smaller, more narrow eyes typically represent coldness and/or evil), overexaggerated emotions, and the use of fewer words to tell a story than their traditional Western comic counterparts.

Other notable differences between Japanese and Western comics include how manga is read and how it is created. The reading orientation for manga is very different from Western comics because when original Japanese manga is translated into English, the art is not flipped. Therefore, most manga titles read back to front, right to left (as opposed to books in English which we read front to back, left to right). Also, unlike Western comics, which are usually created by a team or by one person over an extended period of time, most manga titles are created by one person who must produce a large amount of work in a very short period of time. Also, unlike traditional comics published in the United States, manga does not always end happily or neatly: relationships end, the guy doesn't always get the girl, someone loses, and people die.

Whether in spite of or because of these differences, manga is especially popular with American teens today, largely because it is often action oriented and fast paced, episodic, and a glimpse inside daily life in Japan. The following lists present recommended manga series (manga is series oriented; a one-volume publication is rare) that we think belong in every middle or high school library or young adult collection.

Manga for Older Teens (ages 15–18)

- *After School Nightmare!* series by Setona Mizushiro
- *Antique Bakery* series by Fumi Yoshinaga
- *Deathnote* series by Tsugumi Ohba
- *Dragon Head* series by Minetaro Mochizuki
- *Emma* series by Kaoru Mori
- *Fushigi Yugi* series by Yuu Watase
- *Hana Kimi* series by Hisaya Nakajo
- *Hot Gimmick* series by Miki Aihara
- *Kare Kano* series by Masami Tsuda
- *Nana* series by Ai Yazawa
- *Ranma ½* series by Rumiko Takahashi
- *Real* series by Takehiko Inoue
- *Rurouni Kenshin* series by Nobuhiro Watsuki
- *Sand Chronicles* series by Hinako Ashihara
- *Train + Train* series by Hideyuki Kurata

Manga for Younger Teens (ages 12–14)

- *Azumanga Daioh* series by Kiyohiko Azuma
- *Bleach* series by Tite Kubo
- *Dramacon* series by Svetlana Chmakova
- *FLCL* series by Hajime Ueda
- *Fruits Basket* series by Natsuki Takaya
- *Fullmetal Alchemist* series by Hiromu Arakawa
- *.Hack//Legend of the Twilight* series by Tatsuya Hamazaki
- *Initial D* series by Shuichi Shigeno
- *Inu Yasha* series by Rumiko Takahashi
- *The Kindaichi Case Files* series by Kanari Yozaburo and Satoh Fumiya
- *Miki Falls* series by Mark Crilley
- *Naruto* series by Masashi Kishimoto
- *Negima!* series by Ken Akamatsu
- *Neotopia* series by Rod Espinoza
- *Sorcerers and Secretaries* by Amy Kim Ganter
- *Tokyo Mew Mew* series by Mia Ikumi and Reiko Yoshida
- *Usagi Yojimbo* series by Stan Sakai
- *Yotsuba&!* series by Kiyohiko Azuma

Who Are Some of the More Renowned Authors and Illustrators of Graphic Novels?

As with any format, hundreds of well-known writers pen graphic novels. In addition, the comic-publishing industry is overflowing with artists who often work as a team to complete the "illustrations" for graphic novels. Although some creators do serve as both the writer and the illustrator, it is more common to see a graphic novel created by a writer/illustrator twosome or as a collaborative project with a writer, a penciller, an inker, a letterer, and sometimes a colorist. Some of the most well-known writers and illustrators of graphic novels include Jeff Smith, Neil Gaiman, Alan Moore, Art Spiegelman, Will Eisner, Frank Miller, Osamu Tezuka, Chris Ware, Terry Moore, Colleen Doran, Andy Runton, Judd Winick, Kean Soo, and Scott McCloud.

What Other Graphic Formats Might Appeal to Teen Readers?

Other formats that might be of interest to teens which fall under the graphic novel umbrella include graphic nonfiction, comic books, and picture books.

Graphic Nonfiction

Although books classified as graphic nonfiction generally fall under the umbrella term of "graphic novels," they are not novels. Graphic nonfiction covers a range of subjects with just as much diversity in content as in artistic style and intended audience, such as poetry, biographies, and historical timelines. The following graphic nonfiction titles have been selected to demonstrate this variety:

- *Last Day in Vietnam: A Memory* by Will Eisner
- *Pyongyang: A Journey in North Korea* by Guy Delisle
- *The Magical Life of Long Tack Sam* by Ann Marie Fleming
- *The Case of Madeleine Smith: Treasury of Victorian Murder* by Rick Geary
- *The Cartoon History of the Modern World Part 1: From Columbus to the U.S. Constitution* by Larry Gonick
- *Malcolm X: A Graphic Biography* by Andrew Helfer and Randy DuBurke
- *Houdini: the Handcuff King* by Jason Lutes and Nick Bertozzi
- *Barefoot Gen, Volume 1: A Cartoon Story of Hiroshima* by Keiji Nakazawa
- *To Afghanistan and Back: A Graphic Travelogue* by Ted Rall
- *Safe Area Gorazde: The War in Eastern Bosnia 1992–1995* by Joe Sacco
- *Persepolis: The Story of a Childhood* by Marjane Satrapi
- *The 9/11 Report: A Graphic Adaptation* by Ernie Colon and Sid Jacobson
- *To Dance: A Ballerina's Graphic Novel* by Siena Cherson Siegel and Mark Siegel
- *The Complete Maus: A Survivor's Tale: My Father Bleeds History/Here My Troubles Began* by Art Spiegelman
- *Satchel Paige: Striking Out Jim Crow* by James Sturm and Rich Tommaso

- *Journey into Mohawk Country* by H. W. Van den Bogaert and George O'Connor
- *Action Philosophers: Giant-sized Thing* by Fred Van Lente and Ryan Dunlavey

Comic Books

Not to be confused with a book-length graphic novel, a comic book is a 32-page, staple-bound, serialized comic that is available monthly, bimonthly, or quarterly. Comic books are considered periodicals and can be purchased as part of a periodicals standing order. However, because most comics publishers—with the exception of DC, Marvel, and Archie—do not offer direct subscriptions for individual series, most major library subscription agents do not carry comic books. Some companies, such as Diamond Comic Distributors, Mile High Comics, and Midtown Comics, specialize in providing comic book subscriptions, and most of these agents are willing to work with libraries. If you choose not to work with a subscription agent, you can always purchase issues separately at a local comic book store or set up an account with a comics retailer.

Web Comics

Also called online comics or Internet comics, these are serialized comic books published in installments online. One of the best things about Web comics, besides being predominantly free of charge to read, is that anyone can create and publish a comic or graphic novel online. Although some Web comics are eventually printed and sold as stand-alone graphic novels, most Web comics continue to maintain an online archive and Internet fan base.

Picture Books for Teens

Picture books, like graphic novels, are a format. Picture books differ from graphic novels in that picture book illustrations are one part of a full-page narrative, while the illustrations in graphic novels correspond directly to the text in each panel. Also, picture books are generally shorter than graphic novels but longer than comic books. The picture book format also covers a range of genres, including science fiction, nonfiction, realistic fiction, mystery, horror, poetry, historical fiction, and the like. In spite of what most people in the library profession think about picture books, all books with 32 pages that contain pictures are not intended for young children. In fact, many picture books would be completely out of place mixed in with the easy readers, as their thematic content and language are intended for an older audience. The following list presents picture books that easily fit under the graphic novel umbrella, incorporating both images and text in such a way that they are both visually and intellectually appealing to teens.

- *Palindromania* by Jon Agee
- *Zoom/Re-Zoom/Minus (−) Equals (=) Plus (+)* by Istvan Banyai
- *Animalia/The Water Hole* by Graeme Base

- *Smoky Night* by Eve Bunting, illustrated by David Diaz
- *The Wolves in the Walls/The Day I Swapped My Dad for 2 Goldfish* by Neil Gaiman and illustrated by Dave McKean
- *The Man Who Walked Between the Towers* by Mordicai Gerstein
- *Black and White* by David Macaulay
- *Who's Got Game? The Ant or the Grasshopper?* by Toni Morrison
- *Patrol: An American Soldier in Vietnam* by Walter Dean Myers, collages by Ann Grifalconi
- *Zen Shorts* by Jon Muth
- *Pink and Say* by Patricia Polacco
- *Jumanji/The Mysteries of Harris Burdick* by Chris Van Allsburg
- *Sector 7/Tuesday* by David Weisner

Audiovisual Formats

Growing up in an exceedingly visual world, where multiple television sets per household are the norm, most teens play video games, and computers and the Internet are as often used for educational instruction as for entertainment, it is no surprise that teens gravitate toward audiovisual materials in the library. In addition to books, library collections today often include music, movies, audiobooks, and video games. Like magazines, audiovisual materials are often a catalyst to get teens in the door of a library. Although some teens do have disposable income, some do not. In the public library, a teen does not need a credit card to check out a movie. All he or she needs is a library card, available free for anyone who fills out an application. This is the beauty of the public library, and this is what makes us such a valuable resource for all teens, but especially those with empty pockets.

As we move into a time where the majority of our entertainment content is available online and is portable, this changes the playing field for libraries and for teens. Most libraries have moved to downloadable audiobooks, and movies aren't far behind, but libraries continue to shy away from downloadable music. We could argue it is because adults aren't clamoring for the newest music like they are for the newest title on audiobook, so the pressure to seek vendors and allocate resources isn't there. But for teens and the LSTs who serve them, the reality is that teens today rarely buy music as teens did ten years ago. Teens expect to purchase music in an online transaction, whether this is from a traditional music store's online presence, like Best Buy, or an online presence only, like Amazon.com or iTunes. Portable music is not the wave of the future—it is now. Where are libraries in that mix?

Is It Really Important to Have an Audiovisual Section for Teens at Your Library?

Yes. Public libraries are repositories of educational materials and cultural materials. In other words, it is a home to books and music and movies. One of the most unique things about libraries, especially for teens, is that they offer services and materials for free. In addition to books, they circulate movies and music to anyone, regardless of their age or socioeconomic class. It is not your responsibility to compete with Blockbuster or the Virgin Record Megastore. It is your place to meet the needs of your patrons—including making leisure materials such as the latest movies and the most popular music and video games available to the public, in addition to instructional and educational videos and audiobooks. Your goal is to be responsive to your customers' needs, and to do this you need to be open to the idea of collecting materials that serve both educational and recreational purposes.

Why Do Teens Like the Audiovisual Formats?

For the same reason they like the Internet and television. Teens today are a visual generation, immersed in a multimedia culture that is both fast-paced and immediate. Music, movies, audiobooks, and video games are also a lot of fun, which greatly contributes to their popularity among teens. As adults, we struggle to provide teens with materials that somehow contribute to education. It can be easy for us to overlook the value of these formats in the face of such "frivolity." However, providing teens with access to movies, music, audiobooks, and video games is as much a part of our job as is helping young people connect with books because all are their sources of information. It is respecting their development needs and it is remembering our own teen years.

Music

Why Should Your Library Indulge Pop Culture?

The answer to this question is philosophical: Pop culture is a real-world reflection of the world in which you, and your teen patrons, reside. Pop idols today are the music icons of tomorrow, and just as you cannot imagine a well-rounded, diverse public library collection without the greatest hits of U2, Beastie Boys, the Beatles, or Elvis, libraries with collections that serve teens should include the music they listen to, including rap, hip-hop, and top-40 music. Music today is as powerful as it has always been, but sometimes we, as adults, forget that just because we don't like the music, it is no less valuable as a medium. Kanye West is no more or less important than Ella Fitzgerald was in her day. In the 1920s and 1930s, people thought jazz was the demoralization of human civilization. Today, adults say the same thing about punk, hip-hop, and rap music. In the present, it can be difficult to see a body of music as culturally significant; however, history has shown that music has the ability to define a generation. Teens are participating in the development of culture as it evolves. Therefore, teens are entwined in what will become known as the defining music of a generation in the same way Madonna and Prince did for Generation X. To exclude hip-hop, rap, or pop music is the same as saying we shouldn't have jazz music in our collections. It is up to us, as professional librarians, to extend our cultural cache, to acknowledge the younger generation's musical tastes, and to provide access to music they want to listen to in order to acknowledge their rightful place in the library community.

What Do You Need to Know About Music for Teens?

There is a lot to know, and it changes daily. With CDs, MP3s, and legal music downloading services, music these days is seemingly as complex as teenagers themselves. Music is as defining for young people as it has always been, and teens today are as enamored with Justin Timberlake and the Jonas Brothers as teens were in the past about the Beatles or the Jackson Five. Music can be an escape. Music can also be a shared language for young people, providing a foundation on which to form alliances. While no particular genre encompasses the musical tastes of all teens everywhere, a few genres are pervasive among young listeners:

- **Contemporary Christian.** The contemporary Christian (CC) genre of music has reappropriated the sound of popular music with Christian-themed lyrics. A diverse genre with a shared premise of Christianity, CC runs the gamut of style from pop to punk as praise and worship. Well-known artists in this category include Third Day, Mercy Me, Point of Grace, Lifehouse, Chris Tomlin, Blue Fringe, Casting Crowns, and TobyMac.

- **New (or popular) country.** Country music has always been more than a sound. For a majority of listeners, including teens, it is a way of life that often portrays a lifestyle about which people are still nostalgic—a simple, self-made, family-oriented, small-town, living-off-the-land way of life. The use of technology is what often distinguishes the sound of old country and new country. New, or popular, country is more influenced by the evolution of preexisting instruments, the introduction of new instruments, and the influence of other genres, pop culture, and musical technology. Some of the most popular artists of new (or popular) country include Taylor Swift, Kenny Chesney, Carrie Underwood, Sugarland, Brad Paisley, Zac Brown Band, Rascal Flatts, and Little Big Town.

- **Americana/alternative country.** The term "Americana" is synonymous with alternative country and usually refers to music created by country bands that play traditional country but bend the rules slightly. Alternative country artists do not usually conform to Nashville's hit-making traditions but instead work outside of the country industry's spotlight, frequently intertwining musical traditions with singer/songwriter and rock-and-roll aesthetics. The biggest difference between traditional country and this genre is the rock influence; Americana is really more of a hybrid of classic country and rock and roll. In fact, a lot of the artists in this category are often played on both country and pop/rock stations. Well-known artists in this genre include Allison Krauss, My Morning Jacket, Wilco, Patty Griffin, and Fleet Foxes.

- **Electronica/techno.** A uniquely American genre, electronica/techno developed in Detroit in the early 1990s and has spread worldwide in the past ten years. Considered an urban genre, the idea behind this style is very simple—it is generally music created through electronic machines such as synthesizers, turntables, and samplers, not live instruments. This is an evolving genre that it is often hard to put one name on. A lot of people who work with this genre refer to themselves as DJs because they are working with turntables. The term "electronica" refers to dance music, like the Chemical Brothers and Ministry of Sound often heard in clubs and raves; however, this genre has also grown to include more ambient compositions by acts like Metro Station, Hot Chip, and M83.

- **Gospel.** Originally born out of blues, folk music, and church hymns, Gospel has become a catch-all for Christian music influenced by blues, rap, hip-hop, country, and rock. It is generally upbeat and up tempo. Well-known gospel performers include Mary Mary, Chris Tomlin, Natalie Grant, Ce Ce Winans, Yolanda Adams, and Rebecca St. James.

- **Heavy metal/punk.** Angry, rebellious, loud, and subversive, heavy metal and punk are fast-paced and aggressive styles of music. Heavy metal is characterized by excessive electric guitar (with whammy bars), drums, and over-the-top vocalizations; repetitive chords, mumbled lyrics, and a rally call of anarchy characterize punk music. After taking a hiatus in the 1990s while Grunge became the subversive music of choice, heavy metal resurfaced in the new millennium with a more industrial sound. Older heavy metal includes the likes of Kiss, Metallica, and Motley Crüe. Older punk includes acts like the Sex Pistols and the Ramones. Newer heavy metal artists include Notwist, Muse, Stained, Linkin Park, and Amon Amarth, while newer punk artists include Against Me!, Rise Against, and Bob Mould.

- **Independent/alternative.** It is important to note that alternative music and independent music are not necessarily interchangeable terms. Originally, in the 1990s, alternative, or alt/rock, was a label given to music that was unlike the majority of music on the popular charts. Independent, or indie, music was music produced on a label that is not corporate, not affiliated with the five big music labels that monopolize the music industry: BMI, BMG, Universal, Sony, and Time Warner. The rise of independent and alternative music happened with the emergence of digital recording technology, which allowed people to create their own product; the rise of the Internet allowed artists to market their own product.

- **Indie rock.** Independent rock is simply music created by rock groups or artists that do not conform to the mainstream trends and who publish on independent labels like Touch and Go Records, Subpop, and Kill Rockstars. Indie rock artists include Vampire Weekend, Animal Collective, Wolf Parade, and Deerhunter.

- **J-Pop.** An abbreviation for Japanese pop, J-Pop is essentially music created and performed by popular Japanese musicians that is similar to American pop music with teen idols and boy/girl bands. Today, popular J-Pop stars include Ayumi Hamasaki and Hikaru Utada

- **Pop/rock.** Pop, or popular, music is perhaps the most widely marketed contemporary musical genre and thus appears to be the most popular, or at least the most pervasive, among the American public, especially teens. The pop/rock genre of music is constantly changing, due in large part to the short-lived nature of fads that define popular culture. Some of the leading pop/rock artists include Daughtry, Pink, John Mayer, Jonas Brothers, Natasha Bedingfield, and Miley Cyrus.

- **Rap/hip-hop.** Rap is basically a spoken-word style of music that is dominated by percussion and often accompanied by turntables. Hip-hop is similar music with a different vocal style. Although rap started out mostly in urban areas, it quickly spread to the white suburbs due in part largely to the aggressive, hard, sexually explicit, and status-oriented lyrics. More than any other genre of music, rap addresses a social struggle. Well-known artists who have been bestsellers in this genre include Run DMC, LL Cool J, the late Tupac Shakur, Beastie Boys, Lil' Kim, and Eminem. Gangsta/hard-core rap was an early form of this genre, sung by gangsters commenting about life in American inner cities. Today this subgenre is epitomized by artists like Jay-Z, T.I., and Lil' Wayne. Hip-hop, which is sometimes considered a descendant of disco, really emerged as a dominant form in the 1980s and is a little less abrasive and more emotionally vulnerable than rap music. Some of the most well-known hip-hop artists today include Rhianna, Beyonce, and Kanye West.

- **Reggaeton.** At its simplest, this is Spanish reggae born in Puerto Rico which then spread through the United States via Miami and New York City. More specifically, it is reggae and dancehall combined with Afro-Atlantic genres, such as merengue and salsa, as well as hip-hop and electronic. Popular acts include Daddy Yankee, Pitbull, Ivy Queen, and Tego Calderon.

- **Soul.** Made world famous by Motown in the 1960s, soul combines elements of jazz, gospel, and rhythm and blues. Some of today's better known soul singers include Alicia Keyes, John Legend, Adele, Mary J. Blige, and Erykah Badu.

Confused? You should be. Recall images of your parents shaking their heads over Led Zepplin, Duran Duran, Nirvana, or whoever was unpopular in your house when you were growing up. No one expects that you listen to, or even like, the music your teen customers listen to, but you should respect it, its influence, and its importance.

Where Can You Find Out What Music to Purchase for This Audience?

You do not have to listen to top-40 music or program your car radio to the local hip-hop station to keep abreast of the music to which young people are listening. You work with your best source of information—the teens themselves. Ask them what they like and make it a point to purchase the preferences they mention. You can also check out various Web sites dedicated to the newest, hippest stuff out there. "All Music" is a great site (www.allmusic.com), as are the online sites for the most popular cable television music channels, including MTV (www.mtv.com), VH1 (www.vh1.com), and BET (www.bet.com). You can also read the leading music magazines, like *Rolling Stone* (www.rollingstone.com), *Spin* (www.spin.com), and *Billboard* (www.billboard.com), for ideas about what music is currently topping the charts. To find out more about the music produced by independent labels, you can read *CMJ* (College Music Journal) *New Music Monthly*, which comes with a CD of new, independently produced music each month, or check out their Web site at www.cmj.com. You can also visit a music store and spend some time browsing, perhaps taking your Teen Advisory Council with you on a "field trip" so that they have an opportunity to provide direct opinions about the collection you are building for them and their friends.

Should You Continue Adding CDs to Your Collection?

Yes, but be aware that as streaming and download options become more pervasive, how libraries connect teens with music will likely change. The best advice is to accept that music is portable, downloadable, and will always be a moving target for libraries who are stuck in the idea of "collecting" it. You need to move to the idea of access to music. Libraries will need to break their habit of choosing or relying on one prevailing format, VHS versus BETA or DVD versus Blu-Ray; get comfortable with new formats being introduced into and leaving the marketplace quickly. Again, if you think about access to the content rather than collecting the content, you will be in good shape. The music, television, and movie industries are also struggling with these issues, so watch how they begin to handle access to their content. Is it offered for free or priced low, available all the time or temporarily, and who is developing Web sites to thwart their efforts? There will always be the gray area of illegal downloading versus legal downloading, and it is good to be aware of Web sites that allow access to all varieties of legal entertainment. Here are a few to familiarize yourself with so that you can provide access to your teens:

- Creative Commons (http://creativecommons.org/). Creative Commons is a nonprofit corporation dedicated to making it easier for people to share and build on the work of others, consistent with the rules of copyright. They provide free licenses and other legal tools to mark creative work with the freedom the creator wants it to carry so others can share, remix, use commercially, or any combination thereof. They work to increase the amount of creativity (cultural, educational, and scientific content) in "the commons"—the body of work that is available to the public for free and legal sharing, use, repurposing, and remixing. Their tools give everyone from individual creators to large companies and institutions a simple, standardized way to grant copyright permissions to their creative work. The Creative Commons licenses enable people to easily change their copyright terms from the default of "all rights reserved" to "some rights reserved."

- Hulu (www.Hulu.com). Hulu is an online video service that offers hit television shows, movies, and clips, all for free, anytime in the United States. Their mission is to help you find and enjoy the world's premium content, when, where, and how you want it. Their library includes thousands of videos, from full episodes of new and archived television shows to full-length movies to sports games and highlights to clips. They are always constantly updating their online selection. You can enjoy most of Hulu's content without signing up for a Hulu account, but you can take advantage of several features if you have an account:

  ○ Maintain a video queue and add videos to it for future viewing.

  ○ Subscribe to shows and Hulu will add new videos for those shows to your queue.

  ○ Rate and write user reviews for videos.

  ○ Activate resume play. Log into Hulu on a particular computer, and as long as you remain logged in, any video will resume playing where you left off previously.

  ○ Create a profile page from which you can monitor your Hulu activity. You can also choose to share your interests with other users through your public profile.

- YouTube (www.youtube.com). Founded in February 2005, YouTube has become the leader in online video and the destination to watch and share original videos worldwide. It has changed how news is reported, putting breaking news in the hands of the average person, and it reinforces the idea that you are being watched and possibly recorded at all times. YouTube allows people to easily upload and share video clips on and across the Internet through Web sites, mobile devices, blogs, and e-mail. YouTube has struck numerous partnership deals with content providers such as CBS, BBC, Universal Music Group, Sony Music Group, Warner Music Group, NBA, and The Sundance Channel.

Movies

The teenage years are a time of identity development in which young adults often struggle with themselves, their peers, and society as a whole. Movies created for a teen audience often address these struggles, both realistically and idealistically, with comedy, dark humor, sarcasm, and drama. Teen coming-of-age movies that aim to be representative of their young adult audience address things like relationships, sexual identity, body image, and popularity. While the movies are not real, a teen can spend two hours watching characters like them or someone they know deal with the same issues that they deal with in their real lives. Movies, like books, can be a great escape from reality. The difference is that the majority of teens watch movies for fun and recreation. The inclusion of popular movies in a library's collection will not only make the library a "cooler" place for teens to frequent; it will also make the library more teen service oriented and teen consumer responsive, which is what really matters. In addition, there is always a chance that the presence of popular movies in the teen area will have a ripple effect on library services, whereby increased library traffic in general will increase general print circulation, computer use, and reference.

You Want to Include Movies in Your Library's Teen Section, but What Titles Are Appropriate for This Age Group?

The great thing about movies is that the rating system created and carried out by the Motion Picture Association of America (MPAA) takes the guesswork and subjectivity out of evaluating movies and assigning each a rating according to the age appropriateness of content. For the most part, some G, PG, and PG-13 movies will be appropriate for a teen movie section in your library, depending on your community. "G" stands for general audience; movies that have received this rating contain no adult-themed content, profanity, nudity, sex, or violence and are considered appropriate for audience members of all ages. "PG" stands for parental guidance suggested; movies that have received this rating may include some profanity, violence, or brief nudity but no drug use. "PG-13" stands for parents strongly cautioned; movies with this rating may contain subject matter that is inappropriate for viewers under 13, including violence, nudity, sensuality, language, or other content that is more explicit than in a PG movie but less than what a viewer might see in a movie that has received the restricted R rating. For more information about movie ratings, visit the MPAA Web site at www.mpaa.org. To search for a rating of a specific title, visit the MPAA database title at www.mpaa.org/movieratings/search/index.htm.

How Can You Find Out What Current and "Classic" Movies Are Popular with Teens?

Again, ask them. Ask your Teen Advisory Council for feedback. Put a survey on your teen Web page asking teens to select their top ten favorite movies from a drop-down box of 50 titles selected by your TAC. Check the "Teen Movies" Web site (www.teenmovies.org) or http://www.hollywoodteenmovies.com for some great information specifically about teens and their movie preferences. You can read movie reviews written by teens and get movie trivia for contests and icebreakers. There is also a place for teens to vote about their favorite current movies on the big screen. For an LST, this is a great place to begin making a list of titles to purchase as soon as they are released.

Should You Just Purchase Popular, Recent Movies for Your Teen Library Collection, or Should You Select Other Videos That May Appeal to This Audience?

A collection of popular materials will circulate with teens. While this is important, it is also equally as important that libraries provide DVDs that a teen might not be able to get anywhere else, including instructional DVDs on teen-oriented subjects like martial arts, snowboarding, and backpacking through Europe on $40 a day, along with educational DVDs like those that address teen pregnancy, violence in the schools, drug addiction, and legal rights. No library can compete with a local retail store with regard to keeping the newest, hottest DVD on the shelves. That's not the library's job, and you shouldn't aspire to be a movie store. You should aspire to have a well-rounded collection of educational and recreational DVDs for teens by including movies that they'll come in looking for and DVDs that they might find interesting once they start browsing the shelves.

Can You Show Movies in Your Library If You Have Them in Your Collection?

Well, this depends on whether a movie purchased by your library comes with a public performance site license. This also depends on whether your library has purchased a blanket Public Performance Site License from an outside source. A Public Performance Site License, available from Movie Licensing USA (www.movielic.com), is a site-based license that allows a library to exhibit movies in a public setting that have been licensed for "Home Use Only." This license is not that expensive, and it can be a great asset when developing programs for teens, such as a summer movie series or thematic movie festivals like "Superheroes on the Big Screen" or "Classics You'd Rather Watch Than Read."

Audiobooks

Fifteen years ago people doubted whether audiobooks would ever make their way off of the library shelves and into the homes of listeners; now it seems that audiobooks are a booming business. In the past, librarians have had apprehensions about whether audiobooks would be accepted and used by teens. Those fears have largely been put to rest by librarians and teachers who have seen and written about students who experienced major changes in attitude about audiobooks. This format has changed teens' opinions not only about reading but about the library and how the library really does have something for everyone.

Like any other nontraditional format, audiobooks have their fair share of skeptics. However, librarians who work with teens know that sometimes it takes a nontraditional format coupled with traditional library services—meeting the needs of the patron and providing an appropriate vehicle for information—to contribute to a positive library and literary experience for a teen. Like some adults, some teens would rather listen to a book than read it. Learning styles differ widely in people, and, again, teens are not different. Some readers are more visually literate and some are auditory learners. Teens are often on the go, and audiobooks can be an excellent form of mobile entertainment, especially in the car or on a long bus ride to or from school.

Even still, many parents, teachers, and even colleagues feel as if audiobooks are not "real" books. If you are wondering if this format is a viable and legitimate method of "reading" a book, know that researchers, classroom teachers, and librarians throughout the country have seen, firsthand, the effect audiobooks can have on reluctant readers, less-proficient readers, readers of English as a second language, and even capable readers who have had limited exposure to good-reading models. Audiobooks often act as a scaffold, helping limited proficiency readers increase both their comprehension and oration skills while allowing struggling readers to engage in positive reading experiences.

The popularity of audiobooks has allowed this format to transition successfully from audio CDs and MP3 files to downloadable content with vendors like OverDrive and Recorded Books. Now all-in-one devices like the Playaway combine digital audio content with a small, battery-operated player. Teens just plug in their headphones and start listening. For more information about portable devices, see Chapter 11 on technology.

Why Should You Collect Audiobooks/Downloadable Audio for Teens?

- Young people who have had limited experience listening to English often listen to books on tape while reading along with a text to hear how punctuation is used in inflection.

- Listening to audiobooks often helps readers improve their own reading fluency or the ability to enunciate while reading aloud without breaking a narrative by stopping midsentence.

- Audiobooks contribute to both vocabulary development and extension, allowing listeners to hear new words and then use context clues to assign meaning.

- Audiobooks encourage active listening and critical thinking, contributing greatly to a reader's listening comprehension skills, skills that are much needed in the real world but rarely taught in the school.

- Audiobooks can capture a character's dialect in a way that is not possible in print, granting a student the opportunity to "read" a book as the author intended.

- Literary devices such as satire and irony often translate better orally than on the page, allowing a listener to experience the material within the context of the writer's intent.

- Classic authors such as Shakespeare and Homer created their works to be heard and not read. Audiobooks provide this authentic literary experience and allow listeners to focus more on hearing the story than on deciphering the text.

- Finally, and most important, an audiobook has a rightful place in the library for both educational and recreational purposes because, just like a print book, an audiobook is capable of pulling a reader into the story and providing a literary experience.

Computer Games/Video Games

Teens play video games. They play them at home, on handhelds, in cars, on buses, in restaurants, in class, at school, and, yes, at the library. This is no revelation for anyone who works with teens. This is certainly no surprise for any LST who works in a library that provides Internet access. Like it or not, gaming plays a large part in the life of a Millennial. They don't know a time without high-quality graphics, realistic sounds, portability, and parents who also grew up playing video games. You can either fight gaming by refusing to allow teens to play computer games in the library and, as a result, lose the opportunity to develop meaningful relationships with these teens, or you can accept gaming, embrace it, and begin working to develop a relationship with the teens who frequent your library, using the computer and video games as a gateway to this age demographic.

Do Video Games Have Any Educational Value?

Yes. If this answer surprises you, then you probably have either never played a video game or not played since the early days of video game development. In the beginning, video games were very task oriented, whereby kids were preoccupied with what was happening on the screen and gave little or no thought to the background story or the characters. In these early games like Atari's Frogger or Nintendo's Super Mario Brothers, the screen featured very little text, the story had little or no plot, and the player had to fill in the backstory by reading the booklet that usually came with the game. As video games have evolved, they have become more literary. Today, the narrative is absorbed into the game through interspersed text segments as well as textual and audio dialogue between characters. Unlike older video games, today's games require players to be active participants in the story, and, something you might not have ever considered, today's advanced computer games contain major elements of literature, including plot, setting, conflict, and resolution. To draw another parallel between reading and playing a video game, character development is a driving force for gamers, allowing players to develop the same sense of character loyalty that readers often experience with their favorite book characters.

You Want Video Games in the Teen Section of Your Library, but Should the Teens Be Able to Check Them Out?

To circulate or not to circulate—that is the question. Like with many questions in this chapter, the answer to this one is situation specific and will depend greatly on your library policy and budget. Some libraries do not purchase any video games for circulation but have a gaming console (like the Playstation 3, X-Box 360, or Nintendo Wii) in house and allow patrons to check out video games like Guitar Hero or Madden Football that can then be played in-house only. Some libraries circulate video games either for free or for a fee. There is no set method for circulating or not circulating this format. While there is no doubt that video games will circulate in just about any library where they are made available, the question is usually whether they will return. There is no standard answer for this question, but it appears that libraries that circulate this format have deemed it valuable enough to educate their patrons on the importance of returning materials and then have budgeted accordingly for lost item replacement costs. Often one decision that holds up the purchasing of video games for a library is the content. Some teens want access to video games with mature content and libraries walk the fence of providing access to these games without bringing a house of pain down on themselves. Many libraries make the decision to purchase games rated only EC, E+, or T and avoid sticky discussions with parents/patrons. Some libraries purchase the latest, hottest video games and pass the responsibility on to the parents. It is good to be familiar with this rating system, similar to the rating system for movies. While many libraries don't follow these guidelines, the reality is that parents do, so knowledge about the rating system can be valuable.

The rating system, created and carried out by the Entertainment Software Rating Board (ESRB), has two parts in which each game is assigned a rating symbol and content descriptors:

- **EC: Early Childhood.** Game content is suitable for players 3 years of age and up and contains no inappropriate material.

- **E: Everyone.** Game content is suitable for players 6 years of age and up and may contain minimal violence, slapstick humor, and/or crude language.

- **E+: Everyone 10+.** Game content is suitable for players 10 years of age and up, and may contain cartoon, fantasy, or mild violence, mild language, and/or minimal suggestive themes.

- **T: Teen.** Game content is suitable for players 13 years of age and up and may contain some violent content, adult language, and/or suggestive themes.

- **M: Mature.** Game content is suitable for players 17 years of age and up and may contain mature sexual themes, intense violence, and strong language.

- **AO: Adults Only.** Game content is suitable for adult players and may contain graphic depictions of violence and/or sex. Games that receive this rating are not intended for players under 18 years of age.

- **RP: Rating Pending.** Game has been submitted to the ESRB and is awaiting a final rating.

The content descriptions provide more in-depth details on what each game contains. The rating system allows the ESRB to give more information to purchasers about the expectations in a given game, including level of violence, references to drugs, tobacco, alcohol, sexual content, level of gore, realism of violence, blood, etc. For more information about content descriptors, visit the ESRB Web site at www.esrb.org.

What Are the Best Selection Tools for Creating a Teen Collection?

The dilemma facing the LST is that your selection processes are driven by selection tools/review journals, while the majority of materials mentioned previously are rarely reviewed. There are no library review sources for teen magazines, popular music, DVDs, comic books, or video games. Some of these items may have reviews, but they are not in our literature and they may be done more by consumers than professionals.

Thus, the first step in teen collection development is realizing that even our best selection tools only offer a slim selection of the materials that best belong in an active, customer-driven teen collection. That said, the following are the big four review journals for teen materials:

- *Booklist.* Their reviews include YA notes at the bottom of titles that have teen appeal for educational and pleasure reading. The real plus in *Booklist,* aside from lots of subject lists, is that teens are not the primary interest. Instead, by reviewing primarily for the public library market, this provides LSTs, especially those working in high schools, with the best information about new adult books with teen appeal. *Booklist* also does the best job of reviewing reference books and as an ALA journal is normally the first print journal to publish the various YALSA lists.

- *KLIATT.* Publishes reviews of paperback books, hardcover adolescent fiction, audiobooks, and educational software recommended for libraries and classrooms serving teens, published bimonthly. *KLIATT,* which used to cover only paperbacks and audiobooks, is very eclectic in its choice of what to review but seems strong in materials that support formal education.

- *School Library Journal.* In addition to their regular reviews in print, *SLJ* has the best Web site of the big four, providing readers with the most free content. *SLJTeen* is a free e-newsletter that provides LSTs in public libraries and high school libraries as well as high school teachers with the latest information about content for teens (books, graphic novels, anime, films, and games), technology (handheld hardware, social networking, and other software), and teen consumer information.

- *VOYA. Voice of Youth Advocates* is a great source for fiction, nonfiction, and graphic novels; they also do genre lists throughout the year that are invaluable because most of their reviewers are practicing teen librarians. *VOYA* is also the only one of the big four to prublish reviews written by teens. *VOYA* does the best job of reviewing science fiction and fantasy, small press and Christian publishers, and professional materials. Through regular columns, it provides fantastic information on graphic novels, teen series, as well as a "best list" in each of its six issues. Trying to serve teens without subscribing to *VOYA* is like trying to build a house without a hammer. It can be done, but it is not going to be easy, or pretty.

In addition to these four, there are two journals from the education community that LSTs with a focus on literature and/or working with teachers need to know:

- *ALAN Review*. The Assembly on Literature for Adolescents publishes the *ALAN Review* three times each year (fall, winter, and spring). The journal contains articles on YA literature and the teaching of YA literature, interviews with authors, reports on publishing trends, current research on YA literature, a section of reviews of new books, and ALAN membership news. The review section is on "clip and file" index cards, but the reviews are often much more in-depth than those found in library journals. Many of the journals are articles from academics about arcane topics in YA literature, but there are enough practical articles to satisfy most LSTs.

- *Voices from the Middle*. ALAN is a division of NCTE, as are those who comprise *Voices from the Middle*, which focuses, as the title implies, on literature for the middle grades. Along with articles regarding teaching young adult literature, there are also reviews, columns, and lists.

One of the best places to learn about new teen fiction is the YALSA-BK electronic discussion list where librarians, and often authors, review, discuss, and debate books, and the issues surrounding them. For graphic novels, the GN-LIB is the best electronic discussion list with a library focus. Jobber catalogs are designed to hype, and they are just as important as journals that review. While there are numerous book jobbers out there, which jobber you use, however, depends on your library's contracts. While you probably can't make that decision, you should, and can, advocate for the jobbers that do concern themselves with teen materials. With the exception of *VOYA*, the problem with all of these tools is that they are all from the view of adults.

In addition to whatever vehicles you've chosen to add teen involvement into the collection mix, there is always Amazon. While the professional reviewers in the teen section are among the best in the field, it is the authentic teen reaction, rants, and reviews of titles that LSTs need to read on a regular basis. Amazon is probably the only free source to get bibliographic information on certain types of materials, such as books with game codes. Don't bookmark the teen page; you should make it your start page on your browser.

The purpose of any collection is to fulfill the wants and needs of a particular library's users. While every library may have a different protocol for this mission, the customer is the bottom line. The challenge of serving teens, of course, is that those wants and needs are innumerable, varied, and changing. Developing any collection for teens is trying to hit a moving target. A teen collection can't be all classics, nor can it be all paperback collections. Can a book be great if no one reads it? Can a book be great if no one wants to read it again because they forget it five minutes after finishing it? If there is a common theme that runs through our ideas on collection development, it is about selecting that which helps teens do their job. These are books that evoke emotional responses among teen readers through the year—core needs create a core collection.

How Do You Maintain Your Teen Collection?

- **Weed.** It is safe to say that even libraries with separate teen collections do not have the luxury of space. Constant weeding is necessary, but not only for space considerations. First, if a teen is browsing the nonfiction area in the 921s and happens upon an M. C. Hammer biography or a book about the Backstreet Boys, that sends a pretty clear message about your collection. Second, weeding is one of the best ways to increase circulation. For example, by doing a big weed in your hardback area you have now freed up space to display at the end of the bookcases and teens get the chance to see the book covers. Third, if possible, consider temporary weeding. That is, prune down the collection to a couple copies of core titles and series and store the rest until you need them in the summer. If not, then either you are forced to have an area overflowing and overstuffed with titles or you weed them—these are not books you don't want; they are simply ones you don't have room for. Sure, storage is a problem, but find a box or two and an area in the basement or on top of a cabinet.

- **Consider buying the YALSA award winners and honor books** (Michael L. Printz, Odyssey, William C. Morris, and Alex). While these books and audiobooks are not always the most popular, they are often great books for readers who want to be challenged. These books also help teens fill reading requirements for an award winner. All of these award winners are announced during the ALA Midwinter Conference and posted to the YALSA site within hours of the announcement.

- **Each year take time to read through the YALSA Selection Lists to find titles of interest for your library.** Buy books on these lists (Best Books, Quick Picks, Popular Paperbacks, and Great Graphic Novels for Teens, and ALEX) that appear to be a match for your community. All of these lists offer a "Top Ten," so this is a good jumping-off point. These lists are usually posted on the YALSA Web site a few weeks after the ALA Midwinter Conference.

- **Consider all of the books reviewed in *VOYA*.** Focus your attention on those that received a four or a five in either popularity or quality. Buy those that are perfect tens. Each year

VOYA puts together this list of perfect tens that represent the best of the best.

- **Buy books that are listed on Amazon.com's Bestseller list for teens.** Although they may not all be classic works, they represent top teen selections purchased by the general public. Also consider those books that are listed as the year's best books for teens, selected by Amazon's editors.
- **Consider any book listed in the various *VOYA* "best" lists.** These books were reviewed favorably by adults *and* teens.
- **Look at circulation reports.** Buy another copy of anything that is getting heavy use, and look at lost-books reports. Buy and replace core titles often.
- **Look at YALSA-BK.** Follow the discussions of titles and learn which titles librarians who post are praising—even if those titles never show up on an award list.
- **Look closely at the monthly catalogs of vendors.** Seek the paperback reprint edition of titles that are circulated heavily in hardback.
- **Ask teens continuously about their preferences.** Survey, open up your Web page to teen reviews, do book discussion groups, conduct exit interviews, conduct an annual favorite book poll, and listen. Ask teens what they are reading and then buy the answer.

Collection Development Concerns

If building an active teen collection were not challenging enough, librarians also face a series of special concerns. Some of these are large societal problems while others are specific to libraries. Let's examine four key issues that consistently arise doing teen collection development work: reaching rampant readers, reaching reluctant readers, reaching incarcerated readers, and reaching readers who only want the best.

Reaching Rampant Readers

The 7th graders who were initially excited by teen romance series might be coming to you by 8th grade for more serious romances. Eventually by 10th or 11th grade the materials in the teen section will no longer be of interest to these rampant readers. Finding materials for this group is often difficult because, although their reading tastes, interest, and abilities have matured, many of the adult books might be developmentally inappropriate. To serve these readers, you need to first understand why they might prefer Patricia Cornwell or Eric Jerome Dickey to Lois Duncan or L. Divine.

While most of the review journals do a good job of informing LSTs about new adult books for teens, it is with the Alex Awards from YALSA where they move beyond the bestsellers and find adult books with unique teen appeal.

Reaching Reluctant Readers

This is normally a boy who wants the book on tape if possible or, if not available, then wants a "thin one." If you are going to understand how to "turn" reluctant readers into willing ones, you must first understand the obstacles:

- **Association with failure.** Does anyone like to do something they are not good at? Of course not, and this is perhaps the most important thing to understand about reluctant readers. For numerous reasons, many of which have been well documented in recent research, plenty of teens don't have good reading skills. By making them read books in school that they can't read, we are setting them up for failure. For teens who are literate, but not in English, this is just as much of an obstacle. Many libraries report great success with audiobooks with new English language learners.

- **Lack of time and energy.** For boys, it might be the opposite. They have too much energy to sit still long enough to read. This is a factor facing most teen readers. Their schedules and secreting hormones don't always allow time or focus for reading. Reluctant readers sometimes just want the action. This was one of the many reasons the *Goosebumps* series was so popular years ago: the characters in these novels didn't have time to learn and grow; they were too busy running for their lives.

- **Negative peer pressure.** A teenage boy "caught" with a big, fat novel in some peer circles will be made fun of by others, but the same boy caught with a music magazine, a book of Tupac's poetry, or a superhero graphic novel will not be heckled. The latter boy is asked to share. The issue is more than developmental; teens will reject certain books merely because adults want them to read them.

- **Not stimulated by ideas.** Novels are about many things, but most deal with themes that require some thought and reflection. Disregarding whether we like or dislike a book and accepting that it is a piece of literature that the teen might like is a viewpoint we should take when working with reluctant readers. Books that produce responses from teens might be best, especially in this culture that is both media heavy and saturated with computer games.

- **No history of reading or reading encouragement at home.** Many nonreading teens come from homes of nonreaders—sometimes for the same reasons outlined here, or sometimes because parents are too busy working two jobs to dive into a good book. Again, this is the opposite of the upbringing and

CD **See Tool 37. Teen Picks Card Template**

daily lives of many LSTs. A number of us learned the value of books and reading from our parents; it is assumed and understood. It is part of our culture, but in many homes, for many reasons, books are an alien form.

- **Can't find the good books to read.** Dr. Kylene Beers, one of the primary people looking at alliterate teens—those who can read but choose not to—tells a great story about middle school teens visiting a school library. All of the kids, except a few boys of course, took books every week. When she asked the boys why they didn't pick a title from all of the good books available, one said, "But which are the good ones?" For a reader, a library full of books is a paradise, but for a nonreader a library full of books is a minefield. Dr. Beers proposes the "good book box," where LSTs could help teens narrow their choices.6 Some LSTs take the same notion with displays called "teen picks." Nonreaders need guidance in finding a book that won't turn out to be for them yet another bad experience.

- **Not a priority.** Admit it. In high school, once you got a car, how much reading did you do? If you played sports, how many novels did you knock off during the season? You went to school all day, participated in an after-school activity, and then went to work at McDonald's for another five hours. Do you think you would still have the energy—and reading does take energy—to knock off a novel? Now, add to that the choices available to today's teens; it is not just deciding to read or watch one of three network channels but making a decision between reading a book and hundreds of cable channels, piles of video games, and the time-sucking hole that is the Internet.

Reluctant readers are not stupid. They are kids who do not choose to read. Treating them like dummies is as counterproductive as pushing Jane Austen down their throats. Because they are reluctant to read, they will need encouragement from adults in addition to materials that encourage them. Not pushing, but real encouragement matched with materials that will help make reading a positive experience. This encouragement must begin with accepting the materials that interest them, not you. It might take some time to build credibility with a reader. Remember they know what you want them to read but it isn't interesting to them. Every adult has topics that don't interest them but rarely does someone attempt to force us to read in those subjects. Reluctant-reader titles take many shapes and sizes. Books like Walter Dean Myers' 300-page *Fallen Angels* have appeared on the Quick Picks list, but so have wordless picture books. In general, fiction books for reluctant readers will do the following:

- Have a hook to get the reader's attention immediately
- Move at a fast pace with only a few characters
- Have a single point of view and few flashbacks or subplots

- Deal with real-life situations and high-interest topics
- Have an emotional impact and are gripping and memorable
- Use short sentences and paragraphs and nonchallenging vocabulary
- Have attractive covers, wide margins, and easy-to-read type face
- Weigh in at less than 200 pages

Nonfiction will meet many of these criteria, but also will do the following:

- Contain diverse illustrations to complement the text
- Adopt a magazine-style layout approach
- Contain first-person narrative and real-life experience

One powerful tool for selecting popular and timely materials for reluctant readers is YALSA's Quick Picks committee. The evolution of the committee has been interesting. It started as the "Hi Lo" committee, meaning high-interest, low-vocabulary group, who found the Fry reading level for each book and listed titles for librarians to use with nonreaders. In the 1980s the committee changed its name to the Recommended Books for the Reluctant YA Reader committee and further evolved, placing more emphasis on the high-interest aspect and less on low vocabulary. In the 1990s the committee changed names once again to the Quick Picks committee, thereby reflecting a change in the committee's intended reading audience. Its annotated list targets teens. Teens then got involved in the selection process, and the committee moved away from looking at the number of words in a paragraph to looking at titles that would hook reluctant readers. Librarians, of course, are not on the real front line in this area—reading and English teachers deal daily with such students. The professional literature in education overflows with articles about methods of instruction, motivation, and encouragement. For librarians, reaching the reluctant reader takes rethinking some attitudes and developing methods to reach this audience. The escalator theory states that the only real reading is book reading. This theory falls in line with our mission, and even a thin book is acceptable for a reluctant reader.

Reaching Incarcerated Readers

As we mentioned previously with the SmartGirl survey, the majority of survey respondents (72 percent) reported that they like to read for pleasure when they have time. One might therefore conclude that not having enough time is a major obstacle to teens reading heavily. The hectic schedule of teen life coupled with the plethora of recreational choices often leaves little time for reading. But there is one group of teens who have a very rigid schedule and few choices: teens in correctional facilities. While incarcerated teens have time for reading, many of them lack skills. Speaking at the 2003 American Library Association conference, Vibeke Lehmann, the Library Services Coordinator for the Wisconsin Department of Corrections, noted that 40 percent of prison inmates in the United States are illiterate.[7] The cycle is easy to see and hard to stop. People who end up in prison often became engaged in illegal acts as teens. While there are hundreds of reasons, it is clear that many became engaged in crime because they were not engaged in school. Again, hundreds of reasons, but many don't engage in school because they don't do well. They don't do well because they can't read well. They can't read well because they never learned, didn't have positive early literacy experiences, were not raised in print-rich environments, and never learned the value of reading for educational reasons, let alone as a recreational activity. Yet, teens in correctional facilities do value recreational reading. If they have access to reading materials that meet their interests and are on their reading level, they will read them. Meeting those interests is not as easy as it sounds. While there are clear guidelines for library services for incarcerated youth that embrace intellectual freedom, there is the reality of working with the correctional system. Any person in a correctional facility is deprived of certain liberties. So these teens find the facility acting "in loco parentis" and determining which materials are appropriate for them to read. Juvenile Corrections Librarian Amy Cheney, creator of Alameda County's award-winning "Write to Read" Program in California, has more than eight years of experience with outreach, program design and implementation, and providing direct service to incarcerated teens. Based on her day-to-day work with teens behind bars, Amy provides the following advice for librarians interested in creating a library collection with a juvenile detention center:

> The collection is the heart of your library. Start with books that you know are relevant, youth will enjoy, AND that you can defend. These books will help set a standard for the institution so that the center's administration trusts your judgment. For example, choose books about people who have made a transformation from foster care, a poor educational background, or criminal activity, but make sure they are engaging, well-written and action-oriented. Let me be perfectly clear: a Juvenile Hall is not a hotbed for advocating free speech and the rights of readers, so pick your battles wisely when it comes to what books you add to the collection. I have found there are enough books written from a poor or "street class" perspective to engage my readers without bringing in "Urban Lit" intended for an adult audience which only serves to polarize or have my collection questioned endlessly by administration"[8]

Amy then goes on to offer the following advice for building a collection within a juvenile detention center:

- Buy new books when possible. Teens behind bars are used to getting discards (and are often discards themselves); new books establish respect and excitement.

- Most juvenile halls have transient populations except in the maximum security units. It's important that your administration enable you to have a fast turnaround of books from purchasing to receiving.

- Consider minimal processing (one stamp, one genre label, and one piece of tape). This helps the books get out to the youth faster, the youth can take part in organizing your collection, and minimal processing makes it easier to discard torn or worn books and replace them with new ones.

- Don't further frustrate already frustrated readers. Buy graphic novels that are stand-alone unless you have the staff, ability, or budget to get future books in the series in a timely manner.

- Have EVERY book on the shelf be a winner. Start with 100 percent high interest. Ultimately, 80–90 percent of your collection should be high interest, with only 10–20 percent dedicated to adding depth to the collection.

- Unless you are going to have the time and staff to educate youth about the Dewey Decimal System, organize your collection around easy access and the honor system: genre stickers such as African American, Latino (I'm talking *Snitch*, not *House on Mango Street*) and Biography highlight the entry points for most incarcerated youth.

- Enlist the teens who use your library in graffiti patrol, upholding the honor system, and taking care of the books.

The following lists of fiction and nonfiction titles are Amy's top selections for creating a collection within a juvenile detention center that, in her experience, appeal to incarcerated teens. Also, according to Amy, many juvenile detention facilities do not allow hardcover books for security purposes. Therefore, only a few very popular titles currently available only in hardcover have been included in the following lists.

Fiction

- *Tyrell* by Coe Booth
- *Kendra* by Coe Booth
- *Tears of a Tiger* by Sharon Draper
- *Forged by Fire* by Sharon Draper
- *Darkness Before Dawn* by Sharon Draper
- *Party Girl* by Lynne Ewing
- *House of the Scorpion* by Nancy Farmer
- *Hot Girl* by Dream Jordan
- *Touching Spirit Bear* by Ben Mikaelsen
- *God Don't Like Ugly* by Mary Monroe
- *Gonna Lay Down My Burdens* by Mary Monroe
- *God Don't Play* by Mary Monroe
- *Too Beautiful for Words* by Monique Morris
- *Last Book in the Universe* by Rod Philbrook
- *Forever My Lady* by Jeff Rivera

- *Hotlanta* by Denene Millner and Mitzi Miller
- *Drama High* series by L. Divine
- *The Rose That Grew from Concrete* by Tupac Shakur (hardcover)
- *Cirque du Freak* series by Darren Shan
- *Retaliation* by Yasmin Shiraz
- *A Girl Like Me* by Ni-Ni Simone
- *Shortie Like Mine* by Ni-Ni Simone
- *If I Were Your Girl* by Ni-Ni Simone
- *Cruise Control* by Terry Trueman
- *Street Pharm* by Allison Van Diepen
- *Snitch* by Allison Van Diepen
- *Black and White* by Paul Volponi
- *Rooftop* by Paul Volponi
- *Rucker Park Set Up* by Paul Volponi
- *Response* by Paul Volponi
- *Bluford High* series by various authors

Nonfiction

- *Gunstories: Life Changing Experiences with Guns* by Beth Atkin
- *Voices from the Streets: Young Former Gang Members Tell Their Stories* by Beth Atkin (hardcover; out of print).
- *A Place to Stand* by Jimmy Santiago Baca
- *A Long Way Gone* by Ishmael Beah
- *A Piece of Cake* by Cupcake Brown
- *Sentences: The Life of M. F. Grimm* by Percy Carey
- *One Hundred Young Americans* by Michael Franzini
- *Permanence* by Kip Fulbeck
- *How to Be a Succesful Criminal: The Real Deal on Crime, Drugs and Easy Money* by Ron Glodoski
- *Cooked* by Jeff Henderson
- *No Choirboy: Murder, Violence and Teenagers on Death Row* by Susan Kuklin Susan (hardcover)
- *Somebody's Someone* by Regina Lousie
- *Makes Me Wanna Holler: A Young Black Man in America* by Nathan McCall
- *A Child Called "It": One Child's Courage to Survive* by Dave Pelzer
- *The Lost Boy: A Foster Child's Search for the Love of a Family* by Dave Pelzer
- *A Man Named Dave: A Story of Triumph and Forgiveness* by Dave Pelzer

- *East Side Dreams; Forgotten Memories; Those Oldies but Goodies* by Art Rodriguez
- *Always Running* by Luis Rodriquez
- *Skulls* by Noah Scalin
- *Custom Kicks* by Kim Smits and Matthijs Maat

In addition, many incarcerated teens are parents, and libraries should be assertive about early literacy programs, such as "Born to Read," which teach these young parents about the importance of reading to their children. Despite obstacles that are inherent to working in the correctional setting, there are plenty of books that teens will find of interest. Reading levels vary widely, as do interests. Amy Cheney's lists of recommended titles are certainly not the only books of interest to young men and women in the correctional system, but they do represent a selection of the most popular books that will likely get teens behind bars reading. Interestingly, there are few young adult problem novels of interest to teen offenders, perhaps because the problems faced by fictional protagonists pale in comparison to the real lives of incarcerated teens. When working with incarcerated teens, libraries have ample opportunities to demonstrate the value of reading. But to what end? What is our real motive? The core work of librarians isn't about books, but about building assets in young people. Reading for pleasure is one of the 40 assets that teens need to succeed, and one area where we can positively impact young people behind bars.

Reaching the Readers Who Want Only the Best

YALSA's Michael L. Printz Award is an award for a book that exemplifies literary excellence in young adult literature. The Printz is meant to be like a teen Newbery award designed to honor the best book regardless of popularity or accessibility. The award is new compared to its cousins the Newbery and Caldecott medals and was not introduced without some controversy. Should there even be such an award? What constitutes excellence, and, for that matter, what constitutes young adult literature? To help answer these questions, the YALSA committee that established the award developed criteria for eligibility and selection. The book must have been designated by its publisher as being either a young adult book or one published for the age range that YALSA defines as young adult, 12–18. Thus, adult books are not eligible. The book can be fiction, nonfiction, poetry, a graphic novel, or an anthology. Books published previously in another country are eligible. There is really only one criterion for selection: literary merit. See Figure 6.14 for a list of the winners and honor books so far.

This is a fine list of books, but also a short one. It represents only the best of the best since the year 2000, but young adult literature has been around since the mid-1960s. While those who are concerned with young adult literature eagerly await each year the answer to the question of which book will win the Printz Award, yet another question lingers: "What if?" What if there had been a Printz award five or ten or even

Figure 6.14. Michael L. Printz Winners 2000–2009

2009 Winner	**Melina Marchetta**	***Jellicoe Road***
2009 Honor	M. T. Anderson	*The Astonishing Life of Octavian Nothing, Traitor to the Nation, Volume II: The Kingdom on the Waves*
2009 Honor	Margo Lanagan	*Tender Morsels*
2009 Honor	E. Lockhart	*The Disreputable History of Frankie Landau-Banks*
2009 Honor	Terry Pratchett	*Nation*
2008 Winner	**Geraldine McCaughrean**	***White Darkness***
2008 Honor	Judith Clarke	*One Whole and Perfect Day*
2008 Honor	Stephanie Hemphill	*Your Own Sylvia: A Verse Portrait of Sylvia Plath*
2008 Honor	Elizabeth Knox	*Dreamquake: Book Two of the Dreamhunter Duet*
2008 Honor	A. M. Jenkins	*Repossessed*
2007 Winner	**Gene Luen Yang**	***American Born Chinese***
2007 Honor	M. T. Anderson	*The Astonishing Life of Octavian Nothing, Traitor to the Nation, Volume 1: The Pox Party*
2007 Honor	John Green	*An Abundance of Katherines*
2007 Honor	Sonya Hartnett	*Surrender*
2007 Honor	Marcus Zusak	*The Book Thief*
2006 Winner	**John Green**	***Looking for Alaska***
2006 Honor	Margo Lanagan	*Black Juice*
2006 Honor	Marilyn Nelson	*A Wreath for Emmett Till*
2006 Honor	Elizabeth Partridge	*John Lennon: All I Want Is the Truth, a Photographic Biography*
2006 Honor	Marcus Zusak	*I Am the Messenger*
2005 Winner	**Meg Rosoff**	***How I Live Now***
2005 Honor	Kenneth Oppel	*Airborn*
2005 Honor	Gary D. Schmidt	*Lizzie Bright and the Buckminster Boy*
2005 Honor	Allan Stratton	*Chandra's Secret*
2004 Winner	**Angela Johnson**	***First Part Last***
2004 Honor	Jennifer Donnelly	*Northern Light*
2004 Honor	Helen Frost	*Keesha's House*
2004 Honor	K. L. Going	*Fat Kid Rules the World*

(Cont'd.)

Figure 6.14. Michael L. Printz Winners 2000–2009 *(Continued)*		
2004 Honor	Carolyn Mackler	*The Earth, My Butt and Other Big Round Things*
2003 Winner	**Aiden Chambers**	***Postcards from the Edge***
2003 Honor	Nancy Farmer	*The House of the Scorpion*
2003 Honor	Garret Freymann-Weyr	*My Heartbeat*
2003 Honor	Jack Gantos	*Hole in My Life*
2002 Winner	**An Na**	***A Step from Heaven***
2002 Honor	Peter Dickinson	*The Ropemaker*
2002 Honor	Jan Greenberg	*Heart to Heart: New Poems Inspired by Twentieth-century American Art*
2002 Honor	Chris Lynch	*Free Will*
2002 Honor	Virginia Euwer Wolff	*True Believer*
2001 Winner	**David Almond**	***Kit's Wilderness***
2001 Honor	Carolyn Coman	*Many Stones*
2001 Honor	Carol Plum-Ucci	*Body of Christopher Creed*
2001 Honor	Louise Rennison	*Angus, Thongs, and Full Frontal Snogging*
2001 Honor	Terry Trueman	*Stuck in Neutral*
2000 Winner	**Walter Dean Myers**	***Monster***
2000 Honor	David Almond	*Skellig*
2000 Honor	Laurie Halse Anderson	*Speak*
2000 Honor	Ellen Wittlinger	*Hard Love*
Source: Young Adult Library Services Association. n.d. "The Michael L. Printz Award for Excellence in Young Adult Literature." Available: www.ala.org/ala/yalsa/booklistsawards/printzaward/Printz.cfm (accessed June 1, 2008).		

twenty years ago—then what book would have been named the winner? Patrick Jones asked this question for the third edition of this book. In February 2001, he and teen librarian Sarah Cornish Debraski e-mailed a ballot to 125 people with knowledge of young adult literature. They asked each person to select for each year their pick of what book would have won the Printz award since 1978. They started with the first year of *VOYA* and went up through the last year before the Printz award was developed. It was easy for the 1996–1999 BBYA list years, as they used the top-ten BBYA lists. For the years before the 1996 list, they selected ten titles from the BBYA list. They used BBYA as their foundation, working under the assumption that the Printz book for every year would, or should, be a BBYA. In 2002, one of the Printz books was not a BBYA book, but Patrick and Sarah believed that the BBYA list is so

Figure 6.15. Retro Mock Printz Winners 1978–1999

Year	Title	Author	Year	Title	Author
1999	*Hole*	Louis Sacher	1988	*Fallen Angels*	Walter Dean Myers
1998	*Tangerine*	Edward Bloor	1987	*Goats*	Brock Cole
1997	*Rats Saw God*	Rob Thomas	1986	*Izzy, Willy, Nilly*	Cynthia Voigt
1996	*Ironman*	Chris Crutcher	1985	*Moves Make the Man*	Bruce Brooks
1995	*Catherine Called Birdy*	Karen Cushman	1984	*Interstellar Pig*	William Sleator
1994	*The Giver*	Lois Lowry	1983	*Running Loose*	Chris Crutcher
1993	*If Rock and Roll Were a Machine*	Terry Davis	1982	*Annie on My Mind*	Nancy Garden
1992	*We All Fall Down*	Robert Cormier	1981	*Let the Circle Be Unbroken*	Mildred Taylor
1991	*The Silver Kiss*	Annette Curtis Klause	1980	*Jacob Have I Loved*	Katherine Paterson
1990	*Weetzie Bat*	Francesca Lia Block	1979	*After the First Death*	Robert Cormier
1989*			1978	*Gentlehands*	M. E. Kerr

*"Where is the 1989 list? According to Betty Carter in an e-mail to the authors, before 1989 the BBYA list was known by the year in which the bulk of the books were published. For example, the 1988 list covered 1988 books (and some from 1987). Yet the announcement of the 1988 list in 1989 caused confusion. So in 1989 the dates changed to match the year the list was announced, instead of the books' publication year. It appears that there was no BBYA list that year, but if you check copyright dates, you'll see no break in years represented" [Cornish, Sarah, and Patrick Jones. "Retro Mock Printz: The Best of the Best of the Best of Young Adult Literature from the VOYA Years." *Voice of Youth Advocates* 25, no. 5 (December 2002): 353–157].

comprehensive, involving both a committee and teen input, that it is highly unlikely that the best YA book of the year would go unrecognized by BBYA. Also, not using the BBYA would have been a logistical nightmare. They looked at several factors, such as reputation of the book and author over time, other awards the book has won, the impact of the book on how people read, wrote, and/or reviewed YA literature, and the placement of the book on the various rankings produced by YALSA.[9]

Figure 6.15 includes the winning titles for 1978–1999 selected by the librarians and educators who participated in the Retro Mock Printz. While this is not a YA literature textbook, this is a nice initial reading list for teens and LSTs who want only the best of the best.

Conclusion

So, are these titles the best books for teens? Earlier we wrote about the importance of collecting materials that address the basic needs of teens, whereby core needs create a core collection. A collection full of fiction, nonfiction, magazines, video games, DVDs, and music that explores or celebrates an adolescent's journey, while at the same time addressing the issues of independence, excitement, identity, and acceptance, will be both accepted by teen library users and promoted by teens to their peers. Good collection development is not only about allocating our resources but also about giving teens a plethora of good reasons to allocate their most valuable resource—time—to a school or public library.

Sources Cited in This Chapter

1. SmartGirl.org. 2007. "Report on Teen Read Week 2007 Survey." Available: www.smartgirl.org/reports/7482493.html (accessed June 1, 2008).
2. "Teen Reading Habits and Perceptions Survey." Survey conducted November 26, 2008–December 31, 2008. www.surveymokey.com (unpublished results).
3. Smith, Michael W., and Jeffrey D. Wilhelm. 2006. *Going with the Flow: How to Engage Boys (and Girls) in Their Literacy Learning.* Portsmouth, NH: Heinemann.
4. Faulkner, Brooke. E-mail to author. January 15, 2009.
5. Gravett, Paul. n.d. "An Introduction to Manga." Available: www.paulgravett .com/articles/manga_intro/manga_intro.htm (accessed February 17, 2009).
6. Beers, Kylene. 2002. *When Kids Can't Read What Teachers Can Do: A Guide for Teachers 6–12.* Portsmouth, NH: Heinemann.
7. Lehmann, Vibeke. 2003. "How to Be a Prison Librarian: Preparation for a Foreign Land." Sponsored by Library Services to Prisoners Forum. American Library Association Annual meeting, Toronto Canada, June 19–24.
8. Cheney, Amy. E-mail to authors. February 3, 2009.
9. Cornish, Sarah, and Patrick Jones. 2002. "Retro Mock Printz: The Best of the Best of the Best of Young Adult Literature from the VOYA Years." *Voice of Youth Advocates* 25, no. 5 (December): 353–357.

Recommended Sources for Further Reading

Alexander, Linda B., & Sarah D. Miselis. 2007. "Barriers to GLBTQ Collection Development and Strategies for Overcoming Them." *Young Adult Library Services* 5, no. 3 (Spring): 43–49.

Aronson, Marc. 2008. "Being and Nothingness." *School Library Journal* 54, no. 10 (October): 31.

Barr, Catherine, and John T. Gillespie. 2009. *Best Books for High School Readers, Grades 9–12,* 2nd ed. Westport, CT: Libraries Unlimited.

Barr, Catherine, and John T. Gillespie. 2009. *Best Books for Middle School and Junior High Readers, Grades 6–9,* 2nd ed. Westport, CT: Libraries Unlimited.

Bartel, Julie, and Pamela Spencer Holley. 2009. *YALSA Annotated Book Lists for Every Teen Reader.* New York: Neal-Schuman.

Brehm-Heeger, Paula. 2008. *Serving Urban Teens.* Westport, CT: Libraries Unlimited.

Brenner, Robin. 2007. *Understanding Manga and Anime.* Westport, CT: Libraries Unlimited.

Chance, Rosemary. 2008. *Young Adult Literature in Action: A Librarian's Guide.* Westport, CT: Libraries Unlimited.

Crawford, Philip Charles. 2008. "Why *Gossip Girl* Matters." *The Horn Book* 84, no. 1 (January/February): 45–48.

Creel, Stacy L. 2008. "Graphic Novels and Manga and Manhwa...Oh, My!" *Voice of Youth Advocates* 31, no. 3 (August): 197.

Fraser, Elizabeth. 2008. *Reality Rules! A Guide to Teen Nonfiction Reading Interests*. Westport, CT: Libraries Unlimited.

Frolund, Tina. 2008. *The Official YALSA Awards Guidebook*. New York: Neal-Schuman.

Gallaway, Beth. 2009. *Game On! Gaming at the Library*. New York: Neal-Schuman.

Gorman, Michele. 2003. *Getting Graphic! Using Graphic Novels to Promote Literacy with Preteens and Teens*. Columbus, OH: Linworth Publishing.

Gorman, Michele. 2008. *Getting Graphic! Comics for Kids*. Columbus, OH: Linworth Publishing.

Honig, Megan. 2008. "Takin' It to the Street: Teens and Street Lit." *Voice of Youth Advocates* 31, no. 3 (August): 207–211.

Hubert, Jennifer. 2007. *Reading Rants: A Guide to Books That Rock*. New York: Neal-Schuman.

Hughes-Hassell, Sandra, and Ernie J. Cox. 2008. "Urban Teenagers, Leisure Reading, and the Library Media Program." *School Library Media Activities Monthly* 25, no. 1 (September): 56–58.

Jobe, Ron. 2002. *Info-kids: How to Use Nonfiction to Turn Reluctant Readers into Enthusiastic Learners*. Ontario, Canada: Pembroke Publishers.

Jones, Patrick, Maureen L. Hartman, and Patricia P. Taylor. 2006. *Connecting with Reluctant Teen Readers*. New York: Neal-Schuman.

Oakley, Trevor. 2008. "Circulating Video Games." *School Library Journal* 54, no. 4 (April): 30–32.

Reynolds, Tom K. 2005. *Teen Reading Connections*. New York: Neal-Schuman.

Scholastic. 2008. "The 2008 Kids and Family Reading Report" Conducted by Yankelovich and Scholastic. Available: www.scholastic.com/aboutscholastic/news/readingreport.htm.

Snowball, Clare. 2008. "Teenagers Talking about Reading and Libraries." *Australian Academic & Research Libraries* 39, no. 2 (June): 106–118.

Thomas, Rebecca L., and Catherine Barr. 2008. *Popular Series Fiction for Middle School and Teen Readers: A Reading and Selection Guide*, 2nd ed. Westport, CT: Libraries Unlimited.

Thompson, Jason. 2007. *Manga: The Complete Guide*. New York: Del Ray.

Walker, Barbara J. 2005. *The Librarian's Guide to Developing Christian Fiction Collections for Young Adults*. New York: Neal-Schuman.

Welch, Rollie James. 2007. *The Guy-friendly YA Library: Serving Male Teens*. Westport, CT: Libraries Unlimited.

Zbaracki, Matthew D. 2008. *Best Books for Boys: A Resource for Educators*. Westport, CT: Libraries Unlimited.

Booktalking

Even the best, most well-funded collection needs to be promoted to let teens know that the collection exists and that it is filled with good material. One of the best ways actively to promote a collection is through word of mouth: words in the form of a booktalk coming out of the mouth of a librarian visiting a classroom or other group setting. While booktalks do take place informally, this chapter answers the basic questions about formal booktalking—a time-tested, research-tested method of connecting young adults and libraries.

What Is a Booktalk?

A booktalk is a paperback blurb as performance. Like a movie trailer, a booktalk should whet a teen's appetite for the real deal. Just as the copy on the back of any teen paperback is designed to entice the teen reader to pick up the book and purchase it, a booktalk is a presentation designed to motivate the teens in the booktalk audience to check out the books being promoted. A booktalk is not a read-aloud, a review, or a literary criticism of a book. Instead, it is a performance, sometimes written, but most often ad-libbed, to excite the audience into reading the book. It is not a summary; it is a sales pitch.

When they are done right, booktalks sell reading as an activity. Your goal is to persuade, convince, and even manipulate your audience to sell a product. Your tools are your sense of humor, creativity, and knowledge of books. You don't need to be a Nike commercial, but you should be aware of what teens respond to in advertising: humor, directness, and anything that's not preachy.

Who Is the Audience for Booktalking?

The teen audience is a tough crowd. Very few teens would cheer upon learning that someone from the library is coming to their class to talk

The key to booktalking is similar to that of readers' advisory: find and promote books to which readers will respond.

about books. Often, LSTs are asked to visit "reading classes," which tend to be classes filled with teens who have reading problems or issues and who may lack the motivation or the skills to read well or often. Sometimes, the situation is exactly the opposite and the LST is asked to present booktalks to a high school honors English class in which students are reading the great works of Western literature rather than the latest teen coming-of-age novel. Normally, the audience is somewhere in between and the students have a wide range of reading interests, levels, and experience. The common denominator is that they are teenagers; thus, booktalks must always consider the developmental and emotional needs of teens. Books don't always have to be YA novels, but they should speak to the interests and needs of teenagers. Look for the four core goals of adolescence—acceptance, independence, identity, and excitement—in the books you choose for booktalks. Keep in mind that the needs of high school students differ from those of junior high or middle school students.

Teens, however, are not the only audience for booktalks. Teachers, school librarians, activity directors, principals, volunteers, security guards, and parents could be among the many adults who are present while you booktalk to their charges. This matters because these adults will be working with these teens long after you have finished with your booktalks and left for the day. These are the people who might have an opportunity to talk about these books with teens once you are no longer in the picture, so it is in everybody's best interest to sell the books to all who are present, including teens and their grown-ups.

It is also vitally important that you keep the lines of communication open between you and these adults. E-mail them recommended titles with reviews, request books from the library and put them on hold for them, and send them reviews, galley copies, and candy. Do whatever works to make sure these adults are in the loop about new and exciting reading materials for teens. As true as it is that it takes a village to raise a child, it is equally true that it takes a village to raise a teen reader.

What Are the Top Ten Justifications for Booktalking?

1. Booktalking contributes to increased circulation. Booktalkers all over the planet can regale you with hundreds of success stories. Booktalking works. The advertised books fly off the shelves, garner reserves, and, as word of mouth spreads, remain popular long after the presentation.

2. Booktalking promotes the library as a place of recreation for teens. With the concern that books, reading, and libraries are no longer "relevant" to teens, booktalking reminds teens that libraries offer more than just the Internet. In this way, booktalking should be counted as programming since the goals are very much the same.

3. Booktalking allows the LST to work with schools and to get his or her face seen by students. This certainly has advantages for all other aspects of teen work—programming and readers' advisory in particular. For the school librarian, it allows the students to see them in another light, not merely as someone writing passes or enforcing discipline but as a source of presenting information and entertainment. The more teens see librarians as connected to and aware of what they like to read, the more they will rely on and expect good customer service in the form of readers' advisory. Booktalking increases customer service credibility.

4. Booktalking promotes teen collections efficiently, especially when the booktalk supports a school assignment for outside reading. Rather than having 30 students come to the library at different times and getting different levels of service and expertise when finding a book to read for school, one booktalk session levels the playing field and provides the students with the information they need. It is also more efficient to have one LST present to 30 students once rather than have those 30 students asking, "What's good to read" over the desk, if they bother to come to the library at all.

5. Booktalking provides LSTs with the opportunity to use their creative talents for the good of the library. No one got into this profession to sign up people for computers. Many people working in libraries, in particular those working with youth, have that creative urge that needs to be flexed for the good of the library as well as for the LSTs' morale. Booktalking provides LSTs with the opportunity to share their creativity with customers, coworkers, managers, and, most important, teens. Teens who see librarians enjoying the activity of booktalking see adults excited about reading, and that experience changes everything for the better.

6. LSTs reach more teens in one day of booktalking than they will probably see throughout one week within the walls of the library. How many high school students, not counting those who are homeschooled, homeless, or truant, will you see if you are at the reference desk in a public library from 10:00 a.m. to 2:00 p.m. during the school week? Zero. How many would you see if you spent one day visiting every classroom of just the 9th grade? Of course, it depends on the size of the school and the number of classes, but let's say 300. Okay, now which number is larger: zero or 300? If there is even one sentence in your job description about serving teens, booktalking should be on your monthly schedule because numbers like that are hard to ignore.

7. Booktalking is one of the few library activities whose primary audience is the nonlibrary user. There are two ways to increase circulation: to motivate current users to check out more materials or to create new users. Booktalking can accomplish both

tasks. While many in the audience may know you and the books you are talking about, chances are there are just as many who don't have a clue about the library or the books. There is no doubt that booktalking reaches nonusers, but it is just as important to remember that booktalking shows library users new possibilities. Lots of teen library users have functional and specific reasons for coming to the library: to get a certain book, to check their e-mail, to wait for a ride. Booktalking does in the classroom what we don't have the time or the opportunity to do with these functional users: show them the bigger picture. While booktalking is limited by how many titles you can cover in a 50-minute class period, what is not limited by the time available is the message: There's a lot of good stuff in the library beyond that computer screen.

8. Booktalking is the most effective method for actively promoting reading. We can sit at our desks and bemoan the fact that kids don't read, or we can go out there and actively engage teens with books, selling the act of reading as an enjoyable way to pass some time.

9. Booktalking increases the audience's awareness of the library as a resource. The first step to getting people moving toward an action is to increase their awareness. The booktalking visit is a vehicle to promote everything LSTs do for teens, so use every booktalking opportunity to hand out a list of the books you are promoting or information about how to get a library card, library hours and locations, paying (or reading down) fines, upcoming programs, and how the library can provide homework help.

10. Booktalking provides LSTs with opportunities to build relationships with teens. Before and after any booktalking session, it is a given that some teens (often the ones who are readers) will come up to speak with you. Are these kids you've seen in your library before? Probably. But have you, between reference questions and paper jams, had a chance to listen to them talk about the books they've read? These classroom visits will provide you with the perfect opportunity to take a few minutes and really listen to these teens as they talk about, and ask questions about, books. Additionally, these classroom visits provide you with opportunities to build relationships with teachers and other adults by promoting programs, creating collaborative assignments, and sharing information.

What Are the Models for Booktalking?

Booktalking is a lot like storytelling, and the main thing for LSTs to remember as they prepare to deliver a booktalk is to evoke a sense of performance. This does not mean you must become an entertainer, but you should recognize that the booktalk situation—a person standing in front of the room before an audience—is a performance setting. This doesn't mean you must be theatrical or dramatic, but it does mean you should understand some basic concepts of performance, especially the importance of knowing and respecting your audience. The bottom line when it comes to delivering successful booktalks to teens is that it is not about you—it is about them. Think about these four experiences as a way to model your booktalks:

- **Paperback blurb.** When written correctly, the copy on the back of a book is all sizzle and no steak and it is written with one sole purpose: to sell the book. While perhaps a little shorter than most booktalks, the key questions are there: Who are the characters? What is the conflict? Why should the reader care?

- **Movie preview.** You see the main character, get a sense of the theme or mood of the work, and often witness a sneak preview of some of the best scenes or lines. It's short, powerful, and designed to sell the product.

- **Pop music single.** A classic radio single is catchy and it rarely clocks in at over four minutes. There is often a hook or memorable part and repetition of the song title so teens know what to search for when they go looking to download it from iTunes.

- **Joke.** Short, often funny, and usually ends with a punch line— a surefire way to keep teens coming back for more.

What Are the Rules of Booktalking?

The rules of booktalking are fairly well established. Beginners to the craft should be very careful to abide by them; seasoned veterans know which ones can be bent or broken.

Of all of the established rules for giving a booktalk, the single most important rule is to have realistic expectations. Some teens will be more than happy to show interest, ask questions, and check out books, while others will merely look on with bored indifference. Remember that indifference is a well-honed attitude for many teens, so try not to take it personally. Besides, hundreds of things happen during the course of a day that could make a teen indifferent to the promotion of reading. Home life, homework, and hormones all affect the atmosphere you walk into. The good news is the research is on your side: booktalking works; it may not always work for every student every time, but it will motivate teens to read.

There are rules, and then there is the prime directive—remember your audience. When you are writing, attempt to visualize not only yourself giving the talk (that will help with performance) but also your audience. As you plan a ten-minute booktalk summarizing every key scene in the book, can you visualize your audience sitting in rapt attention? See the sidebar for some basic Dos and Don'ts for creating and delivering successful booktalks to teens.

The cardinal rule of booktalking is simple: sell, don't tell.

DO
- Have realistic expectations
- Bring books with you to check out
- Memorize talks and have cheat sheets
- Vary the themes/types of talks
- Keep good records of visits
- Come prepared to ad-lib and interact
- Vary length of talks
- Start strong and end strong
- Be organized, cool, and confident
- Relax and enjoy yourself
- Measure success
- Learn from your mistakes

DON'T
- Booktalk books you have not read
- Booktalk books you did not like or would not recommend
- Gush
- Give away the ending/the secret/the surprise
- Give a book review
- Label by gender/race/other
- Oversell
- Read aloud unless it is absolutely necessary
- Talk about sex/drugs/violence without clearing it with the teacher
- Booktalk books you don't have in multiple copies
- Be boring

What Are the Most Common Types of Booktalks?

Everybody who uses booktalks as part of their bag of tricks has a different way of doing booktalks. It is helpful to observe other techniques and styles, but you should develop your own unique style. This may take some practice and thought, as every book you meet will lend itself to several different ways of being booktalked. Following are the most common types of booktalks. As you observe others booktalking, you will begin to see these types emerge and you will also begin to recognize which type works best with the YA books you encounter.

- **Mood.** The goal here is to convey to the audience the general "mood" of the book. This works best with scary books, and reading from the text can be part of this technique. But setting the mood can work equally well with a genre like humor or realistic fiction. To set the mood, you can use props, dialogue from the book, or lighting. If you have a flair for the dramatic, this is where you can let it all out. Beginning with a particularly dramatic booktalk is a good way to show teens that they are in for something interesting. For the most part, a mood-based talk aims to share the experience of reading the book with the audience. This works well with senior high students who might be more appreciative of an author's language. Why summarize Maya Angelou when you can let the power of her words do the work? Titles that lend themselves to this type of booktalk include *Stuck in Neutral* by Terry Trueman, *You Don't Know Me* by David Klass, *The Rag and Bone Shop* by Robert Cormier, *Speak* by Laurie Halse Anderson, and *The Love Curse of the Rumbaughs* by Jack Gantos.

- **Plot.** This is the most common—and seemingly the easiest—technique. Hit the high points of the story just as if you were telling a friend about a book or movie. With a booktalk, the hard part is to know when to shut up. If you tell too much, few will want to read the book because you've told everything, including the ending; if you tell too little, the audience won't be interested in finding out what happens. If there is a failing with most booktalkers, it is to include too much plot, too many characters, and too much action. You have to keep it simple so the audience can track your words, form the images, and still want to hear more. Practice stopping before you think you should and get comfortable leaving people wanting more. Finding the right stopping point in a book's plot is what makes booktalking more art than science. Titles that lend themselves to this type of booktalk include *Tomorrow When the War Began* by John Marsden, *Thirteen Reasons Why* by Jay Asher, *Memoirs of a Teenage Amnesiac* by Gabrielle Zevin, *Project X* by Jim Shepard, and *The First Part Last* by Angela Johnson.

- **Character.** The preferred method for many booktalkers is to present the booktalk in first person. As many teen novels are told in the first person, this really allows the audience to experience the "voice" of the book. Some booktalkers who do this go all out, using costumes and accents, while others will merely read from the text. Presenting in first person can be tricky and sometimes confusing to the audience, but when it works, it is very effective and memorable. It will only work, however, if you are comfortable with these techniques. If you are not, teens will see through it and reject it. Take the risk and reap the benefits. Titles that lend themselves to this type of booktalk include *Ender's Game* by Orson Scott Card, *I Am the Messenger* by Markus Zusak, *Tyrell* by Coe Booth, *Whale Talk* by Chris Crutcher, and *Looking for Alaska* by John Green.

- **Scene.** Rather than telling the entire plot, going into details about all the characters, or reading a great deal to set the mood, this type of talk presents one part as a representative of the whole. This technique works well with thrillers or adventure novels. The key is to find one scene to share that really captures the essence of the book. You'll need to give some background to the story, but like some movie trailers, one exciting or comic or scary scene can be enough to give the audience a taste. Titles that lend themselves to this type of booktalk include *Nick and Norah's Infinite Playlist* by David Levithan, *Little Brother* by Cory Doctorow, *Stormbreaker* by Anthony Horowitz, *Fat Kid Rules the World* by K. L. Going, *Upstate* by Kalisha Buckhanon, and *Repossessed* by A. M. Jenkins.

When you are booktalking nonfiction, especially biography and history, you can use any of these techniques. A "scene" talk for a self-help book might involve doing one of the quizzes. For a poetry book, you might consider reading one or more poems. While there are variations from the four forms—plot, form, character, and scene—they do represent the frame on which most booktalks are built.

How Do You Write a Booktalk?

The most critical part of booktalking is selecting material. This requires knowledge of your collection as well as the interests of your readers. As you select materials, use the same tools and techniques you use to build a collection, including print and online review resources, booktalking Web sites, and teen lists of recommended books (Amazon is a great resource for this). Although plenty of published sources are available on booktalking in print and on the Web, eventually you will have to sit down and write some original material. Use the existing talks to get your feet wet. Once you are comfortable with the process, start writing your own and testing them out gradually on an audience with whom you feel comfortable.

The books you select to booktalk will certainly vary based on the teacher's needs and the reading levels and interests of the audience. You may choose to booktalk only new books, but remember that this will limit teens' access to the books since most libraries do not buy multiple copies of hardcover books. You may choose books on a theme or subject, but remember that the books you present need to have more going for them than just a shared theme; they need to be interesting, appealing, and lend themselves to the booktalk format. It's best to strike a balance between fiction and nonfiction, between serious books and funny ones, between popular authors and lesser-known writers, between classics and contemporary works, and between books you like and those you love. Like all things, booktalks need to be customer focused, and the reading interests of the teens—not the teacher or LST—need to drive the selection of materials. Keep your audience in mind; balance between books that appeal to girls and guys, readers and nonreaders, those who have and/or take the time to read and those who read only for an assignment. The more you think about your audience or potential audience, the more prepared you will be to deliver the booktalks. There comes a time when you will read a book that is wonderful and amazing but, sadly, not the easiest book to sell in a booktalk. Set it aside, and ask around for others who like the book to describe it to you because they may give you the perfect hook or description for a booktalk. Some titles make it very easy by selling themselves, but others may need more effort, and even a smaller number are titles that can't be forced into a booktalk situation. Once you begin reading with booktalking (and your audience) in mind, titles will begin to sort themselves. The more you read, the bigger your booktalk arsenal will be.

After choosing books, it is time to start writing the talks. Some people write down every word, while others merely read the book and sketch some notes. Some people start with the blurb as the framework and then fill in more details, while others take extensive notes as they are reading the book. Most people read the book all the way through, but some read just as many pages as necessary. Some people, especially when booktalking nonfiction titles and graphic novels, scan illustrations and project them, while others stay as low-tech as possible. There are endless numbers of ways to prepare, to write, and to present, but the bottom line remains the same: Sell, don't tell.

How Do You Start a Booktalk?

The best thing to do first is read books with booktalks in mind; this will help you pick and remember phrases, characters, etc., to use in your booktalk. Often there is a sentence or setting that screams "Booktalk me!" When these jump out at you, use them—the author spent a lot of time crafting those scenes and selecting those words, so let them do their job with teens. Look to use the following five items as you read and craft your booktalk. At first, stick with only one so your booktalk doesn't get too long or complex. As you gain experience, try combining two and see where it takes you. Refresh old booktalks by using a different angle. Teens may respond to a book they previously ignored.

- **With a character.** Use a quotation or description, but in the first sentence of your booktalk give the audience a good (or bad, depending on the character) first impression of the character. If you use a quotation, do it with a different tone of voice. This gets attention and it helps announce that something is different about this book.

- **With a question.** A question forces the audience to pay attention because they want the answer.

- **With an action.** Share something that a character does that is dramatic and attention-grabbing: an act of violence, daring, or even stupidity.

- **With a shared experience.** Open with something in the book that the audience has probably felt, done, or said. Again, your first sentence might best be a question.

- **With a shocker.** Many books have shocking incidents. Rather than building up to them, use them as a point of departure. It is a cheap way to build excitement, but it works.

What Goes in the Middle of a Booktalk?

Many LSTs consider the middle of a booktalk the hardest part to write. If you get stuck, focus on creating a beginning and an end. The middle will happen once you have established a structure for your talk. Here are some things to keep in mind when it comes to crafting a memorable middle:

- Keep it simple and use short, declarative sentences.

- Follow a narrative. Go from point to point without detours.

- Keep it to a few characters. The more people you talk about, the more confusing your talk can become for both you and your audience.

- Repeat things. In information literacy instruction, you always repeat what you want people to remember; the same is true of booktalking.

- Choose your words carefully. A booktalk is not the time for a vocabulary lesson. Make sure the words, images, and allusions are appropriate for your audience and their grade level.

- Read sparingly. Your task is to sell the book, not to recite it. Reading takes your eyes off of your audience and your audience's eyes off of you.

- Watch timelines. You don't want to cover three years' time in one talk. The book's time frame will help determine this, but events should not happen too far apart.

- Watch your watch. Movie trailers and pop songs last about two to four minutes. Any booktalk over four minutes should be pretty special.

- When in doubt, leave it out.
- Edit, edit, edit.

Most booktalk presentations are timed to last a class period. To allow time for asking and answering questions, handing out materials, taking attendance, and allowing for teens to look over the books, plan your booktalk presentation to last around thirty minutes. How many titles you can booktalk in that time period will be up to you; some people do 10 to 15 separate booktalks within a half hour while others choose to provide longer booktalks for fewer titles. Like a band putting together a set, there should be some mix in timing. Try a variety until you get comfortable with what works best for you. Ask teachers what they prefer and talk to, observe, and pick up tips from your booktalking colleagues. If you will be spending an entire day with one teacher, booktalking to every one of her English classes, it might be a good idea to prepare a longer list of titles so you can mix it up and not bore yourself or the teacher by talking about the same ten titles all day long.

How Do You End a Booktalk?

The average booktalk should be between two and four minutes. Any less time, and it is hard to get to the sizzle; much more, and you are giving away too much steak. The thing to remember is that the last line should be memorable, and an excellent punch line is often the title. But don't force a booktalk to an awkward conclusion just to work in the title, and doing it every time probably borders on compulsive and annoying. The rule is simple: End with whatever it takes to get at least one teen in the audience to say, "What happens next?" or "I want to read that!" When this happens, remember how you ended that booktalk and file it away in your bag of tricks.

How Do You Turn a Booktalk into a Performance?

Paperback books almost always have a great hook or tagline on the cover or in big letters on the back of the book. They introduce the character, describe the conflict, outline the emotions, or ask a question that can be answered only by reading the book. This hook is what gets you interested, and when it works, it's the answer to the question, "Why should I read this book?"

Booktalks can have hooks in the same way. Just as a hook is what makes each book different and memorable, each booktalk can have a different spin. Sometimes the hook will come naturally out of the book, while other times it takes more creativity to develop the hook. At first, you may be so concerned with remembering all of the character's names that you don't want to think about adding anything to your talk. But after a while, especially after booktalking the same titles a few times, you will notice what types of things work with an audience. Experiment with books you know well, turn the booktalk upside down and inside out, change a "mood" booktalk into a "plot" booktalk, use an accent or vary your voice, truly memorize it, and add movement for drama. It will make it interesting for you and you might catch the ear of a reader with a different approach. Using hooks ensures that you sell as well as tell.

What Are Hooks on Which to Hang a Booktalk?

Once you have decided on the type of booktalk to use for a particular title, it is time to think of the hook that catches even the most discriminating customer. Again, try these hooks with your tried-and-true booktalks because it may renew your interest in a title and sell it in a way that connects with new teens. When you observe others doing booktalks, try to identify the hooks they use. You will find your own favorites, those hooks that come to you easily and those you have to work a bit harder to achieve. They are all great ways to reel your audience, teen or adult, into books.

- **Audience participation.** Look for ways to get your audience involved. Have them answer questions. Include sound effects. Repeat "taglines." Do your booktalk as part of a larger presentation. Overall, remember to let teens participate in your presentation.

- **Diary.** Many YA novels are written in a diary format, with a conversational tone and an often self-absorbed teen narrator. Reading aloud from a specific meaningful, exciting, or emotional diary entry is an excellent way to hook a teen reader.

- **Empathy.** Almost every writer of teen fiction is aiming to build a character that young readers can relate to and care about. Present in second person or talk about the character's emotions with the teens sitting in front of you. If they can understand the character's plight and start to care a little about the character, then they will care about reading the entire book. The first two lines of *Speak* by Laurie Halse Anderson are perfect for 8th graders. "It is my first morning of high school. I have seven new notebooks, a skirt I hate and a stomach ache." These are four common experiences teens can relate to and share with the main character.

- **Expect the unexpected.** Books with an unexpected ending have a built-in hook; tell a little bit about the story and then let your audience know that the end of the book is something he or she will totally not be expecting. Two great books for this hook are *The Rag and Bone Shop* by Robert Cormier and *Lucas* by Kevin Brooks.

- **Experience.** Lead into a talk by relating a personal experience, or, better yet, do a short booktalk pretending the events that happened to the character actually happened to you. *Shattering Glass* by Gail Giles and *Olive's Ocean* by Kevin Henkes both lend themselves to this hook.

- **First sentence/one sentence.** Some books have such well-crafted, dramatic, and spellbinding first sentences that a discussion of those sentences could be the center of a booktalk. There are too many titles to mention here, but three favorites are *The Chocolate War* by Robert Cormier, *Feed* by M. T. Anderson, and *Monster* by Walter Dean Myers. This hook works well at the end of a class period if you have only a few minutes left but not enough time to do a full booktalk for any of these titles.

- **Your own gimmicks.** Maybe your gimmick is magic or riding a unicycle. Use what works for you. Part of getting through to teens when booktalking is presenting yourself as someone worthy of the teens' time.

- **Giving up control.** Let the audience pick the title they want you to booktalk from your pile or list of books. It helps you gauge what sounds interesting to teens, and it also puts them in the driver's seat. This may sound risky, but there is actually very little risk, as teens will be choosing from a predetermined list of books you are already prepared to booktalk.

- **Gross-out.** Younger teens, in particular, enjoy a gross-out. From the adventure novels of Gary Paulsen, to the pulp horror fiction of Stephen King, to photos found in many books about mummies, there are plenty of opportunities to turn the stomachs of teen listeners. *The Secret Family: Twenty-Four Hours Inside the Mysterious World of Our Minds and Bodies* by David Bodanis and *Phineas Gage: A Gruesome but True Story About Brain Science* by John Fleischman will elicit great groans, especially right before lunch.

- **Headlines.** Just as the television show *Law and Order* talks about being "ripped from the headlines," plenty of young adult titles, both fiction and nonfiction, mirror current events. Make the connection obvious and use it.

- **Kiss-and-tell.** Teens are interested in sex. Talk with the teacher first to get an idea of how much (if any) freedom you have to discuss sexual content. Even then, you will want to allude to the sexual aspects of a book rather than playing kiss-and-tell. A well-placed pause or look will let the audience know the good stuff is contained between the covers. This can be the payoff for those teens who are listening carefully—they get the joke or innuendo before those teens who checked out. This can be something as subtle as reading the list of boyfriends from *The Boyfriend List* by E. Lockhart to reading the shocking first couple of paragraphs from *Doing It* by Melvin Burgess. You could also consider projecting the last page of *A Bad Boy Can Be Good for a Girl* by Tanya Lee Stone, which is the "blank page" inside the school's copy of Judy Blume's *Forever* with advice from girls in the school about boys to absolutely avoid as they are only out for one thing.

- **Know a secret.** Is there any more intriguing question to most teenagers than "Do you want to know a secret?" Since many teen novels are built around this simple premise of a character hiding a dark secret, this is almost a foolproof way to structure a booktalk. Tell a little about the characters, hint at the secret, get ready to reveal it, and then stop. You could build a whole list—fiction and nonfiction—around this hook. Great YA books with a secret include *Madapple* by Christina Meldrum and *Hero Type* by Barry Lyga.

- **Link.** Link a book with a current movie, or link a popular fiction title with a nonfiction title. Link a book that students have read in class with one you are booktalking. Look to connect pieces of the teen world with the literature written for them. This works really well with graphic novels based on television shows or novels that have been made into movies.

- **Next line.** This, the easiest hook of all, works best with scene-based talks. Set the scene, build the action, and then just as a character is about to do or say something, stop, pause, and then hold up the cover of the book.

- **Pantomime.** Adding a little bit of movement every now and then will make talks more entertaining for the audience and for you—just remember not to go overboard.

- **Props.** Show materials from the book. This works well with first-person talks. By using the middle of Chapter 6 from *White Darkness* by Geraldine McCaughrean, sunglasses, and the imaginations of the teens, a quick trip to Antarctica is within your grasp.

- **Repetition.** Repeating the title or the tagline is a great way to hook a reader. Plus, repetition adds rhythm to the talk.

- **Risk.** Ask for a page number from the audience and then begin reading at that point—you never know what you're going to get and neither does the audience. It's risky, but it's a great way to give teens some power.

- **Sound effects.** From knocking on the door to imitating the sound of a beating heart, let sounds rather than words carry key parts of the booktalk.

- **Unifying experience.** Get everyone thinking about the same thing by asking questions about universal experiences that unify a group, like driving, friendship, being dumped, or dealing with parents.

- **Vocabulary.** Begin a talk by asking the audience to define certain words. Repeat these words throughout the talk, and then come back to them at the end. Using the word "reputation" is a great lead-in to *Sandpiper* by Ellen Wittlinger.

- **Xerox.** If you were booktalking *Curious Incident of the Dog in the Night-time* by Mark Haddon, you might pass out copies of various maps or math equations from the book. You might choose anagrams from *An Abundance of Katherines* by John Green, or pass out a deck of playing cards for *I Am the Messenger* by Markus Zusak. Other books that have short, easy-to-read documents (letters and comics, for example) would work, as well.

Adding hooks such as these, as well as those you develop, will help ensure that a booktalk presentation is something more than an LST standing in front of the room describing a bunch of books. What booktalk hooks do for you is add to your tool kit of proven methods for constructing a talk that you can use at a moment's notice depending on your audience.

Can Booktalking Be Learned, or Must an LST Be Born with That Gift?

Every booktalker, like every storyteller or reference librarian, has a different "style." Style can be copied, but it can't be taught. However, techniques for booktalking can be learned. Often people will see someone else booktalk and say, "I couldn't do that," which is exactly the case; no two people could, would, or should booktalk exactly alike. You can learn some of what to do and what not to do from watching another booktalker, but in the end you are going to have to go out there and just do it in order to develop your own style. If you are really brave, we recommend inviting a trusted colleague (who has experience booktalking to teens) to watch you or record you and give feedback. You will be able to gauge reaction in the moment, but a little distance can give you perspective about what tools you need to help you improve.

After accepting that booktalking, like storytelling, is a performance, and admitting that you want to influence your audience, you will begin to handle your booktalks differently. You will learn to perform rather than recite your talks, and you will learn your own performance style. Your goal is to inform, to entertain, to whet the appetites of ravenous readers, and to inspire reluctant readers. By arousing the audience's curiosity, by using sound, movement, repetition, and other hooks, by creating empathy for characters, and by evoking emotions, all while entertaining them with a lively presentation, you will succeed.

What Are the Elements of Booktalking Success?

- **Know the crowd; don't be too proud or too loud.** The teacher needs to tell you as much as possible about the classes you will be visiting. You don't want to go into a class of lower-level readers and present books they can't read, nor do you want to visit a group of students with high reading levels or

> Anyone can learn to booktalk, but it takes practice to master the art.

sophisticated tastes and talk about series mysteries. To help you get the information you need, we recommend sending the teacher a questionnaire about his or her classes, preferences, and areas of interest several weeks before your visit.

CD See Tool 24. Planning a Booktalk Visit

- **Speak to feelings, not lofty ceilings.** Characters, emotions, and stories to which teens can relate—these are the things teens look for in books. Teens are notoriously egotistical, so they will be looking for something familiar in your talks, from characters that look and act like them to settings that seem all too familiar. What they are not looking for is elements of style or literary devices. The group may have a variety of different reading levels and interests, but teens share certain emotional similarities. Teens may expect you to booktalk books they don't like (those they are assigned to read for class), so building credibility right out of the gate is important. You get one shot to make that first impression, so make it good.

- **Don't just speak out, seek out.** Involve the audience as often as possible. In a performance setting, an involved audience gives energy back to the performer. If other peers are involved, the audience is more likely to become interested in the booktalk.

- **If you want a reaction, create an action.** The worst thing during a booktalk is total silence. If you want your audience to react, you need to create situations for them to react to. Be sure to let the teacher know you want interaction and can handle it. Let the books do the work: tell the one-liners in funny books if you want to hear laughter, or read the graphic descriptions of horror in Stephen King books to get a groan.

- **Use your style, not cards from a file.** When you write your talk, you will probably not have a hook in it right away. Only through practice and experience will you move from file cards to re-creating the talk as something to be performed rather than read. One trick is to tape the booktalk on the back of the book. Teens will be focusing on the book as you hold it up, and, if necessary, you can sneak a peek at your notes.

- **Think stage, not printed page.** Again, write your booktalk, but think about adding movement. Think about adding sounds or props as you write. Challenge yourself by working one of the hooks into a talk already in your file. Moving around the room will help you, but it will also keep the teens in the back of the room engaged.

- **Be yourself and lose yourself.** You have to be yourself when you speak in front of a group. Teens, in particular, will pick up on any falseness in your presentation. Your goal is to relax and leave your ego (and self-consciousness) at the door. Once that happens, the audience will naturally be more engaged because the authenticity will be there. One thing you do not want to do is load down your talk with slang or attempts to be something you are not; aim for candid and you're bound to land somewhere in the land of authenticity.

- **No matter what you try, answer the question why.** Hooks are gimmicks, and like most gimmicks, they only go so far. You can never get away from the central point: providing a group of teens with the reasons why they should take their precious time to read a certain book.

- **Remember needs, not just deeds.** When deciding which books to booktalk, focus on what is really happening in the book, the "journey" the teen protagonist is experiencing, rather than just the "plot" or the action. Chances are the characters are grappling with issues or feelings like independence, acceptance, identity, and excitement. Those are the real selling points.

What Do You Need to Know to Schedule a Booktalk?

To ensure successful booktalks, most booktalkers develop formal or informal policies for scheduling and carrying out classroom visits.

Some LSTs ask that all booktalks be scheduled at least two weeks in advance, that a booktalking session must last the length of one period, and that teachers must stay in the room (and not read the newspaper). Some booktalkers don't mind doing all six or seven class periods in one day, while others won't do that many in a row. If you choose to combine classes, remember that this might mean that different grades and reading levels are in the same room. Also remember that part of scheduling is also considering the best time of day for booktalks. Since booktalking requires more of your energy and the class's energy, the end of the week is not a good time to schedule a visit. Additionally, classes first thing in the morning or late in the afternoon are also notoriously difficult. Classes right after lunch are the most fun and challenging because the Twinkie rush usually kicks in during the middle of the presentation. Trying to arrange several mini-talks for multiple classrooms during one period is also very difficult. Darting in and out of rooms every ten minutes is too confusing for the teachers, provides too little interaction with the teens, and will likely leave you feeling very discombobulated. Finally, remember that each school is different, so accept the fact that the first visit might not go perfectly.

How Do You Structure Your Booktalks into a Cohesive Presentation?

After you have written your individual booktalks, you need to structure them into a presentation. If you have seen the group before, you don't need to go through the whole "introduction" section and you can jump right into talking about the books. However, if it is your first time to visit

CD **See Tool 24. Planning a Booktalk Visit**

When it comes to planning a booktalk, it's important to do a thorough interview with any teacher you will be working with for the first time. The more you know about the makeup and needs of each class you'll be visiting, the greater chance you'll be successful throughout the day. It's just as important to take some notes during each visit and, as you plan the next visit, make these changes in order to improve the experience for everyone.

CD **See Tool 7. Booktalk Evaluation**

with a class, be sure to introduce yourself and your library and provide a brief explanation about what you have planned for the next 30 minutes to an hour, including talking about several books, time for questions and answers, followed by time for them to look at the books and check them out if possible. Once you have been doing this for a while, you can put together a list of books you know cold. Pass out this list and ask the audience to tell you, based on the title and a one-sentence tagline, which book they want to hear. You need to decide how many books you cover given the time you have. When a band puts together a concert, they break it up into sets. In that set, they structure the songs to a particular effect. Lots of bands begin with an "old favorite" to get immediate recognition, then play new material, and encore with more old favorites. That's a good model to keep in mind when putting together booktalk presentations.

What Are the Elements of a Successful Booktalk Presentation?

- **Always prepare more than you need.** You don't want to run through all of your titles in 20 minutes and mutter, "Any questions?" Have long and short versions of presentations for titles so you can stretch or shorten depending on the time factor and audience reactions.

- **Booktalk in teams.** This means that LSTs need to prepare less material, but it also has other advantages. It allows both people to utilize their booktalking strengths and it helps keep the energy level high. It also provides an opportunity for you to learn new techniques and gain inspiration from other people's material. You also give your audience exposure to another LST, who is sure to have a different set of titles than you. Finally, you can have a lot of fun playing off of each other.

- **Check out books.** If possible, bring multiple copies of titles with you on the visit that you can check out in the classroom. It will answer any immediate need that teens have for the book that might cool before they can get to the library. There is the risk that you will lose a title, but the idea is to get the books into the hands of teens. Work with the school librarian prior to the visit, so he or she can pull titles you will be booktalking. If you cannot bring books with you, take names and place reserves.

- **Consider audiovisual.** Some people use PowerPoint to display the book jackets or illustrations from nonfiction titles. Some LSTs do booktalks over the PA system or on the in-school cable channel. You could use AV to complement your booktalks, or you could film a quick video to replace your visit occasionally. Background music or even sound effect tapes can also be effective when they are not overdone or played too loudly. You might also consider incorporating multimedia into your talks, especially with graphic novels or other formats that lend themselves to more visual presentations. This might be as simple as projecting images on a wall using a laptop computer and LCD projector or as difficult as producing original book trailers (like movie trailers, only about books) and then uploading them to YouTube. You might also consider showing some of the existing book trailers currently available on the Internet from various YA publishers. For more information, see www.bookscreening.com.

- **Craft smooth transitions.** The transitions between your talks need to be smooth to give the impression that your "act" fits together rather than being a random selection of books. Try to make the last word of one booktalk be the first word of the next. If doing horror stories, a basic transition is, "If you thought that one was scary, then . . . "

- **End with a bang.** Save your best talk for last. Be careful of the timing, though; you don't want your best talk cut off by the bell.

- **Find movie tie-ins.** For a first booktalk, consider a title they recognize, one with a movie tie-in or one that a movie was based on.

- **Give something away.** End the booktalk presentation by putting something in the teens' hands. It could be a book list, a flyer about a program, a bookmark, an evaluation form for your talk, or a reading interest survey.

- **Incorporate other formats.** In addition to talking about some of the library's newest books, highlight some of your library's recent AV acquisitions, especially DVDs and Playaways.

- **Keep notes handy.** Some people bring a written booktalk with them, while others speak entirely from memory. A good compromise is a "cheat sheet" listing the names of the major characters and one- or two-word reminders of the outline of your talk so you can get from point A to B without forgetting the highlights.

- **Make a list.** No matter how hard you try to work in the title of a book, many kids are just not going to remember it. List the titles you are going to talk about, then also list similar titles. If possible, show these supplemental books as part of the presentation. Make sure you distribute a copy of the list to the teacher and the school librarian and make a copy available at your library so visiting teens (who of course will not remember to bring the list they received in class) can find the book you mentioned during your visit. Another step is to label books on the list that are available at both the public library and the school library. The goal is to get teens reading. Where they get the books doesn't really matter.

- **Relate inside information.** If you can relate any personal information about the author, it makes the book more real to the audience, especially if you can tie the author or the content of the book to your city or to a recent current event.

- **Relate personal experiences.** Don't bore them with the story of your prom, but dig deep for any personal experiences for which teens can relate. These personal anecdotes will help break down barriers, and they are a great way to create connections.

- **Talk with the teacher first.** As much as you may want to be a one-person show, you need the teacher's help, especially considering they have the power to help (or hinder) you in setting the mood for the class. If you want the teens excited and even talkative, let the teacher know. If not, the teacher may feel the need to settle them down when you are trying to "get them up."

- **Use a known author.** In the beginning, you are establishing credibility. Choosing a Stephen King book establishes the common ground between their interests and your resources. You don't need to sell Stephen King, but you do need to sell the idea that your library has "good stuff."

- **Use your captive audience.** Give them a short survey to solicit responses about whatever topic will help you plan better services. Ask them about their music or programming interests, or any other kind of information you would like to collect. If possible, provide them with an opportunity to share their contact information for news about future programs and library events for teens.

What Does a Booktalk Actually Look Like?

Here are sample booktalks that illustrate many of the hooks described earlier. Some of these are variations of talks that first appeared in the NoveList database or in previous editions of *Connecting Young Adults and Libraries*.

Shattering Glass by Gail Giles

"I've had a long time to think about it and I still ask myself the same question. Why did we follow Rob all the way to the end? Of course we hung out with Rob, he was our leader. Simon Glass, on the other hand, was the biggest loser in school, a nobody, we all hated him. So, why did we agree to help Rob with his plan to make Simon Glass the most popular guy in school? Looking back on it, I see that Rob was using all of us, but he was the coolest guy in school, so we went along with everything. The lies, the manipulation, the deception. At first, it seemed like a game, harmless, even a little fun. But it became pretty clear that it was about something else for Rob. It was about power. And by going along with Rob's plan we got something only Rob could give us...his approval. In the end Rob's creation had a mind of his own, but when things turned ugly, I turned my anger on the creation, not the creator and I went along with Rob all the way to the end, the bloody end."[1]

Airborn by Kenneth Oppel

Although he's just a cabin boy, Matt Cruse hopes to someday be the captain of his own airship. For now though, he feels privileged to be able to serve aboard the luxury liner *The Aurora*. He is learning everything he can about the ship, and he gets to travel to exotic destinations. He even had a taste of adventure last year when they came across a hot air balloon in distress. In the bottom of the balloon's basket lay an old man, dying. As the smallest and lightest member of the crew Matt was swung out in midair to rescue the man. As Matt begins to determine the problem, the old man opens his eyes, and with a look of true wonder and amazement asks Matt, "Did you see them? They were . . . beautiful! Not birds really, but, with wings." Matt sensed it was important to the old man so he agreed that he had seen the creatures. The old man looked directly into Matt's eyes for several seconds and then he knew that Matt had not seen the creatures. He closed his eyes, his breathing went shallow and his heart stopped. Now it is a year later, and on board *The Aurora* is Kate, granddaughter to the old man, who believes what Matt was told. Kate has her grandfather's logbook from the balloon in which he recorded his sighting of the marvelous creatures and she intends to prove her grandfather right but needs Matt's help to find the truth. As they approach the same area where Kate's grandfather was discovered, *The Aurora* is boarded by sky pirates, and during the battle the great ship is damaged and plummets out of the sky landing on an uncharted island.[2]

Memoirs of a Teenage Amnesiac by Gabrielle Zevin

It was a fluke. A coincidence. An accident. It was the luck of the draw. Now Naomi can't remember anything. A fall down the stairs as she went back to get the yearbook camera has left her with no memory of her life after 6th grade. Think about that—what has happened to you since you were in the 6th grade? Because the fall leaves Naomi with no memory of her boyfriend. No memory of her parents' split. No memory of a half sister. No memory of high school. Naomi searches for her past as she tries to figure out the truth about her life and who she is. If you had to piece together the past four years who would you trust to tell you the truth? How would you know the difference?

Thirsty by M. T. Anderson

Chris is a pretty normal teenager. He's got a couple of good friends who take turns insulting one another. There's Rachel, the girl of his dreams who sits near him in English class. There are his parents, who fight all the time. There are all the trappings of teen years, including Chris's passion for McDonald's, which he notices grows stronger by the day. It must be just a growth spurt, he thinks as he tries to figure out why he is hungry all the time. Chris is a pretty normal teenager. He's got these friends who he hangs out with. One day they are walking down by the lake that is a landmark in their town. They start up with each other again, but the teasing gets too personal and Chris gets angry. He pushes his pal Tom down on the ground near the lake. A violent urge overtakes Chris. His mouth begins to water. He looks down at Tom, and then glances at the water. That is when Chris finds that he has no reflection. Chris is a pretty normal teenager, except for two things: he's a vampire and he's very, very thirsty.

You Don't Know Me by David Klass

"You don't know me." John, who claims his father named him after a toilet, is cut off from the world. He lives most of his life in his head and believes that no one knows him. Not his mother, who is rarely home and spends her time working to make ends meet. To his mother, John would say, "You don't know me." Not his father, who left home when John was four, never to return. To his father, John would say, "You don't know me." And certainly not the man who John calls "the man who is not my father." That is his mother's boyfriend. That is his mother's future husband. That is the man who terrorizes John on a daily basis. Hard slaps to the head, harder and more brutal verbal abuse. To this man, John would say, "You don't know me." At school, well, teachers try, but they are too busy. There are friends, but sometimes friends fight. And then there is Violet, the girl he longs for, but certainly she does not know him. John doesn't know all that much about life, but he is learning. He is learning the hard way. He learns that "your real enemy is someone who knows you, knows all about you. That person who knows you best is the person who can harm you the most." So, if no one knows him, John figures, he can't be hurt. John is wrong—very tragically wrong. Because more than sticks and stones can break bones. What John is going to know most about is simple: pain. John lives most of his life in his head, which is a safe place to be, because in the real world, he's about to get his ass kicked.

Getting Away with Murder by Chris Crowe

A lot people think the civil rights movement began with a courageous act of nonviolent resistance by Rosa Parks on a bus in the big city of Montgomery, Alabama, in December of 1955—and that's true, to some degree. But in many ways, it was a cowardly act of violence in a little-known town in Mississippi in August of 1955 that was the start of the long march for civil rights. Maybe the Supreme Court said that black and white children should go to school together in *Brown v. the Board of Education*, but things like that didn't matter much in rural Mississippi, where the drinking fountains were still labeled "white" and "colored."

That was the world that 14-year-old Emmett Till entered into August of 1955 when he ventured down from Chicago to spend the summer with his cousins in this little backwater town. This was the world that 14-year-old Emmett Till came face to face with when he entered the store owned by a white couple named Roy and Carolyn Bryant. Roy was away for the day, working a second job. Emmett Till walked into the store and something was said. Did Emmett Till "whistle" at Carolyn Bryant, did he say something suggestive, or did he merely say "bye, baby," when he left the store on August 24, 1955, in rural Mississippi? News spread throughout both the black and white community that something had happened at the store, and all hell was about to break loose.

A couple of days later, on August 28, Roy Bryant and his pal J. W. Milam showed up at the door of Emmett Till's uncle and asked for the "boy who did the talking." They took Emmett from the house and drove him to the boondocks. And they beat him. And they shot him. And they killed him. And then they buried his clothes. And then they strapped his body to a piece of scrap metal and let it sink into the Tallahatchie River.

But the murder is really just the beginning of the story. Emmett Till's body was fished out of the river and returned to Chicago. His mother demanded that the funeral be held with an open casket so the world could see "what they done to my boy." The black newspaper the *Chicago Defender* ran a photo of Emmett Till's bashed-in face lying in the coffin. In the court of public opinion, Bryant and Milam were guilty. But in a courthouse in Mississippi in 1955, things were different when the case went to an all-white jury. Do you want to bet on the outcome? Do you want to know how easy it was for people like Bryant and Milam to get away with murder?

America by E. R. Frank

This is the story of America. This is the story of Now and Then.

Then: America was born to a drug-addicted mother. In the past 15 years he's never had a real home for long. He is caught in the system; sometimes he is lost within it.

Now: America is in a residential program, listening to Dr. B. trying to get him to talk. Dr. B. wants to know why America tried to take his own life. What's wrong with America?

Then: Is America white? Is he black? Does it even matter? Yes, to the rich white family who adopted him as a baby but who turned him away when he started turning his color.

Now: In his file, it probably says something like "America is a lot of trouble." "America might be crazy." It might even say that America might be a murderer.

Then: His mother gave birth to America and rejected him. Then she took him back, and she left him behind again.

Now: America lies in his bed at night, trying not to cry, trying not to hear other kids screaming. America wants to fly, let his spirit soar, even if he's locked in his room.

Then: So another family comes along and says they love America. Mrs. Harper adopts him and teaches him to read. But if Mrs. Harper is so good, then why is her brother so evil?

Now: He's working in the kitchen, but he's always getting in trouble. America hates carrots and he throws them away. They remind him of the past: of then, of that, of it.

Then: Mrs. Harper's brother showed America the carrot peeler, showed him how it can peel away skin. White skin, black skin. Does it even matter?

This is the story of Now and Then. This is the story of America.

Conclusion

It seems simple enough: read a book and tell someone about it. Of course, those of us who do it know there is so much more to it, including planning, preparing, and evaluating. Despite all of the help offered in this chapter, many things are not covered. We recommend doing some further reading online and in print. Many librarians who are also master booktalkers have written comprehensive books and/or created exhaustive Web sites with advice as well as sample talks. Once you have a solid grasp on what a booktalk is and how you can make it happen, it's time to jump in and give it a try. If you have a regular group of teens who hang out in your library, consider inviting them to a pre-booktalk booktalking session after school one afternoon. Provide them with snacks and let them know you're looking for constructive criticism before you actually have to deliver these talks to their peers. If your barrier to booktalking is stage fright or fear of public speaking, there are books out there to help overcome those barriers. If your barrier is fear of teens, then that is something you need to get over if you plan on serving this age group. If your barrier is your administration, refer to the discussion of the advantages of booktalking at the beginning of this chapter. If your barrier is a lack of booktalk experience, this is the easiest one to control. Get out there and make it happen, and you'll soon notice that it gets easier and more fun every time you have the opportunity to turn some teens on to books.

Sources Cited in This Chapter

1. Reynolds, Tom. Booktalk. August 20, 2008.
2. Debraski, Sarah Cornish. Booktalk. August 23, 2008.

Recommended Sources for Further Reading

Belden, Dreanna. 2008. "Harnessing Social Networks to Connect with Audiences: If You Build It, Will They Come 2.0?" *Internet Reference Services Quarterly* 13, no. 1: 99–111.

Braunstein, Stephanie. 2008. "Partner with Outreach as if Your Library's Life Depends on It. . . . It Quite Possibly Does." *Louisiana Libraries* 70, no. 4 (Spring): 37–40.

Brookes, Joanna, and Ryan, Rebecca. 2007. "A Tale of Two Libraries: Outreach is the Focus." *Public Libraries* 46, no. 4 (July/August): 9–12.

Burhanna, Kenneth J. 2007. "Instructional Outreach to High Schools: Should You Be Doing It?" *Communications in Information Literacy* 1, no. 2 (Fall): 74–88.

Erdman, Jacquelyn. 2007. "Reference in a 3-D Virtual World: Preliminary Observations on Library Outreach in 'Second Life.'" *The Reference Librarian* 47, no. 2: 29–39.

Pfeil, Angela B. 2005. *Going Places with Youth Outreach: Smart Marketing Strategies for Your Library.* Chicago: ALA Editions.

Suellentrop, Tricia. 2006. "Get Out of the Library!" *School Library Journal* 52, no. 9 (September): 39.

Vogel, Victoria. 2008. "Library Outreach to Teens with Physical Challenges." *Young Adult Library Services* 7, no. 1 (Fall): 39–42.

Outreach and Partnerships

We define outreach services as activities that take place outside of the library setting. Outreach refers to either a community relations function (promoting services) or actual service delivery, such as booktalking, in a location outside of the four walls of a library. Sometimes these two areas of outreach overlap, with one area helping set the stage for the other. The community relations mode also means networking, attending meetings, or being present in other settings that allow you to bring the library's services for teens to a particular table. The result of this networking can be new partnerships, which are the foundation for future outreach.

What Is Outreach and Who Is the Audience?

Outreach is taking the library out into the community, to anyone and anywhere who will have you. It can be as basic as taking flyers for your new programs to the high school or as formal as speaking to the local Rotary Club about your services to teens in a juvenile detention center. It can be as tricky as coordinating multiple visits with multiple supervisors to teens in group homes to get them all library cards so they can check out books you have brought. Perhaps the most important concept in all of outreach is "face time." That is, getting your face (and message) in front of teens or to the people who work with them who could use your services. Sometimes face time means presenting, sometimes it means staffing a booth at a school function, sometimes it means delivering a service, but often it means showing up so you have the opportunity to interact one-on-one with teens, or those who serve them. The problem with face time is it is a long-term investment in a library environment consistently concerned with short-term results.

The limit to who is involved in outreach is limited by your imagination, your community, your resources, your administrative support, and your willingness to connect with community partners. The possibilities and levels of involvement are endless and varied. School visits are a good place to start, with lots of probable "nonusers," and you have a somewhat

Outreach is about partners, new ideas, old scenarios, and endless possibilities!

captive audience with other adults around to reinforce ideas and information after you have gone. Students are all in the same situation—they all have to do a science fiction book report—but what they really need are suggestions for books they might actually like. Assigning a science fiction book report does not mean that the LST or teacher has a great list of titles for the students to choose from, but if you can provide that service everyone wins. You get face time with the teens who probably never see you, they hear about a variety of books that will help them with an assignment and hopefully make them think differently of the library next time around, and the teacher sees the value of you as an educational partner.

When you visit a middle school, the target audiences for your services are the students, teachers, and administrators. However, the audience for outreach services isn't always so obvious. Sometimes you have to search a little harder for your audience, and sometimes you get lucky and one outreach event leads to others. For example, once you establish a relationship with one group, a juvenile detention center for example, you can begin to look at groups that splinter off from your original contact: teens on probation, teens in foster care or group homes, judges, court system, the adults who run those facilities or provide education and other services. You can also investigate other groups associated with the detention center, such as mental health, Alcoholics Anonymous/Narcotics Anonymous, anger management, religious groups, career classes, and GED classes, to see if you can be of assistance. Often the library will have materials or services to provide to these groups that they may find helpful or about which they may be unaware. One of the most important questions to ask any partner at an outreach activity is, "Whom else should I see?" While most cities of any size have some sort of youth services collaborative, it is most often the unofficial networks that net the best results. While cold calling a potential partner often works, it is better if you can get a current partner to make the introduction or smooth the way. Look to the human services agencies in your city or the United Way network. Often youth-serving councils or coalitions exist already, and if you find they don't, there is no reason you can't start one, beginning with the library, police, school districts, mental health, and parks district.

Why Should a Library Actively Reach Out to the Community?

The simple answer is because libraries thrive when the community in which they exist thrives, but also because, when you really think about it, no one funds a library only to shelve books; they fund a library to be a viable participant in the community. Real estate agents understand this and it is time that libraries do as well.

When you begin to do outreach, your library becomes seen as a viable part of the community. The first thing that happens when staff begin going out into the community on a regular basis is promotion of the library to nonusers (and their parents, who may also be nonusers). You will immediately tap into a population that you always knew existed but never quite knew how to reach. Since we rarely see or hear from these people, this group seems the most at need. They are unaware of the value and resources that the library provides and are therefore unable to use or support it.

One reason promotion of the library is useful, especially at budget time, and when comparing outreach services to in-library services, is circulation statistics. Your use of materials will increase, and in turn the circulation statistics will increase, which is important to note, not only how many items are being checked out but what types of items. The types of materials being checked out and requested can give you insight into what types of services or programming would appeal to those customers. But those are relatively short-term reasons.

We want people to use the materials and resources that we work hard to select, we want the library to prosper and to be important in people's lives, and we want to connect people to ideas and experiences that will improve their lives. You already have the people who are coming in your door; they understand how it works. The people you never see are the ones who need you and the library. Whatever the circumstances, some people in our communities would use the services of the library if it were a little more convenient. Sometimes the attitude is that if they really wanted to use the library, they would find a way: "Well, we are here, open 10:00 a.m. to 9:00 p.m. during the week...what more do they want from us?" Our libraries' services must realign with our customers, where they live and spend their time. Our teen customers, when asked, almost always tell us the main thing they would change about the library is its hours. They really do want to use our resources, but it doesn't fit into their schedules. If we can't change when we serve teens, since few libraries ever add hours in the evenings or on weekends, then LSTs need to focus on where we serve our customers.

Why Is Outreach So Important in Teen Services?

Teens use products that are marketed to them. The goods and services we are marketing may not be cool, but they are quality; they are free, will help them in the short and long term, and will help them save time. Outreach is direct marketing at the most fundamental level; visiting school is like going door to door, except each door opens to 30 potential customers. Every teen is a potential library customer.

When you provide outreach to teens, many things are happening:

- You are reaching teens who aren't aware of the library and the resources available. These teens may already be library users, but you might turn them on to a new service or a hot new title that is outside of their current use and reading habits.

- You are giving positive attention to teens who may equate adults with only bad attention. We are a benevolent people.

- You open a flow of communication between the library and teenagers. Part of face time is letting teens meet someone on the "outside" that they may need when they visit the library. People like to go where at least someone knows their name.

Outreach is about meeting teens where they are: their time, their turf, their technology.

- You are gathering opinions and ideas about the library and your services from teenagers.

Outreach can't just be about telling; it is also about listening. When you give teens a chance during a school visit to ask questions or offer opinions, you'll find them more receptive to information if it comes in the form of an answer rather than a speech.

What Services Are Best Delivered as Outreach?

Just about every service we talk about throughout this text can happen just as well on the road as within a library. If our true interest is on the outcomes and not on numbers, on making a difference rather than just making a hash mark on a stat sheet, then where services are delivered is not important. The taxpayers pay for library services, not just a building. Thus, LSTs can deliver many services outside of the library, such as these:

- **Collections, by taking library materials to specific locations.** This might involve deposit collections in classrooms, juvenile detention centers, group homes, courtrooms, shelters, or other locations. It is bringing the materials to the teens rather than expecting them to come to us.

- **Information services, virtually.** We need to conceptualize our online reference services more as an outreach service and less as a technical service. If outreach is bringing library services to people where they live or work or congregate, then certainly our virtual services allow teens to use the library from their bedrooms, cars, or phones.

- **Booktalking to teens in a classroom or group setting.** For more on the advantages of this, as well as tips for successful booktalks, see Chapter 7.

- **Programs such as book discussion groups.** Which is easier—to try to get ten kids to come to a public library at the same time for a book discussion group, or for the public librarian to work with a school to do the discussion *at* the school? What matters is the outcome, not the location.

- **Programming.** Cultural, crafts, entertainment, etc. We'll talk about how to do programming later, but once we focus on outcomes, it is easier to conceive of outreach programs. If we want teens to have a positive library experience, where is it written that it must take place in a library? Given the difficulty of arranging teens' schedules along with access issues, it makes more sense for one librarian to travel than to expect 10, 20, or 200 teens to do so. For some programs with huge appeal, such as an author or performer visit, a school or recreational center might be the only venue large enough. Most meeting rooms are too small, and unless we do it off hours (which you might argue is a form of outreach as well), the commotion caused by such a program is sure to impair normal library operation and staff. Related to this, libraries can also sponsor programs or events at locations in the community, such as a skate park, shopping mall, or a movie theater.

- **Summer reading promotion.** The visit to promote summer reading is a staple of public librarians, even if there is virtually no evidence that this has direct impact on participation. Thus, LSTs need to begin to document the success of these visits and make them more than just show-and-tells.

- **Programs to at-risk teens or groups.** Given shrinking resources, we need to justify our outreach efforts. One common way is to determine what gives the most bang for the buck. These are normally the school visits, often to English classes, to do booktalking and/or information literacy instruction. But, are those really the kids who most need library services? Many of those teens *do* have access to the library, *do* have computers at home, and *do* have resources (time, money, supportive parents) who will get them to a library. What about teens who are parents? In GED programs? In jail? In alternative schools? Those teens might not have the resources, and more likely are in need of the information or programs we can deliver off site. The need is greater, but this doesn't mean the results will be as spectacular. If we think outreach is only about numbers, then we'll keep doing the summer reading program show-and-tell; but if we realize that outreach is about outcomes, then LSTs will begin to look at what might be best for the most vulnerable teens in the community, and not what's best for library statistics.

- **Simple promotional activities.** Staff a table at your local middle or high school's open house in September, or during a parent/teacher night, or in the cafeteria during lunchtime. Also, send library card applications to all the media centers. Students can return completed application to the media center, the media center gets them to the library, and then staff process and mail cards to students.

- **Information literacy instruction.** In the school setting, this is often done in the library, but public libraries need classrooms to take this show on the road. The instruction can be with teens, with teachers, or even with parents. For more information on information literacy instruction, see Chapter 5.

What Are the Benefits and Drawbacks of Outreach?

The benefits are twofold. The library benefits from more members of the community being aware of it and using it, and the library, because of connections made throughout the community, has the chance to be seen in a different light—as a proactive entity and as a community hub.

When LSTs work with teachers, it creates a laundry list of benefits for teens, such as the following:

- Ability to obtain materials easily
- Better understanding of how libraries work
- Clearer assignments
- Increased access to information
- Increased access to information technology
- Increased access to recreational reading
- Innovative programs to meet their needs
- Library staff with better understanding of their needs
- Reduced frustration in using libraries
- Reduced stress in using libraries

Teens in the community who receive outreach services from the library are more informed, read more, and are generally more aware of the possibilities offered by their local public library.

The bottom line, of course, for students, teachers, and the community is that teens do better in school. While people will argue endlessly about how money is spent within the educational system, there is probably agreement on one thing: Everybody wants kids to do well in school, no matter how "doing well" is defined.

Outreach from the school library into the classroom makes a difference, especially when it is backed up by funding for staff, collections, and technology. We can only infer, for there is not yet any research to document this, that students with access to a public library that funds teen services, and where the LSTs are involved in collaborative activities with schools, will excel. Public librarians do school cooperation because it works for teens, plain and simple, not because it makes their job easier or because it is fun, but because they know that library partnerships can increase student learning and achievement.

But more than knowing it works, it is what your public wants you to do. Gallup polls have indicated that formal education support is seen by the public as an important role for public libraries to play, the assumption being that the purpose of this role is to support student learning and achievement. Education/instruction was seen as the sole province of the schools and, within the schools, as part of the school library media program. Technology requires that public libraries get involved in information literacy; it is not only about educating your customers but about empowering your teen users. The need for constant training and instruction about new information technology has forced public library LSTs to take another look at their role in supporting student learning and achievement. If public library staff receive the proper instruction and training, then they can become full participants in the education of their customers. Communities no longer see the formal educational institutions as the sole providers of learning, in part because of the recognition of the need for lifelong learning.

So, if outreach and partnerships are so wonderful, why are they not more plentiful? The drawbacks to outreach vary with the types of services you provide. A drawback that cuts across the board is that the more you promote the library, the more people come into the library. It might sound odd, but you may have the mind-set that this is the exact outcome desired, but other library staff may think differently. The type of people coming into your library may change; staff may have to learn to serve customers they would rather not serve at all—teenagers. If you are out beating the bushes for customers, then you need to have staff back at the branch who are ready to serve them, no matter their needs. Some other drawbacks include the following:

- Once you start providing outreach services, everyone wants a piece of you, and there may not be enough staff to go around. This is almost always objection number one: "We need you on the desk." Yes, but teens in schools and shelters also need the LST. Why is the desk, especially in large systems with telephone, chat, and e-mail reference available to any customer who walks into any library, still the holy land? Is "the desk" where the action is? Is it where your customers are between 9:00 a.m. and 3:00 p.m.? Most likely no.

- Staff at facilities and schools change, and the new person may not even understand what type of service you provide. Schedules, rules, and interest may change the services you provide, and they may want more of you or less of you or things you cannot provide.

- The hours that work for a correctional facility or other community partner may be the exact opposite of your work schedule, and this may include weekends.

- Administration does not see the value—they like to put your picture on the cover of the annual report but your funding does not reflect that prominent position.

- Library staff don't know or understand what you do, mainly because you are outside of the building. Therefore, you must not really be working. You need to bring back the goods and let your coworkers, who often are carrying a heavier desk schedule, the results your outreach is bringing. In this case, you might want to tell the story in terms of what it is doing for the library—in other words, what is in it for them.

- Once you start to see how many people need outreach/library services, it is difficult to say no to any opportunity.

How Do You Begin Developing an Outreach Program to Reach Incarcerated Teens?

On a recent ALA panel, several libraries spoke about their service to teens in the corrections system. Services ranged in length, budget, and frequency, but all noted similar challenges with regard to diverse reading level and ability, censorship, and funding.[1] Working with the corrections staff at the center is crucial to assist them in understanding the goals of the program and what materials the library will bring to the facility.

Correctional facilities are charged with maintaining safety and security, and depending on your relationship with the facility, certain materials may be viewed as contrary to that goal, which is all the more reason to establish the requirements of the facility up front. Regular communication with correctional officers and directors about your library services and the type of materials being used and taking every effort to understand the rules and regulations they operate within will only improve the relationship and the outcome. The more this happens, the better access libraries have to teens in correctional facilities. There are several libraries with successful programs around the United States: Johnson County Library's (Kansas) "Read to Succeed,"[2] Pima County's (Arizona) Juvenile Detention Center Library,[3] Hennepin County's (Minnesota) "Great Transitions,"[4] Austin Public Library's (Texas) "2nd Chance Books,"[5] and Alameda County's (California) "Write to Read"[6] to name a few.

In addition to supplying books and magazines, many libraries promote reading in correctional settings using techniques similar to those used in a school setting:

- Booktalking
- Book discussion group
- Book review programs
- Creative writing workshops
- Guidance programs
- Poetry slams
- Read-alouds
- Readers theater
- Storytelling

For more information about developing a collection for teens behind bars, see Chapter 6.

What Are the Obstacles with Outreach and How Do You Overcome Them?

Staff and money are the two biggest obstacles. Lack of support from your boss or administration can also be tough to overcome. A community that does not see the value of the library and is not open to the idea of the library trying new and innovative ideas can be a challenge that may take time to change. When you first begin outreach you may encounter people who are not opposed to working with the library but are genuinely surprised that the library offers such services. This will surprise you because you are obviously willing to provide the service, and more, with the right connections. Part of your job is to educate the public that the library does actually offer such outreach services. Keep educating them because people change jobs and forget.

Even with time and money as an obstacle you can start small, but smart, by following a plan similar to this one:

> "Ever since you guys have been coming to the JDC [juvenile detention center], I've read a lot more books than before, and I have found a healthy way to escape reality and to relax. In books, you can be in a million places in a million ages."
>
> —Incarcerated teen, Johnson County (KS) Juvenile Detention Center

- Focus on one school, one staff person, for 4–6 hours a month.

- Focus on one activity: doing booktalks.

- Be realistic about the time it takes to put together a good book-talking list.

- Take advantage of the tools (this book for one) that are out there to help you with booktalks that will make those students remember you and the books.

- Partner with the school librarian, one with whom you already have a personal or professional relationship.

- Have the school librarian look ahead to the assignments he or she knows are coming, which sadly the librarian may not always know.

- Get e-mail addresses of the teachers you will be seeing and ask them what types of books their students like or don't like.

- Have the school librarian/teacher report any success stories that you aren't around to see.

- Track your progress: check the circulation on titles of books before you go out to talk about them and then monitor the status of those titles for the next several months.

- Compile numbers of how many students you were able to see in 2 hours and how many teenagers were served in the library while you were gone by the staff person "on the desk."

- Invite your supervisor and anyone else to come along to observe to dispel whatever notions they had in their head of what outreach is. Let them see it and you in action. Worst case, tape it or have people write letters on your behalf—administrators listen to the public, especially parents whose teens picked up a book because you told them about it, and this was a first.

- Continue the outreach discussion, within your library and outside as well. Decide on one or two talking points and consistently and stubbornly bring up the subject.

There are ways to help with changing the mind-set of your community. For the most part it has to come directly from the library and eventually from talkative people who have enjoyed your services. Once you have figured out who your target audience is—let's say a middle school—then you need to be at meetings, in-services, new teacher orientation, luncheons, and anywhere else you can be promoting your services. You'll want to visit the target school in the late spring, two weeks before school is out, and introduce yourself to the school LST. He or she will most likely be packing up the library and students won't be checking out books, so the LST may have a minute to talk if he or she isn't helping with field day. Give the LST a flyer, a sample booklist, and your card, and tell him or her you would love to present free booktalks for the students at the school once they get settled into the school year. Underline the word *free*. Be sensitive to the fact that the first few weeks are chaos. You might mention that the booktalks work great if a class has a book report due during the first quarter, that you will use a mix of titles owned by the school and public library, and that you will give them a list beforehand in case they want to pull the books for checkout. Think like they think: What will help them do their job better? The worst thing to do is to come on too strong with too many ideas and projects; most school-based LSTs are already way too busy, and this will put them off. Instead of telling the school everything you can do right from the get-go, focus on a small project that proves you can work together. From that success, all other collaborations flow.

One of the best ways into a school is if you have a personal relationship with someone who works at the school and can vouch for you. After hitting a school district hard with promotions and getting nowhere, it was a school librarian moonlighting at the public library who took a chance with having the librarian come to give booktalks to her 6th graders. She spread the word in an e-mail, and at a meeting soon after the visits the library received several calls from other middle schools interested in having booktalks at their schools. A personal recommendation was all it took. A mistake that many LSTs make in working with schools is trying to work with *every* teacher. You'll have more success if you focus on one or two teachers. Your outreach program, as a whole, will grow from these personal relationships as teachers with whom you have been working tell their peers.

> Outreach is all about being proactive, building relationships, and being present in the community.

Are There Ways You Can Reach Out to Teens Without Leaving the Building?

While direct, face-to-face service is the best way to connect with teens outside the walls of the library, there are alternatives. When we think about outreach in a physical sense, we think of places teens gather by choice or by force. So we should continue to think in those terms in the virtual world. LSTs are no strangers to social networking, and as more virtual communities develop and grow as a common place to which teenagers flock, libraries should be ready to provide outreach services to those communities just as they would do for a new school, shelter, or community center. The specifics of what services libraries provide and to which communities will vary. Today most libraries have a MySpace page as well as a presence on Facebook. Next year it might be a new social networking tool. It's not the application that matters; it's the opportunity to communicate with teens outside the four walls of the library. The most important question to ask yourself is, "What technology can I use or borrow to assist my library in connecting with the teens in this community?" The best way to find those communities as they develop is to ask teens.

Any outreach is about relationships. For some this connection is easiest in the physical world, and for others this connection is easiest in the virtual world. Building those relationships remains the goal. A strong relationship with the library and a caring adult equals strong teens equipped with the resources they need to conquer the world and find a great book.

What Kinds of Partnerships Can You Form?

Partnerships are the agreements you craft with schools or businesses to make outreach as well as in-library services happen. Partnerships can be a real plus for libraries by extending resources, providing easy access to another organization's customer base, and increasing the library's visibility in the community. Both partnerships and outreach are exciting, difficult, creative, satisfying, and often the best way to spend your time and money. Although working with other organizations can be daunting in the beginning, we promise the outcome will be worth it.

The term "partnership" is used generically to describe three very specific types of activities that libraries engage in with other institutions:

- **Communicative.** This is where the library merely seeks to team up with another organization for the purpose of getting out its message about services in general or about specific programs or projects. A communicative partnership may be as simple as an agreement with a local gaming shop to post flyers, a school to make announcements, or a cable station to air PSAs produced for the library by teens. In a communicative partnership, you are often asking for very little, and it is usually centered around receiving access to your partner's audience.

- **Cooperative.** A simple way to think about this type of partnership is quid pro quo, or "this for that." In such partnerships, the library asks for something (coupons from businesses, space in a newspaper, access to the partner's audience, etc.) but is expected to provide something as well, perhaps only recognition of the gift. Libraries are good at asking for things but not as good at providing something in return to those who work with them. "Cooperative" might also mean an arrangement to bus in teens from an after-school program, do a project with another youth-serving agency, or develop a booklist with a school librarian. Cooperative partnerships will require you to invest more, but you will also get more in return.

- **Collaborative.** Communicative and cooperative partnerships normally involve the library advancing its goals and the partner advancing its goals; a true collaborative partnership means both groups create new goals within the context of the partnership. A collaborative partnership takes a while to get started due to the process of identifying needs, establishing roles and trust, setting goals, and finding resources. While the other arrangements may be handled with simply a phone call or e-mail, a collaborative partnership means sitting down together to write down who is going to do what, why, when, and where.

An inverse relationship exists with these three types of partnerships. Collaborations take the most time, but normally have the highest payoff, while a strictly communicative relationship requires little but generally provides little in return. The types of partnerships LSTs engage in will

Figure 8.1. Potential Community Partners

Formal Education Organizations	Youth-serving Agencies (Cont'd.)	Commercial/Media Outlets (Cont'd.)
Public schools	Church or temple youth groups	Cable access
Private schools	4-H	Newspapers
Charter schools	Junior Achievement	Beauty shops
Alternative schools	Boys/Girls Clubs	Used car lots
Home schools	YMCA/YWCA	Music stores
Special programs	Explorers	Video stores
Adult education	Summer programs	Coffee shops
GED classes	After-school programs	Bookstores
Adult literacy classes	Homeless youth programs	Sporting goods stores
Community colleges	Dropout programs	Supermarkets
Colleges and universities	ROTC	Department stores
Parent/teacher groups		Hot Topic, or other teen clothing and accessory stores
Teachers' professional associations	**Cultural/Recreational Organizations**	
	Art museum	Malls
Governmental Departments	Science museum	Formal shops
Police	Theater groups	Skating rinks
Anti-gang task force	Dance companies	Putt-putt
DARE	Music groups	Entertainment centers
Fire	Young audiences/Youth performers	Arcades
EMS	Arts council	
Health	Local historical society	**Other**
Parks and recreation	Improv comedy groups	Political clubs
Housing		Social clubs
Community development	**Commercial/Media Outlets**	Adult service clubs
Elected officials	Martial arts	Professional associations
Jails/juvenile detention center	Sports teams	United Way
Juvenile court/community service	Fast food/pizzeria	Health Communities Project
	Hobby shops	Voluntary Action Agency
Youth-serving Agencies	Radio stations	Ethnic clubs
Boy/Girl Scouts	Television stations	Neighborhood associations

depend on many factors, but primarily you should look to partners who will help you reach the teen audience outside of the library setting.

How Do You Move from Outreach in the Community to Developing Partnerships?

This takes a little longer, but it comes from doing consistently good work at various outreach sites. It also comes from taking the initiative, showing up at meetings for projects, sharing ideas, and helping to plan. People in other agencies need to start thinking about the library as part of the team, the solution, an agency with something to offer, and a partner that respects them. For example, a diversion program requires first-time teen offenders to attend a drug and alcohol film discussion group with their parents. The library is asked to do a presentation to both groups about resources the library has to offer, such as information about local laws and the corrections system in your area, resources for drug and alcohol counseling, resources at the local schools, lists of activities for teenagers, and other services. The corrections system is not the expert in gathering information—the library is—so they called the experts to let you do what you do best.

Who Are Your Potential Partners in the Community?

Every community that is big enough to have a library is also big enough to have one or two possible partners. Partnerships begin with you asking one question: Who else in your community touches the lives of teens? The follow-up question is: What do you have to offer to each other in order to create a viable partnership? Every community is different, but every community is also all the same, in that there are several groupings of potential partners (see Figure 8.1).

Certainly every community is different, but almost all have one thing in common: the yellow pages in print and online. It is still the best community directory available to the LST. The other common element in every community is the teens. Ask where they go, whom they listen to, and how they spend their time. A key to outreach and partnerships is to find avenues of opportunity to interact with teens outside of the library. To do this you need to know where to find them. The best thing you can do in any partnership when your partner thanks you for your participation is to thank them for the opportunity and then say, "Whom else do you know that might be interested in this service?" Outreach is all about building relationships.

You Want to Partner with a For-profit Business: How Do Private/Public Partnerships Work?

For a long time public libraries steered clear of partnerships with for-profit entities and focused on the multitude of nonprofit and civic organizations. There are a few challenges up front:

- The appearance of favoritism
- Pushback from library staff
- Groundwork needed for a for-profit partnership to work

When you think about the reasons libraries haven't looked to these businesses previously, you could venture a guess that a partnership with businesses simply seemed complicated and messy. Different worlds, different rules, unfamiliar players, and the problem libraries often fall into, thinking we have nothing to offer. But there has been a shift in many libraries.

Johnson County Library (JCL) in Kansas began offering gaming in 2005, and even with adequate funding for this program they began to see the difficulties in sustaining this type of programming. A newly hired staff member (who came from the private sector) asked why the library didn't partner with local businesses. An unspoken shiver of fear ran down the backs of longtime staff members, as they touted the mythical party line: "We don't partner with for-profit entities." Fortunately, no one could track down the root of this myth, so the newly hired staff member decided to make a plan that would allow the library to pursue these types of partnerships. The plan included these steps:

- Compiling a list of gaming businesses to approach
- Developing a list of concerns to address about partnering with for-profit entities
- Encouraging administration to begin working on a policy that would enable the library to engage in for-profit partnerships in the future

 **See Tool 10. For-profit Partnership Letter**

The main concern was that the library needed to offer all potential for-profit partners the opportunity to partner with the library to avoid the appearance of favoritism. The library sent letters to all local gaming businesses, detailing JCL's plan to offer regularly scheduled gaming programs.

Interested partners would supply the newest gaming system and highlight/test new games, supply prizes, and advertise the library program in their stores. The library would add the business's logo to the advertisements, allow advertising in the meeting room where the gaming program was held, and give the business access to their demographic (in this case, teenage males 13–17 years old). Of the 20 businesses contacted, only one business responded: GameStop. The group felt they had equally extended the opportunity to all potential partners in a fair manner, so they set up several meetings with the GameStop manager who had responded to the inquiry. The results over the next three years were six large gaming tournaments (two per year), which the library could not have funded on its own.

The partnership wasn't smooth. Some of the challenges included these:

- Planning. The library plans four to six months ahead, and GameStop works in a shorter time frame (often the week of the program).

- Balance and understanding. Each entity had to learn the strengths and weaknesses of the other. GameStop had the latest and greatest equipment and the library had the space and teen patrons. The library was able to offer access to the latest and greatest equipment to teens on an equal footing.

In spite of these challenges, the library was able to successfully (with no bloodshed or cries of impropriety) partner with a for-profit business with whom it had no prior relationship. It took staff with a fresh outlook to help dispel a library myth, and now the library can proudly say that it does partner with private entities and is always looking for future partnerships within the for-profit world.

This is an example of a fairly small partnership, but regardless of the size of your plan, it is important to remember a few things:

- **Coordination.** If five people from your library all ask the same business for a sponsorship, the library loses. We become ineffective by not focusing on a goal larger than today or one branch, but rather gathering a group of like-minded staff and planning the pursuit of a partnership.

- **Communication.** Remember that the private business may not have experience with a public agency like the library, so be clear and identify which type of partnership you are looking for—communicative, cooperative, or collaborative.

- **Education.** If you find a business that you suspect will be a good partner, you may need to have several meetings to discuss the values of each member; be prepared for the business to be unfamiliar with standard library policies like privacy. Don't take their lack of knowledge personally and use this as a chance to talk about your shared goals and how the library's values play into it. Draw a clear line between what the library can and cannot take part in.

- **Patience.** Partnerships may take awhile to pay off. For example, one library partners with the local arena. The arena gives the library free tickets to family-friendly events and the library holds drawings for its library patrons. The arena gets advertising inside the library focused on the drawing/family event and the library offers its patrons access to events and a collection connection based on the type of event (previous events have included topics such as dinosaurs and the circus). The arena originally asked for their logo to be on the library Web site with a link back to the arena. The library decided they were not comfortable with that level of advertising. After two years of building this relationship with the arena, the library proposed that the arena run a short video advertising the library's community artist program in the arena concourse during upcoming events. The library was given unprecedented free advertising and access to event-goers numbering around 15,000. When the partnership began, neither entity knew what the limits would be but continued discussions made this possible.

- **Customers.** Think about what your customers want and expect. It may be different from what you think. For example, the state of Kansas entered into a partnership with American Century Investments[7] to promote reading throughout the summer and offer a chance to learn more about college savings. During summer reading, at more than 150 libraries across the state, families registered to win a $500 Learning Quest college savings account.[8] After participating in this program for two years, the library received staff complaints of "too much advertising in the library" and patron complaints that they thought their branch was *not* participating in the program. Patrons thought the partnership was normal and for a good cause because they saw that the end result—education—was right in line with the values of the library. While it is important to think these partnerships through, it is also important to keep an open mind and do your research. As the Johnson County Library had offered the opportunity to sponsor their gaming events to all local gaming businesses, so did the state of Kansas. Each year the opportunity to manage the Learning Quest fund is put out for bid, thus avoiding the appearance of favoritism. It is also good practice to talk with your administration and foundation, for two reasons: you never know what plans they have cooking with which you wouldn't want to interfere, and you never know what type of assistance they could lend.

Why Should All LSTs Work with Teachers?

Often teachers and LSTs have the same goals: to get the library, books, and reading into the lives of their students. The LSTs at the schools can do their part and be the intermediary, but it can be easier and more reliable to work directly with teachers. They know what assignments they are planning for the year; they know their students; and they see them every day. The combination can be very powerful for all parties involved. You get access to a variety of teens to spread the word about the library, the teacher is able to hear about important resources at the library, and the students make a connection with the public library, get great information, hear about books they might enjoy, and enjoy a temporary break from listening to their teacher. It's a win all the way around.

From consistently booktalking (twice a year) at a middle school for the past four years, we know one LST who was invited to participate in the following community activities and events solely based on her interest in the lives of local teens: judging a science fair, leading a poetry workshop, teaching catalog instruction, overseeing an author visit, conducting a writing workshop, helping plan and carry out a talent show, speaking during career day, staffing a jewelry-making party, and attending many staff lunches. And did we mention the fleece vest with the school name and logo she was given as a token of appreciation at the end of the year?

What Are Some Obstacles to Working with Teachers, and How Can You Overcome Them?

For most LSTs, working with teachers is one of the single most frustrating experiences in the profession. In a perfect world, teachers would open their arms to librarians and welcome them into their world of ongoing opportunities for students. Unfortunately, it doesn't always happen this way. School librarians are not always in the loop when it comes to planning assignments in a majority of schools around the country. Teachers are very, very, busy people, and most librarians have yet to make a convincing case that teachers should change their planning methods to incorporate the library/librarian.

You might need to start by educating teachers as to what the library provides and what you do as an LST. You need to be flexible and accepting of the limits of what a classroom teacher can do. Meeting teachers halfway can remove most of the obstacles—if you want them to give up class time for you, you need to be prepared to be flexible enough to meet their needs. One LST was trying to get into a middle school, but the teachers only wanted to free up class time for formal library instruction pertaining to an upcoming research project. So the LST struck a deal: one outreach visit of catalog instruction/Internet searching for the research paper and then one outreach visit of booktalking to occur on the day after research papers were handed in. This is a break for the teacher, the students, and a perfect opportunity for the LST to spend more time with the students. The teacher and students get the research help they needed and the LST gets to connect twice with the same group of teens, showing them the homework side of the library and the fun side of reading.

What Is the Best Way for an LST in a Public Library to Develop a Working Relationship with a School Librarian?

The best way to work with school librarians in your area is to learn about where they are and how you can best be a part of their world. Like teachers, school librarians have a million things on their plates and very little help to get everything done. As an LST in a public library, your job in creating successful partnerships with school librarians is to develop a solid working relationship. The next step is to continually find ways to keep the lines of communication open. Keep the following four basic things in mind when developing relationships with school librarians.

Start Small

This seems easy enough, but even this first, simple step can contain some pitfalls. Librarians in schools are no different from most teachers in that they feel they have too little time and too few resources. Work around their schedule and share your resources with them, like journals or advance reading copies of young adult books you receive from publishers. The message you want to send is, "We can help each other." School librarians have their own problems, and you'll recognize them because you have many of them in common. They know all about teachers not notifying them about assignments. They will be amazed that you expect a teacher to pick up the phone to call you or write you a letter when that same teacher will not even walk down the hall to tell them. Their problems are your problems, and hopefully both of you will be willing to help each other find solutions. Unfortunately, you looking good can make a school librarian look bad. For example, you work with a teacher and set up a time to visit and do some booktalking. The school librarian might look bad because he or she didn't or doesn't offer this service. If teachers begin to take you up on offers for library instruction or other services, then the question arises: Why is this not being handled in the school by the school librarian? To rectify this situation, plan all outreach to your local school with the full knowledge of the school librarian. It's also a good idea to involve the school librarian in both the planning and implementation of any outreach event. The librarian might not have time to join you, but he or she will likely appreciate the gesture (and get the unspoken message that you are not stepping on his or her turf). The best road to cooperation is to work cooperatively. School librarians often feel underappreciated. Find ways to provide them with recognition because it's a smart bet they are not getting much in their school. Thank-you notes go a long way in building a reciprocal relationship, and once in a while a letter to the principal is also a nice touch. If you have put together a successful program with a school librarian, write this up as a press release filled with quotations from participating teens and teachers and distribute it widely.

Keep It Simple

While everyone might be on the same page about working together, the truth is that school librarians often feel overwhelmed. Therefore, although they might agree on the principle of cooperation, the reality of making it work may seem time-consuming. Instead of your laundry list of cooperation opportunities, pick one small project the two of you can work on together. It might be a required reading list for next school year, a cooperative book club, or maybe customizing some of the tools in this book's LST Tool Kit. Choose one project that needs both sides working on it. After planting the seed, larger projects involving more cooperative planning will become possible. As your relationship grows and strengthens, so will your role as allies.

Expect Some Resistance

Some school librarians may feel they have absolutely nothing to gain by working with you—they know their teachers and what they need. If they "tell you" about those teachers, then maybe those teachers will take their business elsewhere. There is a subtle competition between libraries just like there is competition between branches in a library system. You have to find what you can "exchange" to get the school librarian to help you and to create a win-win situation. Sometimes you can figure it out, but sometimes you just have to ask the question: "Now, what can I do to help you?"

Learn to Navigate the School Maze

Like libraries, all schools are different in how they are governed and run on a daily basis. It often seems that the first "official" contact for a formal partnership between the local public library and school library comes at an administrative level, with a library director contacting a school superintendent. Best case scenario is your director writes the superintendent, expresses ideas for working with the schools, and asks for permission to begin making contacts. What happens next also depends on the particular library or school system. You might need to work through another layer, meeting with a curriculum supervisor or maybe the school system's coordinator for media services. Often, after talking with the school librarian, you can contact teachers directly or work through a department chairperson. If you can invite yourself or, better yet, get invited to a department meeting, you have finally reached the teachers. After you have formally met them at these department meetings, you can begin making individual contacts.

We know that public library–school library partnerships seem like a no-brainer. Unfortunately, and although we know that nothing would help young adults more than for these two institutions to work together, we also know that it can be difficult for LSTs, school librarians, and teachers to find the time and opportunity for a reciprocal exchange of ideas and services. One of the best ways to find common ground is to focus on information literacy. After you have read Chapter 5, take some time to make a list of ways public libraries can (and often already do) contribute to the development of information-literate teens. This knowledge will not only help you plan better programs, services, and partnerships; it will provide you with a framework for working with your local schools.

Libraries are sold on cooperation. Our history shows the advantages: from the development of library systems, to the creation of automation networks, to interlibrary loan—libraries know it works. Teachers, however, have a different mind-set and different values. The key to success in developing partnerships with educational institutions is for LSTs to learn those values, ask good questions of our educational colleagues, and let them tell us how we can best support student learning and achievement rather than merely telling them how wonderful we are.

If you don't know the answer to at least seven of the questions in the sidebar quiz, invite your local school librarian to lunch or sit down for coffee. Knowledge really is power, and it makes for more successful and dynamic partnerships between you and your local school libraries.

What Are the Elements of Successful Partnerships with Schools?

The elements of success for developing a partnership between any school and public library can be remembered using the mnemonic FASTING:

- **Fitting in.** Preexisting curriculum dominates school planning, and a vast amount of material has to be covered in a relatively small period of time. Teachers want to cover as much as possible

Take the following quiz to see how well you know your school librarian colleagues:

- What are the full names of the librarians at your local middle and high schools?
- Do they work full time at one school or are they shared between buildings?
- How many classes and students do they see and instruct in a day?
- When was the last time the school district had an increase or decrease in funding?
- Do their school libraries have a formal collection development policy?
- Are the school libraries open to all students before and after school and during lunch?
- Are their local school library programs tied to your state curriculum standards?
- Does your state require teaching credentials or certified school librarians?
- What effect has the No Child Left Behind (NCLB) Act had on school libraries in your area?
- What is the Strengthening Kids' Interest in Learning and Libraries (SKILLs) Act?[9]

and many "resent" an interruption to that schedule, whether it be school assemblies or library activities. The best way to counteract this is to carry out programming that complements the existing curriculum. When you tie in your work to the school's state-mandated standards and achievement tests, you not only create a fan out of teachers and school librarians but also directly complement student achievement and student learning.

- **Asking.** It seems obvious, but the need to gather information before you embark on a partnership is paramount. You need to know what schools are in your service area, who works there, and myriad other data. This information is not going to fall in your lap. Be proactive; go out there and get it.

- **Scheduling.** Many LSTs spend time preparing extensive "back to school" flyers for teachers during the summer and then drop them off at the beginning of the school year. Then they are dismayed when the document produces no results. If you do not already know this, the start of the school year is the *worst* time of the year to give school teachers anything because they are doing daily triage to keep their heads above water. Ask the school librarian for a good time to share material with the teachers.

- **Teaching.** The process of cooperation is really one of teaching and educating. Teaching teachers about libraries, teaching administrators about teens, and often teaching other staff about how to teach students.

- **Intervening.** Always be on the lookout for those "teachable moments" with teachers in which you can educate them about the myriad of services and programs available via public library staff.

- **Networking.** Make yourself available to attend department meetings, staff retreats, in-services, or any other meetings where groups of teachers will be congregating.

- **Goal setting.** As we mentioned earlier in this chapter, success breeds success. Once you have one success with one teacher, word will spread. Once you have an "in" with one teacher, it is highly likely that his or her colleagues will soon be seeking you out.

The most important thing to remember is that both teachers and school library media specialists can serve as distribution channels to teens. Many teens cannot or are not allowed to go to the public library. By partnering with school staff, LSTs can make connections with teens who cannot come to us.

How Do You Develop and Maintain Successful Working Relationships with Your Community Partners?

- **Find your champions.** Look for people in high places who will tell your story for you. Your best, ongoing advocate in the community is the one who suggests to his or her colleagues that the library also belongs at the table when it comes to planning how to best serve teens in your town.

- **Share your core values.** Make a list of your core values as an LST. Share these values with your partners so that you know you're all on the same page from the beginning of any collaboration.

- **Celebrate your success.** Nothing brings a team together in the short term like winning. Celebrate each success, no matter how small.

- **Share the credit.** Nothing tears a team apart in the long term like an individual taking singular credit for the work the group did as a whole. Share credit and blame in equal measure to keep everyone happy and committed to the cause.

- **Be an active collaborator.** Attend meetings. Share your thoughts. Return the e-mails and the phone calls. Good partners make something happen once; great partners make something happen over and over again for the good of the community.

What Are Some Ideas for Developing New and Innovative Outreach Programs?

When done right, library services for teens is about more than what happens inside the walls of your library. The following outreach and partnership success stories feature LSTs who have engaged in the following activities:

- Attended and presented at district in-services for school librarians or teachers. This gives LSTs a chance to explain the library's outreach services and how they can add value to the school day. The key to these presentations is to stay on a couple of themes and push just a few services. Don't overwhelm your audience with the quantity of services you can offer; instead, impress them with the quality of a few services and how they can help their students.

- Attended literacy nights at schools where teens, young children, parents, and grandparents have different stations (crafts, etc.) to visit. Also use incentives.

- Attended a Title 1–sponsored family night with a reading booth created by the school and public librarian working together.

- Created and carried out "Born to Read," "Reach and Read," "Raising a Reader," or other programs aimed at working with teen parents. Contacts for these programs are often made through partnerships with hospitals, health clinics, and alternative high school programs.

- Celebrated Banned Books Week with programs held at both the school and public library celebrating challenged and banned books.

- Created a cooperative literary magazine involving the school, the public library, and the local chapter of the National Writer's Union.

- Created cooperative employment programs between school-based interns and libraries.

- Developed a partnership with a local judge and probation officer so that juvenile offenders could do their community service hours at the library.

- Developed a tutoring program held in the public library in conjunction with a local fraternity.

- Developed a sexuality education program in collaboration with a local high school to provide booklists of fiction and non-fiction about teen health issues and the prevention of sexually transmitted diseases.

- Hosted information literacy programs for and with homeschool associations, GED classes, or other "nontraditional" students.

- Hosted, in conjunction with a local high school and college, a college fair in the public library including speakers, Q&A sessions, and handouts about pursuing higher education.

- Joined forces with a local middle school to develop a grant for after-school programming. The grant, from 21st Century Schools, was funneled through the schools but the public library subcontracted to hire staff to provide programming.

- Met on a regular basis with librarians from schools, community colleges, and other institutions to discuss issues, brainstorm problem solving, and share resources.

- Organized a mentoring and homework help program, held in the library but sponsored by the high school honor society.

- Organized teen library volunteers to donate some of their time to various social services agencies such as Meals on Wheels.

- Partnered with an assisted living center where members of the Teen Advisory Council had the ongoing opportunity to visit the residents and drop off books.

- Partnered with the District Attorney's Office to offer at-risk teens ages 16–19 career counseling, workshops, fine waivers for their library cards, computer training, book discussions, and information about college scholarships and the armed forces.

- Set up a cooperative materials delivery system with a local middle school and high school. This program allows students to place reserves on public library materials from their school library. These are delivered regularly from the public library to the school, and all materials are returned to the school so that teens who do not have access to the local public library can still benefit from the collection.

- Set up a library card outreach program to register local teens for library cards during school-sponsored open houses or parent/teacher nights.

- Arranged with the local school library media center to make library card applications available to all students. Once applications have been signed, send and process library card applications and return to school. Or, better yet, work to process library cards on site.

- Sent newsletter to high school librarians announcing events, programs, and resources.

- Set up a deposit collection at a local group home so that teens who do not have a permanent address can still check out books from the local library via their temporary address. This can also work in partnership with foster care placement centers, hospitals, rehabilitation centers, alternative high schools, and homeless shelters.

- Shared collections: once school is over, teens choose books to take from the school library to be used in the public library during the summer.

- Shared the Accelerated Reader (AR) Program. During the summer time, the school library houses the AR computer at the public library who then uses it as their teen summer reading program. (Note: check with your AR or similar representative about your ability to do this based on the site license.)

- Spoke at career day to inform teens about careers in library and information science.

- Teamed with a local newspaper and cable news station during Teen Read Week to provide full media coverage of events.

- Teamed with a local newspaper to jointly sponsor an online creative writing zine.

- Teamed with a local newspaper to publish book, movie, and music reviews written by teen patrons.

- Teamed with a local social service agency to provide programming as part of a free breakfast/lunch program during the summer, using large numbers of teen volunteers to plan and carry out accompanying programs for younger children.

- Worked with a high school teen parenting center to create a deposit collection for teen moms at the school's day care. They've also worked with the school to plan and carry out pre-school programming for the children of teen moms.

- Worked with local sports teams to provide guest readers in schools and public libraries during Teen Read Week.

- Teamed with a community access cable station to produce and air a television show produced by teens, who not only wrote, performed, and taped each episode, but also brainstormed topics for each show and built the set.

If you examine the award-winning programs listed in each edition of YALSA's *Excellence in Library Services to Young Adults*, you'll notice that a large majority of them incorporate outreach and/or are built on partnerships. If you look at the book *Running a Successful Library Card Campaign*, the number one success factor for most programs was a commitment to taking the library out of the physical building and establishing partnerships within the community to provide financial support, develop a new patron base, and share resources. Finally, one of the clear messages of the youth development movement is that no one can do this work alone.

What Are Some Best Practices/Models for Outreach and Partnerships?

We have given you many ideas for providing outreach services within your community but we suggest you look around your own community, state, and region to find places and people to work with to expand your library's services. The several successful programs that follow can offer inspiration and solid advice.

A+ Partners in Education

Howard County Library
Columbia, Maryland
www.hclibrary.org

In September 2002, Howard County Library and the Howard County Public School System launched a countywide initiative called A+ Partners in Education. Their vision is to expand the educational opportunities and enhance the academic achievement of each student. Their mission is to ensure every Howard County Public School System student has and uses a Howard County Library card to borrow materials and access e-resources. Since its inception, numerous libraries and schools have requested information about how to replicate such a partnership. Howard County Library and the Howard County Public School System celebrate the remarkable accomplishments achieved during the A+ Partners in Education initiative, which expanded in 2007 to include Howard Community College.[10]

A Captive Audience: Serving Teens in Crisis in Charleston County

Charleston County Public Library (CCPL)
Charleston, South Carolina
www.ccpl.org

In September 2005, the Charleston County Public Library (CCPL), under the leadership of Young Adult Services Manager Andria L. Amaral, developed a plan to reach out to community organizations serving teens in crisis, establishing successful partnerships with Crisis Ministries Homeless Shelter, the Florence Crittenton Home for pregnant teens, Carolina Youth Development Center (CYDC), and the South Carolina Department of Juvenile Justice. Library staff visit these centers on a monthly basis to provide booktalks, stimulate discussion, and promote CCPL materials and services. With cooperation from facility management and caseworkers, staff have made library cards available (in some cases for the facility, in others for individual teens), and each month they bring teens a variety of fiction, nonfiction, and graphic novel choices. Visits to the Florence Crittendon Home also include a presentation on the importance of early literacy and tips for reading aloud to young children. The partnership with CYDC, an emergency shelter and residential facility for abused, neglected, and abandoned youth, also started in late 2005, with staff visiting the facility once a month to provide booktalks and materials for checkout. The teens and the center responded well, and once CYDC staff became aware of all that CCPL has to offer, they started to bring groups on field trips to the library to participate in on-site programs and borrow materials much more often. In just one year, CYDC attendance at library events increased by over 1000%. The CYDC outreach coordinator Pam Chamberlain said, "This has made our kids better readers, expanded their knowledge about people and the world and given them an awareness of what's going on in the community. They are beginning to develop a love for reading."[11]

Attention Home: Serving Teens in Detention Centers

Laramie County Library
2200 Pioneer Avenue
Cheyenne, Wyoming 82001
www.LCLSonline.org

Teen Librarian Beth Cook conducts a monthly book club with local teens in Cheyenne, Wyoming, who have been court-ordered to spend time in a juvenile detention facility/school called Attention Home. The school runs in tandem with the local school district but it is a privately owned, nonprofit company. Cook partners with an English teacher at the facility who coordinates the space, clearance, and snacks. The book club was started through the ALA Great Stories Book Club, and after the group finished the first three grant-provided books they decided to continue the program. In spite of the high student turnover rate, the program today is in its third successful year. The club reads a variety of books, with staff selecting titles of varying degrees of difficulty and interest to meet the differing wants and needs of participating students in 7th–12th grade. Although this program has been funded by the school in the past, club sponsors secured a donor to support the book club in 2010 (participating teens are given a new book they are allowed to keep each month.) According to Cook, "The books are often a great segue for the teens to talk about their lives, school, their life experiences and especially what their plans are when they 'get out.'"[12]

Conclusion

If we want to connect young adults and libraries, we must do it on their turf and not just on ours. Through partnerships with schools and other agencies and various outreach opportunities, LSTs can provide outstanding services and programs for teens who, for one reason or another, are unable to visit our libraries. However, we cannot do any of this alone. Outreach is about more than making presentations in the community. It's about building bridges, and if we want to be seen as a "player" then we need to get ourselves to the tables of educational, cultural, recreational, and governmental institutions who share our values and our mission of reaching all teens in our community.

Outreach provides LSTs with not only a chance to tell our story but also to listen to teens tell their stories about why they do or don't use libraries. Every visit to a classroom is an opportunity to get ideas from teens about what we can do better. Sometimes this conversation will be in the form of a paper or an online survey; sometimes it will be a casual Q&A session with local teens. The most important thing to remember is that the teens we meet in the classroom, in the shelter, or behind bars are the ones who most need what we can, despite the obstacles, do for them by providing information and an outlet for creativity and self-expression.

Always remember that outreach is a continuum, from a simple visit, to a classroom to talk about books, to a complex million-dollar deal to develop a library card campaign with local vendors. There is value in every kind of outreach, so don't discount the small opportunities or shy away from the big ones. In all things, find the opportunities that are local, have support, can be attained within your resources, and have a payoff for teens in both the short and long term. Finally, always remember that the ultimate goal for both outreach and partnerships is to extend our reach outside our walls so that all teens in our community know that the library is a resource waiting to be tapped.

Sources Cited in This Chapter

1. Carpenter, Devo, Tricia Suellentrop, Jack Gantos, Patrick Jones, and Amy Cheney. 2006. "Books Behind Bars." Panel sponsored by the Young Adult Library Services Association. American Library Association annual meeting, New Orleans, June 22–28, 2006

2. McLellan, Kathy and Tricia Suellentrop. 2007. "Serving Teens Doing Time." *Voice of Youth Advocates* (December): 403–407.

3. Morgan, Deanna. 2008. "Juvenile Detention Center Library Like No Other." Fox11AZ.com. June 12. Available: www.fox11az.com/news/top stories/ stories/KMSB_20080612_dm_jh_library.27f7b5ee.html (accessed February 19, 2009).

4. Jones, Patrick. 2004. "Reaching Out to Young Adults in Jail." *Young Adult Library Services* (Fall): 14–17.

5. Austin Public Library. n.d. "Gardner Betts Juvenile Justice Center Outreach Program: Program Description and History." Available: wiredforyouth .com/secondchance/about.cfm (accessed January 19, 2009).

6. Holzmeister, Karen. 2007. "County Library Program Honored." *Oakland Tribune*, January 23.

7. Kansas State Treasurer. n.d. "Kansas Learning Quest Education Savings Program." Available: www.kansasstatetreasurer.com/prodweb/cs_main.php (accessed: November 30, 2008).

8. Learning Quest Savings. n.d. "'Get a Clue' about Summer Reading and a Chance to Start Saving for College at Kansas Libraries." Available: www.learningquestsavings.com/learningquest/press/press_release_07132007.jsp (accessed November 30, 2008).

9. Brehm-Heeger, Paula. 2008. "What's Going On?" *School Library Journal* (February): 27.

10. Gross, Valerie J. 2005. "A+ Partners in Education: Linking Libraries to Education for a Flourishing Future." *Public Libraries* 44, no.4 (July/August): 217.

11. Amaral, Andria L. E-mail to authors. February 21, 2009.

12. Cook, Beth. E-mail to authors. February 24, 2009.

Recommended Sources for Further Reading

Alessio, Amy. 2002. "Community Teen NETwork." *Public Libraries* 41, no. 4 (July/August): 196–197.

Angier, Naomi, Rebecca Cohen, and Jill Morrison. 2001. "Juvenile Justice Outreach: Library Services at Detention Centers." *PNLA Quarterly* 66, no. 1 (Fall): 16.

Angier, Naomi, and Katie O'Dell. 2000. "The Book Group Behind Bars." *Voice of Youth Advocates* 23, no. 5 (December): 331–333.

Bajjaly, Stephen T. 2003. *The Community Networking Handbook*. Chicago: American Library Association.

Block, Marylaine. 2007. *The Thriving Library: Successful Strategies for Challenging Times*. Medford, NJ: Information Today.

Crowther, Janet L., and Barry Trott. 2004. *Partnering with Purpose: A Guide to Strategic Partnership Development for Libraries and Other Organizations*. Westport, CT: Libraries Unlimited.

Doyle, Joyce. 2008. "Reaching Out to Teens: Eight Ways to Draw Teens into Your Library." *Voice Of Youth Advocates* (October): 312–313.

Farmer, Lesley S. Johnson. 2002. "Encumbering Grants: Managing the Money." *Book Report* 21, no. 1 (May/June): 12–14.

Francisco, Grace, and Shelly G. Keller. 2001. *Joint Ventures: The Promise, Power, and Performance of Partnering*. Sacramento: California State Library, 2001.

Jones, Patrick. 2002. *Running a Successful Library Card Campaign: A How-To-Do-It Manual*. New York: Neal-Schuman.

Levine, Thomas H. 2008. "Beyond Open Houses: School Promotes Cross-cultural Understanding among Teachers and Language-minority Families." *Journal of Staff Development* 29, no. 1. (Winter): 29–33.

Madenski, Melissa. 2001. "Books Behind Bars." *School Library Journal* 47, no. 7 (July): 40–42.

McCook, Kathleen de la Pena. 2000. *A Place at the Table: Participating in Community Building*. Chicago: American Library Association.

McLellan, Kathy and Tricia Suellentrop. 2007. "Serving Teens Doing Time." *Voice of Youth Advocates* 30, no. 5 (December 1): 403.

Pfeil, Angela B. 2005. *Going Places with Youth Outreach: Smart Marketing Strategies for Your Library.* Chicago: American Library Association.

Pitman, Nic, and Nick R. Roberts. 2002. "Building Relationships: Forming Partnerships Between the School and Public Libraries." *The School Librarian* 50, no. 2 (Summer): 69–70.

Pittman, Karen J., Nicole Yohalem, and Joel Tolman. 2003. *When, Where, What, and How Youth Learn: Blurring School and Community Boundaries.* Hoboken, NJ: Jossey-Bass.

Ryan, Sara. 2001. "Be Nice to the Secretary and Other Ways to Work Successfully with Schools." *Journal of Youth Services in Libraries* 14, no. 3 (Spring): 15–17.

Sullivan, Edward T. 2001. "Connect with Success: A Few Tips for Public Library–School Cooperation." *Journal of Youth Services in Libraries* 14, no. 3 (Spring): 14.

Programming

Programming with and for teens is often one of the most rewarding experiences for LSTs. Although teen programming can be scary for those of you who have never done it, the good news is you're only a newbie once. We promise that the first one is always the most stressful, and it will get easier with each program you plan and carry out. If this is your first time planning and carrying out programs for teens, you may feel out of your element as you begin. You may know about story times and preschool crafts but have no experience programming for older kids. Or maybe you are new to libraries and those older kids leave you weak in the knees. Whatever your situation, rest assured that programming for teens gets easier as you go and that there are many resources out there to help you plan, implement, and evaluate these programs—starting with this chapter. The most important thing to remember when it comes to programming for teens is that this is your opportunity to go from merely supplying a collection of materials for teens and responding reactively to information requests, to proactively developing events to meet the needs of teens.

Rosemary Honnold's books *101 Teen Programs That Work* and *More Teen Programs That Work* are both full-length texts that provide lots of practical information about planning all types of teen programs. We will include some of that in this chapter, but in addition to giving you "fish" (lists of program ideas and models to borrow and steal), we also want to teach you to fish by providing you with a way of planning teen programs. The most frequently asked question about teen programs at training workshops is "What is a good program?" In reality, this is probably the last question that needs to be asked. If you have followed a planning process that involves youth and uses information derived from surveying your community and your collections, then the answer to that question becomes obvious: It depends. It depends on the resources available to you and those already in the community. It depends on what your teens want, but also on what the library wants to achieve. The best way to start thinking about teen programming is to first get an idea of what teen programming is and why it matters.

IN THIS CHAPTER:

✔ What Is Teen Programming and Why Is It Important in the Lives of Young People?

✔ How Is Programming for Teens Different from Programming for Children?

✔ What Are the Keys to Developing Successful Teen Programs?

✔ So How Do You Plan Teen Programming?

✔ How Do You Implement a Teen Program?

✔ How Do You Evaluate a Teen Program?

✔ What Are Examples of Successful Teen Programs?

> Programming is youth development in action, and when it's done right, it's also a lot of fun!

What Is Teen Programming, and Why Is It Important in the Lives of Young People?

A program is defined as a library-sponsored activity that takes place outside of the context of reference services and is designed to inform, entertain, or enrich a group of people as well as promote the use of the library and its collection. With teen users, put the accent on entertain and add the word "fun." Now that we know what it is, let's determine why it matters. Simply put, successful programming for teens meets all seven of the basic needs of adolescents. While no 13-year-old is going to come to the desk and ask, "Do you have an event that will allow me to exert myself physically in a structured environment with clear limits, while providing me with opportunities for creative expression or meaningful participation with peers and adults?" chances are good that he or she will get involved in a poetry slam, role-playing game night, library lock-in, tie-dye program, or talent show. The building blocks for these programs are the seven basic developmental needs of teens, along with the idea that teens just want to have fun.

Teens find value in programs that speak to their desire for these things:

- Physical activity
- Competence and achievement
- Self-definition
- Creative expression
- Positive social interaction with peers and adults
- Structure and clear limits
- Meaningful participation

Successful programs for teens also help in these ways:

- Increase use of the collection and other core services
- Inform, entertain, and enrich teens
- Attract new users or convince current users to use the library differently
- Promote the library in a positive light in the community
- Increase youth involvement opportunities
- Support healthy youth development

Perhaps one of the best and most familiar models for teen programming takes place in the children's room at toddler time. Most toddler programs are limited, highly interactive, and focused on the child having a positive experience. We don't follow the same model for toddler time as we do for preschool programming because it is not developmentally appropriate. Now, that said, how do we justify programs we spend hundreds of dollars on when only five kids show? It may be true that those five attendees enjoyed the program, but the five teens would have enjoyed it as much,

One of the unique things about teen programming is that quantity does not always equal quality. For example, a teen book discussion group with 50 kids in attendance is, on the stat sheet, a huge success. For the 40 or so kids who read the book and never got a chance to speak, it is a total failure. We need to plan programs that focus mainly on the benefit to teens, not programs that merely improve library program attendance.

and probably more, if they were surrounded by hundreds of their peers.

We can determine the program's likely outcome by looking at the scope of the program. While there is certainly a place in libraries for big, blowout performances in front of a passive yet enthusiastic audience, there is just as much value in the small, highly interactive programs. Most of the research about programming tells us that it needs to be intense and extended. One-shot deals don't really make a big difference in people's lives. Thus, the smaller, more intense programs, like book discussion groups, teen advisory councils, or literary magazines, will help you, and teens, meet more of your goals.

Programs should be fun, but they can also be fundamental in building assets for teens. Youth involvement in programming shouldn't be limited to setting up chairs or passing out pencils but should consist of real opportunities. You need to focus on how to get teens to attend programs and, as this chapter outlines in detail, how to plan programs that will do just that. But you also need to think about what happens to teens after they leave the program. You continually need to ask yourself these questions: How did that program build the 40 Developmental Assets? How did the library contribute to healthy youth development? How did the library contribute to making the community better? You need to ask these questions for your own evaluation and for your community, your directors, and your funders.

One final word about the importance of developing and carrying out programming for teens: When programs for teens are done right, they often help libraries meet both their mission statements and goals, including creating lifelong library users; enriching the community; providing a safe learning environment; providing opportunities for the community to get involved; helping teens with their informational, educational, and recreational needs; providing access to social and cultural ideas; and encouraging young people to share knowledge and ideas with one another and the community.

How Is Programming for Teens Different from Programming for Children?

Before we jump into the actual planning of teen programs, let's take a minute to examine the similarities and differences between programming for children and for teens.

Similarities include:

- **Enjoyment.** Everybody, regardless of age, wants to spend time doing something they enjoy—they want to have a good time, be relaxed, laugh, and smile. Enjoyment comes easy to children, but teens are becoming aware of the challenges of adulthood and they face activities that may not always be enjoyable, such as homework or after-school jobs. They are aware of their time and must balance and choose activities based on the perceived enjoyment level.

- **Atmosphere.** Children, teens, and adults all gravitate toward a warm, inviting, relaxed atmosphere. Libraries need to extend that type of welcoming atmosphere to teens in conjunction with programming.

- **Age appropriateness.** Generally, for programming purposes, libraries define teens as young people between the ages 12–18 or students in grades 6–12. This definition may vary with the educational setup; for example, if 6th grade is in the elementary building, it might make sense to start your teen programming at 7th grade or the middle school level. With children, certain tasks become easier as coordination and understanding develop. This also applies to teenagers. Many teen programs require higher levels of physical, emotional, and intellectual development. Teen programs are appropriate to teen development, and this might leave out 11-year-olds or it may include them—it depends on the program. Similarly, a preschool story time may leave out 18-month-olds or include them, depending on the program. It's also important to recognize that programs and special events you plan for older teens will not be appropriate for younger teens, like anime clubs that show more adult-oriented films, college prep classes, and health programs intended for an older audience about sex, sexuality, etc.

- **Enrichment.** When done well, programs for all ages should somehow enrich the participants' lives, from teaching something new to expanding existing horizons.

Differences include:

- **Mobility.** Preschoolers are put in the car and taken to a story time; teenagers make the choice to come to the library and attend your program, and they need to get a ride or walk. By the time they are old enough to drive, most teens have active social or work lives that make a library program just one of many options available to them.

- **Parent involvement.** Parents are "programmed" to bring their young children to the library—not so with teenagers. For their teenagers, parents are more likely to pay for "enrichment programs" or to take teenagers to school for events and activities. We have to "reprogram" parents to think of the library as an option for their teens. So many children's programs are created to allow parents and children to interact, but teens, especially young teens, want to avoid being seen with their parents at all costs.

- **Choices.** Younger children don't have the choices about how to spend their free time that teens do. From sports, to volunteering, to after-school activities, teens have a lot of time dedicated to other pursuits. A key to programming is to complement those activities rather than compete with them.

- **Teen attitudes.** While some teens do view the library as a place for information and fun, this is not the popular view. Add to that the attitude that anything "studious" is not cool and you have a lot of peer inertia pulling teens away from library-sponsored events.

- **Staff attitudes.** A child's opposition to authority can be short-lived or cute, so most children are greeted with acceptance by library staff. However, many adults perceive that teens have an "attitude." This can be the case, but it may also be that teens feel a little out of their element and don't mask it well. Generally, the attitude given by staff at the front door is the attitude that can be expected from the participants. If you think teens are stupid and don't listen, then that is probably what you will get. If you think teens are interesting people with value who can follow directions and be creative, then that is probably what you will get.

Now that you have an idea of why programming is important in the lives of young people, how teen programming relates to most libraries' missions and goals, and how programming for teens differs from programming for children, you can consider how to plan, implement, and evaluate successful teen programs.

What Are the Keys to Developing Successful Teen Programs?

- **Choose a popular topic.** While trying to guess what is popular with teens is not easy, an LST should be able to determine which topics have broad popularity by asking, by looking at the collection, and by observing what teens are doing online and listening to, reading, and discussing with friends. Just as important are topics that enjoy deep rather than broad popularity. For example, the majority of teens are not interested in subjects like anime and cosplay, live action role-playing games like Dungeons & Dragons, or slam poetry, but teens who are interested in these topics are usually fanatics who look for any opportunity to pursue their interests.

- **Partner with schools, school groups, and other youth-serving organizations.** Whether the partner provides information or an audience, these programs will succeed in terms of attendance, and you may be able to capture the partner group's audience for other library programs.

- **Promote, don't just publicize.** The role of your library's marketing and community relations department is to provide you with publicity materials; your job is to use those materials to promote your programs.

- **Make connections to what is happening in the lives of teenagers.** This means planning and carrying out programs that cover necessary topics like PSAT or SAT prep classes, funding for college, alternatives to college, etc. You can also make connections to the calendar, to the curriculum, and to the state education standards.

- **Think "hands-on."** The best model for teen programs is not story time, in which you perform and the audience watches, but toddler time, in which you provide an interactive experience consistent with the developmental needs of the child. Too often LSTs use the children's performer–audience model, and this doesn't work as well for teens. Most teens want to do, not just watch.

- **Youth involvement.** Teens can be involved in so many ways, from coming up with ideas, to preparing promotional materials, to actually doing the program themselves. What matters is that teens have an opportunity to "own" a program. Once they feel vested in it, they are more likely to show up, participate, and bring their friends.

- **Define success and tailor expectations based on the needs of your library and teens.** A teen book discussion group with 50 teens in attendance might be a "success" on the stat sheet, but it won't be for the teens who attended but didn't get a chance to speak. While there are some exceptions, remember that in many teen programs there is an inverse relationship between the quantity of attendees and the quality of the experience. At the same time, you must define your expectations. To say, "Well, the three teens who were here enjoyed it" works for a book discussion group or a hands-on craft activity because these kinds of interactive programs work well with small groups. To say this for a large-scale gaming tournament or a Battle of the Bands doesn't work because limited-interaction programs intended for large groups need an audience to be successful. You need to be honest with yourself, but you also need to be honest with your superiors to help them understand that teen programming is not as simple as children's programs. It is not just a matter of booking a performer, putting out some flyers, and waiting for the parents to bring the kids. Moreover, while there is nothing wrong with enjoyment being the only "outcome" of a children's program featuring a clown, teens need more than that. If you are to focus on the outcomes for teens, you must stop focusing so strongly on the output for the library.

So How Do You Plan Teen Programming?

If planning is your strong suit, plan away, but remember to keep your audience in mind. When planning for teens, don't set everything in stone. Instead, be flexible and allow others to have input, especially the teenagers. If you are the spontaneous type, great, but don't forget you are planning for teens, and if they need to get a ride or must choose between your program and another activity, they may need a little advance warning. Plan large events like a Battle of the Bands many months in advance, but keep some board games around for an impromptu and unadvertised game afternoon.

Some people get stuck here: the planning process seems overwhelming so it gets put off, for a long time. Look at what other libraries are doing and copy, study, and borrow their programs. Start small; it can be incorporated into the other programming at your library. Plan one program a quarter as you begin, and then gather input and keep your ears open for suggestions and feedback. As you become more comfortable with teens and programming, teens will begin to look to the library as an option. As you experience success with programs, not only will you gain confidence, but you will also gain further interest in programming as teens start to look forward to happenings at the library.

This is, of course, true only if the funds are available for more teen programming. The most common statistical argument is that if 25 percent of the bodies that walk in the library are between the ages of 12 and 18, shouldn't this equal 25 percent of the budget allocated to teen services? This should be the case, but it usually isn't, or if it is, the librarian is keeping it quiet. However, most LSTs providing teen programming are experienced at making the most of their budgets. LSTs become resourceful and inventive, which can often result in some very interesting programs. You can also try to tap the usual sources of fund-raising: soliciting donations, finding corporate sponsors, and asking the "Friends of the Library" to financially underwrite programs. However, these sources can make for shaky services and tense LSTs. The optimum situation would be to have a specific budget for teen services or teen programming that is not dependent on donations but could certainly be enhanced by them. This may take time to set up, and it may mean working with your business office, director, or manager. It may take explaining—or even proving—the value of teen programming to your community. But working toward a stable budget is worth the effort for you and the teens in your community.

Here are some other things to keep in mind when planning teen programs:

- **Ask teens to pitch in.** Ask teens to brainstorm, plan, implement, and evaluate the programs, both those that library staff have planned and those that are the product of a teen advisory council or outside presenter.
- **Be cognizant of teens' schedules.** Plan programs during times when teens are available and looking for something to do, like a Friday night, right after school, or during the middle of the day in the summer.
- **Be creative.** Think outside of the box and try new things.
- **Be almost spontaneous.** Not every teen program needs to get on your library's "master program schedule" six months in advance. Sometimes, like with craft programs, it just happens because you've noticed a teen interest in a certain subject or activity.

(CD) See Tool 3. Battle of the Bands: Band Information Packet

(CD) See Tool 4. Battle of the Bands: Individual Band Information Sheet

(CD) See Tool 5. Battle of the Bands: Invite Letter

(CD) See Tool 6. Battle of the Bands: Time Line

(CD) See Tool 38. Teen Program Planning Chart

(CD) See Tool 39. Teen Program Planning Form

(CD) See Tool 40. Teen Programming Survey

Let's address the actual steps for planning a program for teens, beginning with defining your audience.

Who Is Your Audience?

The audience for your teen programming may start with "library teens," but it will soon expand to include a variety of teens. Be aware of the developmental stages of the age groups you are targeting. If you want the high school crowd (15- to 18-year-olds), readers' theater may not appeal to them, but having the high school drama club or forensic club help you with an improv comedy night featuring other high schoolers and their friends might do the trick. Obviously certain programs will appeal to certain ages, but you can be aware of the other activities that are being offered or not being offered to specific age groups and what about the activity appeals to a certain age range.

- **12- to 13-year-olds.** This group is interested in being teenagers in every possible way. Their opinions are unfiltered and they will go where they are invited because they are too young for things they deem "cool." Programs that often work really well with this age include basic crafts like making braided hemp bracelets, duct tape wallets, and bath salts. Other programs that are successful for this age group include origami, basic cooking classes, polls and quizzes, babysitting safety programs, scavenger hunts, and PG film festivals.

- **14- to 15-year-olds.** This group is able to remember topics and discussions from one month to the next. While they don't always get a regular opportunity to be creative, they have the ability to express their emotions through writing, acting, and group discussion. Teens this age are often looking for opportunities to self-identify, analyze, and contemplate their place in the world. They can assist with crafts as well as participate. Successful programs for this age group include poetry slams, book discussion groups, video contests, journal making, health and wellness seminars about high-interest topics, comic book design, digital photography, online scrapbooking, and higher-level crafts like altered book workshops, geekwear jewelry (made out of recycled computer parts), and making paper. PG-13 (no one under 13 allowed) film festivals are also successful with this age group.

- **16- to 18-year-olds.** This group is able to give opinions while taking multiple factors into consideration and craves the practical application of information. They have developed niche interests. Programs that often work with this age group include prom programs (where you gather gently used dresses, shoes, and accessories from the community and hand them out to participants via some kind of "boutique"), SAT and ACT prep classes, music production and video game design workshops, and one-shot programs about high-interest topics like writing a résumé, car maintenance, crafting the perfect college entrance essay, getting your manga published, or alternatives to college. Informational programs and forums about high-interest topics like sexuality, protecting the environment, and abusive relationships are also a good bet for this age group.

While teens may share age-related interests, to assume what topics or programs will interest the teens in your area is risky. You must be willing to listen, observe, and react. Just because you are not personally interested in a topic or subject does not excuse you from providing that subject through a program or activity. You do not have to do it alone; find partners in your library or community who do have an interest in such topics and assist them in providing an opportunity for teens to learn and enjoy.

Once you have an idea of who you will be serving, the next step is to consider the types of programs you can offer at your library.

What Types of Teen Programs Should You Offer?

In the beginning you need to separate the pipe dreams from potential teen programs to get the most out of your ideas, energy, and budget. A great idea does not always turn out to be executable, and some of the craziest ideas often end up being the most fun teen programs. Think big, brainstorm with teens, look around you for ideas, read books about library programming best practices, and always stay tuned to pop culture and the things in which teens have an interest so that your programs are timely, relevant, and engaging. Also, remember that planning and carrying out programs for teens in your library doesn't have to be a one-librarian show. Ask for help, recruit volunteers, and, most important, get teens involved. Teen programming can take many shapes and have several levels of involvement:

- **Staff-led programming.** Library staff member plans, implements, and evaluates the program.
- **Teen-led programming.** Library staff member plans the program with participating teens, but teens actually implement and help evaluate the program.
- **Staff presenter.** Someone on your library's staff (not always the teen librarian or LST) who has special knowledge or expertise that would appeal to teens gives a presentation.
- **Teen presenter.** A teen who has special knowledge or expertise that would appeal to other teens gives a presentation. This presenter might be paid or a volunteer.
- **Outside presenter.** Adult from the community presents information or performs an activity that appeals to teens. This presenter might be paid or a volunteer.

How Do You Determine Programming Topics?

You start by figuring out what teens want and need. Teen involvement has been mentioned as part of the planning process, but gaining this

A great way to develop a teen program is to identify a topic you find interesting that might also be interesting to teens (e.g., knitting, learning to play the guitar, graphic design). Not only will planning and carrying out this program be of interest to you, but it will also be an opportunity for teens to see you learning something new and, potentially, struggling with a new set of skills.

CD See Tool 28. Staff Proposal for Potential Teen Program

CD See Tool 25. Presenter Agreement Contract

Another excellent way to come up with programming ideas is by looking at how teens are already using your library. What Web sites are they visiting? What magazines are they looking at? Most important, what books are they checking out or browsing while hanging out in the library? While not every program needs to have a clear and direct connection to the library's collection, materials still matter because if kids are interested in reading about a topic, researching it online, or watching a movie about it, then they might be interested in learning more about it through some sort of related program.

involvement may take some time, especially if your library is new to teen programming. Teen involvement is important because it will make your programs better; teens are more likely to participate in something they had a hand in planning, and the program will have more of a "teen flavor" than if an adult had planned it. When you are involving teens in planning, ask all of the questions, have the teens talk it through, and hit some of the details to help them understand the process you go through every month. Let them know up front the budget, time limitations (if any), and library rules that are nonnegotiable. Discuss the time and supplies the program will require.

You could also begin by asking yourself this question: "Dewey" or "Don't we know the best topics for teen programs?" Brainstorm through the Dewey areas, listing every possible subject that might make for an interesting program. Or if you don't want to brainstorm on your own, Figure 9.1 offers a fairly exhaustive list of programming ideas classed by Dewey decimal numbers.

Determine what types of programs appeal to teens at your library. Most teen programming can be separated into six basic categories:

- **Cultural.** These programs give teens the opportunity to explore artistic or intellectual pursuits. Cultural programs might include a pottery demonstration, open mic night, short story read-aloud, international cooking program, or a program that focuses on hip-hop.

- **Educational.** These are programs in which participating teens have an opportunity to learn something educational about topics of interest such as vegetarianism, SAT prep, the environment, or the history of rap music.

- **Informational.** These programs offer direct information about issues or matters that affect teens, including seminars and workshops about writing a résumé, getting a job, hair weaving, taking care of your first car, or learning how to cook with a microwave.

- **Opinion.** These programs allow teens to give their input and engage in open dialogue about community issues and about library services and collections. These types of programs can provide avenues for teens to express their opinions and often include poetry slams, book discussions, TAC (Teen Advisory Council) meetings, formal and informal polls, political group meetings and events, and expert-facilitated discussions about timely issues that focus on health, well-being, safety, and personal experiences. Opinion programs provide teens with opportunities to share their opinions and take a stance on particular issues as well as allowing other teens to observe the responses of their peers.

- **Recreational.** These programs combine things teens enjoy with the potential of learning something, including a skateboarding demonstration, gaming tournament, dance competition, or sewing class.

(continued on p. 244)

Figure 9.1. Programming by Dewey Number

Number	Program	Description
000	Digital Art and Graphic Design	Demonstration and interactive, hands-on workshop.
000	Computer Guts!	Teens take apart and explore the inside of an old computer to see what's inside the machines they use every day. Advanced teens can try putting it back together to see if they can make it work.
000	Buying a Computer 101	Demonstration and interactive workshop on how to purchase a new or used laptop or desktop computer.
000	Geek U (also called "Hard Wired")	Basic technological training that lets teens learn a new application or sharpen old technology skills with a new project each week (e.g., Google Maps and mashups, listening to music online, creating a wiki, designing an avatar); include Web challenges and prizes for participation.
000	Read-to-me Buddies	Teens volunteer to read to small groups of children.
000	Storytelling Program	Middle school and high school drama classes and English classes learn how to tell stories; include visits to the library for field trips.
000	Teen Story Hour	Research shows teens love to hear stories read aloud, although adults often stop doing "story times" once kids learn to read by themselves. Pick a high-interest YA title and read a chapter aloud a day at a set time during the summer or after school one day a week. For one-shot read-alouds, read short stories or high-interest fan fiction.
000	Trivial Pursuit Competition	Questions to answer each week; teens write down an answer, you pull out a winner and offer a prize.
000	Trivia contest during Teen Read Week or Teen Tech Week	Contest follows TRW or TTW theme; teens earn an incentive each time they come in and answer a question correctly.
000	Guinness Book of World Records contest/quiz	
000	Techno Teen Volunteers	Teens volunteer to be responsible for troubleshooting computers and printers and providing one-on-one instruction for library patrons.
000	Web Design Workshop	Teens learn the basics of creating their own Web site using code, or teens can learn how to insert images and text and how to publish a site to the Internet.
000	Zine Sceen	Teens create a zine (print newsletter) featuring art, writing, and reviews of books, Web sites, music— all content created for and by teens. Naming the zine can be an entirely separate program!
000	Amp Your MySpace	Based on a book by the same name, teens learn (and teach others) how to modify their personal social networking site by adding images, backgrounds, and creating original layouts. This program can apply to any popular social networking site where teens have their own virtual spaces.
000	Viral Library Videos	Teens create original, library related, 30-second videos about life in the library, which are then posted to YouTube. Videos can be voted on by participating teens.

(Cont'd.)

Figure 9.1. Programming by Dewey Number (Continued)

Number	Program	Description
000	Podcasting	Teens use Audacity Freeware to create and edit library-related podcasts.
100	Astrology	Demonstration and interactive workshop.
100	Chinese Horoscopes	Demonstration and interactive workshop.
100	Fortune-telling	Demonstration and interactive workshop.
100	Tarot Card Class	Teens learn the basics of tarot and have a reading done.
100	Dream On	Interactive dream interpretation workshop.
100	Hypnosis	Demonstration and interactive workshop.
100	Handwriting Analysis	Demonstration and interactive workshop.
100	Just Breathe!	Workshop focusing on coping with stress from school, extracurricular activities, and work; teachers might include massage therapists, yoga instructors, Reiki instructors, other professionals trained in stress reduction exercises.
300	Prom Project	Collect gently used and new prom dresses and accessories (including shoes, jewelry, and handbags) from members of the community and then host a boutique where teens can shop for free for their big night.
300	Feeling Freakish?	Based on a book by the same name, a discussion for teens about feeling comfortable in their own skin; conversation facilitated by medical professional who serves teens who can address puberty.
300	GLBTQ?	Positive Q and A session for, by, and with teens who have questions, in general, about sexuality (his or her own, a friend's, a parent's); conversation facilitated by a professional counselor.
300	Sexplanations!	Honest, open forum for discussion (facilitated by person in the medical field) in a safe environment where teens can ask questions (submitted via some type of secret submission) and get answers.
300	Money 101	Workshop or ongoing series of classes focusing on finance and investing, where teens learn how to manage their money, balance a checkbook, open a checking account, bank online, and make smart, well-informed financial choices about investing in their financial future.
300	6R Movement	Monthly, environmental craft program that provides teens with opportunities to create new and innovative items out of recycled materials. The 6Rs include reduce, reuse, reclaim, redesign, recycle, and renew. Incorporate facts (perhaps as a trivia game) into the program about how we can all help save the environment by doing small things every day. Facilitate conversations about "going green" during each program. For more information about this program, see the *VOYA* MVP article in the October 2008 issue.
300	Get a (Summer) Job!	Basic tips on interviewing for a summer job and filling out an application; could be held in conjunction with a job fair featuring employers who hire teens in the summer.

(Cont'd.)

Figure 9.1. Programming by Dewey Number *(Continued)*

Number	Program	Description
300	Where the Jobs Are: Present and Future Opportunities	Workshop with a job counselor to help teens learn current and future employment trends.
300	Know Your Rights!	Demonstration and interactive workshop about teens and the law, focusing on their rights; conversation facilitated by an attorney, youth advocate, or police officer.
300	ASVAB (Armed Services Vocational Aptitude Battery) study workshop	
300	Military Careers	Presentation and discussion about the four branches of the military and possible careers under each branch.
300	Forensics 101	Demonstration and interactive workshop about forensic science.
300	So You Wanna Be a Cop?	Demonstration and interactive workshop about careers in law enforcement and police/detective work; special guests might include police officers from the K-9 Unit, SWAT Team, Sexual Crimes Division, and Homicide.
300	Boy Scout Badge programs	
300	Girl Scout Badge programs	
300	Study Hall	Teens use the meeting room for studying before or during final exams.
300	Shhh!	After-hours study space in the library during final exams; provide snacks.
300	Now What? Making Decisions about What Happens after High School	Workshop where teens learn about resources at the library that will help them find a job, select a college or trade school, buy a car, etc.
300	GED workshop	
300	LearnATest	Free practice tests for the PSAT, SAT, and other standardized tests
300	PSAT Study Night	Provide a quiet space, some food and drinks, and a few tips on how to ace the PSAT.
300	SAT/ACE Preparation Workshop	Teens learn time management and test strategy techniques.
300	Surviving the College Application Process	Teens learn about the process of applying for college and receive tips on (and feedback about) writing an entrance essay; also include information about the decision-making process most libraries use to select applicants.
300	Virtual [and Print] College Tour	Teens (and parents) learn about online and print resources available at the library related to college information.
300	You Got into the College of Your Dreams! Now What?	Workshop about paying for a college education, including information about scholarships, grants, work study programs, and loans.
300	Mehndi (Henna Tattoos)	Presentation and hands-on workshop; to save time, have a presenter do a visual demonstration on one teen and then allow teens to create tattoos on one another in pairs.

(Cont'd.)

Figure 9.1. Programming by Dewey Number (Continued)

Number	Program	Description
300	Got Ink?	Teens learn about tattoos (pro and con) and get a temporary tattoo from an actual artist who draws on the skin using pen ink instead of the traditional needle and ink.
300	Hole in Your Head	Pro and con session about body piercing that addresses how piercings are done, health issues, and healthy maintenance of existing body piercings; discussion facilitated by professional piercing artist.
300	Fast Food Nation!	Based on a book by the same name, this facilitated conversation is all about the scary truth about fast food and how teens can make smart decisions when eating out, on the go, or in a hurry.
300	Scary Stories and Urban Legends	Performance by a storyteller followed by a chance for teens to tell their own stories and talk about the truth behind various urban legends.
400	Sign language demonstration and interactive workshop	
400	Word Nerd	Using dictionaries, teens create fake definitions of words, then have a contest to fool others.
400	Rhyme Time	A contest to come up with the most words that rhyme in the shortest period of time; great for an icebreaker.
400	Hieroglyphics demonstration and interactive workshop	
500	The Armchair Scientist	Based on the book *How to Fossilize Your Hamster*, this program is all about interesting (and strange) experiments teens can do at home.
500	Fairly Scientific	A science fair in reverse; teens learn about various fields of science, talk to professional scientists about their work, and learn what science fair judges look for when they judge student entries.
500	We're Going Natural!	Presentation by a naturalist, followed by a chance for teens to interact with animals; especially the ever-popular snake, bat, hissing cockroach, and anything else creepy, crawly, or slimy.
500	Math Mentors	High school honors students tutor middle school students or elementary students in math basics.
500	Astronomy 101	Demonstration and interactive workshop for novices about stargazing and the constellations.
500	Chemistry Magic	Demonstration and interactive workshop about the various principles of chemistry that allow scientists to create explosions and other unexpected chemical reactions that create new and unique (and sometimes gross) materials like slime.
500	Birds of Prey	Demonstration and interactive workshop about birds rarely seen in the wild like eagles, buzzards, falcons, vultures, and owls.

(Cont'd.)

Figure 9.1. Programming by Dewey Number (Continued)

Number	Program	Description
600	Hot Movies, Hot Topics!	If you have a public performance site license to show movies, select hot new movies that somehow address timely, relevant topics in which teens will have an interest like friendship, self-reliance, suicide, teen pregnancy, depression, making a change in the world, the environment, etc. Follow each movie with a talk-back session led by a health care professional or other subject-area expert.
600	Teen Health Forum	Library-sponsored, all day forum and health fair during the weekend about health topics of interest to teens like depression, stress, eating disorders, sexuality, peer pressure, acne and skin care, etc. Invite local health practitioners and local youth-serving health organizations to sponsor sessions, teach breakout sessions, and participate in the information fair.
600	Yoga Workshop for Beginners	Invite local yoga instructor to teach basic poses and breathing techniques in a one-shot or ongoing series of classes.
600	Get Fit Smart!	One-hour workshop about eating right, staying fit, and being smart about exercise. Content might include food guides, a healthy "diet" versus a scary diet fad, developing an exercise routine, using a nutrition calculator, and accessing online resources to create nutritious meal plans.
600	Auto Repair 101	Invite a local mechanic to show teens how to change a tire, read warning lights, change windshield wipers, etc.; market this to young women who think auto repair is a "guy thing."
600	No Lemons!	Interactive workshop for teens interested in buying a used car. Content might include questions to ask seller, checking the car's history with the VIN number, inspecting the body for damage, etc. http://www.samarins.com/.
600	Bikes, Scooters, Skates, and Boards! How to Buy 'em, Fix 'em, Improve 'em, & Move 'em	Based on a book by the same name, this program is all about nonmotorized modes of transportation. Really, the book's subtitle says it all for content you can include in this workshop.
600	Low-rider Cars	Demonstration and interactive workshop; invite local owners to show off car modifications and talk about low-rider culture and community.
600	Model Cars, Planes, and Rockets	Demonstration and interactive workshop; invite a local model maker to share personal tips and techniques.
600	Motorcycles	Demonstration and interactive workshop; content might include how to get a motorcycle license, how to buy the right bike, street safety for bikes.
600	Pet Nation	Invite employees or volunteers from a local animal shelter to talk about their work, show potential pets, talk about volunteer opportunities, and answer questions.
600	Exotic Pets!	Demonstration and interactive workshop about nontraditional pets such as ferrets, snakes, sugar gliders, iguanas, etc. Content might include parade of pets, legality of exotic pets, and pet care.
600	Sweet!	Candy making demonstration and hands-on design workshop.

(Cont'd.)

Figure 9.1. Programming by Dewey Number (Continued)

Number	Program	Description
600	Chocolate Fest	Snacks and library-based activities related to finding information; include contests, quizzes, and scavenger hunts about chocolate.
600	Delicious Dish!	Demonstration and interactive workshop on how to prepare quick and healthy snacks.
600	Japanese Cooking for Manga Fans	Manga readers will love the opportunity to create simple Japanese dishes using ingredients found in every Western kitchen. *The Manga Cookbook* will be especially useful, as it provides step-by-step instructions for preparing authentic onigiri (rice balls), yakitori (skewered chicken), oshinko (pickled vegetables), udon (Japanese noodles), and okonomiyaki (Japanese-style pizza).
600	Ice Cream Social	Homemade ice cream workshop.
600	Pizza-tasting Contest	Teens rate the best pizza in town.
600	Food Fear Factor @ the Library!	Hand out rain ponchos and barf bags at the beginning. It's funny, but it will also help with the mess. Teen participants eat disgusting food in rounds. If you throw up or give up, you're out! Disgusting foods might include octopus, oysters, baby food, anchovies, clam milkshakes (blended clams, clam juice from can, and buttermilk), sardines, pickled eggs, spoonful of mayonnaise, Vienna sausages (and their juice), vegemite, sauerkraut, baby formula, potted meat, and cold canned spinach.
600	Dreds, Braids, and Weaves	Hair care basics for African-American teens; invite a local salon owner to give tips, do sample braids and weaves, and talk about hair care products.
600	Best Face Forward	Invite a representative from a company (like Aveda, Mary Kay, or Proactive) that sells skin care products to teach teens about basic skin care.
600	Generation T	Based on a book by the same name, use the book to create innovative new T-shirt designs out of existing T-shirts teens can bring from home.
600	Teen Alternative Fashion Show	In this program, participants create and model unique designs created out of alternative materials like recycled fabric, rubber, duct tape, bubble wrap, and more. For more information about this program, see the *VOYA* MVP article in the October 2007 issue.
600	Insparation!	Based on a book by the same name, teens can create original bath salts for a little self-pampering.
600	Babysitting Clinic	Workshop conducted by the Red Cross; provides teens with basic information and a certificate of completion.
600	Books for Babies	Workshop conducted with other agencies; targeted to pregnant and parenting teens.
600	Parenting 101	Ongoing series of beginner workshops for teen parents (moms and dads), taught by professionals who work with teen parents; topics might include information about medical, housing, and financial services available to them as well as the importance of reading to their child.

(Cont'd.)

Figure 9.1. Programming by Dewey Number (Continued)

Number	Program	Description
600	Résumés That'll Have 'em Raving!	Teens learn how to write a stellar resume and cover letter for job-seeking purposes.
600	Clever Codes and Ciphers	Demonstration and interactive workshop about writing and solving codes and ciphers.
700	Share Your Secret!	PostSecret is an ongoing community art project where people mail in their secrets anonymously on one side of a postcard. For your program, provide blank postcards and a place for teens to post their secrets for one month. At the end of the month, collect postcards and mail to PostSecret. To find out more about PostSecret: http://postsecret.blogspot.com/.
700	Mask Making	Demonstration and interactive workshop.
700	Origami	Interactive, hands-on workshop where teens learn about the history and the art of Japanese paper folding.
700	Comic Book/Manga Swap	Invite teen comic book/manga readers to drop by the library and trade popular titles with one another.
700	How to Draw Comics and Manga	Invite a local comic book artist (inker, penciller, letterer) to your library to do a live demo of drawing techniques; if you do not have a published comic book artist who lives in your area, search artists portfolios online by zip code or contact a local art school or college or university with an advanced art program.
700	Manga Mania	Invite teens to meet and discuss new manga titles during this monthly program; encourage attendees to help select new manga series for the library collection or fill in gaps in the existing collection.
700	Anime Addicts	Invite teens to meet and discuss new anime titles during this monthly program. See *VOYA*'s "The Anime-ted Library" article in the April 2005 issue for more information about creating an anime group at your library.
700	Jewelry Design Workshop	Teens create jewelry out of a variety of materials including hemp, beads, wire, paper beads, etc.
700	Calligraphy Basics	In this class teens will have an opportunity to learn the basic calligraphy strokes; invite local calligraphy artist to help teach class.
700	Candle Making	Demonstration and interactive workshop.
700	Duct It!	Invite teens to create cool stuff out of duct tape; provide a few samples, but allow teens to make whatever they want.
700	Paper Airplanes	Demonstration and interactive workshop; on completion of workshop, engage teens in a flight competition.
700	Puppet-Building Workshop	Invite teens to work with a local artist to create large-scale puppets; encourage students to return to the library to carry out puppetry programming for younger children in the library.

(Cont'd.)

Figure 9.1. Programming by Dewey Number (Continued)

Number	Program	Description
700	Scrapbooking Club	In this ongoing club, teens learn about different techniques and share their scrapbooks and techniques with one another.
700	Altered Books Camp	In this week-long camp (two hours a day for one week), teens learn a new technique each day as they work on an ongoing altered book project. You can provide books that have been weeded from your collection or teens can bring one from home. See *Alter This: Radical Ideas for Transforming Books into Art* by Alena Hennesy for daily techniques.
700	Fit to Be Tie-dyed!	Pick a nice day and set up your tie-dye program outside; encourage teens to bring their own T-shirts to dye. For an easy tie-dye program, buy a kit from a craft store. If you want to do it yourself, there are plenty of directions on the Internet.
700	Screen Printing	Invite a local artist to teach teens techniques of screen printing; if possible, create screens and actually screen print on T-shirts.
700	Air Brushing	Demonstration and interactive workshop that focuses on graffiti-style art.
700	Sports Card Collecting	Demonstration and interactive workshop; invite a local seller/collector to talk about collecting as an investment.
700	Photography Contest	Invite teens to submit original photos for contest; winning photos are posted both in the library and on the library's Web site.
700	Break Beat: Hip-hop Dance Workshop	Invite a local hip-hop dance instructor to teach a class on the basics; invite a local DJ to provide music for the event.
700	Hip-hop Symposium	Invite a panel of record company representatives, songwriters, attorneys, librarians, and other community members to discuss music and hip-hop culture.
700	Rock the Library!	Invite local teen bands to perform during a live "Battle of the Bands" competition. This program can be inside the library after hours or outside during the day.
700	Drum Circle	Performance and interactive event featuring drummers from the community; teens have an opportunity to make a drum and learn the basics of drumming as a group activity; encourage attendees to participate in a drum circle at the end of the workshop.
700	Get a REEL Job	Workshop about finding and succeeding in a career in film and television.
700	Clowning Around	Teens learn basic clown techniques, gags, and makeup; teens can volunteer to perform for children's programs at the library.
700	Acting 101	Teens learn the basic techniques of theater arts and improvisation; topics might include selecting props and costumes, staging, imitating mannerisms, and delivering lines with dramatic impact.
700	Stage Makeup Workshop	In this hands-on workshop, teens learn how makeup is used in theater, television, and movies; encourage teens to practice on one another once they have learned a few basic techniques.

(Cont'd.)

Figure 9.1. Programming by Dewey Number *(Continued)*

Number	Program	Description
700	Much Ado About Dancing!	Introduction to ballroom dancing, including the waltz, tango, merengue, mambo, and samba; invite a local ballroom dancing instructor to teach a one-shot program or ongoing classes.
700	Murder Mystery at the Library	Highsmith (www.highsmith.com) provides a kit, or you can write a "script" of your own by plotting a murder, planting some evidence, and asking a few of your teens to play key characters in the drama.
700	Juggling Workshop for Beginners	Invite a local juggler to teach the basics of juggling; if you have a proficient juggler in your area, invite him or her to do a live demonstration of advanced juggling skills using multiple pins or objects and other exciting materials like fire and knives.
700	—	Monopoly, Scrabble, and other board game tournaments
700	Cheat! A Club for Video Gamers	Invite teens to join you once a month to trade cheat codes, play games, and select gaming strategy guides for the library. Unlike traditional video gaming programs, this type of program is about creating a community of gamers who come together to socialize, talk about video games, and help the LST develop a gamer-friendly library collection.
700	Old-School Video Games Challenge	Introduce the teens in your library to old-school video gaming with the likes of Pong, Pac-Man, Tetris, Space Invaders, Asteroid, and other classic Arcade-style games that are now available, free of charge, on the Internet. In the summer or during spring break have an ongoing tournament where teens play a new game each day.
700	Chess Club	Invite teens to play chess, learn from one another, and socialize with their peers; consider inviting adults to help facilitate and teach. This makes a great intergenerational program.
700	Boxing 101	Boxing demonstration and interactive workshop
700	Roughing It!	Demonstration and interactive workshop about camping, hiking, backpacking, and survival skills for the great outdoors.
700	Snow Sports 101	Demonstration and interactive workshop about both skiing and snowboarding; content might include sport basics, safety, and appropriate weather gear.
700	Yo-Yo Tricks	Demonstration and interactive workshop featuring basic yo-yo tips and tricks.
700	Martial Arts Workshop	Overview workshop about several types of martial arts including capoeira, aikido, kung fu, tai chi, karate, judo, and tae kwon do; for an all-day program, invite local martial arts masters and black belt students to give live demonstrations.
700	NASCAR 101	Informational workshop about NASCAR basics; live demonstration of driving techniques.
700	Sk8rNation	Combination live demonstration/workshop for teen skaters; content might include a demonstration of skate techniques, board repair, board safety, skater culture, etc.

(Cont'd.)

Figure 9.1. Programming by Dewey Number *(Continued)*

Number	Program	Description
700	Sound Off!	Teen open mic night where teens have an opportunity to perform for their peers.
700	Live Your Sports Passion	Workshop about career opportunities that somehow involve sports.
800	Who Said That?	In this trivia contest, participating teens match the quote to the person who said it. Include a variety of quotes from those spoken by famous people, movie lines, song lyrics, and pop culture phrases.
800	Battle of the Books	Librarians select titles for teens in participating grades. The public library buys several copies, and librarians make up questions and act as timers and scorekeepers. Some state-sponsored BOTB contests have Web sites and a list of approved books each year. To see if your state participates, contact your state library.
800	Online Research 101	Introduction to online databases and writing a solid research paper.
800	Middle Earth Madness	Test your teens' knowledge of Tolkien's *The Hobbit* and the *Lord of the Rings* trilogy.
800	Spooked!	After-hours event where teens have a chance to hear ghost stories and local urban legends from a professional storyteller.
800	Journaling	Hands-on workshop where teens have an opportunity to create an original journal (book binding machine with recycled paper and cardstock for a cover or notebook with time to collage a cover from recycled magazines); invite a local writer to talk about the act of journaling/self-reflective writing.
800	Book P(r)eview	If you pick up advanced reading copies (advanced review copies [ARCs], also called "galleys") during conferences or receive them from publishers, encourage teens to write book reviews from these advanced copies. Also encourage participating teens to look for typos and do basic copy editing and submit feedback to publishers. Teens get to keep each ARC they review.
800	Tales of Terror Writing Contest	Teens compete to write and/or draw the best scary short story or mini comic; categories might include horror, manga, or comic format, ghost story, and real-life tales of terror.
800	Fan Fic Group	Local teens who write fan fiction come together to share stories, critique one another's work, and create a social network of fandom; a group blog, wiki, or social network site might be a good place for publishing this group's writing.
800	Guys Read!	Join author Jon Scieszka and create your own all-male book discussion group for guys in middle school or high school. For more information, see the official "Guys Read" Web site: www.guysread.com.
800	—	Book club based on your state's annual teen book award: teens vote locally for their favorite books.
800	—	Mother/Daughter or Father/Son book group
800	Mad Libs Poetry	Teens fill in the blanks and create their own version of famous poems.

(Cont'd.)

Figure 9.1. Programming by Dewey Number *(Continued)*

Number	Program	Description
800	Magnetic Poetry	Teens create their own magnetic poetry kits and spend some time composing poems. To be green, use recycled magnets, like those that are often found on phone books or given away by local businesses. If the library hands out magnets as a promotional item for any event, hang on to the leftovers and use them for this type of program.
800	Poetry Café	Held in conjunction with National Poetry Week in April, host an evening program with cake and coffee and encourage teens to read their own poetry or the works of their favorite poets.
800	Poetry in the Dark	Host an outdoor poetry reading during the evening with a little candlelight to help establish ambience.
800	Power of the Pen	Creative writing program for teens; encourage teens to post their poems in a special gallery on your library's Web site or on your library's social networking site. If this is a monthly program, consider publishing an anthology of teen poetry, fan fiction, or short stories in print or online each year.
800	Slam It!	Slam poetry/spoken word demonstrations, live performances, and facilitated discussions.
800	Teen Graffiti Board	Use butcher paper to cover a wall, pole, or other flat surface in your library. Teens then have the opportunity to leave a message, write poetry, or share a book recommendation on the "graffiti wall." If you have windows in your library, hold a "window graffiti" day and encourage teens to doodle on the windows with special window/glass markers you can buy at a craft, art, or hobby store.
800	Library Lock-in	Invite teens to join you for an all-night, after-hours program in the library where attending teens have an opportunity to take over the library, use the computers, and sleep amid the stacks. This program is not for the faint of heart, as it should begin when the library closes and end when the library opens again in the morning. For safety purposes, all attendees are "locked in" for the entire event.
800	Book Swap	Pull interesting teen books from your book sale and invite teens to exchange books from their collection with those you have available. Put exchanged books back onto the book sale shelf for resale.
800	Breakfast Club	During the breakfast hour, invite teens in your middle school or high school to join you once a month in the school library to provide input on materials selection; participating teens get the first chance to check out new materials.
800	Lunch Bunch	During this mid-afternoon book discussion group, teens bring a sack lunch and the library provides drinks and dessert. In a school library, this is a great way to meet the needs of middle schoolers or high schoolers who are looking for a place to hang out during the (often dreaded) lunch hour.
900	—	Programs, quizzes, or other activities to celebrate, commemorate, or explore various historical events (Juneteenth, Holocaust, 9/11, etc.).

(Cont'd.)

Number	Program	Description
900	Six-Word Memoirs	Invite teens to craft and share their personal six-word memoir. If teens need some help, refer them to *Not Quite What I Was Planning: Six Word Memoirs*. Here are some great examples from the book: Mixed blood. I am America's future. —Holly Santiago I colored outside the lines. —Jacob Thomas Asked to quiet down. Spoke louder. —Wendy Lee
900	Who Am I?	Demonstration and interactive workshop about oral history and creating a family tree; good intergenerational program.
900	Rooting Into Your Past	Genealogy demonstration and interactive workshop.
900	—	Local history programs involving teens and technology (digital and still photography, digital video, and podcasting) to record the community's past.
900	Name Game	Program where teens find out the meaning of their names.
900	—	Visit from the Society for Creative Anachronism or another organization that focuses on historical reenactments.

Figure 9.1. Programming by Dewey Number *(Continued)*

- **Technological.** These programs might fit in a few of the previous areas but they have a technological slant, like a video game design class, graphic design workshop, online safety seminar, or digital photography scavenger hunt.

The type of programming you choose depends not only on the interests of your teens but also on the resources available. It's not just money, but also space, time, support, and your own internal resources, that must be considered. While there are many types of teen programs, there is really only one type of LST to do programming: one who has a high threshold for rejection. While these categories hold potential for all kinds of library programs, in most libraries, the tradition of story times and other preschool programs runs deep. While children's librarians create lots of innovative programs, they also have plenty of staples. LSTs focusing on teen programming are usually making it up as they go along, with little history of programming success or failure.

That said, there are a few teen programming staples worth exploring, such as craft programs and book discussion groups. In addition to these topic-based programs, teen summer reading programs and special YALSA-sanctioned weeklong celebrations, including "Teen Read Week" and "Teen Tech Week," and a few other annual celebrations, like "Banned Books Week" and "Free Comic Book Day," are growing in popularity and serve as important models for all teen programs. Finally, many public libraries have created after-school programs to provide a little bit of everything: tutoring, activities, and reading promotion.

Craft Programs

Craft programs usually fall into two categories: process oriented or product oriented. Process-oriented crafts are more open-ended with a greater focus on the experience and less on the finished product. For example, providing supplies for teens to decorate their own picture frames or create anything they want out of duct tape is process oriented. If you want teens to take the lead and use their creativity, open-ended programs work best. You supply the materials and they supply the ideas. Product-oriented crafts allow participating teens to come away with a specific product. You choose the materials, prepackage everything, teach them the details, and let them follow the preprinted directions. Examples of product-oriented crafts include creating a mosaic table for the library or painting a mural. There is a time and a place for both types of programs, but process-oriented craft programs are normally more engaging for teens who want to infuse a product with their personality and generally have more freedom during the creative process.

Often teens are attracted to activities that are not like the things they do in school. This is where the library fits in, as a bridge between school and free-time activities and interests. The great thing about teen craft programs is that, more times than not, teens have the manual dexterity, creativity, and independence to tackle new things on their own. Many times giving them the supplies and some initial instructions is all that is required. One LST was concerned because he had never scrapbooked, but he knew it might be a popular program. He read several books, asked questions of several people he knew who did scrapbooking, bought the supplies they recommended, and was prepared to scrapbook—though he wasn't quite sure what to do. He laid out the supplies, scissors, paper, and glue and several books with tips on how to scrapbook. Once the program got started, he realized the teens knew way more than he did and that it did not really matter what he knew because there was no right way to scrapbook. Afterward, he mentioned it was the most relaxed program he had done in a while, mainly because there wasn't a lot of hand-holding. He had a chance to talk with some of the teens he knew from other programs and meet some new teens for the first time. If you are doing a craft program that is fairly involved and has many specific steps, it will be to your advantage to practice the craft at least once. Be sure to think through how you will teach a group of teens to master the steps and if each person needs supplies or if everyone can share. Although most librarians assume teen craft programs will mostly pull in girls, remember that craft programs can be guy-friendly as well. If you're making jewelry, make sure to provide more masculine beads and hemp rope. Duct tape is always a hit with guys, and, of course, incorporating power tools (if you can) into your program is always a hit. Other ways to get guys involved is to pull them in during the planning process. Once they have helped to disassemble computers to make key chains out of motherboards or to break CDs for mosaics, they are more likely to stay to complete the program so they can walk away with a finished product.

You may get comments about these craft programs not being library related. People may not understand that teens, like adults, are interested in learning new skills, ideas, or activities. No matter what the craft, the library has materials that relate to and support the program. For environmental crafting (see Figure 9.1 for some ideas), consider booktalking *Re-Creative: 50 Projects for Turning Found Items into Contemporary Design* by Steve Dodds and *ReadyMade: How to Make [Almost] Everything: A Do It Yourself Primer* by Shoshana Berger and Grace Hawthorne during your program. You can also put environmental documentaries (*11th Hour* and *An Inconvenient Truth*) on display with other green-friendly titles like *The Green Book: The Everyday Guide to Saving the Planet One Simple Step at a Time* by Elizabeth Rogers and Thomas Kostigen and *Green Chic: Saving the Earth in Style* by Christie Matheson and hand out bookmarks created in-house with environmentally friendly Web sites and tips for doing one's part to save the earth.

Finally, craft programs can be a big initial draw and a gateway to other types of programs. One LST used crafts as the draw and added her interest in history to make the program more meaningful. She combined quilting and the history of the Underground Railroad, booktalked several historical fiction YA titles, told them a bit of history, and taught them the basics of hand quilting. You may not have experience as a quilter, but you can booktalk while a quilter from the community provides a demonstration. Another LST had older teen girls demonstrate their hobby of knitting to their peers while he provided the snacks and yarn. Yet another LST hired the high school girl he bought coffee from every morning at the local coffee shop to teach other teens how to make the jewelry he saw her wearing.

Book Discussion Groups

Book discussion groups are a natural, but they may take time. To get a core group of teens to attend, start with teens who show an interest in participating and let them guide the group. Book discussion groups break down into two types: either everybody reads the same book or everybody reads what they want and discusses the story or the genre their books share. One group is relaxed and everyone talks about what they are reading, which is almost always something different. The LST offers suggestions—new books or books he or she has recently read— and the teens offer their suggestions. The only constant is when they meet. Another group always reads fantasy, and they choose their books three months at a time so they can be advertised. Also, if one of the members misses a month, he or she still knows what the book is for the next month. One group is sponsored by the Friends of the Library; the LST gets a list of popular books that are in paperback for the group to choose from, she booktalks each title, and she gives the teens time to examine each title and make their decisions. They choose a title and the Friends group purchases paperback copies for each participant to read

There will always be people who will question your judgment or inquire about the legitimacy of any teen program. The best answer to this will always be, "We're building community." While a person might not question the legitimacy of a library-sponsored, monthly quilting bee for senior citizens, this same person might wonder about the validity (and use of precious library resources and funding) of teens creating duct tape wallets, making metal flowers out of recycled soup cans, or learning to knit using the tape inside recycled cassette tapes.

and keep. The more choices you can give teens, the better the group experience. It may take a month or two for the group to settle down to a consistent group of readers, but never get too comfortable because your group will constantly be changing. Friends, siblings, and girlfriends and boyfriends will come and go and add their unique flavor to the group. The most important thing about a book discussion group is that social engagement is the key. If participating teens are not interested in that month's book, encourage them to talk about what's happening in the news, what's going on in their schools, or what's up online. Also, remember that you are there as a facilitator, not the book group know-it-all.

Teen Read Week

Teen Read Week (TRW) is an annual, weeklong national literacy initiative sponsored by YALSA encouraging teens to read books for fun on a regular basis. Celebrated annually during the third week in October, TRW's main theme is "Read for the Fun of It," with a subtheme that changes each year.[1] Originally developed to help build connections between teens and libraries, YALSA held the first national Teen Read Week Celebration in 1998. In the past decade, this weeklong celebration has grown into a nationally recognized program on a mission to encourage teens to read both for pleasure and for educational purposes. YALSA's Teen Read Week Web site is a wealth of information, including a description of the current year's theme, advice for librarians who are new to TRW, theme-specific programming ideas, and resources that include informational Web sites and books about the year's topic, promotional materials created by ALA specifically for TRW, a sample press release, a public service announcement (PSA), a proclamation, official logos with graphics, and a place for participating librarians to register, share ideas, and provide feedback. YALSA also hosts a TRW wiki with hundreds of subtheme programming ideas, Web site resources, and display ideas submitted by LSTs from around the country. Whether you do thematic programming for TRW based on the annual subtheme selected by YALSA or not, special programs and events during this week will allow you to get the word out to local teens that the library really is a teen-friendly zone. Use this week to shine a spotlight on what your library has to offer young people by highlighting the teen advisory council, ongoing classes and events, and materials that teens might not know exist in the library collection, such as graphic novels, manga, teen magazines, and comic books.

The following are some other ways to promote teen reading, in general, in your library.

What Are You READ!ing? Contest

This program idea, based on the celebrity READ! Posters published by ALA Graphics, can be a great kickoff for Teen Read Week. Hold a contest a few weeks before the start of TRW asking teens to submit the name of their favorite book along with a short write-up explaining why they like the book. Select some of the best entries and photograph these teen winners with their favorite books. ALA has made this incredibly easy in the past few years by creating "READ! CDs" that contain pre-designed READ@ posters and bookmarks.

Read-in

Since finding a time to read can often be a problem for busy teens, set up a "Read-in" at your library and invite local teen readers to bring their pillows, blankets, and sleeping bags and fall into a book for an hour or two. Provide refreshments, hand out reading incentives, and give away reading-related prizes like gift certificates to a local bookstore or comic-book store. This kind of program is always more fun if you can do it after hours, so, if possible, hijack your library one evening and turn it into the ultimate teen-friendly zone for some uninterrupted quality time with the books.

Scavenger Hunt @ the Library

Place a handful of "special" bookmarks in books throughout the library. If a teen patron checks out one of these books during TRW, he or she is an instant winner. A prize can be as simple as a nice bookmark or a small-denomination gift certificate to a bookstore. This simple event can take place throughout the week and does not require much money or a major investment of time. It is also a great idea to do this in addition to several specific programs since it is ongoing and promotes the use of the collection.

Get Carded @ Your Library!

This idea, taken from ALA's "Get Carded @ Your Library" campaign to promote national Library Card Sign-up Month, could be a weeklong event during TRW whereby a teen can get an incentive prize simply by showing up at the library and flashing his or her library card. These prizes, which should be simple and promote library use, might include a free print card, a free copy card, or a "get out of library card debt free" card (if this is legal within your library system). For teens without a library card, this is the perfect opportunity for them to get signed up. The "Get Carded" poster from the ALA online store is a great promotional item for Teen Read Week in October or Library Card Sign-up Month in September.

Coffeehouse for Teens

Invite teens to drop by and share a latte or an iced coffee one afternoon or evening at the library during Teen Read Week. Create a friendly environment, play some music, and have a few icebreakers ready to get the group talking. This is also a great time to ask participants to share their favorite books, authors, movies, and music.

Teen Tech Week

Teen Tech Week (TTW) is also an annual weeklong national initiative sponsored by YALSA to "ensure that teens are competent and ethical users of technologies, especially those that are offered through libraries such as DVDs, databases, audiobooks, and videogames." Teen Tech Week also "encourages teens to use libraries' nonprint resources for education and recreation and to recognize that librarians are qualified, trusted professionals in the field of information technology."[2] Like Teen Read Week, TTW has a main theme of "Get Connected @ Your Library" with a different subtheme each year. On YALSA's TTW Web site you can find excellent resources for promoting technology for teens in your library, including programming ideas, marketing and promotional help (including a sample press release and PSA), contests for teens, online resources, and a link to the wiki. On the TTW wiki you will find more resources, including ways to promote this annual celebration in your library and various links to technology resources. Capitalize on this national, weeklong celebration by promoting existing technology programs at your library or by creating new and innovative technological programming for and with teens at your library.

The following are some ideas that vary in technical know-how needed, so there's something for the technophobe as well as the techno-geek librarian.

Create Your Own Avatar

http://avatarmaker.abi-station.com/index_en.shtml
Teens can create their own personalized avatar (an image that you create to represent yourself online) to upload and use online.

Create Your Own Quiz!

www.quizyourfriends.com
Teens can create their own quizzes to share with their friends and family about their likes, dislikes, personal trivia, etc. What's really cool about this site is that once a teen creates a personal quiz, he or she can e-mail the quiz to friends or add it to his or her MySpace and Facebook site using the provided html code.

Wild Wiikend!

By now you're probably all familiar with the Wii (pronounced "we"), Nintendo's fifth-generation gaming platform. If you haven't already done so, buy a Wii for your library and watch the teens come pouring in to play live-action sports games like baseball, golf, and bowling, or unusual video games like "Trauma Center" where players use the Wiimote to perform surgery in an operating room. Make a Wiikend of it and just set the Wii up in your library on a Saturday and Sunday during TRW. If you cannot afford to buy a Wii for your library, we highly recommend looking into renting one or borrowing one from a teen patron for a wild Wiikend.

Old-School Video Games Challenge Program

Introduce the teens in your library to old-school video gaming with the likes of Pong, Pac-Man, Tetris, Space Invaders, Asteroid, and other classic arcade-style games that are now available, free of charge, on the Internet. This program can be an ongoing program, and it works especially well during the summer months or during TRW when you can introduce a new game each day.

Computer Gaming Tournament

Gaming tournaments can take place in a library in one of two ways: using computers in a lab that share the same network or establishing a separate network between gaming computers (and this is what would take place if patrons brought their own laptop computers). A central computer with the master game program will need to be in place so that all participating computers can communicate with one another and participate against one another. Think virtual reality; for all participating teens to be interacting in the same virtual "room," they need to be able to share their location and their virtual actions. If none of this makes sense, and you still want to host a gaming tournament, I highly recommend you ask local teens who have expressed an interest in participating in such a tournament. (Trust me when I say that these teens know more than we ever will know about this sort of thing.) Additionally, I recommend asking your library's IT department for help and/or advice.

Banned Books Week

Developed by ALA almost 30 years ago, "Banned Books Week" (BBW) continues to be a popular annual celebration in libraries around the country during the last week of September. According to the BBW Web site, this weeklong celebration is about honoring "the freedom to choose or the freedom to express one's opinion even if that opinion might be considered unorthodox or unpopular and stresses the importance of ensuring the availability of those unorthodox or unpopular viewpoints to all who wish to read them."[3] On ALA's official "Banned Books Week" Web site you can get a basic guide about why we celebrate banned and challenged books and a list of activities for celebrating BBW. Here you will also find a list of the most challenged books of the twenty-first century, a list of frequently challenged books, and the most frequently challenged books and authors of the previous year.

To get you started, the following are some programs and promotional ideas for celebrating Banned Books Week in your library.

Banned Books Display

Take ALA's list of the most popular banned or challenged books in the past century and create an eye-catching and informative display. Consider creating a "jail" with bars out of cardboard to house the books, or use the American flag and the words "You're Free to Read Anything You Want in This Country!" as a backdrop for your display.

They Don't Want You to Read This!" (Banned Books Made into Movies) Film Festival

If your library has a public performance site license to show movies, select a few teen-friendly movies that were once banned or challenged books. Titles that would be great for an event like this include *The Golden*

Compass, Of Mice and Men, Harry Potter, James and the Giant Peach, The Grapes of Wrath, Bridge to Terabithia, and *To Kill a Mockingbird.*

"We Read Banned Books" Read-in for a Cause

Invite teens to drop by and participate in an all-night "read-in," spending one entire night locked in the library, reading books that have been banned or challenged in the past century. To make it even more fun, consider encouraging participating teens to ask friends and family to sponsor their participation by pledging X dollars per hour of reading completed. As a group, select a local, literacy-based nonprofit organization to be the recipient of all donated funds.

"If It Pleases the Court..."

Invite a local, high school debate team to put a banned or challenged book on trial. If possible, tape the proceeding and upload it to YouTube for everyone to see.

Free Comic Book Day

Like the name of the annual daylong celebration implies, Free Comic Book Day is a "single day when participating, comic book shops across North America and around the world give away comic books absolutely free to anyone who comes into their stores."[4] Although this happens in comic book stores, libraries can get involved by partnering with their local, independent comic book shop. If you do not already have a relationship with the owner of your local store, now is the time to drop by and introduce yourself. The way Free Comic Book Day works is that comic book publishers print a certain number of comic books each year specifically for this day. Then retailers purchase copies of these comics for a very low rate per copy. So technically, these "free" comics are not free for retailers. So as a partner, offer to provide the bookstore with a certain amount of money in exchange for the owner adding a few hundred extra copies of certain teen-friendly comics when they place their order several months in advance. You might also consider offering your local comic book store free publicity in exchange for a predetermined number of free comic books to be handed out in your library. Publicity might include promoting the store on your library's Web site or MySpace page, stamping every free comic book with the name and address of the partnering store, and putting the name and logo of the partnering store on all flyers and posters in the library promoting the event. To find a local comic book store participating in this annual event, see the Free Comic Book Day Web site, which provides a free store locator online (www.freecomicbookday.com/fcbd_locator.asp).

Summer Reading Programs for Teens

Although a majority of libraries around the country create and carry out traditional summer reading programs, the intended audience is usually children, occasionally addressing the developmental and recreational needs of preteens and teens. For libraries that have made an effort to create a place for teens within the library community, it is imperative that there be some segment of a library's summer reading program that speaks directly to the needs of teens. In addition, a summer reading program for teens should allow participating teens to be directly involved in the creation of the program, providing an opportunity for teens to provide input during the developmental phase as well as during the program itself.

Currently, the Collaborative Summer Library Program (CSLP) provides a national teen summer reading program for 48 states in the United States. CSLP is a

> grassroots consortium of states working together to provide high-quality summer reading program materials . . . by combining resources and working with a commercial vendor to produce materials designed exclusively for CSLP members, public libraries in participating states or systems can purchase posters, reading logs, bookmarks, certificates and a variety of reading incentives at significant savings. The participating systems and states develop a unified and high-quality promotional and programming product. Participants have access to the same artwork, incentives and publicity, in addition to an extensive manual of programming and promotional ideas.[5]

For libraries that are not currently a member of CSLP, it is possible to create an individualized teen summer reading program that incorporates reading activities, contests, and special events specifically for participating teens by making changes to an existing summer reading program for younger readers. Some things to keep in mind when creating a teen-friendly summer reading program include the following:

- **Keep it simple.** Develop a simple reading record (in print or online) where teens can keep track of their hours. If possible, allow teens to print off prize and fine waivers online once they have reached hourly benchmarks.

- **Make it possible for teens to get involved on many levels.** The goal of any summer reading program is to encourage reading for fun during the summer. Provide prizes throughout the program, for completion of 5 hours, 10 hours, 15 hours, etc.

- **Allow free choice when it comes to selecting reading materials.** Reading books count, but so does reading online, as does reading more nontraditional materials like teen magazines, comic books, and graphic novels.

- **Incorporate the Internet.** Teens spend a lot of time online, so it makes sense to incorporate the Web into your programming and publicity. Many libraries with successful teen summer reading programs allow teens to enter and keep track of their hours read online via their library's teen Web site.

- **Select teen-friendly prizes.** Popular prizes for teen summer reading programs might include flash drives, keychains, drawstring backpacks, or travel coffee mugs with the library's logo and teen Web site URL, free print cards, and paperback books.

- **Incorporate fine reduction into the program.** Fine waivers make great prizes, and an initial fine waiver coupon handed out at sign up is an excellent motivator for teens who might not otherwise participate in a teen summer reading program.

- **Seek community partners.** Many local businesses and national chains are happy to help you develop a teen summer reading program by providing seed money, free books, other prizes, or free food or services to participants. You'll never know unless you ask.

- **Make it fun.** Throw a party for all teens who finish the program. If your budget allows, hold a drawing at each library location for teens who finish the program. Prizes for these drawings might include a gift card to a teen-friendly store or restaurant, movie tickets, or a coupon for waiving a fine in the future. If you have the budget for it, consider having a systemwide drawing for a major prize like a video iPod, Nintendo Wii, Playstation Portable, or even a laptop computer for one lucky teen reader.

> To make a summer reading program more teen-oriented, we recommend asking teens for ideas about theme, feedback on the artwork and design, and help crafting the parameters of the program as a whole. The more teens are involved in creating the program, the more likely they are to participate.

After-school Programs

Some of the most successful programs for serving teens after school are the ones directed to those classified as "at risk." While this term has different meanings, generally it speaks to teens who, due to socioeconomic circumstances, are likely to engage in risk-taking behavior and/or drop out of school. Successful programs for at-risk youth not only focus on specific needs of at-risk teens but also attempt to overcome the obstacles that prevent these young adults from succeeding. All programs for at-risk teens are built on the premise that "information is empowering." The idea is that the way out of poverty and the path away from destructive behavior is through education, information, and knowledge. Although many such programs were built without knowledge of the developmental assets model, the success of most can be directly related to how well and how often they do help teens as they transition to adulthood. Successful after-school programs usually have some things in common:

- Time, space, and resources for finishing homework
- Tutoring for teens who need help
- Engaging activities that allow teens to be active
- Opportunities for teens to interact with other teens
- Opportunities for teens to help create something, be it a print or online zine, mural, library garden, or teen Web site or social networking site

To create a successful after-school program, you need to make sure you have dedicated staff who can oversee the program, space for teens to hang out, and administrative support for the program. The next step is planning teen programs so that they are engaging, audience appropriate, and (hopefully) driven by teen interest.

Houston Public Library (HPL) in Texas has a great after-school program called "After School Zone" that began in 2007. Like many libraries around the country, HPL realized that several of its neighborhood libraries were becoming extremely busy during the after-school hours with unsupervised middle school students. The students would come in from their school day and want to use the computers or just hang out with their friends while they waited for their parents to pick them up. In response to the adult customer backlash, long lines to use the Internet, and uneven staff-to-student ratios, HPL designated libraries that were within walking distance of schools to be "After School Zones." Libraries that participate in the "After School Zone" program have giant yellow signs (that look like the "Caution" traffic signs) placed in prominent areas to warn customers that the library is likely to be busier and louder than normal between the hours of 3:30 p.m. and 5:30 p.m. There is also a brochure available that informs customers about "Alternative Libraries"—libraries located in the same geographic area of the city that do not see heavier traffic during the after-school hours. Programming is a major component of the "After School Zone" program. Utilizing meeting rooms in a nontraditional manner, librarians provide unstructured programming throughout the two-hour period after school, including "open tech time" where teens have access to wireless laptop computers and "open gaming" where teens have access to two Nintendo Wii's and a PlayStation 2. In addition to these less structured programs, teens also have opportunities to participate in more structured programming during the after-school hours including crafts, homework help, special topical workshops and presentations, interactive games and activities, and programs that focus specifically on life skills and careers. A traveling group of 15 MacBook computers and accessories are also available to support innovative technology programs at each branch like podcasting, video game design, Runescape Clans and LAN (Local Area Network) parties, and film making.[6]

How Do You Implement a Teen Program?

So you did your planning and now the day has come for the program. Teen volunteers are yet another avenue for promoting and assisting with programs. Think back to a party you attended in high school or college. If there was no one in the room, house, or gym, did you have a strong desire to go in? No. You did another loop around the block, hit the "quickie-mart," and made another pass to see if anyone else showed up. Not much has changed; not many teens want to be the first one at a program.

So what can you do to make this transition a little easier? If you have teen volunteers who know you and are comfortable in the library, ask one or two to come early and help set up. They can actually help set up, and they can act as teens who were the first to arrive. If you are already talking to them and things seem normal, other teens might not fear walking in and joining the party. If you can't manufacture "first arrivers," have a task for the first teens to help with in some way: separating, unloading, rearranging—anything—and talk to them while this is going on. Ask them to find a radio station that they like. The music will fill the empty space and up the "cool" factor. One LST schedules teen programs on Saturday afternoons following her Teen Advisory Council meetings. This works for several reasons: the teens picked the time of the advisory council meeting, they are more likely to stay longer for something than to come back at a different day and time, and parents are more likely to want to drop off teens for two to three hours than for one hour. What errands can you do in one hour? That parent or older sibling usually ends up waiting around the library, and after about forty-five minutes they give their teen the "we-have-to-go" look. But two to three hours, depending on the program, means a stop for groceries, time spent at another child's soccer game, or a visit with another adult.

The perfect setting for teen programming has an accessible, teen-oriented collection and an area where teens can be themselves without stares and comments from curmudgeonly adults. See what you already have on your side and make it work for you. Most libraries have a separate meeting room that you can use for programming and community meetings, so bring in carts of new books and magazines from the collection, play music, bring food, and, if possible, employ teens to decorate. Other libraries have no separate room, and the teen collection is surrounded by a seating area of its own. During business hours, hold teen programs that lend themselves to the space, but schedule more animated programs for after hours so teens can be themselves and you don't have to worry about complaints.

When and Where Do You Do Teen Programs?

You need to find what works for your teens, your library, and your community. Trial and error, teen involvement, and planning can give you many answers. Look at your programming from different points of view. There's the school year point of view, which focuses on days off, early dismissal days, holiday breaks, and the sports schedule, and there's the community point of view, which focuses on church youth nights and other church activities as well as any other events aimed at teens in your community. You will go crazy if you try to pick a day or time when nothing else is going on, but it doesn't hurt to be aware of other activities in the community. You may be able to add onto what another organization is doing, or you may need to schedule around it. You may also realize the conflicting activity is aimed at a small group of teens, and there won't be a conflict. Ask teens for preferred times or for days that are typically bad for them. During the school year, a generally bad time for all library programming for teens is Friday, when high school teens are heading to sporting events; everyone is happy to be out of school, and the library is the last thing on their minds. During the summer, the opposite may be true. Try the same program in several different time slots. You may hit on one that works better than the other. Don't get discouraged if the secret to the perfect time slot for programming eludes you. Do the best you can and continue to try new dates/times until you find something that works.

> Remember that programming for teens is not the exclusive property of public libraries. A lot of people in the community do teen programming, so look for partners who are also aiming to get teens involved and provide meaningful opportunities for teens to be engaged with their peers in a safe, developmentally appropriate environment.

It is also just as important to ask yourself when a program should start and when it should end. In most cases the answer rests on the length of time it will take a teen to accomplish the activity or task provided. A common time for a program is one hour. Be sure to factor in a little socializing time at the beginning to act as an icebreaker so teens have an opportunity to find out where everyone goes to school or talk about the newest movie. Also incorporate time for food and drinks in the beginning of the program and end the program with a little more socializing time, which might include talking about books, new music, or what they liked about the program. If you are practicing a craft, keep track of the time it takes you to learn the new skill and then factor in time for five to ten teens doing the same, with you assisting a few of them.

When you are planning, promoting, and implementing your teen programs, you should be mindful of the habits of parents. Most parents automatically take their young children to the library for story time because their parents took them to story time. But if the library was not on the parents' radar for programs or activities when they were teens, then they will probably not automatically think of taking their teenagers to the library for programs. Educating or training parents to connect the library with teenagers is our job. That connection happens at the reference desk, during checkout, during adult programs, on the Web page, while speaking to the PTA, on back-to-school nights, and any other time or place you encounter parents. This education of adults should include parents, but also teachers, youth group leaders, counselors, coaches, and, of course, other library staff—adults who are in a position to disseminate information to teens and their parents.

Providing the same program at multiple locations is a great idea and the benefit is twofold: it will allow teens who really enjoyed the craft to return and be your expert and it allows staff to share lessons learned, giving you the chance to refine your program by changing what didn't work, adding whatever you forgot or needed more of, and getting different ideas and reactions from the teens who attended.

How Do You Promote a Teen Program?

See Chapter 10 for promotion ideas.

If Only One Teen Shows Up, Do You Cancel the Program?

Absolutely not. That one teen made a decision to show up for the program, so consider it your chance to ensure that you not only carry out the program but begin developing (or continue to develop) a meaningful relationship with this teen. So often library programs are judged based on how many people showed up. Unfortunately, this way of thinking works directly against those of us who work with teens. With teen programming you need to change the way you think about the numbers game. Realize that teens are choosing to come to your program. Let's go over that again—teens are *choosing* to come to your program. So what does that really mean for your numbers? It means when you look at the 50 toddlers who are present for a sing-along at your library, those 50 two-year-olds were put into the car and brought to the library by adults. Those children may have had a great time at the program, but was it an independent choice? Probably not. Teenagers make the choice to come to the library and attend your program. They find a way to get to the library, and after the program they will have to find a way to get home. Some of them have been awake since 5:00 a.m. when their bus picked them up for school, and some will not sleep again until midnight after finishing hours of homework and chores. So keep this in mind when you plan a program and only one teen shows up. More than likely, that one teen made a conscious decision to attend your program, not because a parent strapped him or her in the car seat to travel to the library but because he or she really wanted to be a part of whatever you had planned that day. Also keep in mind that that one teen has friends, whom the teen will more than likely bring along next time he or she wants to do something at the library.

Back to the numbers game: Also keep in mind that high attendance statistics do not always equal a great program. If you have a fantasy book discussion group and five teens show up, think for a minute—five is not a lot, but would you really want more? How would a discussion go with 10, 15, or 20 teens? It probably wouldn't go—the discussion would get out of control, not everybody would get the chance to talk or have their opinion heard, and the next time they might be less likely to come back. Ultimately, what matters is whether the goals and objectives of the program were met, not how many teens were in attendance. Go back to the fantasy book discussion group—what are the objectives? Promoting fantasy books, giving teens a chance to talk with other teens about the books they love, helping teens express their thoughts and views on books and other issues, providing a little socialization, building decision-making skills, and practicing listening and interacting with others. For teens, these objectives are best met in a smaller group; teens will be comfortable expressing their opinions among people they know, and the LST will be better able to facilitate the group and get to know each teen.

Do small numbers at teen programs mean it was unsuccessful? Probably not, but be prepared for people to use numbers as the measure of success. A great way to even out this disparity is to begin to keep an anecdote file called "More Than Just a Number." This document of anecdotes, or stories, will help you define your success. These anecdotes should be shared with administration in addition to your monthly program statistics so that everyone can see the difference you are making in the lives of teens in your library on a daily basis.

Word of mouth is the ultimate marketing tool when it comes to actively promoting teen programs.

What Do You Do If You Host a Program and No One Shows Up?

Chalk it up to experience. It has happened to the best of us and it is bound to happen again. The goal is to make sure your tenacity and perseverance remain intact. There may be a hundred reasons why the program was not as successful as you had hoped. The important thing is to keep trying. In fact, you might figure out the factor that got in the way last time. Ask the teens who do show up to a program what else they might like to do at the library, and you might be surprised at their answers. Remember that each program is not an end; it is a means to gather more input from teens about future programs. The most important thing is to learn from mistakes and to evaluate what went right *and* what went wrong with every program. Personally, remember that an LST who excels at teen programming is one who takes risks and is persistent.

How Do You Evaluate a Teen Program?

Perhaps the first step in evaluating teen programs is to look inward and adjust your expectations. The clown show organized for hundreds of preschool- and elementary-age kids is not analogous to the small book discussion group for teens. If anything, those huge summer children's programs are the exception, not the rule. Classes that help seniors learn to surf the Net, show parents how to read to their babies, or teach genealogists how to use the library's collection are the "norm" for public library programming. Our bosses want numbers, but LSTs need to work with administration (and, for that matter, other staff) to advocate a different measurement for teen programs. In a sense, the main number we need to focus on is always the same: 40. How did the program build one or more of the 40 developmental assets in young people?

Surveys and written evaluations can get you the raw data you might need for a report, but it can miss the heart of the program and what the teens who attended thought. Teens will answer the questions put in front of them, but if you don't ask the right questions you may never receive the most useful comments. Adults don't want to answer hundred-question evaluations, and teens don't either. To actually get something out of online or paper surveys that ask teens for feedback about programming and other library services, you need to develop a short and sweet list of questions. If you ask for more than yes or no, which you should, then make sure your questions are asking for information you really want and will use. The two most important pieces of information to capture in a teen program evaluation are how they found out about the program and if they have other suggestions for future programs. Although adults might answer these questions with no problem, chances are good you may get many "I dunno" and "no" answers from teens. To get more specific answers, provide a list of possible answers, for example: "How did you find out about the program?" (a) a friend, (b) a parent, (c) school, (d) library Web site, (e) library MySpace page, (f) a flyer, (g) other. For a question about possible future programs, also provide a list of options like (a) open mic night, (b) jewelry making and other crafts, (c) book group, (d) manga/anime club, (d) technology programs (graphic design, Web design, etc.), (f) other. At the very least, you will find out what advertising avenues are working (or not working) and the level of interest in different categories of programs; at the most, you may get suggestions for other programs you haven't considered.

Some teens are more comfortable talking about what they experienced than writing about it. Keep this in mind when you evaluate a program. Consider doing verbal evaluations (also known as "exit interviews") with a few teen participants after each teen program. Remember that the more you engage a teen in discussion, the more likely you are to get solid information about what they liked or didn't like about the program. Follow-up questions are also very important when conducting verbal evaluations. Consider the following exchange:

LST: What did you like about the poetry coffee house?
TEEN: The poetry.
LST: What else?
TEEN: I thought all the different people were cool.
LST: Did you like being able to read your own poetry or listening to other people's poetry?
TEEN: Listening to other people's.
LST: Would you come to a poetry workshop where teenagers could share their poetry and get feedback?
TEEN: No, I don't write poetry.
LST: Would you come back for a poetry slam that was a competition?
TEEN: Yeah, maybe. Could we rap?

This teen isn't interested in a workshop-type poetry program, does not think rapping is considered poetry, is comfortable with the idea of performing in public, wouldn't be scared off by a competition, and is content listening to others perform. Other programs that might appeal to this teen are a poetry slam, open mic night/karaoke, battle of the bands, comedy improv, or a gathering of local musicians talking about songwriting. When doing verbal evaluations, provide teens with examples or scenarios and ask their opinions to narrow down what their answers mean for you and the library. It may take a little longer than a paper or online survey, but giving teens a chance to follow up on their answers will result in a better evaluation.

The other anecdotal type of evaluation is not as invasive; it involves eavesdropping and watching body language. If teens are having a truly rotten time, it will be hard to hide. And truthfully, most teens wouldn't go to the trouble of hiding it—they would leave or disengage from the activity. Watch how the teens interact with one another, the activity, and the LST. Do they stick around after the program is technically over? Do they ask for it to continue? Do they ask when they can do it again? When parents come to collect them, do they want to go? Do the teens explain what they did, give the play-by-play, when talking to parents or friends? Do they mention the program to other staff at any point? Do they remember you because of the program the next time they are in the library? Do they come back to other programs or to the library in general? This type of evaluation is critical for teen programming, especially since most teens are not accustomed to being asked for their honest opinions by an adult in a position of authority.

> When it comes to teen programming, success is sweet, but the simple truth is that failure is a better teacher.

> Evaluation of any teen program should be twofold: by you and the teens who attend the program.

(CD) **See Tool 27. Staff Evaluation of Teen Program**

(CD) **See Tool 34. Teen Evaluation of Program**

Hands down, evaluating a program can be one of the hardest things to do when it comes to programming for teens. However, evaluating a program can only make it stronger the next time, and with every lesson comes a little more success the next time around. In addition to self-reflection and asking teens to help you evaluate a program, get feedback from another staff person whom you trust to help you with a program and whom you know will be candid. Also consider asking a teen you have known for a while for his or her opinion. One LST uses a staff evaluation after programs that affect staff beyond those who helped with the program. For example, a "Battle of the Bands" may affect circulation staff, information staff, and branch managers, not to mention the maintenance staff, especially if you blow the power grid. Other staff members may not have much knowledge of the program, but you can get a feel for the level of disruption in the building. This can go a long way toward good staff relations, and staff members may see some ways to make your program better. They may even be willing to help with future programs.

Finally, remember that even programs that do everything right are still not slam-dunk, guaranteed successes. A lot of obstacles go hand in hand with programming for teens. Let's acknowledge that we won't top the numbers of the people doing children's programs; more important, we don't want to do so. Teen programming is about quality, not quantity, and your job is to develop programs for and with teens that encourage teens to get involved.

What Are Examples of Successful Teen Programs?

At workshops, we always allow the audience to share successful program ideas. There isn't enough time to get the entire rundown. Sometimes there is time for nothing more than a TV Guide–style summary. With this in mind, look again at Figure 9.1, which includes some programs based on what we've heard on the road, read about on electronic discussion lists, or learned about in the professional literature. In some cases, there is really nothing more than an idea or subject area; in others, we've provided a little more detail. These programs represent a sample of programs being done around the country, urban and rural, large systems and one-branch libraries.

Conclusion

Programming for teens isn't easy, but when it works, it's worth it. Sometimes teens will value a program because they learned a skill, sometimes because they created a craft. While crafts don't directly tie in to the larger mission of most libraries, they do tie in to something just as important: providing teens with an opportunity to engage in meaningful activities. Are crafts meaningful? Are book discussion groups meaningful? The fact that a teen chooses to participate gives that activity meaning. Programming allows LSTs to turn our core values into activities that teens will value.

Sources Cited in This Chapter

1. Young Adult Library Services Association. 2008. "Teen Read Week 2008." Available: www.ala.org/ala/yalsa/teenreading/trw/trw2008/index.cfm (accessed July 28, 2008).
2. Young Adult Library Services Association. 2008. "Teen Tech Week News." Available: www.ala.org/ala/yalsa/teentechweek/ttw08/ttw.cfm (accessed July 28, 2008).
3. American Library Association. 2008. "Banned Books Week Celebrating the Freedom to Read September 27–October 4, 2008." Available: www.ala .org/ala/oif/bannedbooksweek/bannedbooksweek.cfm (accessed July 28, 2008).
4. Free Comic Book Day. n.d. [Home page.] Available: www.freecomicbook day.com/ (accessed July 28, 2008).
5. Collaborative Summer Library Program. n.d. [Home page.] Available: www.cslpreads.org/index.html (accessed July 29, 2008).
6. Daniel, Heidi. E-mail to author. August 28, 2008.

Recommended Sources for Further Reading

Alessio, Amy. 2008. *Excellence in Library Services to Young Adults*, 5th ed. Chicago: American Library Association.

Alessio, Amy, and Kimberly Patton. 2006. *A Year of Programs for Teens*. Chicago: American Library Association.

Coleman, Tina, and Peggie Llanes. 2008. *The Hipster Librarian's Guide to Teen Craft Projects*. Chicago: American Library Association.

Edwards, Kirsten. 2002. *Teen Library Events: A Month-by-Month Guide*. Westport, CT: Greenwood Press.

Frew, Julie, and Lettie Haver. 2008. "Opening Your Doors to Teens: Creating Sustainable Young Adult Programs." *Indiana Libraries* 27, no 1: 38–41.

Honnold, RoseMary. 2002. *101+ Teen Programs That Work*. New York: Neal-Schuman.

Honnold, RoseMary 2005. *More Teen Programs That Work*. New York: Neal-Schuman.

Jones, Ella. 2009. *Start to Finish YA Programs: Hip-Hop Symposiums, Summer Reading Programs, Virtual Tours, Poetry Slams, Teen Advisory Boards and More*. New York: Neal-Schuman.

Kan, Katherine L. 2006. *Sizzling Summer Reading Programs for Young Adults*, 2nd ed. Chicago: American Library Association.

Kunzel, Bonnie, and Constance Hardesty. 2006. *The Teen Centered Book Club: Readers into Leaders*. Westport, CT: Libraries Unlimited.

Ott, Valerie A. 2006. *Teen Programs with Punch: A Month-by-Month Guide*. Westport, CT: Libraries Unlimited.

Spaces and Promotion

Collections and programs are products, but if you want teens to use them you'll need to promote them effectively. Promoting programs, not to mention core services, is something most libraries struggle with, not just the LST. We put out the flyer and then we hope that teens show up. Unfortunately that's not promotion or marketing; it is wishful thinking. Similarly, we build a collection and believe just having it is enough. Maybe it was enough before there were chain and online bookstores like Barnes and Noble and Amazon, but just having books on the shelf is not enough anymore. Thus, the past decade has seen a renaissance in young adult spaces, in both smaller suburb libraries and large urban libraries. Additionally, librarians have embraced urban sociologist Ray Oldenburg's concept of the "third place" in the past couple of years, striving to make the library a neutral space for teens that is neither home nor school where young people can meet friends, study, listen to music, and basically just kick back and hang out.[1]

Whether it is a new building (Loft at ImaginOn in Charlotte, North Carolina), a joint use facility between a library and a local youth-serving organization (Palos Verdes Library District's "Annex," located in a retail area neighboring the library), or a repurposed area in an existing library (TeenSpot in Cincinnati, Ohio), libraries are making a commitment to teens by creating spaces that specifically meet the educational and recreational needs of teens. We get teens to attend our programs through promotion; we get them to use our collection through creating attractive spaces.

Libraries get more money every year, more books, more programs, and sometimes more staff, but rarely more space; thus, space is perhaps the single most valuable commodity available to LSTs.

What Are the Elements of Successful Teen Spaces?

You must first realize that every library already has a young adult space—the entire library. Teens use libraries holistically and even the best, "coolest," and newest teen space isn't going to serve all teens. While in many ways a secondary school library is, in and of itself, a young adult space, there is still work to be done. Many of the design elements found in the public library teen spaces will work just as well in a school.

In the public library, teens are all over the place. The purpose of a teen space is to centralize the recreational, informational, and educational resources for teens. This means more than just a rack of paperbacks, some bean bag chairs, or a neon sign. It also means more than just a fiction collection. In large libraries, teen collections should include nonfiction, music, DVDs, books on CD or MP3, magazines, comic books, and graphic novels. Teen spaces should be comfortable, set apart from the children's section, and easy to navigate. They should also be set up to accommodate teen users, including spaces for group work, lounging, sitting on the floor, or private time within the confines of the teen space as a whole.

Teen spaces will vary from library to library, but every library needs one. Like a teen who wants his or her own room, this is about identity—one of the most basic developmental needs. However, there are other benefits:

- A teen space will help reduce challenges.

- A teen space can become a focal point for services, programs, and recruiting volunteers.

- A teen space sends a message, if done right, by blowing away the stereotypes of libraries, and librarians, by presenting a fresh, fun, and flexible environment.

The elements to remember when creating a teen space are numerous but important. They include:

- **Americans with Disabilities Act (ADA).** Make sure when planning your teen area that you understand the ADA requirements regarding accessibility. Aim to build access into the design of the area as integral, not as an afterthought. ADA regulations provide merely the minimum requirements, so these guidelines should be the starting, not the ending, point.

- **Ambience.** Colors matter. Too much overwhelms and too little is visually unexciting. Comfortable furniture also goes a long way in creating a welcoming ambience. However, ambience is about more than just furniture and a coat of paint. Don't throw out a few beanbag chairs and paint a wall bright blue and assume the teen vibe is now present. Ambience is about creating a welcoming physical environment, but it is just as much about attitude. You can have the hippest teen space ever, but if the staff isn't welcoming, then none of that matters.

- **Art.** Like music and technology, art is a staple of the teen years. Therefore it makes sense for the library to be a great place for hanging teen art, hosting teen art shows, and even providing a space for teens to meet and work on art projects. A teen-created

> Building a new teen space? Don't forget to ask teens in your community what they'd like to see in "their" space.

mural is also a nice way to brighten up your space while at the same time sending out a message to teens that this is their space. The William K. Sandford Town Library in Loudonville, New York, transformed a small study area in their teen room into the Got Art? Gallery that features work by local teens.[2]

- **Branding.** The big question is always do you call it the teen area, the young adult area, or something else. It depends. If you have done all of these things, especially youth involvement during the planning process, then the name is irrelevant. The space will have an identity based on how you plan it rather than on what you call it. Lots of libraries spend time developing names, often involving contests among teens, and a name like "TeenSpot," or "The HYPE," or "The Loft at ImaginOn" does establish the space as a "brand" that can be leveraged in other promotions.

- **Collection development.** You can build the most beautiful teen area in the world, but if your collection development isn't just as responsive, teens might come to hang out, but they won't find anything to hang on to that will make them want to return.

- **Comfort.** There are many reasons teens hang out at the local coffee place: relaxing atmosphere, comfortable furniture, wireless access, snacks, and no shushing. There is no reason the library cannot offer those same amenities as well as staff who can help teens with their homework, recommend new music sites, suggest the newest graphic novel, and help them design their MySpace page.

- **Community space.** In addition to the teen area, LSTs need to be advocates for a community space within the library. Not only can this space be used by all library departments; it will provide LSTs with an extra place to carry out teen programming.

- **Computers.** A library without computers is pretty much unheard of these days. However, many libraries group all of the computers together and then get upset when teens "take over" the space. Your best bet is to include teen-only computers in both your design and budget for a teen space. If you are redesigning an existing space and there are no wires, consider laptops and wireless access. Even if you have wired computers, providing laptops for in-library use will expand your services.

- **Displays.** There is an array of subliterature about library displays, so there is little to add other than these words: You don't have to do it yourself. Unless you are a creative dynamo with artistic talent, visual merchandising background, and a lot of free time, let teen volunteers take over this task. They can do it just as well as you and then you can spend time developing programs, doing outreach, and building the collection.

- **Food and drink.** At home most teens manage to read, use a computer, listen to music, snack and sip without spilling a drop.

Libraries, however, have had long-standing prohibitions against such activities. I am sure you have better things to do with your time than be the "Doritos Police," so I recommend your library adopt a more user-friendly, flexible set of rules for food and drinks that stipulate no eating or drinking near the computers. While this may not fly in all libraries, experience tells us that the libraries that do allow their patrons to eat and drink in their spaces spend less time confiscating contraband snacks and sodas and more time building relationships with their patrons.

- **Fun.** Perhaps the most compelling reason to do any, or all, of these things is simply to try to make the library a "fun" place to hang out and spend time.

- **Library promotion.** Walls and kiosk space, the ends of shelves, the insides of shelves, and maybe even the floor could be used to promote library programs and services. Try to get your Friends group to purchase a good multipurpose display fixture, preferably with a slat wall. You can also have teens paint bookends, design murals for inside shelves, or create an original corkboard from recycled corks for your weekly "What's happening today?" display.

- **Light.** The lighting in most libraries is pretty substandard. In the young adult areas, which often get tucked in an alcove, it is even worse. You can build it, but if they don't see it, then they won't come. Putting the teen area near a window will allow natural light to enter and it will provide the opportunity to see and be seen. The Phoenix teen space's fiber-optic ceiling effects is the ideal. This may be unattainable, but it does remind us that ceiling space is perhaps the most overlooked and underused part of most libraries, especially teen areas.

- **Location.** It is easier to name the locations in a library where a young adult area does not belong: next to the children's room, circulation desk, reference area, or quiet study/reading area. In addition to a location with traffic, the location must afford some privacy, yet at the same time allow staff to observe the area, for safety and customer service. It's also important to acknowledge that the teen area doesn't have to be a traditional space in the library. In the Waupaca Area Public Library in Waupaca, Wisconsin, the teen area is actually a 1,400-square-foot space underground aptly named the "Best Cellar," with booth seating, a gaming area, a large-screen television, sound domes, and a 12-foot computer bar.[3]

- **Magazines.** Teen magazines seem like a no-brainer, but many teen library collections only include a handful of teen periodicals. In addition to the standard teen periodicals like *Seventeen* and *Teen Ink*, consider offering titles that address topics of interest to teens including music (*Rolling Stone*, *Guitar World*), sports (*Sports Illustrated*, *Skateboarding*, *Wrestling USA*, *American*

Cheerleader), humor (*MAD Magazine*), gaming (*Electronic Gaming Monthly, Nintendo Power, Game Pro*), pop culture (*US Weekly, People*), teen celebrities (*J-14, Tiger Beat*), fashion (*Elle Girl, Cosmo Girl*), and popular comic books (*Exiles, Astonishing X-Men, Captain America*).

- **Merchandising.** Displays are not merchandising; they are tools of merchandising. Merchandising is as much a philosophy as it is a practice. Paperbacks are the cornerstones of merchandising because of their size. You can cram more of them attractively into a small area, and their covers are often more attractive than their hardback relatives. Whether we want to admit it or not, teens do judge a book by its cover, so shelve books face out whenever possible. If you look at the vast literature on merchandising, you will realize that most teens seek books rather than a book, so make sure they can browse your collection easily and that there are various displays throughout the library, both timely (horror for Halloween, Banned Books, Printz Award winners) and topical (new manga, poetry, not your mama's "classics," and books by teens for teens), to help increase your circulation of titles teens might not see if they have to look through every book in your collection.

- **Multitasking.** Today's teens have been raised with unfettered access to technology, including computers, the Internet, cell phones, and PDAs—sometimes all at the same time. Multitasking with all these technologies is a phenomenon of the Net Generation, and many grown-ups have little understanding about how teens can be doing their homework while at the same time listening to music, instant messaging with friends, and watching television. Whether you agree with it or not, this is how many teens do homework, so it is a good idea to make sure your library space for teens not only accepts this behavior but provides headphones.

- **Music.** Teens and music often go hand in hand, so it makes sense that new-generation library spaces for teens incorporate music into their design and service. Moving away from the idea that libraries need to be exclusively noise-free at all times, many libraries now play ambient music, especially in their teen spaces. In keeping with the idea that music is an important component of teen culture, it's important that teen spaces in libraries provide options for listening to, sharing, and recording music including the availability of headphones, computers with CD burners (with appropriate copyright notices posted all over them), and Internet access to popular music sites. Providing access to music in your library's teen space can be as high tech as sound pods or as low tech as providing charging pods and/or cords to charge iPods and other MP3 players.

- **Passive youth involvement.** In addition to involving youth directly in focus groups or on advisory councils when gathering

> When in doubt, weed it! Research shows that too many books crammed on a shelf is a turnoff for a reader searching casually for something interesting to read.

information about building and maintaining a successful teen area, there has to be a place for passive youth involvement. This could be a simple suggestion box (make sure you also have a space next to the suggestion box where library staff can respond to the questions or requests so teens know their suggestions and opinions are being heard) or "Teen Picks" cards, whereby teens can recommend their favorite books and other materials to library patrons.

- **Photo wall.** Sometimes the best advertising you can do is put up a bunch of photos of successful teen programs in your library. This will not only help you promote future programs, but it will also provide a level of ownership for your regular teens who will see themselves in the display. If you take photos on a regular basis for teens' social networking sites, ask for permission to keep some of the best ones for this always-evolving photo display. These photos can be hung on a bulletin board, be framed and hung on a wall, or decoupaged onto a piece of plywood for a more permanent piece of art for your teen space.

- **Plugs and power.** If you have ever been stuck sitting on the floor, waiting in a line next to the trash can at the airport because you need to charge your cell phone and there is only one outlet for the 150 passengers waiting to board, you know how frustrating it can be to be stuck somewhere with no plugs or power options. The library can be like that for teens, especially when they are doing homework after school or working on a project over the weekend. As you plan your teen space remember that more is better when it comes to outlets now that most teens are walking around with a cell phone, iPod, and laptop computer in their backpacks, all of which need to be charged regularly.

- **Post the house rules.** Consider having the teens who helped plan your teen space help set the rules for the area. Also remember that this is not the time for a laundry list of rules and prohibitions. Hit the highlights, be succinct, and be clear in your expectations of your teen patrons. It's also a good idea to focus on what teens can do as opposed to what they cannot do in the library. Simple really is key. The Loft at ImaginOn in Charlotte, North Carolina, has three rules: Respect yourself. Respect each other. Respect the space.

- **Privacy.** The "Do not disturb!" sign on a teen's bedroom door is a pretty universal symbol of adolescent angst. Teens like and need privacy, but it's important to design your teen space with a balance: booth seating, comfortale couches in a circle, and a computer bar interspersed with nooks for studying or solitary chairs placed strategically away from crowd for a little independent reading.

- **Put the books with the teens.** When teens enter a library, particularly boys, they make a beeline for the computers. Some go to MySpace, some to Runescape, some to check e-mail, and others to surf the Web looking for personal information. In other words, teens use computers to build their personal cultures, to explore their interests, or both. But while they are on the computers, where are the titles that might help them in their quest? On a shelf half a room away. Place books near the computers, printers, and copiers. Place them on tables and chairs where teens gather. Place books by the phone, checkout desk, and other high teen-traffic areas. The worst that can happen is that the books don't get checked out and need to be reshelved.

- **Quiet space.** It is not in the teen space and certainly not near a service desk, but there does need to be a quiet place for teens to study. Everything about teens' multitasking and being able to talk is true, but never 100 percent of the time. Sometimes, especially around high school exams and the PSAT, what teens need more than anything else is a quiet place to study because many don't have that at home and libraries are their only option. If you have an unoccupied meeting room, consider engaging volunteers to help you staff it so teens can have a quiet place to study after school or during the busiest hours of the weekend. Post signs to let everyone know this is a teen-only quiet zone.

- **Relaxed rules.** The most important part of a successful teen area in a library is not the computers or the comfortable furniture but the tolerance level of the library staff.

- **Rules plus.** A few dozen public libraries around the country have created teen-only spaces in their library. In ImaginOn, the Public Library of Charlotte and Mecklenburg County's Youth Library, there is a designated teen space on the second floor called the Loft. As you enter this area, a sign reads "The Loft is for teens 12–18 only. If you are under the age of 12 please visit the children's library downstairs. If you are over the age of 18, please visit the parent lounge or the Main Library located a block and a half down from ImaginOn." If you have the luxury of a separate library space for teens within your building, consider maintaining it as a developmentally appropriate, teen-only zone in your library.

- **Shelving fixtures.** When it comes to shelving in your teen area, think outside of the box. Consider installing slat wall shelving, zigzag shelving, book display units, and hanging periodical shelving to store and display books and other library materials.

- **Signage.** Although we often lament the fact that teens don't read signs, if you make it big enough and hang it in an open area that is hard to miss, teens will take notice. Aim for big, bright, and bilingual. Also, be sure to avoid library jargon and teen slang. Finally, remember that signage is more than just a sign at

> A teen area is not just about the physical space but about an "emotional space" where teens can behave like teens.

the entrance of the teen area. You need directional signage throughout the building that will direct teens to their area.

- **Study space.** The pedagogy of teaching has changed dramatically over the past couple of decades, from teacher as guru to guide by the side. The idea has been to move away from lecture and memorization (except for those standardized tests) and move toward group work and shared learning experiences. If you want teens to congregate in the teen area of your library to do homework or work on school projects with other teens, your library's teen space needs to accommodate these tasks, including computers where multiple users can work together, tables for spreading out work, comfortable chairs for reading, and also individual spaces where teens can do homework or study on their own.

- **Technology.** These days, access to technology is one of the core services libraries provide to users. This, coupled with teens as digital natives (having grown up with computers and technology at their fingertips), means that LSTs need to not only embrace technology but be an early adopter of all things technical in order to stay current and relevant to teens.

- **Think like 7-Eleven.** When you go into a convenience store, to get to milk, you must go past the candy, chips, and soda. Using that retail mind-set when deciding what belongs in the teen area, consider housing the study guides and classics in close proximity to the graphic novels, teen magazines, or teen computers. This provides a "reason" for teens who may not normally find the young adult area, perhaps because they are not regular library users or avid readers, to visit the teen collection and be exposed to all that a strong young adult collection can offer.

- **Traffic.** Start by looking at the traffic patterns of your library: Where do teens enter the building? Where do they leave? Where do they congregate when they are in the library? What areas do they avoid? Build your teen space within these traffic lines so that teens know a separate space exists just for them. Library developers and architects often build a teen area in the back of the building, with the idea that hidden equals private. Unfortunately, hidden also means out of sight, and out of sight often means out of mind. If teens don't know a separate space just for them exists, chances are good that they will not use it.

- **Youth involvement.** While this is last on the list, it is first and foremost as an element of success for developing great teen spaces. From planning to implementation, teens should be involved in all aspects of the project, including choosing the furniture, designing the layout, naming the place, and even maintaining the space. When teens have this kind of opportunity to be involved, ownership is a natural by-product, and getting

Through well-thought-out, forward-thinking facilities planning, committed collaborations, and open-minded adults, libraries will become increasingly important and significant to teenagers instead of becoming irrelevant places of the past.

—Kimberly Bolan, *Teen Spaces: The Step-by-Step Library Makeover* teens to feel ownership of the space is the primary key to success. Remember that it is not helpful just to say, "What do you want?" to a group of teens who have no experience in picking fixtures for a library; instead, it is your job to facilitate and guide teens on the choices available. Allow them to dream, but if you don't provide some guidance, then you'll get disappointment rather than excitement.

Whether you are planning a new space or redesigning an old one, these elements of success should enable you and your teens to create a place of their own in any school or public library.

What About Virtual Library Spaces for Teens?

Creating original and innovative virtual library spaces for teens (including teen library Web sites, blogs, forums, and presences on social networking sites) is just as important as creating actual physical spaces where teens feel comfortable spending time. Although this topic is addressed more completely in the technology chapter, it is important to acknowledge the value of a virtual library presence for teens since a high percentage of young people spend time online every day. According to a national survey of teenagers conducted by the Pew Internet & American Life Project in 2007, 93 percent of young people between the ages of 12 and 17 are online, 89 percent say the Internet helps make their life easier, and 55 percent use online social networking sites. According to the same survey, 48 percent of teens visit social networking sites daily.[4] Taking these numbers into consideration, creating a virtual space for your library will not only help you reach teens in your community who might not otherwise utilize the library, but it will also serve as a promotional tool for sharing information about the library's services, programs, and materials for teens.

How Do You Go About Creating a Plan for Promoting Your Library's Services for Teens?

A key part of having a successful library program for teens is developing a promotional plan. Promoting a library's services to teens is a twofold process: sell the idea (the library is a helpful and entertaining place where teens are welcome) and then sell the programs and collection. An attractive teen space within the library is a nonverbal message to teens that they are welcome, but in order to get teens to attend programs and use library services you are going to need to be more proactive in your promotional planning.

First, get every staff member involved. For the best output from your promotional efforts you and your staff need to be excited about your

> A teen program is not a success if nobody knows it exists.

library's services for teens. This does not mean wearing clown makeup and doing cartwheels every time you mention a teen program, but it does mean being knowledgeable about what's going on, being enthusiastic, and being friendly to anyone who comes in looking for information. If library staff are not excited or enthused about the program why should you expect a teen to be?

Second, remember that it takes more than putting a flyer on the table to market a teen program. Flyers don't hurt and they are great to give to adults, the newspaper, radio, or cable access station to use in promoting the program, but flyers on a table is the beginning, not the end, of promotion. Don't waste time printing flyers; instead, spend time building relationships with teens and encouraging them to attend a program and bring a friend. Word of mouth is always your best bet when it comes to promoting teen programs.

Third, use your resources. Promote your upcoming programs and special events on your library's Web site, Facebook site, or MySpace page. Send out informational e-mails about upcoming events to other youth-serving organizations and offer to mail them flyers to distribute about upcoming events. If they are also on a social networking site, ask them if they would consider linking to your event blurb or library page. If your library system has many branches, make sure all branches know about upcoming programs so they can help you promote the event. Don't forget to contact local schools to ask for help promoting the library's services to teens, and remember that those flyers you create to promote in-house should also be posted out in the community in places where teens frequent, like bus stops or subways, convenience stores, the mall, and local teen hangouts like the pizza place and movie theater.

Finally, create promotional materials that will be of interest to teens. If you are a one-person department, or what Renee Vaillancourt dubbed "a YA lone ranger,"[5] you may be responsible for creating the advertising materials for your programs. Many computer programs can make this easy work, but it's even easier to engage a teen volunteer to help with the design and layout of flyers and online content. If getting the teen on the computer is not possible, let him or her choose graphics, colors, and fonts—anything that will give your promotional items a teen touch. Once you have engaged a teen, remember to be specific about your intent and what the end product should be. The last thing you want to do is not use a promotional material created by a teen because it does not provide accurate information or does not represent the library appropriately. Whether you or a teen is designing the promotional copy, remember to stay away from graphics featuring "teens" or an artist's interpretation of "teens" because it may become dated quickly. The best thing to do is stick with interesting color palettes and original images that incorporate simple elements of design, like bold shapes, silhouettes, and lines. Think about the most popular brands and the symbols they use, usually not a person but an object or shape, such as Apple's trademark white fruit, Target's bull's-eye, the Nike swoosh, or McDonald's unmistakable initial logo.

What Are Some Best Practices for Promoting Your Library's Materials and Events for Teens?

In addition to the distribution of promotional materials in print and online, there are many ways to promote your library's teen space, collection, and upcoming events and special programs. Here are some things to keep in mind when searching for promotional outlets, planning promotional materials, and developing strategic partnerships that will help you promote your library's teen events:

- **Be a good host.** Encourage community organizations that cater to teens, but lack meeting space, to hold events at the library. Ask, in return, that they pass out flyers for upcoming teen events and/or allow someone from the library to speak briefly to their group about what the library has to offer teens.

- **Be bilingual.** Whenever possible and applicable, make sure that programs are promoted to your bilingual communities, via their primary language newspapers, radio stations, television stations, and online venues. If there is a majority second language spoken in your community, translate your flyers into this language or create bilingual promotional materials.

- **Billboards.** Very expensive, but doable and very effective, especially if placed near teen locations such as skate parks, schools, and malls.

- **Book reviews.** Work with the local paper to publish teen book reviews. If you are in a small market and have trouble getting the newspaper to cover your events, there is a solution. Invite one of the editors to get involved in a teen activity, such as judging a writing contest, so they have a vested interest.

- **Build transportation money into grants.** Transportation for teens is often an issue. If money is the issue, include funding in your programming grant to pay for bus fares or subway tickets.

- **Buy.** Purchase ads in school yearbooks, student newspapers, and school district newsletters to promote teen services to students, parents, and teachers.

- **Cable access television.** While it is true that hardly anyone deliberately sits down to watch a cable access show, teens flipping through the channels might stop if they see a show featuring other teens. Once you have permission, consider videotaping teen programs, booktalks, book discussion groups, and author visits. Include a crawler at the bottom of the screen about upcoming teen events and your library's Web site or social networking site URL. Also remember that many school districts have their own cable access stations.

- **Community.** Get out there and promote the library throughout the community. Participate in community events like information fairs and parades and encourage members of your teen advisory council to also get involved. Participating in something like a parade is not only an excellent promotional opportunity; it raises community awareness about the library as a community resource, and it's an excellent opportunity for youth involvement.

- **Date due receipts.** If your library's circulation system issues a receipt to patrons at checkout, talk to your IT department about printing a brief, teen-centered message on each receipt several times a year (like wishing everyone a Happy Teen Tech Week in March or a Happy Teen Read Week in October). This way everyone who checks out a book will see that the library not only offers programs and services to teens but also cares enough to share this information with patrons of all ages.

- **E-mail distribution lists.** When teens attend an event, gather e-mail addresses. If the event is ticketed, or if teens are registering to win a prize during the event, include a space for their e-mail address on the ticket or prize entry form. Use these addresses to create an e-mail distribution list for promoting upcoming events. Remember to include a notice at the bottom of e-mails sent to list members letting teens know that, to be removed from the list, all they need to do is reply with "Unsubscribe from this list" in their subject line.

- **Fast-food connection.** Work with local fast food chains to market library services through signage in each restaurant and printing the library's logo and Web site on wrappers, cups, placemats, bags, and pizza boxes.

- **Flyers.** While flyers should never be your only method of promoting an event, they are helpful for letting parents who visit the library know about what's happening for teens. They are also good for sharing with schools and other youth-serving organizations who are willing to help you promote your services for teens. Flyers can also be used to stuff in books being checked out, added to existing displays, and handed out during every reference transaction. Remember to include the following on all flyers: name and time of event, library address, Web site, phone number, age and registration requirements, description of event, and library logo.

- **Giveaways.** Giving away free stuff is always a bonus. If you have the means, consider including a prize raffle or drawing during every teen program. These can be advance reading copies of books, $5.00 print cards, or gift certificates to local restaurants. If you can only do this once a week or once a month, promote it as an ongoing event in your teen space and list the winner in a prominent place each week or month.

- **Homegrown "read" posters and bookmarks.** Hire a photographer or use one of your teens with photography skills to take pictures of teens in various locations around the library holding their favorite books, CDs, DVDs, graphic novels, or magazines. Use these photos to create posters you can frame and hang in your teen space or on bookmarks you can hand out to teens both inside and outside of the library. Thanks to ALA (American Library Association) Graphics, this process is now very simple. All you need is the Read CD boxed set, which comes with software that includes predesigned "Read" posters and backgrounds and type styles.

- **Linked.** With today's technology it is easy to create connections and develop a social network for your library by linking to other local and national youth-serving organizations as well as local schools on your library's Web site, MySpace page, or Facebook site. On your social networking site, search for local organizations and schools to see if they have pages. If they do, send them a friend request.

- **Lists.** Recommended reading lists are a great way to share information passively, especially for a teen who might not be comfortable asking a librarian for a book suggestion. You can create both thematic reading lists ("Books That Will Make You Cry," "Teen Health," "Supernatural Sci-Fi") and timely lists (required summer reading, Teens' Top Ten). Put them everywhere—on shelves, in books, on a table at the entrance, at the checkout desk—and change them often. Since these lists serve as both readers' advisory and a marketing tool, be sure to include the library's physical address, contact information, and Web site.

- **Mouse pads.** You can design and order customized mouse pads with your library's teen Web site on them for less than $2.00 a piece. Order these in bulk from an online retailer and you can probably get an even better deal. Distribute these throughout the library system, hand them out to teens who frequent your library, have them available at outreach events, and pass them out to teachers and encourage them to use them in their schools' computer labs and classrooms.

- **Parks and recreation departments.** These city- or county-funded agencies are great promotional partners for the library. Once you have developed a relationship with this group, encourage them to advertise library programs (or perhaps your teen summer reading program) in their promotional materials listing summer events and classes.

- **PowerPoint presentation.** Put together a simple, short PowerPoint presentation describing your library's services for teens. Burn this presentation to a disc and have it ready to distribute to teachers in your community or upload your presentation to the Internet using a free site like SlideShare (http://www

.slideshare.net/) to maximize exposure. You can also create accompanying handouts for last-minute library presentations in the community.

- **Public service announcement.** A PSA is an educational message designed to focus attention on something of interest to the general public that can be written and then printed in newspapers or magazines or recorded and then aired on television, radio, or online. PSAs, which should be noncommercial, nondenominational, and nonpolitical, are a great opportunity for meaningful teen involvement. You might even consider working with a local personality or hip-hop group to produce a public service announcement and/or video about using libraries. Remember, one of Tupac's first big public successes was performing as part of a rap contest to celebrate the Enoch Pratt Library's hundredth anniversary.

- **Parent-Teacher Associations and other connectors.** Parents still have a big influence over the life and times of their teenagers, so don't write them off. Parents who are involved in school organizations are good resources, and they are often connected and can help spread the word to people and places where you do not have access.

- **Radio remotes.** Radio stations make great partners, especially when it comes to publicity. Do a few informal surveys and find out from teens about favorite local radio stations. Then contact the frontrunner and set up a meeting to talk about developing a mutually beneficial partnership. Offer to put the station's logo on print and online promotional materials in exchange for the opportunity to air a teen-created public service announcement or time to talk on air about upcoming teen programs and special events. Also consider inviting your partnering radio station to come out and do a live radio remote (with all the bells and whistles like contests, giveaways, and radio personality appearances) for big events like summer reading kickoff or Teen Read Week.

- **Regularity.** Planning and carrying out regularly scheduled programs is one of the best ways to get teens in the door. A regular schedule of events will allow teens to plan accordingly, tell their friends, and begin to develop the habit of always showing up at the library when they know things will be happening. This might be an after-hours program every Friday night, a gaming or writing club on the first Monday of every month, taking photos for MySpace every Wednesday from 4:00 to 7:00 p.m., or showing a new anime movie every other Thursday at 3:00 p.m.

- **School announcements.** They happen in every school, every day, so they are a great outlet for sharing information quickly with a large body of students. Talk to your local school about mentioning upcoming special events that will be of interest to their students. If your school has a cable station, talk with them about airing a teen-created, 30-second commercial about what the library has to offer teens.

- **School bus ads.** Work with your local school district to put library promotional ads on every school bus in the district that serves middle school and high school students. Since many teens, especially in middle school, ride a school bus, it makes sense to work with schools to post ads that impact both the school and library, like advertising Teen Tech Week in March, teen book clubs year round, or the teen summer reading program in the last month of school.

- **School newspaper.** Pitch stories about library programs, new resources, and any changes in service to your local school's print or online newspaper or blog. Also consider paying for a discounted ad in a school newspaper.

- **School visits.** This is harder and harder to do with class time sucked up by studying for standardized tests, so a school visit needs to be connected to the teacher's goals, not your agenda. Also remember that there are plenty of other ways to do school visits outside of the normal and formal way of moving from class to class. Ask for permission to set up a booth at the school open house to sign up teens for library cards or set up a table with information about the library at the school entrance during a parent/teacher conference night. You can also ask about setting up a table in the cafeteria or school library several times a year to promote big teen programs or shared initiatives between the public and school library, like Teen Read Week or National Library Week.

- **Signs in front of schools.** Instead of a blank marquee sign all summer, ask schools to post a positive message about the library's summer reading program, especially if your library is located next to or close to a school.

- **Student ambassadors.** Recruit student ambassadors who can earn community service credits by volunteering to help market the library within the walls of their schools and also out in the general community. This type of marketing model is also called the "street team" model, whereby members of the team (in this case, the student ambassadors) are the bridge between the public library and the school library as well as the general community. Their job is to create hype for the public library's services for teens using word of mouth. This type of viral marketing is especially great for big events, but it will also work to spread the word about the library being an open and welcoming environment for teens looking for homework help or a free place to surf the Internet.

- **Sunny days.** If the weather permits, hold a program outside. The last thing teens who have been cooped up in school all day

> Encourage every staff member to "sell" the library's programs to teens; proactive and friendly customer service is the best promotion of all.

want to do when they get out of school is go back inside a building, especially when the weather is beautiful outside. Read-alouds, slam poetry workshops, and TAC meetings are all a great fit for an outside venue.

- **Teens as spokespeople.** Always let teens tell their stories about why libraries matter to them and why they should matter to their peers. In writing, on video, or over the radio, aim for maximum teen involvement. Partner with school drama, speech, or related clubs to find well-spoken, animated teens who are ready to help promote the library.

- **Use the calendar.** Plan programs for those special celebrations: Teen Read Week, Teen Tech Week, National Library Week, Free Comic Book Day, Teen Summer Reading, National Library Card Sign Up Month, and Banned Books Week—that come with "canned" promotional materials to download and/or purchase.

- **User guide.** Create a user guide for teens in your library that includes general information (location, hours, Web site), homework resources (both in print and online), staff contact information, volunteer opportunities, information about the TAC, and a blurb about what's available in your collection. It should be informative, yet entertaining. Think like customers. Don't do a user guide about "remote access databases," but instead do one called "How to use the library when the library is closed." It is the same information, but you are telling the story in a way that interests the user.

- **Video promotion.** With the birth of YouTube and other online video-sharing sites, viral videos created by teens are the new-generation marketing tool for libraries. Run a simple keyword search on YouTube for "teen" and "library" and you will see how school, public, academic, and even special libraries around the country are airing 30-second "commercials" highlighting their services and spaces and more in-depth "infomercials" focusing on special events, users, and even staff introductions online. Video promotion is also a great way to highlight your collection, with three-minute, teen-created book trailers. See the technology chapter for Web sites where teens can create professional-grade videos with little or no training.

- **Web sites.** In the age of library 2.0, the best library Web site for teens should be one that allows for teen input, in both the design and the actual content available on the page. Before you design a teen Web site be sure to get input from teens in your community. Once your Web site is up and running, make sure you have a balance of information and teen-created content. General information should include the library's address, hours, staff contact information, link to the catalog, and calendar of upcoming events. Teen content developed on the front end (as opposed to content created by the Web master behind the scenes) should include teen artwork, music, and videos created in-house. Other things to include on your Web site that will allow for maximum teen participation are a blog where teens can post and an electronic bulletin board where teens can interact with one another. So teens can interact with you, the collection, and other teens, include links to the library's social networking sites (MySpace, Facebook) and photo sites (Flickr). If you have the capability of offering Instant Messaging Reference, include a link to the chat widget on your library's site.

- **Youth involvement (again).** Ask your teens how they want to get involved and how you can best promote your services to them. The ideas will probably not be much different from the ones you've read here, but teens' responses will validate them for you.

What Are Some of the Most Outstanding Teen Spaces in Libraries?

The following teen spaces represent some of the best and brightest new, repurposed, and renovated teen library spaces throughout the county and world. Although most of these teen spaces exist within larger, all-ages facilities, some are housed in youth-only facilities, some exist as stand-alone teen libraries, and some are joint-use facilities shared by public libraries and other youth-serving organizations. The one thing all of these spaces have in common is that they all share a similar mission: to meet the informational and recreational needs of teens in a developmentally appropriate space.

Annex: A Teen Library at the Mall

Palos Verdes Library District
627 Silver Spur Rd. Suite 210
Rolling Hills Estates, CA 90274
http://www.freedomcommunity.com/annex.html

In collaboration with Freedom4U, a local California nonprofit organization that seeks to provide youth with programs that focus around creative arts, the PVLD created a 1,500-square-foot teen space in a retail area located between a golf shop and a barber shop next door to the main library called the Annex. The mission of the Annex is to provide 6th–12th graders with a supervised, dedicated space that complements the services of the Peninsula Center Library and Freedom4U's programs. The mission of this teen space is to provide opportunities for safe, constructive interaction in a comfortable environment; a collection of high-interest, up-to-date circulating library materials such as paperbacks, magazines, comics, graphic novels, and other formats of special interest to young people; access to games, computers, and other sources of information and entertainment; activities sponsored by Freedom4U and PVLD; and a place where teens can meet, talk, hang out, and have fun. On weekday afternoons and evenings, the Annex is operated by PVLD staff and volunteers for group study, recreation, and library services and programs. On weekend afternoons and evenings, Freedom4U staff and volunteers operate the Annex to host safe social events such as a coffee house, unplugged music, jazz, improv, comedy, drama, life skills workshops, mentoring programs, and similar activities. Freedom4U and the PVLD share all costs for the Annex.[6]

HYPE (Helping Young People Excel) Teen Center

Detroit Public Library
5201 Woodward Avenue
Detroit, MI 48202
http://www.ready2xl.com/
www.detroitpubliclibrary.org

The HYPE Teen Center, located within DPL's Main Library, is 3,884 square feet of video game consoles, big-screen televisions, performance spaces, quiet study areas, CDs, DVDs, free Wi-Fi, and books. Use of the center is restricted to teens between the ages of 13 and 18 who have a valid Detroit Public Library card. The center's design, game collection, music collection, video collection, and book collection were selected with input from the library's teen advisory council. Within the HYPE Center teens will find comfortable listening and viewing stations for CDs and DVDs, three 42-inch televisions, a big projection television, 10 PCs, and a selection of Windows, Apple, and Linux Machines. The room also includes several video gaming consoles and a wide variety of video games. The space also includes a raised stage for theatrical and artistic performances, three quiet study rooms, thousands of teen books, and free Internet access for teens who bring in their own laptops. The room itself has comfortable modern furniture throughout but preserves the original 1923 room's bookshelves, other woodwork, and an amazing Pewabic tile fireplace with representations of Aesop's fables.[7]

Loft at ImaginOn

Public Library of Charlotte and Mecklenburg County
ImaginOn: The Joe & Joan Martin Center
300 East 7th Street
Charlotte, NC 28202
www.imaginon.org
www.libraryloft.org

ImaginOn: The Joe & Joan Martin Center is located in the heart of Charlotte, North Carolina's urban cultural district in downtown. The only one of its kind in the country, this joint-use facility is a collaborative venture between the Public Library of Charlotte and Mecklenburg County (PLCMC) and the Children's Theatre of Charlotte. ImaginOn's teen library, commonly referred to as the Loft at ImaginOn, is located on the second floor of ImaginOn. The Loft's collection includes fiction and nonfiction for teens, the classics, CliffsNotes, a script library, the latest movie releases on DVD, books on CD and MP3, music CDs, graphic novels, manga, comic books, and teen magazines. The four thousand square foot space is comprised of comfortable chairs, café tables and stools, booth seating, and desktop computers. The entire loft is Wi-Fi accessible and all computers are equipped with Internet access, the Microsoft Office Suite (including Publisher, PowerPoint, Word, and Excel), and advanced graphic design and multimedia software including Photoshop, Dreamweaver, and Flash. Laptop computers are also available for teens to check out for in-house use with a valid PLCMC library card. Adjacent to the Loft is Studio i, a 1,225 square foot state-of-the-art film and music studio where teens have the opportunity to create original live action and animated films and music compositions. Visitors to Studio i have the opportunity to engage with blue screen technology, stop-motion animation, paper cutout animation, claymation, shadow puppet animation, and digital music production. Studio i also includes a stand-alone music booth where teens have more privacy to lay down original tracks or voice recordings. All computers in Studio i are equipped with professional-grade graphic design, music composition, animation, and editing software, including Stop Motion Pro, Pinnacle Studio 9, Acid Music Studio, Garage Band, and Adobe Photoshop Elements.

Mediateka: A Young Customers' Library

Mediateka
Pl. Teatralny 5
50-051 Wroclaw
Poland
www.mediateka.biblioteka.wroc.pl

The Mediateka in Wroclaw, Poland, was created in cooperation with the city of Wroclaw and the Municipal Public Library in Wroclaw in order to best meet the informational, educational, and recreational needs of the teens and young adults in the community. Although Mediateka's collection and services are predominantly aimed at young people ages 13–25, people of all ages are welcome to visit the library. Mediateka's mission is to be both a library and a meeting place where young people in the community come together. The goal of the library is to be a place where young people feel comfortable asking for help and seeking information. The actual design of the space is to encourage communication and collaboration, with a completely open floor plan divided only by an interesting and unusual media wall or shelf that runs the length of the entire building and a transparent curtain dividing the library's reading room from the rest of the space. Within the library, patrons have access to a coffeehouse and a collection of more than 30,000 items, including books, audiobooks, video games, and software, and more than 50 periodicals and newspapers of interest to young people. The comfortable furniture and lounge spaces encourage young patrons to hang out and spend time conversing with friends or studying independently. The Mediateka also includes a dozen public access computers and the MultiCentrum, an interactive education center where teens and young adults have an opportunity to learn new and exciting things defined as supplemental knowledge to that which is taught in the traditional Polish education system. Ongoing programs in the Mediateka include the "Language Café," where young people interested in developing their foreign language skills can converse with presenters in their native language, and the "Living Library," where presenters from various subcultures and demographics (i.e., gay or lesbian teens, ex-alcoholics, formerly homeless teens) discuss stereotypes.[8]

Starbucks Teen Center

Seattle Public Library, Central Library
1000 Fourth Avenue, Level Three
Seattle, WA 98104
http://www.spl.org/default.asp?pageID=audience_teens
http://blog.spl.org/yablog

Located at the back of Seattle Public Library's grand "living room" on the third floor of the Main Library, the Starbucks Teen Center is a 3,900 square foot space that is essentially a long, thin rectangle that stretches along the entire west side of Level 3. Although the library's living room is for patrons of all ages, the Teen Center is specifically reserved for teens and adults who are browsing the YA (young adult) collection or accompanying a teen. With a bold color scheme, comfortable furniture, and a large collection of more than 5,000 items, 30 magazine titles, and a dozen computers, SPL's Starbucks Teen Center is a haven for young people from throughout the city and surrounding King County. Located in the downtown business district, the Starbucks Teen Center also serves thousands of local middle and high school students. Like the rest of the library, the Teen Center is open Monday through Wednesday from 10:00 a.m. to 8:00 p.m., Thursday through Saturday from 10:00 a.m. to 6:00 p.m., and Sunday from 1:00 p.m. to 5:00 p.m.[9]

Teen Annex

Blue Island Public Library
2433 York Street
Blue Island, IL 60406
http://www.blueislandlibrary.org/library/6a.htm

When a local donor offered the Blue Island Historical Society money to purchase a house to serve as a museum, the local public library was able to renovate the space previously used to store historical artifacts into a technology space for teens called the Teen Annex. According to the library's Web site, the purpose of this teen space is fivefold: to provide a safe place for teens to be creative, learn new skills, and just hang out;

take computer classes; offer and attend patron programs; use as a recording studio; and provide a space for staff meetings and training.[10] Additionally, the 596-square-foot space includes computers with Internet access, a collaborative workspace for teens working on projects, computer stations for specific projects (Web site creation, video editing, audio production, etc.), gaming consoles, and board games. The YA collection is housed throughout the rest of the library, with graphic novels and magazines located in close proximity to the Teen Annex. The goal of the Teen Annex is to provide teens with the resources they need to develop and produce original content in the following categories: video production, audio production, graphic arts, 3D modeling and animation, Web development, and interior design. Unlike traditional teen spaces staffed by teen librarians, the Teen Annex was developed and is staffed by the members of the Blue Island Public Library's IT Department. In order to best meet the needs of the town's teens, the Teen Annex is open Monday through Thursday from 3:45 p.m. to 8:45 p.m., Friday from 3:45 p.m. to 5:00 p.m., and Saturday and Sunday from 1:00 p.m. to 5:00 p.m.[11]

TeenSpot

Public Library of Cincinnati and Hamilton County
Main Library TeenSpot, 2nd floor
800 Vine Street
Cincinnati, Ohio 45202-2009
http://teenspace.cincinnatilibrary.org/

Formerly the Public Documents Department, PLCH's new TeenSpot was developed during the Main Library's reorganization as a repurposed space in order to exclusively support the needs and interests of the library's teen patrons. Approximately 8,000 square feet, the space was designed with the assistance of architects, planners, library staff, and area teens, making it a one-of-a-kind destination within the library and the city. The TeenSpot features two study rooms, a vending area with restaurant booths, an eight-foot movie screen for anime and gaming, a lounge area for reading and hanging out, and a magnetic poetry board for releasing creative energy. The TeenSpot collection reflects the broad variety of available formats for material of interest to teens, including a large selection of fiction and nonfiction, biographies, books on CD, manga, graphic novels, and anime DVDs. There are also 24 computers, complete with the Internet and programs like the Microsoft Office Suite, iTunes, Windows Movie Maker, and Audacity. All computers have multiple USB ports, media card readers, headphone slots, and DVD/CD burners. The TeenSpot is open during the Main Library's hours of operation: Monday through Wednesday from 9:00 a.m. to 9:00 p.m., Thursday through Saturday from 9:00 a.m. to 6:00 p.m., and Sunday from 1:00 p.m. to 5:00 p.m.[12] Teens and their parents, caregivers, and teachers are assisted by the professionally trained staff in finding the reference, educational, and recreational materials of interest to them. Staff members also help teachers assemble classroom collections and do research on teen literature topics.[13]

John I. Smith Charities Library

The South Carolina Governor's School for the Arts and Humanities
John I. Smith Charities Library
15 University Street
Greenville, SC 29601
www.scgsah.state.sc.us

The South Carolina Governor's School for the Arts & Humanities is a state-supported public residential high school for emerging artists. With a maximum enrollment of 242 students, South Carolina residents apply and audition to enter one of the school's five programs: creative writing, dance, drama, music, and visual arts. The mission of this unique school is to serve the artistically talented high school students of South Carolina through programs of preprofessional instruction in an environment of artistic and academic excellence. The John I. Smith Charities Library supports this mission through its specialized collections, instructional services, library programs, and extended daily hours of service. The John I. Smith Charities Library is the campus hub where students have unrestricted access to an outstanding print collection of over 15,000 books, over 5,000 CDs that vary from Wagner to G. Love and Special Sauce, over 2,000 DVDs and music scores, and a comprehensive collection of online databases that support the arts and academic curriculum. There are 16 computers in the library and 19 computers in the library's computer lab. A production center is housed next to the library audiovisual room with an additional 4 computers, which allow students to access Adobe Video Collection for film and sound editing, Macromedia Studio products for Web site development, Sibelius and Finale for music composition, Photoshop with a drawing tablet, Movie Magic Screenwriter, and Danceforms to choreograph dances. Digital video cameras, a laptop computer, and LCD projectors circulate to students to use for classroom presentations and projects. The library leads the school community in teaching information literacy skills and applying technology to student learning through classroom instruction and faculty professional development workshops. There are two networked laser printers, one networked color laser printer, and a photocopy machine in the library; there are no charges for printing or copying. The library also does not charge fees for overdue materials or restrict the quantity of items a student or teacher may check out. The custom-designed shelving gives the library a feeling of openness, and comfortable seating and a giant window overlooking the Reedy River Falls in downtown Greenville give the students a bright, welcoming library with a priceless view of the beautiful city park. During the Nine Month Residential School program, the library is open Sunday 4:00 p.m. to 10:00 p.m., Monday through Thursday 8:00 a.m. to 10:00 p.m., and Friday 7:30 a.m. to 5:00 p.m. Summertime hours are 8:30 a.m. to 5:00 p.m.[14]

Conclusion

Most libraries focus on promoting the special, not the everyday. This makes sense, except so many of our teen customers and noncustomers don't know what we do every day. The truth is, all of these good ideas to draw teens into libraries mean nothing if the staff is not friendly, if the collection is not in shape, if there is no teen space, and if the experience is negative. The single most important promotional act you can do in your library is to ensure that every teen who enters your library has a positive experience. When teens have a good experience, they will spread the word. It's this kind of viral marketing that we should all strive to achieve because word of mouth advertising can't be bought—it can only be earned.

Sources Cited in This Chapter

1. Oldenburg, Ray. 1999. *The Great Good Place*. Berkeley, CA: Marlowe & Company.
2. DeLaughter, Maureen. 2006. "The Got Art? Gallery." *Voice of Youth Advocates* 29, no. 2 (June): 132–133.
3. Burington, Peg. 2006. "The New, Improved Best Cellar: Waupaca Area Public Library. Waupaca, Wisconsin." *Voice of Youth Advocates* 29, no. 4 (October): 316–317.
4. Lenhart, Amanda, and Mary Madden. 2007. "Social Networking Websites and Teens: An Overview." Pew Internet & American Life Project, January 1. Available: www.pewinternet.org/pdfs/PIP_SNS_Data_Memo_Jan_2007.pdf (accessed June 13, 2008).
5. Vaillancourt, Renee. 1999. *Bare Bones Young Adult Services: Tips for Public Library Generalists*. Chicago: American Library Association.
6. Orr, Alison. 2007. "Annex: A Teen Library at the Mall." *Voice of Youth Advocates* 29, no. 6 (February): 508–509.
7. Roush, Matt. 2008. "Detroit Library Opening High-tech Haven For Teens." *Great Lakes IT Report*, May 5. Available: www.wwj.com/Detroit-Library-Opening-High-Tech-Haven-For-Teens/2129510 (accessed May 15, 2008).
8. Janus, Anna. E-mail to authors. June 10, 2008.
9. Duncan, Amy, and Marin J. Younker. 2005. "Starbucks Teen Center: Seattle Public Library, Seattle Washington." *Voice of Youth Advocates* 28, no. 5 (December): 380–381.
10. Blue Island Public Library's Teen Annex. n.d. "History and Purpose." Blue Island Public Library. Available: www.blueislandlibrary.org/library/6a.htm (accessed June 6, 2008).
11. "YA Spaces of Your Dreams: Tech Annex." 2008. *Voice of Youth Advocates*. Available: http://pdfs.voya.com/VO/YA2/VOYA200802ya_spaces.pdf (accessed June 1, 2008).
12. Teenspace. 2008. "The New TeenSpot is Open for Business!" Public Library of Cincinnati and Hamilton County. Available: http://teenspace.cincinnatilibrary.org/features/2008-05/ (accessed May 15, 2008).
13. Brehm-Heeger, Paula. E-mail to author. May 21, 2008.
14. Giller, Michael. E-mail to author. June 8, 2008.

Recommended Sources for Further Reading

Bolan, Kimberly. 2006. "Looks Like Teen Spirit." *School Library Journal* 52, no. 11. (November 2006) 44–48.

Bolan, Kimberly. 2009. *Teen Spaces: The Step-by-Step Library Makeover*, 2nd ed. Chicago: American Library Association.

Erikson, Rolf, and Carolyn A. Markuson. 2001. *Designing a School Library Media Center for the Future*. Chicago: American Library Association.

Gallo, Erminia Mina. 2008. "Attractive Displays for Teen Spaces." *Young Adult Library Services* 6, no. 4 (Summer): 32–34.

Goodstein, Anastasia. 2008. "What Would Madison Avenue Do?" *School Library Journal* 54, no. 5 (May): 40–43.

Laperriere, Jenny, and Trish Christiansen. 2008. *Merchandising Made Simple: Using Standards and Dynamite Displays to Boost Circulation*. Westport, CT: Libraries Unlimited.

Lushington, Nolan. 2002. *Libraries Designed for Users: A 21st-Century Guide*. New York: Neal-Schuman.

Manley, Kathy. 2003. "10 Tips for Surviving a Knock-down, Drag-out Media Center Renovation." *Library Media Connection* 21, no. 4 (January): 50–51.

Nichols, Mary Anne. 2002. *Merchandising Library Materials to Young Adults*. Westport, CT: Libraries Unlimited.

Sellers, John. 2007. "Teen Marketing 2.0." *Publishers Weekly* 254, no. 35 (September): 27–29.

Siess, Judith A. 2003. *The Visible Librarian: Asserting Your Value with Marketing and Advocacy*. Chicago: American Library Association.

Also be sure to check out the *Voice of Youth Advocates* "YA Spaces for Your Dreams," a column about teen spaces included in every issue of *VOYA*.

Technology

The third edition of *Connecting Young Adults and Libraries*, published in 2004, was the first edition to include a chapter on technology. Today, one wouldn't dream of publishing a book about how to best serve teens in libraries without including such a chapter. In fact, as you've read through the preceding ten chapters, you will have likely noticed that technology has infiltrated almost everything we do in libraries, from customer service (IM reference) to collection development (books on MP3) to programming (virtual college fair).

We are helping raise a generation of technologically savvy teens, a generation of young people who live in a world where technology is integral to their day-to-day existence. Teens are active consumers of technology, using various tools to connect with the outside world, find and create content, and access information on a daily basis for both recreational and educational purposes.

This is an oversimplification of a teen's day, but here's a general breakdown of how technology might be used by a young person in one 24-hour period:

- Texting friends before school to ask for a last-minute ride
- Checking her Facebook pages at lunch to see if any of her friends commented on her new relationship status
- Listening to his iPod in between classes
- Playing World of Warcraft after school for a few hours with friends online
- Creating a new Playlist in iTunes to burn for his new significant other
- Browsing Wikipedia for information about the Spanish-American War for a paper due tomorrow
- Posting an entry on LiveJournal about today's fiasco in gym
- Using BitTorrent to search for a file of last night's episode of HBO's *True Blood* since she missed it due to her little sister's piano recital

- Uploading the video to YouTube of the fight that happened outside of the gym after school, which he happened to catch on his cell phone
- IMing (instant messaging) friends right before bed to ask about the required reading for first period tomorrow
- Setting the alarm on her cell phone so she can wake up tomorrow and do it all over again

According to a 2009 presentation by Lee Rainie, Director of the Pew Internet & American Life Project:

- 93 percent of teens ages 12–17 use the Internet
- 87 percent of online teens use e-mail
- 97 percent of teens play video or computer games
- 70 percent of online teens use social network sites
- 75 percent of online teens view videos on video-sharing sites
- 68 percent of online teens use instant messaging
- 30 percent of online teens own and regularly update blogs
- 54 percent of online teens read blogs
- 55 percent of online teens use Wikipedia[1]

In the same presentation, Rainie mentioned that almost 75 percent of online teens have created content for the Internet, with

- 39 percent sharing their own creations online;
- 25 percent creating or working on Web sites or blogs for themselves, groups, or school assignments; and
- 20 percent remixing content they found online into their own artistic creations.

Obviously teens are using their time on the Internet to find, consume, and share information or to be productive, creative, and social.

> Our children and future generations have tremendous opportunities in store for them, not in spite of the digital age, but because of it.
>
> —John Palfrey and Urs Gasser, *Born Digital: Understanding the First Generation of Digital Natives*

Are We Raising Teens in Some Technological Utopia?

Unfortunately, no. We still face numerous challenges with regard to teens and technology, including online security, privacy, and personal safety, as well as digital copyright issues, digital harassment, general information overload, and what some critics of technology consider a decrease in the collective attention span of teens due in large part to the proliferation of digital reading.[2]

Additionally, a significant gap exists in how teens perceive their skills utilizing technology for the sake of information literacy and how educators actually see teens using technology efficiently and effectively to find information. In a recent survey of more than 27,000 college students, 79.5 percent of respondents considered themselves "quite Internet savvy" when it came to using the Internet to conduct research. In response, "Many educators believe that students' perceptions about their IT skill levels and Internet savvy are questionable, characterizing their approach to information literacy as do-it-yourself and often relying too heavily on peers rather than on library staff or faculty."[3]

The good news, according to the authors of *Born Digital: Understanding the First Generation of Digital Natives*, is that "the old fashioned solutions that have solved similar problems in the past will work in the digital age, too. Those solutions are engaged parenting, a good education, and common sense."[4]

How Can Libraries Capitalize on Teens' Use of Technology in Their Everyday Lives?

Most public libraries today are in a position to help meet the needs of teens by providing free Internet access, computers that do not filter social networking sites, technology classes, e-books, online homework help, online reference, video editing or graphic design software, and laptop computers for in-house use. The goal is to pay attention to the existing and emerging technologies teens are using to find a way to use these tools to offer existing library services in a more techno-friendly manner. These might include the following:

- Using text messaging to remind teens about overdue books or books on hold

- Providing virtual reference via a free instant messaging service like Meebo

- Using Twitter to keep teens abreast of upcoming events or hot new releases

- Using the bulletin option on your library's MySpace page to market upcoming programs and events

- Providing virtual homework help with a subscription service like Tutor.com

- Posting a teen-created video on YouTube about how to accurately use the library's online catalog to put a new book on hold

- Creating an online "comments" section on your library's Web site for teens to provide feedback about existing services

- Establishing a library account on LibraryThing and then "friending" local teens; staff can then share what they are reading or what's hot at the library as a form of virtual reader's advisory

- Hosting a virtual book discussion group in an immersive environment like Teen Second Life

- Posting photos from your latest teen program on Flickr to promote future library programs

CD See Tool 21. Laptop Circulation Policy and Agreement Form

CD See Tool 23. Photo Release Form

- Using your library's Wii to send a message about an upcoming gaming program to all your Wii friends using the Wii's "message board"

What Is the Role of the LST in Today's Digital World?

Change is inevitable. This is often a hard truth for librarians, especially those who cling to the past or those who are fearful of going out on that proverbial limb and trying something new and different. Thankfully, the majority of LSTs we have come across are more adventurous and willing to try new things, including finding innovative ways to incorporate technology into existing services and seeking out new ways to utilize technology to better meet the needs of teens.

The single most important thing any LST can do in today's digital world is to stay grounded in the rapidly changing digital landscape, stay abreast of the research and best practices, read the blogs, join the electronic discussion lists, attend the conferences, and engage others in the profession in conversations about what they are doing in their libraries to meet teens where they are: online and out in the virtual world.

The second most important thing you can do is be a mentor and a leader, not just a passive bystander and certainly not an impediment. Be an advocate in the library for teens' use of technology, lobbying your administration to create (or update) policies that support access and to set aside budget monies for keeping your library's software and hardware up to date, purchasing emerging technologies, and ensuring that your library's Internet is fast enough to meet the needs of your teen patrons by increasing bandwidth.

A secondary, but no less important, role of the LST in today's digital world is to educate teen patrons about various issues that have become more prevalent as the Internet has become more pervasive.

Information Literacy

Although this topic is covered in depth in Chapter 5, we think it bears repeating that you are the best tool teens have when it comes to learning how to find information online. When most teens are working on a research project, they know that they can type a keyword into the Google search box and something will come up. Your job is to help them understand that what comes up is not always the best source, and sometimes not even a credible source. Even more important, your job is to turn the screen around and help teens navigate your online databases, not do the work for them and then hand them a printout or a URL for an online document. You need to move away from being the information gatekeeper and toward being the educated companion on an information journey.

> In today's digital world, constant change is one of the only things of which we can be certain.

Copyright in the Digital Age

Teens today are growing up in a world where media is fluid, instantaneously viewable, changeable, and deleteable. More important, media today (including photos, music, videos, newspapers, movies, and television shows) are instantaneously sharable, with most teens having immediate access to digital files and the ability to share music, movies, and other digital media online with their friends using peer-to-peer file-sharing software. In fact, according to a survey published by the International Federation of the Phonographic Industry in 2009, 95 percent of all digital music came from an unlicensed source in 2008.[5] For those of us who grew up buying records, or tapes, or even CDs, this number may be surprising, but for most teens today, who have never known a world where they couldn't download music, this number would not be much of a surprise. So how do we educate our young public about something that has clearly become somewhat of a social norm? We educate ourselves about copyright; we model behavior when it comes to showing movies, playing music during library programs, or sharing information with teens in an educational setting; and we enforce the rules we set for teens using our libraries about copying and/or sharing copyrighted music online.

Online Safety

At some point in our childhood most of us were educated about "stranger danger"—the warning born out of a media-driven campaign that strongly advised children not to talk to strangers. Today we're dealing with a new generation of "stranger danger" online, and although the format is different, the message is the same: Stay away from people you don't know, don't "friend" strangers, don't meet people in person whom you met online, and don't put private information online that would help someone you met virtually find you in the real world. The original "stranger danger" campaign didn't work because children assumed "stranger" meant someone "ugly or mean," adults lost their "stranger" status when they spent time, more than once, with a child, and children generally strive to please adults, strangers or not.[6] Today, the same campaign doesn't work for many of the same reasons, only we're dealing with teens who already feel like they know what's best anyway. Like children having a hard time ascertaining what constitutes a stranger in real time, teens today often have a hard time defining a "stranger" in a digital environment because identity is nebulous, social networking thrives on connecting people who don't know one another, and technologies like instant messaging and text messaging make it very easy for "strangers" to manipulate situations and people.

In a recent study, 56 percent of teens ages 10–17 reported posting personal information online, 43 percent reported interacting with people they didn't know online, and 35 percent admitted to having people they didn't know on their friends list.[7] Clearly we still have work to do when it comes to educating young people about the dangers of sharing too much information and "friending" people online to whom they have no connection. This includes teaching teens that nothing online is truly private.

Privacy

Speaking of nothing online being private, this is one of the scarier realities about the digital age for those of us who did not grow up with the Internet. In no other time in history has so much information about average citizens been accessible to the masses. The greatest challenge about this for us is that we have to find a way to help teens recognize the implications this could have on their future while they are still wholly wrapped up in the present. Unfortunately, there is no guarantee that something teens post online today will not end up online in the future, including things posted by them on their MySpace page, on their Amazon.com wish list, on a post to a personal blog, or in response to something on a friend's blog. It's not enough that we teach teens to change the privacy settings on their social networking sites; we need to educate them about how this information might show up in search engines in the future, especially because it is likely in the future that more companies that provide social networking will be tempted to change their policies about safeguarding or releasing private information about their patrons to search engines in order to increase traffic to their sites.[8] Our job is also to remind teens to trust their instincts and click away when something doesn't seem right and to report online victimization and cyber bullying. We also need to make sure we are helping teens make good choices about how they share information online, especially because some teens may have never considered how simple things like sharing passwords, creating revealing IM handles, or posting pictures of themselves with friends in their volleyball uniforms (where the name of the school is clearly visible) on their Facebook page could potentially compromise their safety online.

Is All of This Technology Actually "Dumbing Down" Teens?

In her book *Teens, Technology, and Literacy; Or, Why Bad Grammar Isn't Always Bad*, librarian/technology guru Linda W. Braun makes a strong case for giving teens more credit than we do when it comes to when and how they use various technology tools to communicate. Although we might see a bunch of acronyms (LOL, OMG, TTYL, BRB) and misspelled words (2-nite, l8er, ur, luv) when we look at what a teen is texting or IMing to a friend, teens see a shortcut, or shorthand, language (called "chat speak") that best meets their communication needs. Braun also includes research in her book that backs up the finding that "teens use e-mail, chat, and IM differently based on time, place, need, and purpose" and that teens were not "duped by technology" but instead use it "with a sense of purpose and informed participation that may be surprising to many adults concerned about the influence of computer-mediated communication on the lives of and literacies of the younger generation."[9] Samantha Blackmon, a professor of English at Purdue University, also believes that "blogging, e-mailing and instant messaging without proper punctuation or correct spelling isn't so bad if it means more teenagers are writing for fun."[10] She goes on to explain that informal writing online often helps teens with critical thinking, developing a positive relationship with the process of writing, and communicating quickly in a very fast-paced, digital environment.

We also know not everyone feels this way and that many adults and educators believe this new generation of shorthand communication is actually detrimental to teens' development of writing skills. We acknowledge that both sides have valid concerns. We also know that this debate is not likely to end anytime soon.

Another debate that continues to rage on with regard to the impact of reading online and the intellectual development of teens is whether or not reading online, clicking from hyperlink to hyperlink, and skimming content while scrolling down the page (power browsing), all while navigating (and often being seduced by) flashing images and semirelated links calling to us from the sidebar, is actually making us less capable of reading print materials for a sustained period of time. Are we less capable of reading and absorbing long text passages today than we were five or ten years ago? Are we reading more now than in the past, only getting less out of what we read? Will the proliferation of content online actually rewire how we process information in the future? Is Google actually making us stupider, or are we just globally changing how we process information?[11] The simple truth is nobody really knows the impact reading and doing research online will have on us in the long term.

One thing we do know is that the Internet has opened doors and exposed teens to global communities and perspectives, enabling teens in the United States to share stories, develop friendships, and exchange ideas with teens from around the world. Some of these experiences might include a teen in Washington, DC, chatting with another in Tokyo about a favorite manga series that has yet to be released here, a teen attending a virtual college fair in Teen Second Life to find out more information about attending university in Australia, or two teens from different hemispheres developing a friendship based on their mutual love of Harry Potter fan fiction, which they read and share with one another online on LiveJournal.

Why Should You Allow Teens to Spend Time Chatting Online While Other Patrons Are Waiting to Do "Real" Work?

This is one of the most common questions we receive in workshops around the country. The simple answer is teens have every right to do whatever they want on the computer (assuming it's legal) during their reserved time. You don't stand over a senior citizen playing chess online and ask him when he's going to be done "playing" so that another patron can use the library's computer for "real" work, and you don't do it to the woman who logged on to check her "new moms" bulletin board to see if anyone responded to her post about diaper rash, so why would you monitor what a teen is or is not doing online during his or her allotted time on the computer? You wouldn't. Or, more appropriately, you shouldn't. It's not fair, it's a disservice to your teen patrons, and it's ageism at its worst. You need to be very careful not to make assumptions about how and why teens are using computers; what may look like wasting time may actually be a teen chatting online with a tutor, provided free of charge by the library via Tutor.com, or a teen posting to a classroom bulletin board or engaging in an online conversation for class, or a teen IMing with a classmate about a homework project due tomorrow. It doesn't really matter what teens are doing online because they have every right to spend their time on the computer as they see fit, but it would serve you well to remember that making assumptions about what they are doing and why they are doing it can only lead to judgmental behavior on your part that often contributes to resentment or, worse, all-out battles with teens about how they are spending their time in the library. Finally, you need to remember that libraries all over the country are embracing instant messaging (i.e., chatting) as a legitimate format for providing excellent, all-inclusive customer service to patrons outside of library walls, including online reference and readers' advisory. Be careful not to cast stones about certain behaviors and uses of technologies within the library by teens when you are likely using similar tools to engage in similar activities in the name of "real" library work.

The more complicated answer to this question has to do with the social and developmental benefits of teens' involvement within a participatory culture, defined as "a culture with relatively low barriers to artistic expression and civic engagement, strong support for creating and sharing one's creations, and some type of informal mentorship whereby what is known by the most experienced is passed along to novices." A participatory culture is further defined, at its core, as one in which "members believe their contributions matter and feel some degree of social connection with another." Current research about the benefits of a participatory culture on teen participants include opportunities to learn from their peers, a change in attitude toward intellectual property, and a growth in the development of skills teens will need in the workplace of the future.[12]

Not surprisingly, one of the greatest places for teens to engage in this type of culture is the local public library, where they can go online for free, access various social networking sites, and have the freedom and support to develop and share content, learn from and teach to their peers, engage in discourse locally and globally, and "play" with new and emerging technologies. The heart of participatory culture, like a public library, is community involvement. The blood that keeps this heart pumping is collaboration and networking, both skills that can be honed in social networks and within virtual worlds, both opportunities that we all have the power to make widely available in public libraries for interested teens.

It's Fine for a Public Library to Provide Access to Social Networking Sites, but Why Should Your School Library Allow Teens to Access These Sites?

Unfortunately, this is also a common question that has sadly impacted how school library media centers provide online access to teens. If you work with teens, then you are their greatest ally, the adult who advocates for them in a world where they do not often have a voice. In a school environment, many decisions are made daily by grown-ups without consideration for how these decisions will negatively impact teens in both the present and the future.

One of these decisions that has been made over the past several years in schools around the country is to block student access to social networks and to e-mail and to install computer filters that are so tight that they end up not only blocking access to social networking sites but also essential Web sites. In a 2006 article in *School Library Journal*, a media specialist in California said that not only was her school banning social networking sites but they also weren't allowing students to use e-mail, which she felt negated using the Internet as a teaching tool.[13] In spite of the increase in ways for schools to utilize social networking for educational purposes during the past couple of years, this type of exclusion continues to happen today, with K–12 schools consciously banning student access to sites like MySpace and Facebook as well as virtual worlds like Gaia and Teen Second Life. Regrettably, this lack of access is negatively impacting students' preparation for the twenty-first century. In a recent survey of more than 370,000 students, teachers, parents, and administrators about their views on technology and education conducted by national education nonprofit organization Project Tomorrow, two-thirds of principals said they believed their schools were preparing students to be competitive in the global workforce. In contrast, Project Tomorrow CEO Julie Evans said most tech-savvy students didn't share that view, with less than one-quarter of teen respondents saying they felt that their schools were adequately preparing them for the future. Many students who took the survey also said "the major obstacles to their use of technology at school include filters that block the Web sites they need and administrators who impose rules that limit their technology use."[14] Additionally, according to a survey conducted by the National School Boards Association in 2007, "nearly 60 percent of students use social networking sites to discuss 'education topics.' Yet, 98 percent of school districts use software to block what they deem inappropriate sites, with 52 percent of districts specifically blocking social networking sites in K–12 schools."[15] Today, one can only hope that those percentages have dropped, granting students more access to the sites they need to find information, create and share content, and network with students around the globe.

Thankfully, some school library media specialists, teachers, and administrators out there do advocate for teen access. In a recent article in *Knowledge Quest*, the print journal of the American Association of School Librarians, author Wendy Steadman Stephens instructed school librarians to "leverage their school's investment in digital infrastructure and equipment to teach students everything from copyright restrictions to developing a more nuanced understanding of critical information literacy in online environments."[16] This is exactly how you can be a teen advocate in your schools.

Does Your Library Need a MySpace Profile? A Web Page?

> To best meet the needs of teens, you need to meet them where they are: online.

Absolutely. However, do not attempt to create any kind of Web site or profile or page on a social networking site without teen input. If you choose to go with the Web site option (and more and more libraries around the country are foregoing this option in favor of creating social networking sites), do not create it in a vacuum. Ask teens to help you plan the layout and to create content. The most important thing to consider when you are making a decision about whether to have a teen Web site is maintenance; updating it is mandatory. If you do not have the time, technological know-how, or IT support to keep it fresh, then don't bother taking the time to create it. Teens today live in a world where news is instantaneous and information is readily available and only a click or two away. An out-of-date Web site (and we're talking hourly, not daily or weekly) is about as useful to a teen today as a home phone with a cord. If you do decide to move forward and create a Web site, remember that your site needs to allow teens to both create content and offer feedback. This means including spaces for teens to upload art and pictures, post and comment on the blog or about items in the gallery, tag the online catalog, upload book reviews, and more. Also remember to include areas that allow teens to stay continually involved, including polls, surveys, daily trivia, and a continually changing photo gallery of past events featuring real, live teens. These are the things that will keep teens coming back for more. Additionally, you need to include an up-to-date schedule of programs and events and informational staples like hours, locations, contact information, and information about library services and homework help. Links to other resources are fine, but do not let them dictate your site.

If you do choose to create a page on a social networking site (in lieu of or as an accompaniment to a teen Web site), many of these same rules apply, especially about including the staples. Although most sites will allow you to make a page for free, you still have to keep it updated. In spite of the fact that you see eight year-olds on MySpace, most sites do take time and, to some degree, skill to maintain. Before you even begin creating your page, gather feedback from teens who use your library: What social networking site do they use? What sites do their friends use? What constitutes a "cool" layout? What information would they like to see on the library's page? What add-ons or applications are necessary and which are just clutter? If possible, have a contest to allow teens to design your layout or vote between layout alternatives.

Whatever you decide, remember that teen participation is mandatory and that change is your friend. Do not get too attached to any one format or layout, as it will (and should) change regularly.

Does Virtual Programming Have a Place in Your Library?

Absolutely. Virtual worlds, or immersive environments, like Teen Second Life, Gaia, and Habbo, offer teens opportunities to interact with their peers in diverse environments and to try on new and/or different identities—both developmentally appropriate practices for young people. These online worlds also provide interesting and innovative forums for a new generation of library programs and services for teens, both those facilitated by librarians and those created and carried out by teens.

If you work with teens, you are likely aware of how the formation of identity plays a large role during adolescence. From choosing clothing to changing hair color, teens are limited in how they can alter their appearance in real life. In a virtual world, teens can change their gender, size, shape, even species. Online, teens can be who they want, when they want, and they have ultimate control over how they look to outside observers—something sorely lacking in the real world for most teens. In all virtual worlds, teens create an avatar as their digital representation of self. The ability to modify one's avatar—weekly, daily, even hourly—is one of a virtual world's first draws to teens. In fact, we know of many teens who spent their first days in Teen Second Life doing nothing but altering their virtual alter-egos' physical appearances and then trying on different clothes to further define their new virtual selves. It is normal, even healthy, for teens to try on different identities, and nowhere is this easier than in a virtual world.

Other benefits of virtual, or immersive, worlds for teens include unlimited opportunities for global networking, exposure to new and different cultures and languages, and the chance to be involved with programs they might not otherwise experience, like talking to representatives from NASA (see best practices), visiting with a teen author "in person," or attending an international college fair. These are some of the obvious benefits for teens, but some of the more subtle benefits of teens' participation in virtual worlds that librarians, teachers, and parents might want to know about include practice with reading, writing, and speaking skills and the development of visual/spatial skills and organizational skills, which they learn (and can then apply to other areas) by classifying and categorizing the hundreds of thousands of objects, clothes, and gadgets they gather and store in their virtual world.

Gartner, an international research and consulting company that focuses on technology, estimates that "by the end of 2011, 80 percent of active internet users will have a second life."[17] If this estimate is even close to accurate, then this has huge implications for those of us who serve teens, especially considering that the 2009 Pew Internet Study mentioned at the beginning of this chapter estimates that 93 percent of teens are currently online. Libraries have long been the sole provider of technology for those who do not have access to it at home, and we have a feeling this will be the case for virtual worlds in a few years. The bottom line here is that you don't have to go out and buy an island and start creating original, virtual programming, but you do have to know about virtual worlds, understand the benefits of them, and make them available and accessible to your patrons.

Do Portable Audiobook Devices, E-book Readers, or Video Game Consoles Belong in Your Library?

The simple answer is yes; your library should consider new ways of accessing traditional materials. Technology and portability not only appeal to teens, but teens are increasingly accustomed to digital gadgets—whether they have an iPod Touch or the cheapest MP3 player Wal-Mart has to offer, a PSP, or handheld Yahtzee. Teens may want, and even expect, to see these devices integrated into library collections.

The complicated answer is, it depends. You should answer this question for your library the same way you would answer a similar question about which teen book titles you should add. That answer will be influenced by several factors:

- Library's total collection-development philosophy
- Quality and quantity of school library collections
- Budget, space, and staff available
- Reading interests of teens in your community
- Your own professional values
- What needs the collection should meet
- The roles the library has chosen for itself

The Playaway combines device with content and costs less as a unit. But what about adding devices that allow users to take better advantage of existing digital collections? Much as your library may face the decision of whether to supplement or replace a bank of desktops with laptops for in-house use, you may find yourself considering circulating e-book readers or portable video game consoles. With higher-cost items like laptops, e-book readers, and video game systems, budgeting decisions must reflect not only the upfront expense—and whether teens will be interested in using the new format in the first place—but also the potential for loss or damage and the lifetime cost of batteries. Entrusting teens with a piece of equipment that costs over $100.00 is always going to carry some degree of risk, just as it does with adults. And when teens get huge fines for lost or damaged electronic items, they are unlikely to be able to pay them off without help. In most library systems, high fines block circulation and computer access for that library card, which means one little mistake can keep a teen from being able to enjoy much of what the library offers. Creating payoff plans and policies that allow teens to reduce fines by participating in programs, reading, or volunteering at the library, should go hand in hand with collection development decisions like this one.

The big question is whether e-book readers, video game consoles, or other new technological devices allow you to reach teens in a new way, to uniquely meet teens' developmental needs or expectations for the library, or to otherwise fill a gap in your quest to make the library a desirable destination and service point for teens. If they do, then you measure that potential against the estimated costs and decide what best serves your library's mission and your teens' interests. If it doesn't make sense to circulate readers and consoles, consider expanding the library's collection of downloadable music, audiobooks, and e-books and circulating video games for the latest portable consoles. Maybe a handful of cheap MP3 players—as long as you check their compatibility with your digital collections through NetLibrary, OverDrive, or other vendors—are a better selection decision for now.

How Can You Use Technology to Make the Library More Interesting to Teens?

Creating a space where teens feel comfortable is about making the things they want readily available, including the latest technology. If you set it up right, the library can be a place where teens can come and access technology freely and without constraints. Creating a place teens find interesting is a little bit more of a challenge; it requires you to think outside of the box and often to redefine the role of the library in the twenty-first century. Many libraries have taken up this challenge and are redefining themselves as places not only to find information but to create original content, including digital imagery, podcasts, blogs, digital scrapbooks, animation, machinima, and video games.

The Public Library of Charlotte and Mecklenburg County (PLCMC) is leading the pack when it comes to providing their young patrons with opportunities to create original content with Studio i, a fully functional multimedia production studio located within ImaginOn, PLCMC's youth-only library, which is staffed by technology specialists and high school interns and equipped with professional-grade hardware, software, and a sound booth.[18] Teens who spend time in the studio often walk away with a finished product burned on a CD or DVD that can be shared with friends and family, uploaded to YouTube, or played on the big screen in the ImaginOn lobby.

Other libraries around the country are also developing programs and initiatives that allow young people to learn new skills and create original content. The Buffalo and Erie County Public Library sponsored a

CD See Tool 9. Fine Reduction/Waiver Program (Project Payoff)

five-part program series titled "Bring That Beat Back" in 2008, which helped teens explore hip-hop culture by examining MCing, DJing, hip-hop dance, and graffiti design. In each program the teens received personalized instruction, viewed movie clips and online videos, listened to music (on both CD and vinyl), and participated in hands-on activities, including using a dual CD mixing console, a set of DJ headphones, and speakers to practice their DJ skills.[19]

Teens in Hennepin County (Michigan) have access to Open Tech Labs in four of their community libraries, where they have opportunities to develop rich media content creation skills using software like Scratch, Picasa, ArtRage, Garage Band, and Audacity. The workshops are facilitated by teens or youth workers and youth are encouraged to work on content that is meaningful to them. Some young people work on music projects, and others on animation or game making. Still others use digital cameras to explore photography as a medium for self-expression. The guiding philosophy of the Open Tech Labs is to meet youth where they are—in their skill level, their attention span, and their personal interests. The goal of the labs is to enhance the development of twenty-first-century literacy skills.[20]

Another handful of libraries have also taken the hands-on approach and are creating opportunities for young people to play with new and emerging technologies. Often called a "sandbox" or "technology petting zoo," these kinds of experiential programs provide young people with the chance to play with technologies and technological concepts that are often brand-new to them, from digital photography and animation to robotics and touch-screen technology.

Finally, LSTs who understand that teens often need to be a part of the process are using technology to create a technology-related circle of services. They begin by promoting their technology-related resources or programs online. Teens see the marketed programs or resources and come in to use the technology to produce original content, which they then share online with friends by posting on their LiveJournal blog, on their MySpace page, or on YouTube. Once posted online, these original creations help promote future library programs that involve technology. The circle is complete, and both libraries and teens benefit from the process.

What If You Don't Have the Budget to Buy All of the Newest Technologies?

If you are paying attention to the newest and the latest in technology, chances are very good that you will never have enough money in your budget to stay as up to date as you'd like. The good news is there are a variety of ways to garner financial support to both maintain what you have and add to what you've got. Some funding options include these:

- **LSTA and other grants.** The Federal Library Services and Technology Act (LSTA), available through the Institute of Museum and Library Services, funds dozens of technology-based library programs in each state, each year. Find out more online (www.imls.gov). Many foundations also specialize in technology grants, including the Bill and Melinda Gates Foundation (www .gatesfoundation.org/Grants) and the Michael and Susan Dell Foundation (www.msdf.org). To find more funding sources, visit eSchool News' "Grants & Funding" page: www.eschoolnews .com/tsc/index.php?t=sub_pages&cat=22.

- **Technology donation programs.** These programs generally involve the donation of hardware and software. Examples include the "Computers for Learning" Program (http://comput- ers forlearning.gov/) and "Gifts in Kind (www.giftsinkind.org).

- **Discounted technology.** These programs often provide deeply discounted hardware and software to nonprofit organizations. Examples include the Microsoft Software Donation Program (www.microsoft.com/industry/government/softwaredonation .mspx) and the Cisco Donation Program (e-mail ciag-education@ cisco.com for more information). Tech Soup (www.techsoup.org) offers additional resources for finding technology at a discount.

- **Private/public partnerships.** Companies that deal in software-, hardware-, and technology-related services make great partners for technology-related programs. Examples include Red Octane (creator of high-end metal pads for Dance Dance Revolution, DDR), which sponsors DDR tournaments; GameStop (video game store), which provides prizes; and local gaming places in your area that might donate in-kind for promotion.

- **Private donations.** Many private technology companies (like IBM, Apple, and Dell) donate hardware, including desktop and laptop computers, to libraries in need.

- **Open source software.** Software created and distributed freely to the general public is an excellent way to provide patrons with what they want (graphic design, word processing, video editing, database development, Web design, etc.) without spending a fortune. For a list of available open source software licenses, visit the Open Source Initiative (www.opensource.org/licenses).

- **Hardware rentals.** You can rent video games, gaming platforms, hardware for geocaching, and more.

- **Borrowing materials.** Encourage staff or participating teens to bring in their own gaming systems or games for a library- sponsored program. You not only increase your offerings but have teen approval built into the system with teens bringing in their own games.

Best Practices/Pilot Projects

The following technology programs and initiatives are broken down into two areas: best practices and pilot projects. Like all chapters in this book, we included best practices so you can see some of what we've written about in each chapter as it pertains to real life or, more appropriately, so you can see theory in action. The programs included in this section already have a proven track record of success with incorporating technology into existing programs or using technology as a foundation upon which to build future programs and library services with and for teens. We've included pilot projects for this chapter because technology in libraries, at its core, is about being innovative, taking risks, and trying new things. The pilot projects included in this chapter embody this spirit of risk-taking innovation, using technology to improve existing library services. Both pilot projects were developed with funding from an LSTA grant, and both projects have larger implications for teen services in libraries nationally in the future.

Best Practices

The REEL Focus Project

Livermore Public Library
Rincon Branch Library
Livermore, California
www.ci.livermore.ca.us/library/reelfocus_ala.html

The REEL Focus Project provided 17 young people from lower-income families in 5th–12th grade the opportunity to develop film making, work, and study skills while fostering creative expression through video production. Participating teens attended weekly instructional and drop-in sessions from October 2007 through May 2008, and guest speakers and field trips to film shoots, soundstages, and other film-related locations were included in the curriculum. At the completion of the program, the Liverpool Public Library hosted a student showcase that was attended by family members, community arts supporters, and the public. The students' final video projects were also included on a REEL Focus DVD, which was then made available for checkout from the library.

Teen-Created National PSAs for Teen Summer Reading Program

Public Library of Charlotte and Mecklenburg County
ImaginOn: The Joe & Joan Martin Center
Charlotte, North Carolina
www.cslpreads.org/2007/PSA/yapsa.htm
www.cslpreads.org/2008/ya08.htm

In both 2007 and 2008, Charlotte teens utilized Studio i to create the public service announcement for the national Collaborative Summer Library Program's teen summer reading program, which was subsequently shown in school and public libraries throughout the consortium's 48 participating states each summer. For both the 2007 and 2008 PSAs, participating teens wrote the script, auditioned and cast the actors, created original animation and music, directed the live action or animation, and edited content. In 2008, the teen producers created bilingual versions for Spanish-speaking teens throughout the country.

The Teen Tech Squad

Hennepin County Library
Brooklyn Park Library
Minneapolis Central Library
North Regional Community Library
www.hclib.org

The Teen Tech Squad is a paid youth development and leadership program that began as a pilot project in 2006. Starting out at one location, the project is now at three locations in the county. Using grant funds, each library hires and trains four teens (ages 14–18) to teach media technology workshops for other teens. The youth are provided training and monthly skill-building workshops taught by staff from the Learning Technologies Center of the Science Museum of Minnesota while also being mentored by teen librarians at each location. The teens are taught to use freely available software like Scratch, Picasa, Artrage, Garage Band, and Audacity as well as technology such as digital cameras, scratch boards, and crickets. The teens work up to ten hours per month, and their work includes curriculum development, tinkering time, and time to work on projects to use as demonstrations for teaching. Tech Squad teens learn a wide range of technology skills, develop leadership and problem-solving skills, and investigate the potential of digital media projects for self-expression.

Teen Video Contest: 2008 Election

Johnson County Library
Overland Park, Kansas
http://www.jocoteenscene.org/templates/JCL_InfoPage.aspx?id=8039

During the 2008 presidential election the Johnson County Library partnered with the Johnson County Election office to increase awareness about voting by offering a teen video contest. Teen contestants were challenged to make a video three minutes in length focused on one of four themes: voting early by mail, voting early in person, voter registration, or the new polling locations for Johnson County residents. The winning video won a $1,000 scholarship provided by the Johnson County Election Office. The video was also available on demand through Time Warner Cable and was played as a public service announcement on Johnson County cable channels leading up to the election. All the submissions were also available on YouTube.

Virtual Science Friday

NASA Learning Technologies
National Public Radio
Teen Second Life, Eye4You Alliance Island
The Public Library of Charlotte and Mecklenburg County
Charlotte, North Carolina
http://eye4youalliance.youthtech.info/?p=662

Science Friday is part of National Public Radio's (NPR) *Talk of the Nation* program. It is a weekly show where topics of science and technology are discussed by leading experts as well as listeners who call in to contribute information. This year Science Friday made their audio stream available in Teen Second Life (TSL). A representative from NASA Learning Technologies was in avatar form in TSL on Eye4You Alliance Island, owned by the Public Library of Charlotte and Mecklenburg County, to coordinate the event. Each week she was available to interact with the teens who would be on the island to listen to the audio stream. She also worked as the liaison with NPR so that if a teen on the island had a question about the show in progress, she could text this information to an NPR representative who would then answer the topic on the radio. NASA would prepare posters on the weekly topics and engage teens in helping promote the event, having related discussions or events such as robot-building contests. Teens used read/write, math, and science skills as well as had the opportunity to interact with teens around the world during this live stream.

Pilot Projects

Homework NYC Widgets

http://labs.nypl.org/2008/02/04/web-based-homework-what-do-teens-tweens-really-want/

http://www.imls.gov/applicants/samples/AdvDigitalRes%20Narrative%20Example_NLGOLS.pdf

After realizing their Web-based homework help did not serve tweens and teens effectively, New York City librarians went straight to the audience to learn how students actually do use the Web for homework. Through conversations with 10- to 18-year-olds, librarians discovered the best way to support student homework needs is by serving them where they already are when online via a set of widgets. This information led in 2008 to an Institute of Museum and Library Services' National Leadership Grant (LG-05-08-0149). This grant funding gives the libraries the chance to develop a set of customizable widgets. After heavy testing by teens, the widgets will be launched for use across a variety of platforms. The funding also includes teacher outreach and training so educators will have opportunities to learn about student Web-based homework practices. In the long-term the libraries envision the widgets will replace a static Web site for library homework help. For more information about this project, contact Jack Martin at hjmartin@nypl.org.

Media MashUp

http://gaming.ala.org/news/2008/09/22/imls-grant-awarded-to-media-mashup-project/

www.placonference.org/2008/handouts/1013_321Nelson_Jennifer__116172_Mar12_2008_Time_120207PM.doc

Hennepin County Library in partnership with the Science Museum of Minnesota, the Wilmette Public Library (Illinois), the Public Library of Charlotte and Mecklenburg County (North Carolina), the Free Library of Philadelphia (Pennsylvania), the Seattle Public Library (Washington), and the Memphis Public Library (Tennessee) are developing a best practices framework for innovative technology program implementation. The project evaluates literacy skills developed by youth participating in the creative technology workshops called Media MashUp. Participants' projects and their reflective responses to their work will be evaluated for evidence of twenty-first-century literacy practices, such as higher-order problem solving, collaboration, and risk taking. These literacy outcomes are in demand by employers and reflect significant shifts in the role of education and technology in society over the past 20 years. This project will investigate the implementation process of innovative technology programs at libraries, address libraries' needs relating to program implementation, and establish best practices. For more information about this project, contact Jennifer Nelson at jrnelson@hclib.org.

Conclusion

The one thing we can be certain of when it comes to technology is that everything changes, usually faster than we anticipate and more often than we'd care for. We cannot control this rate of change, but we can control our attitude about change. Nowhere is this more necessary than in the field of technology, especially considering that how we use information, how we transmit information, and how we store information will continue to evolve with time. Not everyone is an early adopter of technology, and that's okay. What matters more is that those of us who work in libraries understand that the field of library services is evolving as rapidly as the technologies we utilize to provide our services, from online reference to online catalogs where our patrons have the freedom to tag our materials. For those of us who work with teens, this is doubly important; we need not only to know and understand how existing and emerging technologies are being utilized by teens in our libraries but also to be ready to adopt the general "I'll try anything" attitude of young people. Knowledge of technology is important, and it can be learned. What cannot be taught is one's willingness to change, to grow, to learn, to branch out and try new things, and, most important, to play. These are the skills that will be required of an innovative librarian in the twenty-first century.

Sources Cited in This Chapter

1. Rainie, Lee. 2009. "Teens and the Internet." PowerPoint Presentation for CES–Kids@Play Summit, January 9, 2009. Pew Internet & American Life Project.
2. Motoko, Rich. 2008. "Literacy Debate: Online, R U Really Reading?" *New York Times*, July 27. Available: www.nytimes.com/2008/07/27/books/27reading.html?_r=1&ref=technology (accessed January 17, 2009).

To keep up to date on best practices involving technology in libraries, we recommend the following:

- Horizon Report (annual) from New Media Consortium and Educause: www.nmc.org/pdf/2008-Horizon-Report.pdf
- International Society for Technology in Education (ISTE): www.iste.org
- Joan Ganz Cooney Center (Publications): www.joanganzcooneycenter.org/publications/
- Learning.now with Andy Carvin: www.pbs.org/teachers/learning.now/
- Pew Internet and American Life Reports: www.pewinternet.org/
- Spotlight: Blogging the field of Digital Media and Learning http://spotlight.macfound.org/
- YALSA Blog (Technology Category): http://yalsa.ala.org/blog/
- YALSA Teen Tech Guides: www.ala.org/ala/mgrps/divs/yalsa/teentechweek/ttw08/resourcesabcd/resources.cfm
- YPulse: www.ypulse.com
- *VOYA* (*Voice of Youth Advocates*, for their technology columns)

3. EDUCASE Center for Applied Research. 2008. "The ECAR Study of Undergraduate Students and Information Technology, 2008." Available: www.educause.edu/ers0808/135156 (accessed January 12, 2009).

4. Palfrey, John, and Urs Gasser. 2008. *Born Digital: Understanding the First Generation of Digital Natives.* New York: Perseus Books Group.

5. International Federation of the Phonographic Industry. 2009. "FPI Publishes Digital Music Report 2009." January 16. Available: www.ifpi.org/content/section_resources/dmr2009.html (accessed January 20, 2009).

6. McBride, Nancy. n.d. "Child Safety Is More Than a Slogan: "Stranger-danger" Warnings Not Effective at Keeping Kids Safer." National Center for Missing & Exploited Children. Available: www.missingkids.com/missing kids/servlet/NewsEventServlet?LanguageCountry=en_US&PageId=2034 (accessed January 17, 2009).

7. Wolak, Janice, David Finkelhor, Kimberly Mitchell, and Michele Ybarra. 2008. "Online 'Predators' and Their Victims: Myths, Realities, and Implications for Parents and Teachers." *American Psychologist* 65, no. 2 (February/March): 111–128. Available: www.apa.org/journals/releases/amp 632111.pdf (accessed January 17, 2009).

8. Palfrey, John, and Urs Gasser. 2008. *Born Digital: Understanding the First Generation of Digital Natives.* New York: Perseus Books Group.

9. Braun, Linda. 2006. *Teens, Technology, and Literacy; Or, Why Bad Grammar Isn't Always Bad.* Westport, CT: Libraries Unlimited.

10. Blackmon, Sandra. 2004. "Prof Says Teens' Grammar Shortcuts OK on Blogs, E-mail." *Purdue News*, July 21. Available: http://news.uns.purdue.edu/UNS/html3month/2004/040721.T.Blackmon.language.html (accessed January 17, 2009).

11. Carr, Nicholas. 2008. "Is Google Making Us Stupider?" *The Atlantic* (July/August). Available: www.theatlantic.com/doc/200807/google (accessed January 17, 2009).

12. Jenkins, Henry, Kate Clinton, Ravi Purushotma, et al. 2006. "Confronting the Challenges of Participatory Culture: Media Education for the 21st Century" (October 19). Building the Field of Digital Media and Learning: MacArthur Foundation. Available: www.digitallearning.macfound.org/atf/cf/%7B7E45C7E0-A3E0-4B89-AC9C-E807E1B0AE4E%7D/JENKINS_WHITE_PAPER.PDF (accessed January 17, 2009).

13. Whelan, Debra Lau. 2006. "Schools Crack Down on Teen Social Site." *School Library Journal* 52, no. 4 (April): 18.

14. Prabhu, Maya. 2008. "Digital Disconnect Divides Kids, Educators." *eSchool News*, October 21. Available: www.eschoolnews.com/news/top-news/index.cfm?i=55665 (accessed January 17, 2009).

15. Barack, Lauren. 2007. "Social Media Buzz." *School Library Journal* 52, no. 12 (December): 20.

16. Steadman Stephens, Wendy. 2007. "Digital Frontier: Schools, Libraries, and Adventure." *Knowledge Quest* 35, no. 4 (March/April): 70–72.

17. Gartner. 2007. "The Five Laws for Virtual Worlds." April 24. Available: www.gartner.com/it/page.jsp?id=503861 (accessed January 20, 2009).

18. Swope, Christopher. 2008. "Revolution in the Stacks." *Governing Magazine* (June). Available: www.governing.com/articles/0806libraries.htm (accessed January 18, 2009).

19. White, Britt. E-mail to authors. January 17, 2009.

20. Nelson, Jennifer. E-mail to authors. January 19, 2009.

Recommended Sources for Further Reading

Coombs, Karen, and Jason Griffey. 2008. *Library Blogging.* Columbus, OH: Linworth.

Cvetkovic, Vibiana Bowman, and Robert J. Lackie. 2009. *Teaching Generation M: A Handbook for Librarians and Educators.* New York: Neal-Schuman.

Farmer, Leslie. 2008. *Teen Girls and Technology: What's the Problem, What's the Solution?* Chicago: ALA Editions.

Harris, Frances Jacobson. 2008. "Teen Tech Week, Despite Limited Access." *School Library Journal* (February 1). Available: www.schoollibraryjournal .com/article/CA6526727.html?industryid=47078.

Holson, Laura M. 2008. "Text Generation Gap: UR2Old (JK)." *New York Times,* March 9. Available: www.nytimes.com/2008/03/09/business/ 09cell.html?ei=5124&en=db877979dd7344a0&ex=1362801600&adxnnl= 1&partner=permalink&exprod=permalink&adxnnlx=1231819407- DxStiNNc91OGEwhCpREn2A.

Ivers, Karen S. 2009. *A Teacher's Guide to Using Technology in the Classroom,* 2nd ed. Westport, CT: Libraries Unlimited.

Lenhart, Amanda. 2008. "Writing, Technology, and Teens." Pew Internet & American Life. April 24. Available: www.pewinternet.org/pdfs/PIP_Writing _Report_FINAL3.pdf.

Lenhart, Amanda, and Mary Madden. 2005. "Teens and Technology: Youth Are Leading the Transition to a Fully Wired and Mobile Nation." Pew Internet & American Life (March 27). Available: www.pewinternet.org/pdfs/PIP_ Teens_Tech_July2005web.pdf.

Rainie, Lee. 2006. "Life Online: Teens and Technology and the World to Come." Pew Internet & American Life (March 23). Available: www.pewinter net.org/ppt/Teens%20and%20technology.pdf.

Tapscott, Don. 2008. *Grown Up Digital: How the Net Generation Is Changing Your World.* New York: McGraw-Hill.

Warlick, David. 2008. *Redefining Literacy 2.0.* Columbus, OH: Linworth.

Youth Involvement

It is easy to blame society for the failure of its young people. It is more difficult to be a part of the solution and to be an ally when a young person needs it most, which usually happens during adolescence.

According to the National Commission on Resources for Youth, youth involvement is defined as "the involving of youth in responsible, challenging action that meets genuine needs, with opportunities for planning, and/or decision-making affecting others in an activity whose impact or consequence is extended to others."[1] The Canadian Mental Health Association further defines *meaningful* youth participation as that which involves "recognizing and nurturing the strengths, interests, and abilities of young people through the provision of real opportunities for youth to become involved in decisions that affect them at individual and systemic levels."[2]

By creating worthwhile youth involvement programs, you are not only contributing to the future but also making a difference in the present by helping teens develop feelings of pride and ownership for their community.

What Does Youth Involvement at the Library Look Like?

If your library is a visible part of your community, then it is a perfect place for teens to get involved. From serving as members of the teen advisory board to volunteering with the summer reading program, teens can offer a fresh perspective and the energy and age diversity that is often missing in libraries. Teens can also get involved in areas you might not have considered, including serving on a library's board of directors, as part of the "Friends of the Library" group, as volunteers and interns, and even as employees. By becoming actively involved in the library and by serving in leadership roles like the ones mentioned, teens are not only giving back to their community but also developing confidence and

IN THIS CHAPTER:

- ✔ What Does Youth Involvement at the Library Look Like?
- ✔ Why Does Youth Involvement Matter?
- ✔ What Are the Goals and Objectives for Youth Involvement with the Library?
- ✔ Who Benefits from Youth Involvement?
- ✔ How Does Youth Involvement Begin?
- ✔ What Is the Role of the LST in Youth Involvement?
- ✔ What Are the Guidelines for Youth Participation?
- ✔ What Are the Different Ways You Can Get Teens Involved in Your Library?
- ✔ You Want to Evaluate Youth Involvement at Your Library, but Where Do You Begin?
- ✔ What Are Some Best Practices in Youth Involvement?
- ✔ What Are the Elements of Success in Youth Involvement?

Your job as a youth advocate is to provide teens with opportunities for meaningful involvement, including developing and carrying out programs that encourage, inspire, and give a voice to young people.

Libraries are for everyone. Libraries that successfully embrace this idea understand that "everyone" means the young, the old, and every person in between.

skills such as communication and teamwork that will serve them throughout their personal lives and professional careers.

If your library is a youth-serving organization (and if any person under 18 years of age walks through your library's door, then it is), it is your responsibility to provide the most complete range of services possible for young people. While this is often easier to do for young children, who are usually escorted to the library by a parent, it can be tricky when it comes to teens. Teens travel in packs, which can be a little overwhelming. Teens also tend to be brutally honest, just as likely to tell you exactly what they think about a program or display as to tell you what's missing from the collection. Embrace these things about teenagers and use them to your benefit. Introduce yourself to the crowd. Invite them to get involved in making the library a more teen-friendly place. Ask them what they want, and then listen to what they have to say.

Youth participation is defined by YALSA as "the involvement of young adults in responsible action and significant decision-making that affects the design and delivery of library and information services for their peers and the community."[3] There are many levels of youth participation because it is as much philosophy as it is practice. Too often, LSTs associate youth involvement with a Teen Advisory Council (TAC). While this is one avenue for meaningful involvement, there are other ways to get teens engaged in the library community. Simple ideas include a teen survey about existing library practices or a suggestion box in your teen area. More complex scenarios for teen involvement include teens sitting on your library's board of directors or becoming active members of your library's Friends group. The level of teen participation will depend on many things, including the skills of the LST and the attitude of the work environment. A library where all decisions are made from the top down by the director without input from staff is probably not one open to putting teens on the library board. The key to turning youth participation into action is to understand why meaningful youth participation matters. Once you have that information it is easier to engage teens in the process and to evaluate existing programs that encourage teen involvement.

Why Does Youth Involvement Matter?

Developmentally, teens need opportunities to be meaningfully involved in things that matter to them and to their communities. To make that transition from childhood to adulthood, teens need to experience positions of responsibility and they need to be in an environment where they are encouraged to make decisions and work with others. Meaningful involvement matters because teens who get involved are developing a sense of responsibility and identity. They are also gaining valuable life skills, knowledge, and self-esteem. So the library might relate the goals of youth participation to improving service, but the goals for teens are about improving themselves. In fact, you could easily demonstrate that an intensive youth participation activity builds and cultivates external assets, such as these:

- Supportive adult relationships
- Community values youth
- Youth as resources
- Service to others
- Safety
- Adult role models
- Positive peer influence
- High expectations
- Creative activities
- Time at home/constructive use of time

Youth involvement can also build internal assets, such as these:

- Achievement motivation
- Caring
- Integrity
- Honesty
- Responsibility
- Planning and decision making
- Interpersonal competence
- Personal power
- Self-esteem
- Sense of purpose

In their Guidelines for Youth Participation, YALSA (Young Adult Library Services Association) goes even further to define how youth involvement is of value to teens by saying, "Youth participation in library decision-making is important as a means of achieving more responsive and effective library and information service for this age group. It is even more important as an experience through which young adults can enhance their learning, personal development, and citizenship while making the transition into adulthood."[4]

What Are the Goals and Objectives for Youth Involvement with the Library?

The answer to this question lies largely in how you envision teens getting involved with your library. If you are considering having teens join an existing governing body such as a library board, foundation, or staff, you need to decide how these teens can best serve as representatives for the library's teen demographic. If you are thinking about creating a new organization, such as TAC that will consist solely of young people, you need to make decisions about how this group can take on a leadership role within the library, how this group can be actively involved in the decision-making process, and how this group can provide input to the library's primary governing body. Any good partnership requires clear goals and objectives. Once these have been established, both the library administration and participating teens will know what to expect (and, just as important, what not to expect) from this joint venture.

Since youth participation is a partnership, the goals and objectives must be mutually beneficial. Also, a true collaboration should create new goals rather than merely allow each group to forward and foster its own agenda. The partnership card is one to play with administration, since most, in budget-tight times, are thinking more and more about looking outside for partners to help with resources. Youth participation activities look inside the library to make partners with our own customers. Youth participation is about providing opportunities to move teens from passive customers to active contributors. In doing so, youth participation is a means of achieving more responsive services for teens while providing teens with the opportunity to build both external and internal assets.

So for the library, the goals of youth participation might be related to improving service, while the goals for teens are about improving themselves. Teens are likely to engage in a youth participation activity for fun, for a school project, for extra credit, and just because they like libraries, so it meets some very practical needs. Yet the work itself and the relationship that youth participation allows teens to develop with the LST and other adults are meeting other goals: the goal of healthy youth development.

Who Benefits from Youth Involvement?

The obvious answer is teens, but libraries (including patrons and library staff) and even the community as a whole benefit from teen involvement. Teens bring a new perspective to the library. Additionally, they bring an authentic voice that will help you develop relevant, meaningful programs for this audience that will reflect both what teens want and what they need from the library. Involved teens are also more likely to bring a new audience to the library. Once teens begin having positive experiences at the library, it is highly likely that they will spread the good news among their friends that the library is not such a bad place after all. So, when done well, everybody benefits, including participating teens, the teenage population served by your library, the library staff, and the community as a whole.

How Does Youth Involvement Begin?

Youth participation begins with adults in the library recognizing that teens can make a positive contribution and respecting the right of young adults to participate in decisions on matters that affect them. LSTs must first be youth advocates before they can facilitate youth participation. YALSA's *New Directions for Library Services to Young Adults* was written to provide in-the-trenches LSTs with a "framework for developing services to teens that are both collaborative and outcomes-driven." Youth involvement is one of the core values identified in this book, and, in fact, turning the value of youth involvement into practice is one of the book's 12 goals.[5] A majority of information covered in this book about youth involvement was built on literature from the youth development field, where most of the models, going back to the work of the Carnegie Council almost three decades ago, emphasize the importance of youth participation. YALSA practices what it preaches by creating a vehicle for allowing youth participation in its own work, such as having teens sit on panels in programs, providing them with an opportunity to share their feedback during one of the Best Books for Young Adults committee meetings during the ALA Midwinter Conference, and by allowing them to freely post on the YALSA blog without parental consent.

What Is the Role of the LST in Youth Involvement?

When it comes to youth involvement, the job of the LST is to guide, not direct; to empower, not exploit. To empower teens you need to first provide them with an opportunity to meaningfully contribute to their community. This requires you to be upfront about your own intentions, expectations, and willingness to hand over the reins. Before you begin recruiting teens, you need to establish how much you are really willing to empower and give over (which means give up) real responsibility. This is not easy; most librarians have "control issues," to put it nicely. They would rather do it themselves (and then complain how busy they are) than give it over to someone else, let alone a teen, for fear that it won't be done right. But teens can, and will, do it right if you really empower them. The best definition of the role of the adult comes from YALSA's *Youth Participation in School and Public Library: It Works*, which states, "the key is to give teens enough structure so they are not overwhelmed, yet enough freedom to be creative and learn from their mistakes." Most of the traits needed to be a successful youth involver are, not surprisingly, the same needed to be a great LST:

- Dedicated
- Flexible
- Good listener
- Good time manager
- Independent
- Patient
- Persistent
- Problem solver
- Reliable
- Risk taker
- Sense of humor
- Trusting

Perhaps the most important of all is to be respectful of teens, of both their ideas and their actions.

What Are the Guidelines for Youth Participation?

YALSA has developed guidelines[6] stating that projects involving youth should have the following characteristics:

- Be centered on issues of real interest and concern to youth
- Have the potential to benefit people other than those directly involved
- Allow for youth input from the planning stage forward
- Focus on some specific, doable tasks
- Receive adult support and guidance, but avoid adult domination
- Allow for learning and development of leadership and group work skills
- Contain opportunities for training and for discussion of progress made and problems encountered
- Give evidence of youth decisions being implemented
- Avoid exploitation of youth for work, which benefits the agency rather than the young adults
- Seek to recruit new participants on a regular basis
- Plan for staff time, funds, administrative support, transportation, etc., before launching the project
- Show promise of becoming an ongoing, long-term activity

What Are the Different Ways You Can Get Teens Involved with the Library?

There are numerous opportunities for teens to become meaningfully involved in their local library community, including the following:

- Friends of the Library Board Member
- Library Board of Directors Member
- Homework tutor
- Reading tutor/book buddy
- Library intern
- Technology tutor
- Team member, library long-range planning committee
- Team member, library materials selection committee
- Part-time employee

- Programming assistant
- Programmer
- Teen Advisory Council (TAC) Member
- Teen Friends Group Member
- Teen Read Week or Teen Tech Week Program committee member
- Teen Summer Reading program committee member
- Volunteer (we have a list of possible tasks for teen volunteers later in this chapter)
- Virtual content creator (library's Web site or social networking site)
- Print content creator (zine, newsletter, and other print communication tool)

If you work with teens on a daily basis, you know that young adults are some of the busiest people in the world. The following are other less time-consuming ways to give teens an opportunity to be meaningfully involved in a library's day-to-day business:

- Suggestion box
- Survey
- Library focus group

Whatever you decide, the most important thing to remember is that youth involvement requires trust on both your part and the teen's. Once you have invited a teen to be a part of the organization, let him or her contribute in a meaningful way, including taking on jobs that require leadership and responsibility. In addition, make it a point to empower participating teens by involving them in the decisions that directly affect them, including programming and collection development.

How Do You Work with Teens as Advisory Council/Library Board Members?

Participation in a library's TAC or on a city council–appointed library board is a great opportunity for a young adult to actively participate in the planning and management of the library's services and programs for its teen population. Additionally, both of these opportunities provide young people with a chance to make positive civic contributions, develop leadership skills, and acquire a sense of responsibility for the community in which they reside.

Teens who wish to serve on a library's TAC have the opportunity to get directly involved in the decision-making process. Similar to their school's student council, a TAC is a select group of teens who will help you make decisions about all things related to teen programming and services in the library. Comprised of a group of young adults who offer both advice and feedback about everything from programming special events to material selection, your library should count the TAC as part of the organization's governing body, meeting regularly, helping you make decisions, and providing input about policies and procedures that directly impact the library's teen population. It is also helpful to have teen participants create a mission statement for the TAC that represents the philosophy of the group, including the priorities, values, and principles that guide the decisions of the organization. Your library TAC's mission statement should provide overall direction and clarify the organization's purpose and meaning. To put it simply, a mission statement is a written description of why an organization does what it does, in 50 words or less. Keep in mind that a mission statement should be simple, giving an overview of the group's responsibility. This simplicity allows for flexibility, which you will need as the TAC and the mission of the group evolve over time. If you want to define the goals and the objectives for the group, create this as a separate document.

Most public libraries around the country have a library board (usually appointed by the city council) that has the responsibility of listening to the needs of the community and reporting back to the council about library development, policies and procedures, and management. Although it is rare for a library board to include a teen member, libraries that view young adult library services as a priority would greatly benefit from having a young adult representative on the board. This would be someone who could offer a unique teen perspective on issues that directly affect this demographic, including the development of teen-friendly facilities, services, and policies, while at the same time serving as an advocate for issues of importance to teens, such as extended library hours and social networking policies.

How Do You Recruit Young Adults to Serve on a Teen Advisory Council?

First, take a look around you. Make a note of the teens you see frequently in the library and make it a point to introduce yourself and to let them know that you are considering establishing a TAC, of which you would like them to be a part. Be sure to get their contact information and then follow through with a call, an e-mail, or a text to let them know you are excited about the possibility of working together. Next, encourage them to invite any friends they think might be interested, as word of mouth is the best form of marketing when it comes to teens. Also, be sure to introduce yourself to any teens you see in the library, making a point to let them know you are around if they need help. Once you've interacted, hand them a comment card that asks for feedback about their library experience. Make sure this card includes a place for teens to leave a name and an e-mail address or phone number if they are interested in becoming involved with the TAC. Also, be sure to leave these cards in areas of the library where teens congregate, next to the magazines, the computers, the graphic novels, or the movies.

Another great way to spread the word to teens is to put bookmarks in the most frequently checked out YA titles, including graphic novels, required reading for school, CliffsNotes, and serials. After you have exhausted places to post the news inside of the library, go out into your community and post flyers in places frequented by teens, such as neighborhood recreation and community centers, churches and synagogues, bus stops, and schools. Also contact local community groups and ask them to spread the word or post a flyer; try the YMCA, 4-H, local homeschool organizations, the Girl Scouts, the Boy Scouts, church and synagogue youth groups, and Boys and Girls Clubs. Once you have done the footwork, sit down and create a simple press release that includes details about the library and how the library is embracing the teen demographic. Make sure to include information about how an interested teen can get involved with the TAC in addition to your contact information. Send this out to the local newspaper, smaller community newspapers, and school newspapers. Finally, be sure to include this information on your library's Web site or MySpace or Facebook site. If possible, include a link to an online (or printable) application for interested teens. While you may want to establish a base number for membership, it is probably best to remain flexible, because many teens will be able to participate only occasionally, and possible new members will surface all the time.

After Recruitment, What's the Next Step for Developing a TAC?

The first thing you need to do is have interested teens fill out an application form for TAC membership. Both for statistical documentation and handy reference, your application should include a place for the teen to provide his or her name, mailing address, e-mail address, phone number, school, grade level, birth date, and a place for a signature from the parent or guardian. The application is also a great place to list the required time commitment, including a place for a teen to acknowledge this commitment formally. The application is also a great place to do a little information gathering about potential council members by asking a series of questions about their interests and strengths. Questions might include these:

- Why are you interested in serving on the TAC?
- What special skills or talents will you bring to the TAC?
- What are some of your hobbies and interests?
- Do you like to read? If yes, what are some of your favorite books, magazines, or Web sites?
- Do you listen to music? If yes, what are some of your favorite genres or bands?
- What character traits will make you a good TAC member?
- What do you like most about the library's services for teens?
- How can we improve the library to better meet the needs of teens?

What Orientation and/or Training Do You Provide for Your Library's TAC Members?

Whether you call it an orientation or simply your TAC's first meeting, make it fun. Provide food, play music, prepare a few icebreakers, and

CD See Tool 30. TAC (Teen Advisory Council) Member Application

CD See Tool 32. TAC (Teen Advisory Council) Welcome Letter

give everybody a chance to talk and get to know one another. This first meeting is also a great time to talk about the goals and objectives for the group. Once you have talked about how the group is going to contribute to the library community, work together to develop the TAC's mission statement. Again, you need to establish their ownership at the onset so the teens know that you are facilitating their activities, not running the show. Allowing the teens to contribute to the mission statement not only helps establish ownership but also provides an opportunity for all of the teens to think about how they can contribute individually to the group's mission. This first meeting is also a great time to confirm everybody's contact information (names, mailing addresses, e-mail addresses, and home and cell phone numbers), to set a schedule for future meetings, and to brainstorm ideas for future projects. This first meeting is also a great opportunity to talk about communication preferences. You may want to consider setting up a TAC blog, wiki, or social network so teens have a means of communicating with you and their fellow TAC members in between meetings. Any required training will likely happen "on the job," allowing you to teach and meet the developmental needs of the group as you go. You might want to arrange training for any staff members who will be working with TAC members, especially for those who have never worked directly with young people. Expect challenges. Expect setbacks. Expect prejudice. Know going into it that it will not always be easy. However, it will be worthwhile, it will make your library a more diverse and teen-friendly space, and it will, in the long run, contribute to the development of a new generation of lifelong library users.

Where Can You Find Out More Information About TACs in Libraries?

In addition to the numerous articles in professional journals and books addressing the development and existence of teen advisory councils in libraries, you can join two really great electronic discussion lists for LSTs involved with these groups. Here you can post questions and read responses from other librarians who are dealing with a large number of the same issues and problems that you might be experiencing. In addition, this is a great forum for collective brainstorming, problem solving, solution seeking, and support and encouragement from other LSTs who share your mission of having a successful TAC.

- TAGAD-L. Teen Advisory Groups–Advisory Discussion. This electronic discussion list, hosted by topica.com, is a discussion forum for the advisors of any public library teen advisory group or board. To subscribe, send an e-mail to tagad-l-subscribe @topica.com.
- YA-YAAC. Young Adult Advocate Discussion List. The goal of this YALSA electronic discussion list is to allow teen library advisory groups and the librarians who coordinate them in school and public libraries to share information and ideas. To subscribe, send an e-mail message to listproc@ala.org. Leave the subject line blank, and in the body of the message type "Subscribe YA-YAAC [first name last name]."

Our professional literature is filled with information about meaningful youth participation. *Library Teen Advisory Groups* by Diane P. Tuccillo (Scarecrow Press, 2004) is a comprehensive book specifically about developing and nurturing TACs. *Teen Volunteer Services in Libraries* by Kellie M. Gillespie (Scarecrow Press, 2004) is all about developing a well-rounded and successful teen volunteer program in your library. A more general book that addresses elements of youth involvement is *Serving Urban Teens* by Paula Brehm-Heeger (Libraries Unlimited, 2008).

Literature dedicated to other professions is just as important, for youth participation is not just a library concern. Many of the electronic discussion lists and journals about youth development, youth and technology, team building, and asset building stress youth participation, such as Deb Fisher's *Assets in Action: A Handbook for Making Communities Better Places to Grow Up* (Search Institute, 2003) and *Teambuilding with Teens: Activities for Leadership, Decision Making, and Group Success* by Miriam G. Macgregor (Free Spirit Publishing, 2007).

How Do You Get a Teen Appointed to the Library Board?

The first thing you need to do is set up a meeting with your library director to ascertain his or her position about the possibility of electing a teen to the library board. Beware of one critical caveat: Without the support of your library director, it will very difficult to proceed. Once you have the support of your library director you need to read the library bylaws that govern the library board's operation. If the bylaws contain an age requirement for participating board members, you need to arrange a meeting with the library board to discuss the possibility of changing the organization's governing bylaws, specifically the age requirement for appointees. Even if no age requirement exists, you still need to set up an appointment with the library board to evaluate their response to the possibility of appointing a teen board member. Again, this will be an uphill battle if you do not have the support of the community leaders, including library administration and officers of the library board. Finally, once you have the support of the board, you need to contact a local city council-person to propose the idea of a teen board member. Be prepared to argue the case for having a teen serve on the board, including statistical information about the number of people between the ages of 12 and 18 who reside in your community, number of teens who have library cards, number of teens who patronize the library, and success stories about teen programming in your library system. Also, take along information about your library's teen advisory council, including tangible examples that highlight how this group has contributed overall to the library, focusing on how youth participation has helped the library achieve effective library services for this age group. In addition, it will be helpful to arm yourself with case studies/success stories about teen board members in other areas of the country, including not only stories about teens who have successfully served on library boards but also on other civic and community-based boards and on special task forces. You cannot overemphasize this last point, for while people say they want facts, they more often just want to hear good stories, and youth participation is loaded with success stories.

A teen volunteer program is an excellent way to get teens involved in the greater library community. However, planning for a teen volunteer program can be a time-consuming process. To be successful and to provide teens with a meaningful experience, it is crucial that you are organized and prepared well in advance of any teen volunteer's start date.

CD See Tool 29. Staff Request for a Teen Volunteer

CD See Tool 43. Teen Volunteer Application

CD See Tool 44. Teen Volunteer Coordinator Checklist

CD See Tool 48. Teen Volunteer Sign-in Sheet

CD See Tool 49. Teen Volunteer Success Story Form

CD See Tool 45. Teen Volunteer Information Sheet

CD See Tool 46. Teen Volunteer Newsletter

CD See Tool 47. Teen Volunteer Parent Information Sheet

What Are the Steps to Creating a Successful Teen Volunteer Program?

The first step is to rally support from administrators. You might need to sell them on the benefits of using volunteers, in particular teen volunteers. You will also need to manage, in particular in a union environment, the concerns of other staff members regarding the use of teen volunteers. Finally, you will need to train yourself and others to trust teen volunteers, many of whom have had little, if any, experience in the workplace. Once you have things in order at the library, it is time to start building a teen volunteer program.

Teen volunteers in the library are a win-win opportunity for the library, the community, and, most important, the teens. The library gains teen input, interaction, and perspective; the community benefits from teens who have had valuable work experience; and teens profit from their involvement in activities that increase their work experience and opportunities that help build assets. Most libraries use teen volunteers in the summer when the need is most obvious and teens are available. While this is the norm, don't forget about using teens as volunteers during the school year for ongoing volunteer tasks, special projects, and other areas of teen involvement.

How Do You Recruit and Select Teen Volunteers?

You can recruit teens from your community in a number of ways: tell the teens you interact with on a daily basis and encourage them to spread the word, blog it on your library's MySpace page, post advertisements inside the library to inform both library staff and habitual library users, send out an e-mail blast to local youth-serving organizations, and, of course, sell the idea hard at local middle schools and high schools. To raise awareness among your school librarian connections, offer to attend a school fair, speak at an upcoming parents' night, or set up a promotional table at the library during lunch to promote the volunteer program and to personally recruit teens.

You should have an idea of the best age range for the teens you want to recruit for your library or library system. Be sure to keep in mind the tasks or duties they will be involved in during the summer. If you use 12- to 14-year-olds they may be reliant on parents or others for transportation, and while 15- to 18-year-old volunteers may not have as many transportation issues, their numerous commitments may limit their availability. If possible, begin to keep a list of tasks that you have in mind for your teen volunteers, including tasks you tend to daily and weekly as well as any special projects you tackle occasionally. This will give you a realistic idea of what tasks teens can help you with as well as identify any projects that are more involved and may require direct adult/staff participation. While you will find some projects or tasks better suited to older teens, others will suit younger teens quite well. When you recruit teens at a school volunteer fair, have a list of tasks available—a list on paper or real-life examples in pictures—for teens and parents to look at so they can get an idea of what the summer will hold for them. Volunteering at the library is not for every teen or adult; if you can show teens examples of what you might ask them to do, you can use everyone's time wisely. If teens, parents, and the library have the same expectations, then you end up with better volunteers. Many libraries offer incentives or a bonus for volunteers, such as exempting them from fines. While this should not be the single draw for teens to volunteer, it may be a nice gesture.

After you have recruited a number of teens, the next step is to interview them to get a better sense of each volunteer applicant. During this brief interview you will also be able to get a sense of each teen's personality and information about how comfortable he or she is with adults and any previous experience in job situations, paid or unpaid. You do not need to subject recruits to a long and exhaustive interview, but it is important to find out pertinent details, such as how often they plan to volunteer, would they like a regular schedule or will it vary depending on other activities and vacation, and what other demands they have on their time. You may find some teens are suited to volunteer work but are really already booked solid for the summer. A regular day and time can work to your advantage so you can plan projects and have any materials ready for certain tasks. Mapping out any one-shot children's or teen programs that teen volunteers can assist with is another way of scheduling, and these one-shot programs may be a better fit for teens who want to volunteer but have a busy schedule. Having a list of tasks can also help teens understand what the library expects of them during their volunteer time. Teens enjoy hanging out with other teens, and often younger teens will feel more comfortable volunteering with other teens. This can work for you because two teens can accomplish a lot together—run a drop-in program, inventory supplies, or organize a paperback shelf—quicker than one teen can alone. At the same time, it is easier for two to get off track when they conspire with each other. You will need to handle friends volunteering together on an individual basis, and you can revisit the decision throughout the summer if you need to do so. The goal for teens is to volunteer; if they can enjoy their friends while doing this without it getting in the way of volunteering, everyone will come away happy.

You will have teens who express an interest in volunteering because their parents are making them. This situation can go sour quickly if there is no motivation to be productive, but there are ways to engage these teens and use their strengths to your advantage. The high school requirement of community service hours may motivate older teens, which usually makes them show up consistently, but they still need to be put to good use. Of course you may have a teen who is not motivated to be a volunteer, no matter the circumstances, and as the adult you will recognize the symptoms. Be prepared to suggest that maybe the library is not the best volunteer opportunity for them.

As a teen volunteer there is nothing worse than realizing that you and the volunteer opportunity are not a match, that you are not useful in this particular role, or that there really is nothing for you to do. As the LST, your job is truly about matching tasks with teens' interests. This will not only make the summer go more smoothly, but you will end up

When it comes to a teen volunteer program, remember that most participants generally want the following things:

- Experience doing a variety of tasks
- Opportunities to do things that are both fun and interesting
- To feel important
- To know that their input and time has made a difference
- To know that they have helped someone

with teens who have a great work experience thanks to the opportunities they have had to use their strengths, be productive, and learn new skills. So how do you select the best teens for the task? Part of this will come from your interview with each teen and the other part will come with experience and common sense. If you are not sure about a task match, give the teen a choice; most teens will pick a task they enjoy, can accomplish, or think is interesting. The more teens volunteer, the better you and they will become at assessing a task and knowing what best fits their skills. Of course, you will have tasks that never seem to find a match, which is simply a marketing challenge. You need to find a way to market that task differently, pair it with another task, or find the right teen for the task. Everyone has something that does not interest her or him, and teens are no different.

In general, certain characteristics lend themselves to certain library tasks:

- **Outgoing/talkative teens:** handing out programs/flyers/evaluations, welcoming patrons to a program, helping patrons with computer questions, assisting with a book sale or in the library's gift shop, helping with programs by being an emcee or host, greeting people at the front door for a large, after-hours event.

- **Creative or artistic teens:** creating bulletin boards or original and unique displays for library materials, reading to children one on one, assisting with story time, creating original content for the library Web site or social networking site, photographing programs/displays and creating or maintaining an online library photo album, blogging about upcoming library events and other programs of interest to teens, planning and carrying out artistic or crafty programs for teens like an altered books workshop or creating geekwear jewelry out of recycled computer parts, or designing a new template for an online or print bookmark of thematically related, teen materials in the library.

- **Quiet/shy teens:** making name tags, developing a library scavenger hunt for children or teens, creating word puzzles or games for younger children, maintaining displays of library materials, making flannel boards for story time, cutting out materials for children's programs.

- **Detail-oriented teens:** doing an inventory of supplies, checking collection for and labeling Accelerated Reader books, making sure newspapers/magazines are in order and labeled appropriately, preparing summer reading packets, and pulling thematically related or award-winning books and/or other materials for displays.

- **Active teens:** helping with children's programs, interacting with grade-school children, helping with crowd control during large events, conducting exit interviews with program attendees, assisting with story time, helping set up or clean up after children's or teen programs.

- **Technologically savvy teens:** creating or maintaining a library's teen social networking site (MySpace, Facebook, etc.); developing and leading a series of introductions to emerging technology classes for grown-ups; filming and editing programs and events; creating and maintaining a library page on YouTube; troubleshooting with staff about library laptops or digital cameras.

What Are Some Potential Tasks for Volunteers?

Figure 12.1 provides a quick list of generic volunteer tasks for teens. School libraries might have different tasks, and certainly smaller public libraries might not have this wide of a range of tasks available for teens. All of these tasks, of course, need to be ones that complement the work of paid staff members, not replace it. Before engaging teens in these tasks, or others that you may think of, make sure you work with your library's volunteer coordinator and union representative, if applicable, to ensure that teens are seen as assets to the organization, not threats.

Figure 12.1. Potential Tasks for Teen Volunteers

Adopt a table—cover tables in butcher block paper so they can be decorated and designed	Make sure the computers have paper and sharpened pencils near them
Adopt a shelf in the teen area	Make up questions for scavenger hunts
Ask customers if they need assistance on the computers	Manage computer sign-ups
Assist in computer classes	Manage mass mailing projects
Assist with an outreach activity in the community	Move and shift books to create shelf space in congested areas
Assist with bilingual story time—recruit from high school Spanish classes	Organize supply areas
Assist in collection development projects (checking lists against catalog)	Page reserve books
Assist with book sale setup, actual sale, and takedown	Photocopy
Assist with crowd control and taking attendance for summer programs	Photograph programs
Assist with program setup and cleanup	Plan, develop, and manage craft programs
Assist with story time	Prepare back-to-school packets
Attend community parade as library representatives	Prepare materials for forthcoming programs
Check YA collection versus standard lists	Prepare summer reading packets
Check collection for Accelerated Reader books and labeling	Prepare PowerPoint presentations
Check in materials	Help produce a mini carnival or other large-scale event

(Cont'd)

Figure 12.1. Potential Tasks for Teen Volunteers (Continued)

Clear drop boxes	Produce a program for parents on books teens should read
Collect reviews	Produce original programs
Compile databases of programs, customers, volunteers, school contacts, etc.	Promote summer reading program to local youth-serving organizations
Conduct inventories of supplies	Pull materials from the Weeding Report lists
Create a book review newsletter	Put on a performance
Create bulletin boards	Put barcodes and stickers on new materials
Create displays	Read one on one to children in the library
Create marketing materials for programs	Recruit other teen volunteers
Create props for displays	Repair books and other materials
Decorate magazine boxes	Review books for *VOYA*
Design and maintain a story time database	Run the laptop/LCD projector for summer video programs
Design covers for periodical boxes	Search Amazon for materials to fill collection gaps
Develop booklists: top ten lists (Amazon model)	Search the Web for homework help sites
Develop activities to support story time	Select and purchase refreshments for programs
Develop MySpace or Facebook page for library	Send mail/e-mail requesting publications
Develop an online photo journal for library	Serve as ambassador in classroom
Develop scavenger hunts, word puzzles, etc. for younger children	Shelf read
Distribute posters/flyers to promote summer reading	Shelve boardbooks and Easy Readers
Distribute flyers and lists at programs and in the community	Sign up children for summer reading program
Do a magic trick or other skill as way of introducing program	Straighten the children's area
Do work outside of the building to keep the library beautiful, such as planting flowers	Straighten the holiday books
Document programs (photos, anecdotes, statistics)	Stuff envelopes
Document their work (journal, scrapbook)	Suggest music, magazines, and other media for library purchase
Doing exit interviews with program attendees	Produce or participate in a teen talent show
Do word-processing on the computer, such as compiling mailing lists	Test out problem CDs and audiobooks

(Cont'd.)

Figure 12.1. Potential Tasks for Teen Volunteers (Continued)

Dust/clean shelves	Train teens to be clowns, puppeteers, musicians, jugglers so they can entertain
Greet customers as they enter the library	Use computer to see how many times certain materials have been checked out
Help troubleshoot computers	Use the library catalog to determine number of copies of specific titles
Help with outreach events	Vacuum out the easy bins
Hold a fund-raising bake sale	Weed young adult collection for condition
Keep statistics for summer programs	Weed and organize vertical files
Locate fun Web pages for kids	Weed magazines, newspapers, comics, etc.
Look through book sale materials for materials to add to collection	Withdraw materials
Maintain display case	Help facilitate group visits or tours
Maintain/update Web page or social networking site	Work one on one with adults on using computers
Maintain displays of materials (books, CDs, audiobooks, graphic novels, etc.)	Write an article for school paper about the library
Make flannel boards	Write and produce a skit to promote summer reading to children
Make nametags	Write reviews of materials that might be of interest to kids or teens
Make sure newspapers and magazines are in order	Write thank-you notes to partnering organizations, teachers, etc.

How Do You Run a Successful Teen Volunteer Program?

Once you have a core of volunteers it is important to have an orientation to the library. Teens can meet one another, you can give the same information to everyone at the same time, and you can engage everyone in a Q&A. Here are some important things to cover with your teen volunteers:

- Check-in/sign-in location or procedure
- Contact/emergency information
- Everyday tasks to do when they arrive
- Length of shifts
- Name tags
- Procedure if they are unable to volunteer for their assigned shift
- Staff break room, restrooms, drinking fountain, and first-aid kit

- Tour of the library including where they can keep their personal stuff during a shift
- Take photos of all volunteers to share with all library staff (and perhaps put on Web site on a special teen volunteer page)
- Dress code

It is important to introduce teen volunteers to other staff members. Make sure that all teen volunteers wear a unified name tag so that library staff can easily identify them. A big task for the LST is to help library staff learn teen volunteers' names by reintroducing teens throughout the summer and taking photos of your teen volunteers to post in the staff room. Teens will see they are part of the staff and begin to understand the true experience of working with adults. In addition to daily repetitive tasks that need to be done, some projects may take special training. You should treat such projects like any other project and clearly lay out the goal, plan of action, examples, and the time line for the volunteer working on the project. At first it may be best to partner a seasoned volunteer with yourself or a seasoned volunteer with a new volunteer depending on the project. Be realistic about the special projects you give to volunteers. Be clear about your expectations for these special projects, especially if it is a more difficult or taxing project. Once you know your volunteers it will be easier to ascertain who can handle a more difficult task. Check in periodically to see if there are questions and be ready to offer suggestions and other resources if needed. If things are moving along as planned, don't forget to express your thanks and acknowledge their accomplishment. Always be prepared to lend a hand with library details or jargon that may be unfamiliar to teens. Also be ready to step in and help (or provide scaffolding) if the frustration level of a teen volunteer rises beyond normal.

Finally, always remember that with everything you do you are building trust and relationships with these teens over time in order to build the developmental assets teens need to transition into adulthood as competent, caring individuals. Working with teen volunteers develops the "empowerment" assets of service to others, youth as resources, and community that values youth. Do not overlook this vital role libraries can play in teens' lives. Libraries can gain as much from having teens work and volunteer in libraries as teens can gain from volunteering at libraries. For many teens this is the first opportunity they have to work with adults who are not family members, whether the work is paid or not.

Something else to keep in mind is that it is important to communicate with other staff about the ongoing work of teen volunteers. There will be a time when you are not at the library, you are busy, or a volunteer is done with a task. From the volunteer's point of view there is a sense of security in knowing the next task, and from the library staff point of view they don't want another person to supervise. Volunteers are here to help, not to become a task for someone else. The best solution is to have a space that is dedicated to your volunteers, a notebook for checking in, a list of tasks for the day, posted schedules, upcoming programs or special projects, and volunteer contact information. The volunteers will always know where to go for their next task, as will any library staff member if there is a question.

Throughout the summer it is important to acknowledge all teen volunteers for their good work. This should not be a one-time thing at the end of the summer but an ongoing process that allows you to praise teens in the act. In other words, catch volunteers in the act when they are positively demonstrating skills or strengths and then praise them for their successes while at the same time explaining the details of the skill or strength they have exhibited. "Thanks for working on the paperbacks; you did a good job," so teens know they did something right. "I appreciate the way you organized the series paperbacks; you really had to think through how you were going to organize the variety of series, look at the space you had in the shelf, and figure out how to make it work. I think other teenagers will be able to find the books they want a lot easier. You also paid attention to the details; the labels you made for each series are spelled correctly, which will help other people who shelve the paperbacks. I also wanted to thank you for pulling out the books that looked beat up or had torn covers; the collection looks a lot nicer now and there is a little more space." Four sentences and the teen is aware of specific things they did well, why it was an important task, and how it will help other patrons. They have an understanding of the value of their task and how the library is working toward better customer service.

Of course if you praise a teen for doing a good job then you must acknowledge a teen volunteer when he or she makes a mistake or does not complete the task according to directions. You are not doing a teen any favors by glossing over a mistake or a project that was done incorrectly. The teen may be embarrassed by your acknowledgment, but by explaining where things went wrong and offering the teen a chance to right the wrong both of you may come away with better skills—you for explaining a project in better detail or realizing a certain task is not volunteer-ready and the teen for listening better, asking questions, and learning to interact with an adult in a give-and-take situation. Will you be able to have this level of interaction with each teen volunteer? Probably not with every volunteer, but hopefully during each teen's stint as a volunteer you will have the chance to observe him or her and give constructive feedback and praise.

All of this attention begs the question of supervision. Who has the time to supervise all of these teen volunteers? Most adult volunteers have a staff person they can go to if they have questions or concerns, and teen volunteers should be treated in the same manner. If you have a large team of volunteers you may need or want to tag-team the summer volunteers, sharing the supervising with another staff member (preferably a teen-friendly staff member who has an opposite schedule from you). This shared duty will give teens another positive adult relationship, and it will lighten your load and give another staff member the experience of working with teens in a positive light. Depending on your volunteer load you may divide teens up by schedule or give your partner half of the teens to supervise. As stated earlier in the chapter, it is important for all staff to be aware of teen volunteers and their tasks, especially if a question about a task arises. By having a mix of daily tasks like reshelving books, straightening the children's area, or maintaining displays and ongoing projects, such as making flannel boards, pulling book reviews, or creating bulletin boards, you can be better prepared for times you are unavailable.

As with any volunteer or work situation, you may run across a teen who is not suited for the task or project you have planned. The teen may have an interest in the project but not the skills. In some situations, retraining may be the solution. We know this may seem like a time-consuming activity but it does not have to be you who retrains the teen volunteer. Other trainers might include more experienced teen volunteers who have worked on similar projects in the past or teens who are working in your libraries as pages. The time that it takes to teach a teen how to use the library catalog to search for a book at another branch, or laminate a poster, or use a copy machine to collate is small compared to the impact it will have on a teen looking for real-life work experiences.

As your summer winds down and your teen volunteers head back to school it is important to send them a note of thanks and appreciation for their time and effort over the summer. Be sure to highlight the difference they made to you, the library, and other patrons when possible. If your budget allows, send out signed certificates of completion with a listed number of completed hours to each volunteer who finished the program. It is also a good idea to hold some type of end-of-summer teen recognition event like a pizza party, ice cream social, or some celebration to thank teens for their hard work. This is also a great opportunity to offer teens who got to know one another during the summer a chance to hang out in a social setting.

For teens who really shined in the summer, be sure to invite them back to volunteer for special projects during the school year. Also be sure to mention that you hope they'll join you again next summer as one of your library's volunteer veterans. Winter and spring breaks may also be times there will be a need for volunteers, so be sure to put the bug in their ears now so when you contact them in a few months it won't be a surprise. Keep a database of teen volunteers, both those available during the summer and those who have expressed an interest in helping throughout the year. Make sure this database has a place for contact information, staff input, and number of hours completed. This information will help you write thank-you notes, create certificates of completion, and write letters of reference or recommendation for many teens who have little or no other work experience outside of the library. You can find form letters for this task online to make the process a little quicker and easier, but be sure to get all of the details from the teens concerning where the letter should be sent and the deadline.

One last thing to keep in mind as the end of summer approaches is to have all teen volunteers fill out an evaluation about the tasks they enjoyed, things they liked, what was difficult or hard to understand, and what they would change for next summer. This is also a great time to conduct an informal exit interviews with participating teens. Talk with them in small groups and really listen to their feedback. It is important not to make this exit interview one during which you spend all of your time on the defensive. If you were unorganized and lost the schedule a few times, sit back and take it because their feedback is valuable for you and for them. The skill of analyzing your actions and others' actions is valuable. Give teens the chance to evaluate themselves, on paper and verbally. This opportunity to look back at what they did well, where they struggled, and what they learned is important, especially when a grade isn't attached, and teens may be able to focus on the process more than the product.

How Do You Create Programming with Teens as Performers?

The best resources we have for programs and special events are the teens who frequent the library. Who better to lead a teen program about how to change a MySpace layout than a teen who spends three hours a day on the site? Who better to present a special costumed story hour on a Saturday morning than members of the local high school's drama club? Who better to paint faces at a new library's grand opening than a teen artist? Who better to lead a program for parents about text messaging shorthand than a teen who texts upward of 200 messages a day to friends on a cell phone? Give the teens in your community a chance to develop programming, and we guarantee you that your programming, as a whole, will be better for it.

These teen-initiated services and programs might include anything from a hands-on demonstration for teens about how to navigate Teen Second Life to a class for adults on using their iPods to develop playlists for car trips with the family. Volunteering in the library provides a teen with the opportunity to give back to the library community. Getting involved in the actual library programming, when a teen moves from helping with a program to being the program, is to bring youth involvement full circle in the library.

How Do You Get Teens Working at the Library?

Real-life work experience within the library is a great way for a teen to learn about how a library works from the inside out. Stories and statistics abound addressing the aging librarian workforce, with major articles in leading professional journals reporting that an unprecedented number of professional librarians will retire in the next 10 to 20 years, leaving a huge gap in the library workforce. It is a fact that 25 percent of librarians will have turned 65 by 2009; 58 percent by 2019.[7] For those of us who work with teens, it is imperative that we provide them with an opportunity to experience, firsthand, the dynamic field of library sciences as a discipline that is continually evolving to meet the needs of an ever-changing information technology environment.

Whether you choose to create internships for teens or allow teens to apply for actual staff positions as pages and assistants, you need to create a job description for the position that includes a description of responsibilities, the time commitment, requirements if there are any, and a list of

Teen programmers have the opportunity not only to actively contribute to the library community but to provide services and programs that are completely out of our scope as adults.

Getting teens actively involved with library programming is a great way to make use of a natural resource, all the while contributing to the diversity of the library by giving teens an opportunity to program for all ages, including young children, fellow teens, adults, and senior citizens.

Remember that today's teen volunteers might be tomorrow's librarians. However, would you have become a librarian if all you did as a volunteer was shelve books all day?

special skills that might be useful. Once you have created this job description, get the word out to the community (both inside and outside of the library) that you are looking for a few good young men and women to represent the teen demographic in the library. Ideas for spreading the word about this opportunity for teens include attending school and community job fairs for teens, placing an ad in the local newspaper and in school papers throughout the city, posting a message on both your library's Web site and MySpace or Facebook page and the city or county's Web site, and letting all local high school counselors know about the available positions. You might also want to consider contacting local government organizations who provide job resources for teens (e.g., the Youth Services Division of the Texas Workforce Commission). Once you have hired teen interns or employees, hold an orientation. During this informational session it will be important to provide each new employee or intern with a letter documenting the expectations and responsibilities for each position. Also, use this time to let the young people ask questions and get answers about how they can best serve the library. Remember to let the teens know that you have an open-door policy and encourage them to come talk to you if they have any problems or concerns about their job responsibilities during their period of service to the library.

You Want to Evaluate Youth Involvement at Your Library, but Where Do You Begin?

Evaluation is an essential component of youth participation in libraries, whether teens are serving on governing bodies or contributing to library services as volunteers and programmers. To evaluate a program is to examine its worth and to compare the goals and objectives that were established at the onset of the program to the actual accomplishments since the program's inception. Continual evaluation of youth involvement not only improves the program but also helps both you and your library assess the effectiveness of established procedures.

The first thing you need to do before undertaking an evaluation of any program is to identify the specific purpose of the program. Then you need to establish realistic parameters, unambiguously defining goals and objectives for the group. Next, monitor and document progress toward the group's set goals and objectives. You can use both informal and formal methods to do this, such as collecting oral and written feedback via follow-up interviews and written surveys or by keeping track of statistical data over a set period of time, including how many youth participate each time the group meets. The final thing you will want to do is set a date for reviewing the evaluative material in order to assess the program: Did the group reach the predetermined goals and objectives? Evaluating youth involvement is an ongoing process. Keep records of all activities and provide multiple opportunities for both formal and informal feedback from participating youth and adults.

There is no "best" way to evaluate youth involvement. Whether quantitative, qualitative, or mixed, the evaluation method(s) you choose to measure the success of teen participation should fit your needs and help you adapt any future programming to fit the needs of contributing teens and the library as a whole, while at the same time meeting the goals and objectives of the program. Look at both outcomes and outputs. Quantitative research methods involve assigning numbers to things (e.g., gathering statistics about the number of youth in attendance at any given program). Qualitative research methods involve gathering empirical data about the opinions, attitudes, and feelings of participants and observers about a particular program. Generally considered more subjective, a qualitative evaluation can take the form of an interview, focus group, informal survey, or comment card.

Whatever your collection methods, we recommend you mix both numbers and stories when tracking a teen program.

Numbers can tell you how many people showed up for a program, but they cannot tell you the impact the program had on a teen. We recommend you keep a "More Than a Number" file on your computer to help you record success stories regarding teens in your library. This ongoing anecdote file will help you give a real human feel to your evaluations, especially when you have to submit these evaluations to your library's administration, board of directors, or external funders.

What Are Some Best Practices in Youth Involvement?

Teens as Advisory Group Members

Award-winning Teen Advisory Group Member

Public Library of Cincinnati and Hamilton County and the Ohio Library Council
800 Vine Street
Cincinnati, OH 45202
http://teenspace.cincinnatilibrary.org/library/tag.asp
http://www.olc.org/news_story082407.asp

Sibongile Sithe has been a member of the Public Library of Cincinnati and Hamilton County's (PLCH) Teen Advisory Board since 2002. In June 2007, 18-year-old Sithe was selected by the Ohio Library Council (OLC) Board of Directors as their "Citizen of the Year" for her noteworthy contribution and positive influence on library services throughout the State of Ohio. According to PLCH's former TeenSpot Manager Paula Brehm-Heeger, "Sibongile is a true advocate for libraries, particularly with one of the hardest to reach groups of patrons: other teens!" In addition to volunteering for numerous local library events, Sithe also served on a teen discussion panel for the local public television station and teen discussion panels at OLC annual conferences.

Oakland Public Library's Youth Leadership Council

Oakland Public Library
Oakland, California
http://www.oaklandlibrary.org/links/teens/ylc.html

Oakland Public Library's (OPL) Youth Leadership Council (YLC) represent OPL at local and national library functions. Members of this group (ages 13 and up) serve as a "junior speaker's bureau" for local businesses, and for the past nine years they have attended the California State Legislation Day to represent OPL and speak about their involvement with the YLC. Members of this group have spoken at City Council meetings about the importance of the library and often serve as ushers during important library events. This group meets for two hours once a month to talk about upcoming events, practice public speaking, and have fun!

Teen Advisory Board at Bluffton Public Library

Bluffton Public Library
Bluffton, Ohio
http://blufftonlibrary.oplin.org/TEENSCENE.htm

Bluffton Public Library's Teen Advisory Board (TAB) meets weekly to plan library events for children and teens. This group of teens, who range in age from 13–18, have an executive board consisting of president, vice president, secretary, fund-raising chair, and newsletter chair. Since their inception, the group has planned and carried out several dozen successful programs for younger children including a Halloween "Monster Mash" program, a "Fireside with Santa" Christmas program, a Lemony Snicket Final Book Release Party, and a Summer Reading Program Sleepover. They also plan a weekly after-school program for local elementary students. According to their advisor Rikki Steingass, what makes this group unique is that they are not dependent on one person to get all of the work done or to tell them what to do. They truly share the workload equally, and all know when it is their turn to lead. Working together as a cohesive group is their strength. In 2008 the group decided to become a Relay for Life team to give back to the community in a different way. The group also publishes a quarterly newsletter called "Teen Scene" that includes book reviews, and each month they take turns doing a bulletin board about a popular young adult author for the teen section of the library.

Teens as Members of the Library Board of Directors/Friends of the Library

Library Advisory Board, Youth Representative

City of Mesa Library
Mesa, Arizona
http://www.mesalibrary.org

In Mesa, Arizona, the public library is governed by a citizen committee formally known as the Library Advisory Board. Teen Alyssa Ratledge is very familiar with this group, as she has served two terms (four years) as a full-fledged voting member of the board.

Friends of the Library Board of Trustees, Student Representative

Montgomery County Public Libraries
Montgomery County, Maryland
http://www.folmc.org/

Erica Cafritz is the student representative to the Board of Trustees for the Montgomery County Friends of the Library, a nonprofit organization whose purpose is to enhance the public libraries through fund-raising and advocacy efforts.

The Princeton Public Library Board of Trustees, Teen Reps

Princeton Public Library
Princeton, New Jersey
http://www.princetonlibrary.org/teens/

Each year the Princeton Public Library (PPL) Board of Trustees invites two teens to serve as formal liaisons to the board. Although their role is purely advisory and they do not vote, teen reps participate in all activities and public deliberations of the board, including discussions about library policy, budget deliberations, and planning. In addition, the reps communicate the board's views and actions to teens via participation in the PPL Teen Advisory Board Program, through postings on the PPL Web site, a bulletin board in the PPL teen area, and via other means.

Teens as Programmers

Teen Second Life Virtual College Fair

The Public Library of Charlotte and Mecklenburg County
Charlotte, North Carolina
http://eye4youalliance.youthtech.info/?page_id=329

In October 2007, Teen Second Life hosted a virtual college fair for teens between the ages of 13 and 17 on the Eye4Your Alliance Island, sponsored by the Public Library of Charlotte and Mecklenburg County. Teens from all over the world helped construct the booths for the fair by building in Teen Second Life with the 3-D modeling tools. They built the stage for the speakers and even provided virtual refreshments. Teens also suggested which colleges they wanted to have present at the fair. Several teens also acted as speakers during the two-day festival, sharing their experiences as entrepreneurs with their family computer company and talking about how their development of programming, design, and leadership skills within the virtual world of Teen Second Life will help them with college and their careers.

Teens as Interns/Library Staff Members

Gaming Committee Member

Johnson County Library
Shawnee Mission, Kansas
http://www.jocolibrary.org/

In 2005 Johnson County Library (JCL) developed a gaming committee to provide gaming systems for several branches and to hold regular gaming programs and tournaments. The staff at JCL quickly realized that although there were a number of staff members excited and interested in gaming, there were very few who considered themselves "gamers." To solve this problem, JCL administration invited several of their teen employees to be a part of the committee in order to offer the most relevant, high-interest gaming programs to their customers of all ages.

Teens as Online Content Creators

Homer Township Public Library's Teen Techies

Homer Township Public Library
Homer Glen, Illinois
www.homerlibrary.org/teens.asp

Homer Township Public Library's Teen Techies Group is comprised of 9th–12th graders who help create Web content for their library's teen Web site. The group created the original teen Web page in early 2000 and a redesign in 2008. The Teen Techies are also responsible for the creation and maintenance of teen blogs and the Delicious account that appears on the library's teen site. Additionally, members of this group help library administration decide what Web 2.0 tools are most useful for reaching teen patrons and offering virtual library services. They help teach computer classes to the community and plan events and contests.

Teens as Teachers

Netguides: Computer and Technology Classes on Demand

The Reading Public Library
64 Middlesex Avenue
Reading, MA 01867
http://www.readingpl.org/netguides.html#about

Tech-savvy teens who frequent the Reading Public Library have a unique opportunity to help patrons with the Netguides Program. Interested high school students are trained to offer one-on-one guidance and personalized instruction to library patrons with software, hardware, and computer applications that may be foreign or difficult for new users, including using e-mail, navigating the Internet, basic computing, and accessing and utilizing hardware and software including computer peripherals, mp3 players, digital cameras, online databases, and Microsoft Office applications.

Hennepin County Library's Teen Tech Squad

Minneapolis Central Library
300 Nicollet Mall
Minneapolis, MN 55401
www.myspace.com/teentechsquad

The Teen Tech Squad, which evolved from a teen leadership program piloted in early 2007, now trains and pays teen interns to facilitate Open

Tech Labs at Minneapolis Central, North Regional, and Brooklyn Park libraries in Hennepin County. Teen Tech Squad members help other youth learn to create video games and animation using software like Scratch, Audacity, and Artrage.

Teens Involved on a National Level

YALSA's Best Books for Young Adults Teen Reading Group

Little Red School House and Elisabeth Irwin High School
272 Sixth Avenue
New York, NY 10014
http://lrei.org/libres/index.html

Middle and high school students (7th–12th grade) read Best Books for Young Adults (BBYA)–eligible books for the entire year (with a minimum requirement of ten nominated titles) in preparation for addressing the BBYA committee. Most students read upward of 25 titles and completed written reviews for all books read. Little Red School House and Elisabeth Irwin High School students have been reading and writing reviews for BBYA titles since 2002. Twice students in the group have traveled to national American Library Association Conferences to share their comments with the committee during a special session open to all conference attendees.

What Are the Elements of Success in Youth Involvement?

While there are no absolute, works-every-time formulas for thriving youth participation activities, the following are some elements of success:

- **Build relationships.** The heart of working with teens successfully is getting to know them and giving them an opportunity to get to know you. Developing authentic, meaningful relationships with teens is not easy, but it is the cornerstone of youth involvement for any youth-serving organization. Ask around and you'll find that most LSTs engaged in youth involvement activities can recall personal relationships they have built with individual teens. They will tell you how those teens remain in contact after they graduate, how they continue to share their successes, and sometimes even how they became librarians themselves.

- **Create a variety of tasks.** As mentioned earlier, not every teen is ready for the same level of responsibility or has the same skills, talents, and interests. So youth participation activities need to provide a variety of ways for teens to participate—not just different tasks, but also different levels of participation and maybe even different venues. Variety is also the spice that keeps teens motivated so that being involved is not boring.

A Teen Advisory Council is not always the best option for teen involvement. Too many libraries create TACs when what they really want is a teen club for hanging out, eating pizza, and scoring a first look at new manga. That's great, but don't call it a TAC, call it a social club. An advisory council needs to advise, so make sure you are asking for advice and feedback and then carrying out their requests and initiatives and holding them responsible for their actions and participation.

- **Define the needs of the project.** If you are asking teens to get involved you need to be able to define how they'll be helping and what's in it for them and for the library. You also need to be able to share this information with your director because although youth participation is an end for teens, to garner support it must also be seen by administration as a way to meet some community need.

- **Encourage diversity.** The library is a great melting pot for teens from public and private schools as well as homeschooled teens. Youth participation in all of its forms is a great way to bring teens from all backgrounds together with the goal of working for the greater good of the library. Your job is to make sure you are encouraging teens from all walks of life to get involved and share their experiences and opinions with the library.

- **Keep it fun.** None of this means much if youth participation is not "fun" for teens. Yes, they can learn, grow, get empowered, build assets, have outstanding outcomes, and all those good things, but they also want to laugh and be acknowledged.

- **Know your limits.** While youth participation certainly can be successful in creating better services, programs, and collections, you need to be upfront with all involved that there are limits. You can and should inspire teens to brainstorm, dream, and create, but you also need to define clearly what is possible. If not, then their voices are just blowing in the wind and everyone's time is wasted.

- **Seek balance.** You need to find the balance between getting the work done and letting teens have fun, between empowering teens to do good work and making sure teens are not being exploited to do somebody else's work, between spending a lot of time with a few teens and less time with a lot of teens, between wanting to direct the work and knowing that facilitating is favored, and between asking for input and enacting all of the input that teens will provide. Finally, successful youth participation means creating a balance between structure and flexibility.

- **Understand your resources.** Budget is one thing to take into consideration, but so are space and staff support. Before you get started you need to find out what resources participating teens have access to when it comes to doing the work of a TAC or group of teen summer volunteers. Do teens involved in youth participation have access to staff computers, phones, areas, and break rooms? Do they get to use the copier for youth participation stuff? What about the digital camera and the programming laptops? Can they post things directly on the library's Web site or blog? Remember, you need more than some food and a meeting room once a month to support youth involvement.

- **Win-win.** Whatever the project is, always remember that both teens and libraries benefit when teens have opportunities to participate in meaningful ways.

Conclusion

Understanding youth participation is a core competency for an LST as defined by YALSA, and certainly we've demonstrated throughout this text how youth participation can be used to connect young adults and libraries. Just because we've given it only one stand-alone chapter doesn't mean it is not important to success in all of these areas. But perhaps the simplest reason to pursue youth participation is because it works. It works for you the LST, for the library, and for the teens themselves. Here is the formula: Teen input to the LST creates successful outputs (circulation, program attendance, etc.) for the library, which equals outstanding outcomes (asset building) for teens.

Youth involvement represents a big shift in professional thinking, moving from services *to* teens and working toward services *with* teens. As discussed, the context from which many LSTs operate does not allow them the opportunity or access to engage in "higher-level" youth involvement activities like many of those described in this chapter or in the work of the Public Library as Partners in Youth Development project. What should be clear, however, is that, as YALSA named its publication on the subject, youth participation *works*. Youth involvement at any level is important, so don't be discouraged if you can't get teens involved in designing your new YA space; instead seize the opportunities that are available and make the most of them. Nothing succeeds like success.

Sources Cited in This Chapter

1. National Commission on Resources for Youth. 1974. *New Roles for Youth in the School and Community.* New York: Citation Press.
2. Canadian Mental Health Association. 1995. *Working with Young People: A Guide to Youth Participating in Decision-making.* Toronto: Author.
3. YALSA Youth Participation Committee. 1997. "YALSA Guidelines for Youth Participation in Libraries." Revised June 2001 and March 2006. Available: www.ala.org/ala/mgrps/divs/yalsa/aboutyalsa/nationalyouth.cfm.
4. YALSA Youth Participation Committee. 1997. "YALSA Guidelines for Youth Participation in Libraries." Revised June 2001 and March 2006. Available: www.ala.org/ala/mgrps/divs/yalsa/aboutyalsa/nationalyouth.cfm.
5. Jones, Patrick. 2002. *New Directions for Library Services to Young Adults.* Chicago: American Library Association.
6. YALSA Youth Participation Committee. 1997. "YALSA Guidelines for Youth Participation in Libraries." Revised June 2001 and March 2006. Available: www.ala.org/ala/mgrps/divs/yalsa/aboutyalsa/nationalyouth.cfm.
7. Gordon, Rachel Singer. 2004. "NextGen: Get Over the 'Graying' Profession Hype." Library Journal (January 15). Available: www.libraryjournal.com/article/CA371074.html?industryid=47106 (accessed March 17, 2008).

Recommended Sources for Further Reading

Asis, Susan. 2006. "Types of Youth Participation Programs in Public Libraries: An Annotated Webliography." *Young Adult Library Services* 4, no. 4 (Summer): 26–30.

Checkoway, Barry, and Lorraine Gutierrez. 2006. *Youth Participation and Community*. New York: Routledge.

The Innovation Center for Community and Youth Development and National 4-H Council. n.d. "At the Table: Making the Case for Youth in Decision-making." Available: www.theinnovationcenter.org/files/Youth_in_Decision _Making-At_The_Table-Report.pdf.

Kirshner, Benjamin, Jennifer L. O'Donoghue, and Milbrey W. McLaughlin. 2000. *Youth Participation: Improving Institutions and Communities: New Directions for Youth Development*, No. 96, Winter ed. Hoboken, NJ: Jossey-Bass.

Issues in Young Adult Services

One of the defining characteristics of adolescence is a young person's struggle to achieve recognition as an independent adult in a society where they are still dependent on others. Most issues related to teens stem from this fundamental contradiction.

This push-and-pull of the teen years reveals itself in libraries as well. While some staff, board members, and administration types want to lump teens into the children's room, others just want to ignore them, figuring there is no reason for a focused effort. Many professional issues revolve around teens precisely because it is a time of transition and vulnerability.

Just like teens themselves, the LST is caught in the middle. All LSTs have a boss to whom they need to answer, policies they need to follow, and work rules to obey. What happens when one or more of those items conflict with the legitimate rights of teenagers in a library? LSTs thus are stuck in the middle, yet for many issues facing teens in libraries there is no middle ground, no shades of gray. The problem with most library policies is they are absolutes, which allow no leeway for circumstances, judgment, and even common sense.

Above and beyond all else, LSTs are advocates for youth. You want to create the conditions in which teens can make their own choices; sometimes, you do this by speaking for them, other times by developing access vehicles for them to voice their opinions directly to decision makers.

In this chapter we present many questions faced by LSTs in school and public libraries at the reference desk, sometimes asked by teens, sometimes not. Each question will identify the speaker; you have to imagine yourself on the other side of the desk. Yes, many of these are fictional questions, but the issues they represent are very real.

Our goal is to present both "sides" of the issue. The foundation for all of these issues begins at home with your own library's policies, which often include the adoption of various ALA policy documents. The ethical foundation of our profession, often spelled out as well in ALA documents, comes into play. The laws of the city, county, state, or nation where you work and live are foundational as well. The issues faced by LSTs do not just come in the form of questions over the reference desk. Sometimes the trickier queries come not from customers but from colleagues and the administration. They may come during a job interview, a performance review, a post-"incident report" meeting, or during budget meetings with administration asking why support (aka dollars) should go to young adults. One of the big issues in serving teens is learning to become a leader and an advocate but also being a "team player" to garner support from colleagues. LSTs often get very frustrated with other staff and higher-ups who don't get it. You need to turn that energy around, stop beating your head against the wall, and instead learn the methods of influence that will allow you to open doors (and pocketbooks) to gain the resources to get the best outcomes for teens. The big issue, of course, arises when these two worlds collide.

Consider this hypothetical scenario: Your director is approached by a juvenile correctional center to provide library services to the teens who reside there. This is good for your director, because it allows her to show cooperation with another government body as well as to have access to funding in the areas of juvenile justice, youth development, and crime prevention. Also, both you and the director can agree that this is an excellent opportunity to show how reading, libraries, and lifelong learning can have an impact on the lives of troubled young people. So, this is a very good thing. The juvenile correctional center is eager to have the service, but there are a few conditions. They present a list of books and magazines you cannot bring, because, in their opinion, they undercut the mission of their facility. A majority of these materials might be by or about African Americans, in particular, resources that speak to the streets. Martial arts books are not allowed due to the potential negative impact they could have on the safety of the correctional officers, and also books with heavy sexual content are prohibited. And also...You get the idea.

You have in your hand your library's policies on free access to materials. You have the Library Bill of Rights, and your own training, that tells you that libraries do not censor; we don't deny patrons, regardless of age, access to certain materials. Your director has the same documents in her hand, but she also has an eye on the bottom line, on the benefits of inter-departmental cooperation, and maybe on winning an award for the service. You can "take the deal" and provide library services that compromise your principles but do give these young men and women behind bars some library service. Or, you can hold fast and thus not provide any service and at the same time not win any points with your director. It would be nice to think a compromise could be reached, but the facility is insistent on getting the last word on what books and magazines kids can read. There is no give there. What do you do? That is just one of many difficult issues or decisions LSTs have to face every day. While you work on the answer to this one, here are a few others to mull over.

Questions Teens Might Ask You

Can You Help Me Find a Term Paper Online?

A collision of values will likely spark most of the tough issues you face. As with most of the issues we explore in this chapter, this one is certainly a case of where you stand depends on where you sit. If you sit in a school librarian's chair, it seems pretty clear that not only would you not help the teen search for and download the paper, but that under your school's policies regarding student conduct you might be required to report even attempted plagiarism. In a public library, which has no code of student conduct, the answer is less than clear-cut, especially if you think beyond the specific incident and look instead at those core values you identified in Chapter 1 to serve as a foundation for all that you do with teens. If you really believe that you should respect the unique needs of teens, this is a good example of "giving them what they want." You will respect their information request, not judge it, and do your best to answer it. Also, if you truly believe in equal access, you likely wouldn't think twice about helping an adult patron find this information or something similar. Then there is the other side of your values, for you also believe in the value of collaboration. Would it not be difficult to collaborate with teachers if you enable or even actively assist teens in plagiarism? Of course it would. You support healthy youth development, yet, clearly, from the developmental assets approach, helping a teen purchase a term paper does not build but erodes assets such as honesty, integrity, and responsibility. So what is the right answer? What do you do?

Do You Have a Copy of *The Anarchist Cookbook*?

This is yet another selection issue, but the question takes on heightened significance post-Columbine and post-9/11. It seems to be the perfect example for discussing issues of intellectual freedom, selection versus censorship, and perhaps even social responsibility. A lot of libraries weasel out of this one by purchasing a copy to show their Intellectual Freedom colors but then not replacing it when it is lost or not buying more copies to fill the (inevitable) hold list. Buying one copy isn't really an answer; if anything, it compounds the problem. It is also a lot harder to say that you cannot purchase this title or similar books whose claim is purely entertainment but then provide instructions on how to do damage to other human beings because on-demand publishing makes it virtually impossible to be out of print. Do you support healthy youth development by purchasing a book that will be checked out by teens who have access thereby to instructions on how to make a bomb? What do you do?

Can I Check Out This Copy of the *Fight Club* DVD?

Contrary to popular belief, there is no law that prohibits a teen from attending an R-rated movie. Instead, it is the Motion Picture Association of America (MPAA) who assigns ratings to movies, which are then commonly adhered to by theaters and the general public. Additionally, the MPAA publicly acknowledges that their ratings are voluntary and therefore intended to be advisory, not compulsory by law. Since there is no law limiting access to an R-rated movie, and public libraries embrace free access and generally treat all materials the same with regard to access, libraries are free to ignore the MPAA ratings and create an in-house policy for who can or cannot check out an R-rated movie. So the real question here is not what all libraries do, but what your particular library's policy is regarding checking out R-rated movies to underage patrons. Some libraries allow anyone to check out anything. Some limit access based on age and rating. Others do not allow anyone under the age of eighteen to check out any movies from their collection. The bigger issue here is often the clash between your professional standards and your community's standards—few members of the public will fight for teens to have the option of renting an R-rated movie, but many of these same people would argue that teens have the right to read anything they want in the library, regardless of content.

Can You Help Me Download Music from the Internet?

Copyright and the digital age are a dangerous mix. While there is some music available online that is free to download, the majority of music teens want to download from the Internet is not available legally. Unfortunately, file-sharing software (like Ares, LimeWire, or Kazaa) has made it very easy for teens to access and rip music from others without paying for it. So while you can make sure your public computer terminals do not allow access to any of the file-sharing software currently available, and you can tape up reminders about how downloading music from the Internet without paying for it is illegal, the bigger question is what, if any, role do libraries have in enforcing copyright? Should you take these opportunities to educate the teen about intellectual property, help him or her find sites where artists have specifically allowed trading and sharing of recordings of their live shows or recorded music online, or simply say no and hope the teen walks away understanding that the library will not play an active role in helping him or her break copyright law? What do you do?

Can You Help Me Find What Started World War II? And While You're at It, Can You Tell Me What Countries Were Involved, and Who Was the "Access" of Evil?

All librarians who work with young people are faced with this dilemma daily: How much help is too much help? When does helping teens with their homework turn into doing their homework for them? On one hand, your job is to help teens by finding and sharing resources. On the other, you want to find a way to teach teens how to do the research on their own so that they can find the information they need. Another issue with this question is providing homework help versus conducting a classic reference transaction; some library staff would not be willing to hand out answers for a teen's homework but would have no problem helping find the answers if the questions came from a grown-up. Some staff might be more inclined to make teens jump through hoops to find the answer to these questions simply because they are teens and they think they should be learning how to find the answer instead of just asking a librarian for help. So the bigger questions here are: How do you strike a balance between solving the problem or finding an answer and teaching a teen how to solve his or her own problem and find his or her own answer, and how do you make sure all library staff are equitable in how they provide reference services to patrons of all ages? What do you do?

Why Don't You Have a Program about Wicca?

The stuff that teens want to know about upsets adults; it challenges them. Before you attempt to hold a program like this, or one on safe sex, or who knows what else, that might touch off a firestorm in your library, make sure that you have your director's approval and support. While this may be the time to present "two sides" of the story, this is not what we normally do in a program. A program for/about/by gay teens doesn't need to be balanced with a born-again Christian telling people how to get out of "the lifestyle." Following this logic, do we invite the Ku Klux Klan to every black history program?

So, you have kids who want a program on a topic you know is bound to be controversial, landing the library on the front page of the paper for all the wrong reasons. What do you do?

Do You Have a Copy of *Playboy* I Can Look At?

That libraries should reflect their community is a given, but what if the community does not reflect library standards? Not just *Playboy*, but most libraries do not stock any materials that contain sexually explicit images. Why not? Libraries generally fall back on the "Well, it will get stolen" excuse, but this does not stop them from purchasing Sunday papers with classified sections, DSMs, Value Line, or nonsecured DVDs and CDs. The "get stolen" excuse is false and most libraries know it. They do not buy pornography because the public would not support it and because they do not believe it is their role to buy these materials. Libraries draw lines; call it selection or call it censorship, or maybe call it making a decision on how to spend the taxpayers' money in a way they can support, but they will give teens what they want, provided everyone is clothed. If libraries really believed in a "give them what they want" policy, then any library serving teen boys would carry *Playboy*. You say you are customer focused, you say you listen to the input of teens, and so the boys in your teen advisory council suggest a subscription for the teen area for *Penthouse*. What do you do?

Do You Have the Book *Dying with Dignity: Understanding Euthanasia*?

You know a teen who has been a patron for years. She has even volunteered on occasion. You notice recently she's been moody, probably depressed. You might say something or try to talk with her, but you never seem to find the time or place. She drops out of sight. The next time you see her she is asking you to help her find this suicide self-help book. Now you've got a ton of questions—you are on record as fighting for access for teens to all materials. When discussion comes up about buying certain controversial materials you are on the side of teens, fighting for equal access for all. You also would be the first person to discipline a circulation clerk who told a teen he or she "shouldn't" be checking out a certain item. But you have a real person standing in front of you and that policy, those positions, might not seem so important now. What do you do?

Questions Parents Might Ask You

My Son Tells Me He Has All These Fines on His Card. I'll Pay Them, but I Want to Know What Books Were Late and What Other Books Are Checked Out.

This one is very much a local policy matter. It is one of those cases where a well-intentioned, necessary policy to protect the rights of young people battles. "Yes, since your son is underage, by law you are responsible for these items, but we can't tell you what they are" is your reply. Teens are beginning to have private lives and they might expect that in a library information will be kept confidential, as they should. While there might be a few exceptions, this might not be one of them. What you don't want to do is what one high school library in Minnesota did: post outside the library the names of everyone who had books checked out (strike one) that were overdue (strike two) and also let the whole school know the names of the overdue books for each student (strike three). While this is the extreme case, more likely you will encounter the parent who is not really interested in spying on her son but, because she has to pay his fines, would like to find out the titles of the books for which she is paying those fines. What do you do?

As Long as I'm Here, I Want to Pick Up Any Books That My Daughter Has on Hold. Can You Get Them for Me?

In branches, many times the person picking up the book is not the person who requested it. You can have policies that enforce against this practice, but they may not be followed in practice. Say Mr. Smith, who comes in every day, arrives at your branch to pick up books for his wife, who is at home sick; more than likely you would allow him to check out those books. To have an "only the person whose name is on the card" policy sounds good on an administrative level, but does not really work well in reality. What do you do?

[Over the Phone]: I Want to Know If My Son Is There. He Was Supposed to Come Home After School. Could You Page Him?

This seems like a no-brainer. A parent calls, wants to talk to her or his child to arrange the ride home, and asks you to page the teen. You might do this without thinking, but is this not a huge invasion of privacy as well? Or maybe they want to know if you could check to see if their son has checked out any books that day, thus proving he has been to the library—they're not asking for the titles of specific books, which almost none of us would give out, but simply for evidence that he was at the library. Do you provide that information? Do you page the teen and when he doesn't show up, tell the caller? By relaying that information have you violated the teen's privacy? What if the mother says it is an emergency? Do you reply, "I'm sorry that your husband was just in a car accident and you would like your son to meet you at the hospital, but our policy is . . ."? So, what do you do?

My Son Has to Do a Paper On . . .

Almost universally, the one type of patron LSTs loathe is the parent doing the research for his or her teen. This presents all sorts of potential problems, not the least of which are your own feelings about the situation. Some parents do this willingly, others out of desperation. Helping them is a challenge; you can't do a strong reference interview, because more often than not they do not know what they need. Since you cannot present them with options to narrow the search, do you broaden the search and give them a lot of materials to take home so the teen can choose the best ones? Often the parent will come in with the teen, but then do all the talking instead of allowing his or her child to ask for help. Worst case scenario: You attempt to isolate the teen and direct the conversation and follow-up questions to him or her, but the parent remains, dominates the conversation, and refuses to allow you to converse solely with the teen about his or her project. What do you do?

Questions Other Community Members Might Ask You

School Vice Principal: We Know That You Have Truant Students Coming Here to Play on the Computers During School Hours. Can You Call Me When You See Any Students from My School Here During the Day?

This is a very hard case. Would you expect a school to cooperate with you, which public librarians always clamor for, when you won't cooperate with them? At the same time, you don't call workplaces to tell them about adults playing hooky from work, do you? There are also some legal issues here, as truancy is against the law in almost every jurisdiction. If it is happening, and you know it but do not report it, what are your personal and your library's legal liability? Are you mandated to be reporters, as with neglect and abuse? If you allow teens to hang out all day instead of going to school, are you supporting truancy or just enabling it? Or is this a right-to-privacy issue? Some libraries, in particular those in close proximity to schools, have the "no students without a pass" rule, while others adopt more of a "don't ask, don't tell" policy.

Occasionally your values will clash with those of your colleagues or the library's policy; you want to collaborate with schools, you want to respect teen's choices, and you also know that a teen spending time out of school is probably not a good sign because you know from the research that truancy is often an indicator of more serious risk-taking behavior. What do you do?

Union Steward: Don't You Realize That All of This Youth Involvement Is Threatening Union Jobs?

Those of you who work within a unionized system know that most unions are suspicious of volunteer jobs. However, youth involvement is not about taking jobs away from adults or replacing people. Instead, it is about creating positive outcomes for teens. It is about side benefits like recruiting for the profession, adding new energy and ideas, and making services more effective. In spite of this, youth involvement is going to scare some people, with or without unions. If you suggest that teens from a performing arts high school might have a role in programming, then isn't that undercutting professionalism? We think not. Instead, we understand that sharing our expertise is the best way for us to demonstrate our professional knowledge. We could train a teen to take your temperature and measure your blood pressure, but that doesn't make him or her a nurse, doctor, or health care professional. Youth involvement, especially in programming, should allow for professionals to be more creative.

Teen volunteers can often take on the jobs that you probably shouldn't be doing anyway (like creating a bulletin board in the teen center, shelf reading, or preparing die cuts for children's story time), thus allowing you more time to focus on core duties of your job like collection development, readers' advisory, and all of the behind-the-scenes work that must get done for a library to continue to function each day. Rather than undercutting professionalism, youth involvement actually contributes to an environment where the true work of an LST is allowed to flourish. But your union steward does not see it that way, so what do you do?

Questions Other Library Staff Might Ask You

This Young Adult Graphic Novel Has Some Nudity (or Explicit Language, or Violence) in It. Does It Really Belong in the Teen Section of the Library?

Too often, library staff use the "I know my community, and this book is not appropriate" excuse to self-censor their collection. Nowhere is this more apparent than in teen collections, especially regarding graphic novels. This censorship is often based on fear of a negative backlash from the community and not *actual* feedback from the community.[1] All library staff should be advocates for the collection in its entirety, and this is as true for the materials in the teen collection as it is for anything else in the library. You, specifically, should be acting as a staunch advocate for all teen materials in your library's collection, including those that espouse your personal beliefs and those that don't, those that you find personally offensive and those that you don't. Of course your library's young adult collection should be in line with the wants and needs of your community, but this alignment should be in tune with your library's collection development policy and not fear of the community and/or your personal beliefs.

As the LST it is highly likely you will face this dilemma (if not with graphic novels then with urban fiction, CDs with parental advisory stickers, or R-rated movies) in your career, and how you deal with the situation will lay the groundwork for how other staff members censor (or do not censor) teen materials. So the next time someone brings you a graphic novel from the young adult collection with a Post-it note indicating a particular page with nudity on it, what do you do?

> We recently saw a T-shirt at a library conference with the slogan "My library has something to offend everyone." Nowhere is this more true than with a teen collection. Your goal is to create a well-balanced collection of materials—not everything for everyone, but something for everyone.

We Want to Save Space and Interfile Our YA Collection with Our Adult Collection or Our Youth Collection. What Is the Problem with Interfiling?

Space is always going to be an issue in libraries, but interfiling your YA collection with another collection isn't always the answer. Teens gauge their importance in a library by space, collections, computers, and programs. So if you interfile your YA collection (and therefore eliminate a stand-alone section of teen materials), teens who use your library are likely to feel like they don't matter. While this is most likely not the case, having a separate YA collection shows teens that the library values them and the materials they want to use. The bottom line: Real estate equals priority. Keep a separate teen section and teens will know they matter.

Here are some justifications for keeping your collections separate:

- Materials selected specifically for teens were intended for a teen audience, not an adult and not a 4th grader (even if this 4th grader's parents assure you he or she reads on a 12th-grade level.) When you interfile teen materials into other collections, you are essentially telling patrons that all materials within your (now) interfiled collection are appropriate for all readers. This can potentially lead to misdirected patrons and unsuccessful searches for teens, parents, teachers, and staff.

- A separate YA collection will allow teens, parents, and staff to zero in with ease on the materials that teens need and want to read. It will also be easier for teens to seek materials on their own and have success finding something they'd like to read. This kind of success using a library is what helps develop lifelong library users.

- Merchandising teen materials is easier (and more effective) when you have a separate teen collection. Additionally, YA materials often get lost within a larger collection, especially if your YA collection was small to begin with, and this lack of visibility directly impacts circulation.

- Conducting readers' advisory with teens is much easier with a separate section of teen materials, simply because staff do not have to wade through thousands of children's or adult titles to find something of interest to the teens being advised.

- Finally, two of the five core values that drive our work with teens are respecting unique needs and equal access. Interfiling the YA collection erodes both of these values.

So the next time this question comes up in a staff meeting, how are you going to defend a separate teen collection within your library?

Questions Your Library Administrators Might Ask You

Why Do You Have *Spin* Magazine in the Teen Area of the Library (or High School Collection)?

Although you might immediately assume your principal or director is concerned about the content of the magazine or the occasionally racy covers, her real objection is to the cigarette and alcohol ads that run rampant in each issue. It is not that she is arguing a moral point, but a legal one, since it is against the law for teenagers to purchase these products. After explaining her reasoning, she calmly informs you that she wants it removed from the library immediately. What are your choices? In the public library, you can compromise and move the magazine to the library's adult periodicals collection; the magazine is still available, but the access is a little harder for teens. In a school library, the choices are probably to lose the magazine or lose your job. What do you do? A lot of issues present themselves here. The first, and one that trips you up again and again, is that you believe in free access and you believe in healthy youth development. What do you say when teens use that free access to obtain information about risk taking or, in some cases, illegal activities? Can you support youth development on one hand and purchase CDs with lyrics that glorify every at-risk behavior? Can you make a case for positive outcomes for youth when at the same time you are providing access to books, magazines, and music that celebrate being a gangster, a pimp, or a cop killer? Is it one thing to carry novels that feature fictional teen characters engaged in smoking and drinking and another to carry adult magazines that promote the latest low-carb beer or popular smokes? If you move *Spin* from the teen section, what's next? *Rolling Stone*, *Vibe*, and *Glamour*, which feature similar ads, will follow and then you are back to a rack of *Boys Life* and *Odyssey*. What do you do?

Why Should We Continue to Support a Teen Collection When Our Main Measure of Success Is Circulation and the Teen Collection Has Lower Circulation Than Children's or Adult Materials?

For the sake of the question, we are going to skip over the idea that circulation is the primary measure of success for any library collection or service area. Going solely on the fact that your director seems to believe that the circulation of teen materials is less than that of adult or children's materials, let's examine the facts: If you look at the numbers every month, the circulation of teen materials is lower. Or is it? Let us say the budget for children's materials is $20,000 and they circulate 80,000 items, but if your YA budget is $5,000 and you circulate 30,000 items, then the teen collection has the higher circulation-per-dollar ratio. You can use the same formula for looking at circulation per square feet or staff hour. Other measures where teen collections do well are output counts such as turnover rate or in-house use statistics. Your job is to find ways to retrain administration to measure the success of the library's teen collection, teen programs, or general services to young adults.

What Are the Standards for Serving Teens in Libraries? How Much of the Collection Budget Should Be Allocated? How Much Staff?

While some states have developed standards for young adult services, most have not. Even state standards cannot speak to every circumstance. Instead of standards, two core documents provide similar guidance. The first is Chapter 5 in *New Directions for Library Service to Young Adults* by Patrick Jones. While every school and public library will have a different complement and arrangement of resources, most libraries will have seven action areas: administration, collections, programs, services, electronic resources, facilities and hours, and staff.[2] Within the chapter each of these action areas is followed by a checklist for resource allocation against which libraries can score themselves. This works on an institutional level; on the professional level, YALSA's "Young Adults Deserve the Best: Competencies for Librarians Serving Youth" spells out what an LST needs to know in the areas of leadership and professionalism, knowledge of client group, communication, administration, knowledge of materials, access to information, and provision of services to teens to create positive outcomes for teens.[3] So the real question is not what are you going to do but what are you going to do first?

Questions You Might Ask Yourself

Where Do I Begin?

Good question. It all depends, but a good place is to ask questions of teens, of colleagues, of community contacts, and of those interested in the library. Learn what works, what does not work, and, most of all, learn what programs, services, or collections garner support in your organization. What is the best way to your director's or principal's heart and thus, hopefully, pocketbook?

Am I Ever Going to Get a Raise? Is My Manager Ever Going to Recognize the Need for Teen Services?

These two questions are together because they converge on a single thread: Sometimes in order to push the youth advocacy agenda most effectively and do the best for teens, LSTs have to stop being frontline librarians and become administrators with a larger scope of influence. Library systems and state libraries that support teen services often have people high in the administration, including library directors, youth services coordinators, and state youth consultants, who "get it," because they too were once LSTs. Moving up the career ladder from the front line to the corner office is easier to do than you might imagine. LSTs need to conceptualize their job as frontline staff, managers, and leaders within the organization. While they may not manage other paid staff, they often manage volunteers and interns, lead systemwide teams, and oversee large teen-focused projects or programs for the library as a whole. Additionally, LSTs often have experience networking, marketing, evaluating, and measuring outcomes. In fact, in most public libraries, teen librarians are better prepared for management than catalogers or adult service librarians specifically because they have this kind of experience working with the community, creating innovative programming and services on a budget, and leading and inspiring a notoriously challenging group of people (teens). If you want to see that teens are treated fairly and provided with excellent customer service, collections, and programming, then the question is are you willing to move into an administrative role in order to shine a spotlight on teen services from an administrative standpoint?

Can the Authors of This Book Help Me?

Yes, the authors of *Connecting Young Adults and Libraries*, 4th edition, are available to conduct workshops at your library, library system, regional association, or statewide association, about any topic related to connecting young adults and libraries. Our workshops are practical, interactive, and, according to most who attend, "inspirational." For more information, contact the authors at connecting4@gmail.com.

Sources Cited in This Chapter

1. Braun, Linda. 2008. "What Are We Scared Of?" Young Adult Library Services Association Blog. July 19. Available: http://yalsa.ala.org/blog/2008/07/19/what-are-we-scared-of (accessed February 21, 2009).

For more real-life scenarios about working with teens in the library, see the LST Tool Kit. These scenarios make great training exercises or opportunities to engage your colleagues in conversations about how you go about best serving teens.

(CD) See Tool 8. Case Studies for Connecting Young Adults and Libraries

2. Jones, Patrick. 2002. *New Directions for Library Service to Young Adults.* Chicago: American Library Association, pp. 57–69.
3. Young Adult Library Services Association. 2003. "Young Adults Deserve the Best: Competencies for Librarians Serving Youth." October. Available: www.ala.org/ala/mgrps/divs/yalsa/profdev/youngadultsdeserve.cfm (accessed January 10, 2009).

Conclusion

So now you know everything there is to know about serving teens in libraries, right? Well, maybe not. Thankfully this field continues to grow and evolve, and new ideas and best practices are constantly being developed and shared in person via workshops and conferences and online via e-mail distribution lists, blogs, and social networks for teen librarians. However, we do hope that the information in this book (culled from our years of experience working with teens and training library staff members around the country to work with teens) will serve as a solid foundation upon which you can build a new generation of services for teens in your library.

Our goal for this book was to answer the question "How do I best serve teens?" by providing you with thoughtful, candid answers to real-life, in-the-trenches questions we have each faced in our careers as teen librarians and youth advocates. Our mission was to make sure you walked away from this book with not only a tool bag of best practices but also a solid understanding of the core philosophy of teen services, which includes respecting teens' unique needs, providing equal access, encouraging youth participation and collaboration, and always promoting healthy youth development. Respect, provide, encourage, and promote— these are the action verbs that make up the "bigger picture" of teen services. Keeping this core philosophy in mind, your job now is to focus on developing programs, policies, spaces, and collections *for* teens, *by* teens, and *with* teens. After all, to offer dynamic and robust library services to teens you must continually think about teens, talk to teens, and, most important, involve teens in the day-to-day process.

If this is your first time working with teens, don't be overwhelmed by the sheer amount of information we have covered in this book. Our intention was to create the ultimate guide, the one you pick up when you need help, information, ammunition, or encouragement. When you get stuck (and you will; we all do) or when you are frustrated with your administration, your teens, or yourself, turn back to this giant pink book and let it do its job; let it help you regroup and find a new idea, an answer to your question, or the inspiration to keep going.

Finally, we hope that you are not the first LST in your library system to read this book. Three editions and hundreds or thousands of workshops by the authors later, the message of this book and the philosophy set forward in this book about recognizing the value of young adults, their right to quality library services, and the passion needed to serve them is alive and well throughout the country. If you are new to teen services, we strongly encourage you to seek out other LSTs within your organization and in your city, state, and region. Teen librarians are a community, and we have never met one who wasn't interested in sharing his or her ideas, stealing your ideas, problem solving, and occasionally commiserating (usually about administration, but occasionally about teens). If you do not know anyone who has read this book, start a book club! Your best ally is a convert and the larger your circle of support, the easier your job.

Almost twenty years ago, Patrick Jones set out to create the ultimate "how-to" guide for librarians and library staff charged with serving teens in the first edition of *Connecting Young Adults and Libraries.* His goal was to motivate the like-minded, educate the uninformed, reassure the anxious, and convert the cynical. Today, with this new fourth edition, our goals remain the same. Thankfully, we have time on our side because right now is a watershed moment for our profession and library services for teens are stronger than they have ever been. This is due, in large part, to people like you who care enough to read the book, do the research, ask the questions, and share the information with colleagues about how to go about developing, implementing, and evaluating outstanding library services for young people in all public and school libraries. Thank you for the work you do every day to connect teens and libraries. It matters, and we're proud to have you on our team. Now go out there and start building connections between the young adults in your community and your library!

Index

About the Authors

Michele Gorman is the Teen Services Coordinator for the Public Library of Charlotte and Mecklenburg County (PLCMC) in North Carolina. She oversees teen services for PLCMC, a system comprised of 24 locations serving a population of approximately 900,000 people, and she also manages PLCMC's teen-only library, the Loft at ImaginOn. In addition to working full time, Michele is a freelance writer and renowned national speaker, certified by the Young Adult Library Services Association as a "Serving the Underserved" Trainer. In 2007 Michele was elected to the YALSA Board of Directors for a three-year term. Michele's books include *Getting Graphic! Comics for Kids* (Linworth, 2008); the third edition of *Connecting Young Adults and Libraries* (Neal-Schuman, 2004), which she coauthored with Patrick Jones and Tricia Suellentrop; and *Getting Graphic! Using Graphic Novels to Promote Literacy with Preteens and Teens* (Linworth, 2003). She has been a contributing columnist for "Teenage Riot" in *School Library Journal* and the graphic novels columnist for *Teacher Librarian*. She is currently the "Getting Graphic" columnist for *Library Media Connection*. Michele can be reached at www.comixlibrarian.com.

Tricia Suellentrop is the Deputy County Librarian for the Johnson County Library in Kansas. She oversees all operations for 13 locations serving more than 400,000 residents. Tricia has been with the library since 1998, serving as the Teen Services Librarian, Youth Services Manager, and most recently Systemwide Services Manager. She received the American Library Association Sagebrush Award in 2001 for outstanding service to young people and the Youth Services Award in 2002 from the Mountain Plains Library Association. Tricia coauthored the third edition of *Connecting Young Adults and Libraries: A How-To-Do-It Manual* with Patrick Jones and Michele Gorman in 2004. In 2005 Tricia was selected as one of *Library Journal*'s "Movers and Shakers" for her work with teens in the correction system. Tricia received her BA in English from Benedictine College in Atchison, Kansas, and her Master of Library & Information Science from Emporia State College in Emporia, Kansas.

Michael Giller, author of Chapter 5, is the Assistant Director of Library Services at the South Carolina Governor's School for the Arts and Humanities in Greenville, South Carolina.